CHILDREN'S RIGHTS AND BUSINESS

Children's Rights and Business: Governing Obligations and Responsibility is a comprehensive legal inquiry into children's rights and business. Relying on insights from various disciplines, the book illustrates the need for a children-focused inquiry on business and human rights. An analysis of the norm legalization process around the regulation of business and human rights, particularly of children's rights, follows the inquiry into existing hard and soft law regulatory frameworks on children's rights and business. The book goes on to evaluate the promise of these frameworks in light of globalized business transactions through the lens of in-depth case illustrations on children's rights in cotton and mineral supply chains and children's rights in large-scale energy and transport investment projects. Finally, it concludes with a normative outlook on governing the children's rights obligations of businesses and responsibility when violations occur, drawing on global governance approaches.

Gamze Erdem Türkelli is a Post-Doctoral Fellow of the Research Foundation Flanders (FWO) File Number: 12Q1719N at the University of Antwerp Law and Development Research Group. She works on human rights and development within international legal debates, with a particular focus on children's rights, business and human rights, hybrid actors and development financing. She holds degrees in Political Science, International Relations (Boğaziçi University, BA; Yale University, MA as a Fulbright Fellow) and Law (University of Antwerp, PhD).

CHILDREN'S RIGHTS AND BUSINESS

Governing Obligations and Responsibility

GAMZE ERDEM TÜRKELLİ
University of Antwerp

CAMBRIDGE
UNIVERSITY PRESS

CAMBRIDGE
UNIVERSITY PRESS

University Printing House, Cambridge CB2 8BS, United Kingdom

One Liberty Plaza, 20th Floor, New York, NY 10006, USA

477 Williamstown Road, Port Melbourne, VIC 3207, Australia

314–321, 3rd Floor, Plot 3, Splendor Forum, Jasola District Centre, New Delhi – 110025, India

79 Anson Road, #06–04/06, Singapore 079906

Cambridge University Press is part of the University of Cambridge.

It furthers the University's mission by disseminating knowledge in the pursuit of education, learning, and research at the highest international levels of excellence.

www.cambridge.org
Information on this title: www.cambridge.org/9781108484169
DOI: 10.1017/9781108681841

First published 2020

Printed in the United Kingdom by TJ International Ltd, Padstow Cornwall

A catalogue record for this publication is available from the British Library.

Library of Congress Cataloging-in-Publication Data
Names: Erdem Türkelli, Gamze, 1983– author.
Title: Children's rights and business / governing obligations and responsibility Gamze Erdem Türkelli, University of Antwerp.
Description: Cambridge, United Kingdom ; New York, NY, USA : Cambridge University Press, 2019. | Based on author's thesis (doctoral – Universiteit Antwerpen, 2017) issued under title: Corporate and corporate-like actors and children's rights : obligations and responsibility in theory and practice. | Includes bibliographical references and index.
Identifiers: LCCN 2019031212 (print) | LCCN 2019031213 (ebook) | ISBN 9781108484169 (hardback) | ISBN 9781108681841 (epub)
Subjects: LCSH: Children – Legal status, laws, etc. | Children (International law) | Tort liability of corporations. | Social responsibility of business – Law and legislation
Classification: LCC K3248.C55 E73 2020 (print) | LCC K3248.C55 (ebook) | DDC 341.4/8572–dc23
LC record available at https://lccn.loc.gov/2019031212
LC ebook record available at https://lccn.loc.gov/2019031213

ISBN 978-1-108-48416-9 Hardback

To Deniz and Selen

CONTENTS

ACKNOWLEDGMENTS

They say that there are two seasons in Quito: the sunny season and the rainy season. Every day begins around 5 a.m. in the sunny season and moves into the rainy season around 2 p.m. in the afternoon. The Volcano Pichincha looms over the city like a piece of décor. It is hard to wrap one's mind around the fact that it is an active volcano that erupted just a short seven years back, in 1999. I am not used to the altitude, there is so little oxygen that it is intoxicating. Two buses and tens of stops later, I arrive at the bottom of a steep hill, the only thing that separates me from my destination. I am a novice at this. I cannot possibly climb this seemingly innocent hill. It must be at a seventy-degree angle to the ground. Thankfully, there are children around to show me the way. I learn that the way to climb such a steep hill is to do it in zigzags, painstakingly, advancing up the hill just a little bit at a time.

This book has been more than a decade in the making, with roots in May and June of 2006, when I was a young graduate student who had traveled to Quito from New Haven to conduct research on children in street situations. From Quito, my research took me to the Ecuadorian Amazon and the adverse impacts of corporate activity on individuals and communities, causing many indigenous families to leave their ancestral homelands in search of livelihoods in big cities like Quito and Guayaquil. That experience brought up questions about what human rights and children's rights duties multinational corporations had under international law and how accountability for business-related wrongdoings could be conceptualized. These questions later led to the doctoral research undertaken at the University of Antwerp's Faculty of Law that constituted the groundwork for this book.

Most of the substantive research, including the data collection, was supported by a doctoral grant from the Special Research Fund of the University of Antwerp. I worked on the conversion of the doctoral project into this book, supported as a Post-Doctoral Fellow of the Research Foundation Flanders – FWO Strategic Research (File

Number: 12Q1719N), based at the University of Antwerp Law and Development Research Group.

This book and the doctoral project that led to it would not have been possible had it not been for the unrelenting support, trust and encouragement of my doctoral supervisor, Wouter Vandenhole as well as the continuous counsel and guidance of Koen De Feyter and Nicola Jägers, who were members of my doctoral commission and provided comments and suggestions on the drafts of my doctoral thesis. I owe an immeasurable debt to W. Michael Reisman, whose "Public Order of the World Community" courses at Yale unleashed my insatiable curiosity and passion for international law and whose scholarship and teaching will forever be an inspiration. I also benefited immensely from interactions within the GLOTHRO Research Network and the ETO Consortium during the preliminary research that went into the book. I am thankful to colleagues from the University of Antwerp Law and Development Research Group; Rachel Hammonds, Arne Vandenbogaerde, Liliana Lizarazo Rodriguez, Ellen Desmet, Vincent Bellinkx and Kata Dozsa have listened to, read and commented on various parts of the research project. I am indebted to Karin Arts, Daniel Bradlow, David Kinley, Radu Mares, Olga Martin-Ortega and Celine Tan, who offered feedback on the preliminary results of the project during an expert seminar organized in August 2016. This being said, I remain solely and completely responsible for the data, interpretations and assertions in this book.

I am also very grateful to the two anonymous reviewers who provided careful appraisal and suggestions on the manuscript, which have in turn helped sharpen its focus and its narrative. I appreciate the time, effort, and attention of Cambridge University Press in the review process, particularly of Tom Randall, tremendously.

I am grateful to my wonderful family, my husband Ali, my son Deniz, my daughter Selen, my parents Ayşe and Kasım Erdem, my brother Çağatay, my parents-in-law Zerrin and Niyazi Türkelli, sister Burcu and my aunt Cüveyriye, who have all supported me and cheered me on as I wrote this book. Thank you.

ABBREVIATIONS

AAAA	Addis Ababa Action Agenda
ACRWC	African Charter on the Rights and Welfare of the Child
ADB	Asian Development Bank
AFD	Agence Française de Développement
AfDB	African Development Bank
AfDB CRMU	Compliance Review and Mediation Unit of the African Development Bank
AfDB IRM	African Development Bank Independent Review Mechanism
AfDB IRP	African Development Bank Independent Review Panel
AI	Amnesty International
AKDN	Aga Khan Development Network
APRAP	Assessment of Past Resettlement Activities and Action Plan
ARIO	Articles on the Responsibility of International Organizations
ARSIWA	Articles on the Responsibility of States for Internationally Wrongful Acts
BCS	Broad Community Support
BEL	Bujagali Energy Limited
BIC	Bank Information Center
CCCMC	China Chamber of Commerce of Metals Minerals & Chemicals Importers & Exporters – China
CEDAW	UN Committee on the Elimination of Discrimination Against Women
CESCR	UN Committee on Economic, Social and Cultural Rights
CoE	Committee of Ministers of The Council of Europe
CRBPs	Children's Rights and Business Principles
CRC	UN Convention on the Rights of the Child
CRC Committee	UN Committee on the Rights of the Child
CRC OPAC	Optional Protocol to the UN Convention on the Rights of the Child on Children in Armed Conflict
CRC OPIC	Optional Protocol to the UN Convention on the Rights of the Child on a Communications Procedure

CRC OPSC	Optional Protocol to the UN Convention on the Rights of the Child on the Sale of Children, Child Prostitution and Child Pornography
CSR	Corporate Social Responsibility
DEG	Deutsche Investitions- und Entwicklungsgesellschaft – Germany
DFID	United Kingdom Department for International Development
DMCC	Dubai Multi Commodities Center – UAE
DRC	The Democratic Republic of Congo
EBRD	European Bank of Reconstruction and Development
ECCHR	The European Center for Constitutional and Human Rights
ECJ	European Court of Justice
ECtHR	European Court of Human Rights
EDFI	Association of European Development Finance Institutions
EIB	European Investment Bank
EJF	Environmental Justice Foundation
ESF	Environmental and Social Framework
ESIA	Environmental and Social Impact Assessment
ESS	Environmental and Social Standard
EU	European Union
FIAN International	Food First Information and Action Network International
FIVAS	The Association of International Water Studies
FMO	Nederlandse Financierings-Maatschappij voor Ontwikkelingslanden – The Netherlands
GC	General Comment
HPP	Hydroelectric Power Project
HRC	United Nations Human Rights Committee
HRW	Human Rights Watch
IACmHR	Inter-American Commission on Human Rights
IACtHR	Inter-American Court of Human Rights
ICAC	International Cotton Advisory Committee
ICC	International Criminal Court
ICJ	International Court of Justice
IDA	International Development Association
IEG	World Bank Independent Evaluation Group
IFC	International Finance Corporation
IFC/MIGA CAO	IFC/MIGA Compliance Advisor/Ombudsman
ILC	International Law Commission
ILO	International Labor Organization
ILO CEACR	International Labor Organization Committee of Experts on the Application of Conventions and Recommendations
IMF	International Monetary Fund

IPCS	The International Programme on Chemical Safety
IPIS	International Peace Information Service
ITUC	International Trade Union Confederation
JICA	Japanese International Cooperation Agency
MIGA	Multilateral Investment Guarantee Agency
MONUSCO	UN Organization Stabilization Mission in the DRC
NAP	National Action Plan
NAPE	National Association of Professional Environmentalists – Uganda
NCP	OECD National Contact Point
NSA	Non-state Actor
OAU	Organization of African Unity
OECD	Organization for Economic Co-operation and Development
OECD Guidelines	OECD Guidelines for Multinational Enterprises
OHCHR	United Nations Office of the High Commissioner on Human Rights
OP	Optional Protocol
PAD	Project Appraisal Document
PCDP	Public Consultation and Disclosure Plan
PID	Project Information Document
PPP	Public-Private Partnership
PROMINES	Growth with Governance in the Mineral Sector-DRC
Proparco	Promotion et Participation pour la Coopération Économique – France
RAP	Resettlement Action Plan
RMI	Responsible Minerals Initiative
RSN	Responsible Sourcing Network
SDG	Sustainable Development Goal
SOAS	School of Oriental and African Studies – University of London
SRSG	Special Representative of the Secretary General
TSDP	Transport Sector Development Project
UGFHR	Uzbek-German Forum for Human Rights – Germany
UN	United Nations
UN ECOSOC	United Nations Economic and Social Council
UN Framework	UN Protect, Respect, Remedy Framework
UN HR Council	UN Human Rights Council
UN WG	United Nations Working Group on Business and Human Rights
UNGA	United Nations General Assembly
UNGPs	UN Guiding Principles on Business and Human Rights
UNHCR	United Nations High Commissioner for Refugees

UNICEF	The United Nations Children's Fund
UNSC	United Nations Security Council
UNSG	United Nations Secretary General
UPE	Universal Primary Education
US DoL	United States Department of Labor
US SEC	United States Securities and Exchange Commission
USGS	United States Geological Survey
WB	The World Bank
WBG	The World Bank Group
WHO	World Health Organization

PART I

Children's Rights, Businesses and Duties

1

Children's Rights Obligations and Business

1.1 Why We Need to Talk About Children's Rights and Business

> Rights offer fora for action. Without rights the excluded can appeal to the charitable nature of others, they can request, they can beg, rely on noblesse oblige, hope that others will be benevolent or co-operative, or even sensible and foresighted. But they cannot demand: they lack the entitlement to do so.[1]

The images of children toiling in sweatshops and earning next to nothing to manufacture big brand goods became a staple during the ending child labor campaigns of the 1990s. In the two decades that followed, when the terms business and children's rights came together, they always did so in the context of child labor. Yet, child labor is but one part of the multifaceted relationship between businesses and children. Businesses engage in value and employment creation and generate investment. Businesses also buy and sell goods and services. By virtue of their activities and decisions, they may come into contact with children not only in the context of child labor but also when children are consumers, offspring of their employees or members of the communities in which businesses operate. Business activity and decisions can affect socioeconomic conditions where they operate, which in turn have a direct bearing on how children live, whether they have to work, whether they have leisure time or even more basically, access to food and housing. The full enjoyment of the rights set forth in the Convention on the Rights of the Child (CRC) also depends on whether adequate resources are at the disposal of children, their families and the communities in which they live. Of

[1] Michael Freeman, "The Value and Values of Children's Rights," in Antonella Invernizzi and Jane Williams (eds.), *The Human Rights of Children: From Visions to Implementation* (Ashgate, 2011), p. 22.

course, businesses do and can contribute to the realization of children's rights and have the potential to generate positive children's rights impacts. For instance, private business is increasingly accorded a pivotal role in the realization of public goals related to sustainable development. This is clearly recognized in the 2030 Agenda for Sustainable Development and the accompanying Sustainable Development Goals as well as the Addis Ababa Action Agenda (AAAA) under the UN Financing for Development framework.

Children's access to resources such as food and clean water, housing, healthcare and education might be put at risk by actors, such as businesses, when they are outside the reach of redress and recourse by virtue of their unclear status in international law. Given the rapid physical and psychological development that takes place during childhood and dictates different "survival and developmental rights ... from those of adults,"[2] the nonrealization of a child's right to, for instance, adequate food and nutrition, healthcare services or education can have long-term negative impacts lasting well beyond childhood. In addition, children are at a higher risk of abuse and exploitation and are affected particularly severely by emergency situations, which include not only disasters but also conflicts and hostilities. The specific nature of childhood also renders children more susceptible to being adversely affected by corporate policies in the domains where children and companies are in direct contact. Moreover, children are particularly disadvantaged in an asymmetric configuration in that "although [their] rights are frequently directly affected by business activity, children themselves are usually dependent on adults to influence company or government decisions."[3] Children may remain invisible in policy-making debates especially when they are not affected directly and in an obvious fashion. Children are excluded from having a public voice in many settings and are hence not consulted by decision makers.

While mainstream legal scholarship continues to insist on a conservative state-centric reading of international law, there is also growing scholarly recognition that the distribution of power in the international arena is no longer accurately reflected in the traditional reading of international law. In parallel, many scholars have argued in recent years for widening the scope of international human rights law to

[2] UNICEF, The Global Compact and Save the Children, "Executive Summary of Mapping of Links between Business and Children's Rights," 21 April 2011, 3.

[3] Ibid.

include actors beyond sovereign states such as intergovernmental organizations, companies, NGOs and even individuals.[4] Though other disciplines, such as international relations (IR), had begun discussing theories of "transnational relations" in the early 1970s,[5] legal scholars largely remained true to a black letter reading of international law, which demoted any non-state actors (NSAs) to a position of legal irrelevance. Despite the fact that "transnational relations" theories did not succeed in gaining a stronghold in the international relations literature and soon met with the revival of state-centered theories,[6] they were precursors to what is a new awakening and a renewed interest in non-state processes and actors which was ignited in the last two decades by debates on globalization. Even as states remained important political players in the IR discipline, scholars started to acknowledge the shifts in power structures starting with the 1990s. Alexander Wendt, a statist constructivist IR theorist, if one may be permitted to use such a characterization, recognized the declining importance of states in the wake of the rise of "multinational corporations, new social movements, transnational and intergovernmental organizations" as early as 1992, yet concluded that sovereign states would continue to dominate the international political arena.[7] More than two decades later, states remain major players in mainstream international law and international relations scholarship. It

[4] Major works include Philip Alston (ed.), *Non-State Actors and Human Rights* (Oxford University Press, 2005); Andrew Clapham, *Human Rights Obligations of Non-State Actors* (Oxford University Press, 2006); Olivier De Schutter (ed.), *Transnational Companies and Human Rights* (Hart Publishing, 2006); Rosalyn Higgins, *Problems and Process: International Law and How We Use It* (Oxford University Press, 1994); Nicola Jägers, *Corporate Human Rights Obligations: In Search of Accountability* (Intersentia, 2002); Adam McBeth, *International Economic Actors and Human Rights* (Routledge, 2011); Surya Deva and David Bilchitz (eds.), *Human Rights Obligations of Business: Beyond the Corporate Responsibility to Respect?* (Cambridge University Press, 2013); Sanae Fujita, *The World Bank, Asian Development Bank and Human Rights Developing Standards of Transparency, Participation and Accountability* (Edward Elgar, 2013); Willem Van Genugten, *The World Bank Group, the IMF and Human Rights* (Intersentia, 2015); Wouter Vandenhole (ed.), *Challenging Territoriality in Human Rights Law: Building Blocks for a Plural and Diverse Duty-Bearer Regime* (Routledge, 2015).

[5] The leading influence on Anglophone literature is Robert O. Keohane and Joseph S. Nye's edited volume on transnational relations: Robert O. Keohane and Joseph S. Nye (eds.), *Transnational Relations and World Politics* (Harvard University Press, 1971).

[6] Thomas Risse-Kappen, "Introduction" in Thomas Risse-Kappen, *Bringing Transnational Relations Back In: Non-State Actors, Domestic Structures and International Institutions* (Cambridge University Press, 1995), p. 17.

[7] Alexander Wendt, "Anarchy Is What States Make of It: The Social Construction of Power Politics" (1992) 46(2) *International Organization* 391–425 at 424.

must nevertheless be recognized that they are no longer the only determinant units of organization or analysis in the global system.[8]

The premise that nation states are the sole addressees of international law has been strongly shaken with challenges arising from interdependence and mobility brought about by globalization. Although states are not and will not – at least in the foreseeable future – become obsolete, other actors besides the state have been gaining not only political but also economic power. It is difficult to focus only on states in attempting to find solutions to today's human rights challenges. The rapid rise of new actors with de facto political, economic and even military power is a reality that needs to be reckoned with, both politically and legally. These actors outside or beyond the state may range from intergovernmental organizations to multinational/transnational corporations and armed non-state groups. These "not a state"[9] actors may operate in ways that limit the jurisdiction of nation states and more significantly, have a bearing on individuals' enjoyment of human rights, as was already recognized in the late 1990s.[10]

In the absence of binding international rules determining the margins of this power, these actors have been enjoying a 'free for all' regime when they operate transnationally, effectively allowing them to escape scrutiny for their actions and decisions. The resulting situation is one where regulation is at the discretion of the actors themselves, as they consider appropriate. Such a scenario has proven insufficient to ensure the enjoyment of human rights by all, especially children.

States continue to serve an important function in society, both domestically and internationally. Likewise, states continue to play an important role in the domestic and international protection and promotion of children's rights. Often, states are the formal authors of the domestic and international laws by which they themselves and others are bound. They can also cooperate internationally to carry out their duties to protect and fulfill human rights. Hence, arguing for a more dynamic legal approach that recognizes actors beyond the state as human rights

[8] Anne-Marie Slaughter, for instance, argues in *A New World Order* that the world is increasingly governed by horizontal and vertical "government networks" (Anne-Marie Slaughter, *A New World Order* (Princeton University Press, 2004)).

[9] The "not a state" comment is an homage to Philip Alston's seminal article on nonstate actors: "The 'Not-a-Cat' Syndrome: Can the International Human Rights Regime Accommodate Non-State Actors?" in Alston (ed.), *Non-State Actors and Human Rights*, pp. 3–36.

[10] Chris Jochnick, "Confronting the Impunity of Non-State Actors: New Fields for the Promotion of Human Rights" (1999) 21(1) *Human Rights Quarterly* 56–79.

duty-bearers does not diminish the significance of states but may as well underpin their position by allowing for strengthened regulation of NSAs both domestically and transnationally.

Given the ever-growing constellation of actors beyond nation states that engage in ventures with the potential to jeopardize the enjoyment of rights by adults and children alike, addressing what the obligations of such actors for human rights are and how responsibility for violations can be attributed and distributed has emerged as a core field of inquiry and research. This book focuses that broader debate specifically on business and children's rights, traces normative developments under international law in this area and offers insights on governing obligations and responsibility in the context of businesses as children's rights duty bearers.

1.1.1 The Many Facets of Children and Their Rights

Various disciplines spanning philosophy, psychology, sociology and the law showcase a true interest in children and their condition. Even approaches that deny rights for children agree on the need to structure other safeguard mechanisms like care or duty.[11] The apparent disconnect between different disciplines in the way they view children, childhood and the condition of children has resulted in similar but parallel universes. In reality, however, the child is not one-dimensional. No one discipline can, on its own, purport to present a complete understanding of the many dimensions of the child. The child is an equally biological, social, cognitive and moral being (among other things) and childhood is at once a period of biological, cognitive, social and moral development as well as a construct. As Lansdown acknowledges, contributions from different disciplines such as developmental psychology, anthropology, sociology and medical sciences are important particularly in providing a comprehensive picture of processes such as children's acquisition of capacity.[12] For this reason, whatever their shortcomings, different disciplines have important insights to offer on the usefulness and merits of

[11] O'Neil and Arneil separately argue for obligations over rights. Onora O'Neill, "Children's Rights and Children's Lives" (1988) 98 *Ethics* 445–463 and Barbara Arneil, "Becoming Versus Being: A Critical Analysis of the Child in Liberal Theory," in David Archard and Colin M. Macleod (eds.), *The Moral and Political Status of Children* (Oxford University Press, 2002), pp. 70–94.

[12] Gerrison Lansdown, *Evolving Capacities of the Child* (Save the Children/UNICEF, 2005), p. xiv.

specifically pursuing a children's rights focus in studying the human rights obligations of businesses and their responsibility for violations.

From the historical trajectory of Western thought back to Ancient Greece, through the theological conceptualizations from Judaism, Christianity and Islam and through the medieval ages, emerge a number of distinct angles from which to view childhood.[13] The first of the emerging "childist ethics" is a "top-down" approach that designates adults as educators and children as subjects from whom to demand obedience. Wall argues that the top-down thinking informs many sources from the writings of Plato, who viewed the child as the "craftiest, most mischievous, and unruliest of brutes"[14] to be restrained and civilized, to some of the major texts of Judaism, Christianity and Islam.[15] The second – "bottom-up" – approach too is traced to religious thought mainly from the medieval ages and is characterized as one seeking to support and nurture children and encourage adults to be more like "children [who] are thought to demonstrate humanity's original ontological goodness, purity, and moral wisdom."[16] Wall describes "developmental" as yet a third approach that puts children on the trajectory of development through the acquisition of capacities en route to becoming adults and cites the writings of Aristotle (who viewed the child as not fully rational yet still a part of society) and Aristotelian-inspired theorists such as Al-Ghazali (for whom the child was an "uncut jewel" ready to be carved into shape), Maimonides (who considered human wisdom to increase with age) and Aquinas (who distinguishes stages of development).[17] It is against this backdrop that theories emerging from the Enlightenment era onwards consider childhood and the status of the child.

The birth of Enlightenment ideas on rights, born out of the desire to transform "subjects" into "citizens," fueled thinking on children along the lines of the developmental approach. As rights and rationality were bound inextricably together early on, the status of those who were presumed to be lacking the requisite "rationality," such as children, was

[13] John Wall, "Human Rights in Light of Childhood" (2008) 16 *International Journal of Children's Rights* 523–543. (Wall makes his case even more extensively in Wall, *Ethics in Light of Childhood* (Georgetown University Press, 2010).)

[14] Wall quotes Plato (Plato, *The Laws*, in Edith Hamilton and Huntington Cairns [eds.], *The Collected Dialogues of Plato* (Princeton University Press, 1961), p. 1379). Wall, "Human Rights in Light of Childhood," p. 524.

[15] Wall, "Human Rights in Light of Childhood," p. 525.

[16] Ibid.

[17] Ibid., p. 526.

still ambiguous. Arneil posits that liberal theory fashions children as "citizens in waiting, human beings who do not yet possess the necessary attributes of citizenship, namely reason, autonomy, and the capacity for having authority over oneself, but will possess them in the future."[18]

Modern moral philosophy too has long been vexed by the question of who is and/or should be a rights-holder, both legally and morally. While the premise that children have legal rights goes by and large uncontested,[19] whether they have moral rights is hotly debated. Other dimensions of the debate cover issues of whether or not children should have rights, whether they should have the same rights as adults and whether children have equal rights as adults. The choice theory, also called the "will" theory, contends that rights flow from the capacity and the ability to exercise them and to demand their provision from others.[20] The association of right ownership with capacity invariably excludes those not in a position to exert this capacity from being defined as rights-holders. Thus, children's designation as rights-holders depends on an evaluation of their capacity to enforce rights.[21] Van Bueren likens withholding rights on the basis of capacity to "conditionality" whereby rights become correlated with and tied to the fulfillment of duties or subject to limitations on the basis of these duties.[22] The main competition to choice theory, interest theory of rights decrees that a right comes into existence by virtue of the existence of a significant interest, which in turn creates duties that others have to carry out. It follows that the one whose interest is protected through the carrying out of these duties is a rights-holder.[23] Because it ties rights to interests, the theory is also called the "welfare"

[18] Arneil, "Becoming versus Being," p. 70.

[19] For instance, Griffin asks: "Of course, children have legal rights. But do they also have human rights?" (James Griffin, "Do Children Have Rights?," in Archard and Macleod [eds.], *The Moral and Political Status of Children* (Oxford University Press, 2002), pp. 19–30). Brighouse questions whether the CRC is flawed for according children legal rights and concludes: "The question of what rights we have fundamentally, or morally, is distinct from that of which rights we should be legally granted." (Harry Brighouse, "What Rights [if Any] Do Children Have?" in Archard and Macleod [eds.], *The Moral and Political Status of Children*, pp. 31–32.)

[20] See: Herbert Lionel Adolphus Hart, "Are There Any Natural Rights?" (1955) 64 *The Philosophical Review* 175–191.

[21] Katherine H. Federle, "Rights Flow Downhill" (1994) 2 *International Journal of Children's Rights* 343–368 at 343.

[22] Geraldine Van Bueren, *The International Law on the Rights of the Child* (2nd ed.) (Martinus Nijhoff Publishers, 1998), p. 4.

[23] Archard, "Children's Rights," in Edward N. Zalta (ed.) *The Stanford Encyclopedia of Philosophy (Winter 2018 Edition)*, https://plato.stanford.edu/archives/win2018/entries/rights-children/.

theory of rights. From the viewpoint of interest theory, the exercise and assertion of rights is not a precondition for the existence of such rights.

The choice and interest theories illuminate two different aspects of what it means to hold rights: the possibility to exercise agency and the entitlement to protection of one's interests. In this regard, both theories have only partial explanatory power and clear limitations. As Federle points out, "neither approach to articulating a rights theory for children challenges the underlying notion of capacity as a prerequisite to having rights."[24] For choice theory, the capacity to exercise rights is a sine qua non of possessing them, for interest theory the lack of capacity warrants the protection of one's interests. Linking capacity to right ownership and exercise, neither the choice nor the interest theory is capable of "fully account[ing] for the limiting effects of capacity."[25]

Situated in the continuum between choice and interest theories are what may be deemed hybrid approaches. For instance, Samantha Brennan advocates a "rights gradualism" approach which grants children rights gradually as they gradually acquire capabilities so that they at first have rights mainly protecting their interest and later on rights mainly protecting their choices.[26] Vallentyne, on the other hand, distinguishes between two different types of rights and argues that "autonomous agents have (mainly) choice-protecting rights, and nonautonomous agents have interest-protecting rights."[27] Vallentyne concludes that children do have both types of rights, starting at the youngest ages with interest-protecting rights and extending, as agency develops with age, to choice-protecting rights.

The gradualist interpretation of rights is closely linked to developmental psychology models. Children's rights discourse and the work of children's organizations (whether nongovernmental, state or international) have been informed very strongly by such developmental approaches. The CRC makes references, for instance, to the "evolving capacities of the child" in two articles[28] and to the "age and maturity of

[24] Federle, "Rights Flow Downhill," p. 343.

[25] Ibid., 347.

[26] Samantha Brennan, "Children's Choices or Children's Interests: Which Do Their Rights Protect?" in Archard and Macleod (eds.), *The Moral and Political Status of Children* (Oxford University Press, 2002), p. 63.

[27] Peter Vallentyne, "Equality and the Duties of Procreators," in Archard and Macleod (eds.), *The Moral and Political Status of Children* (Oxford University Press, 2002), p. 197.

[28] CRC, Arts. 5 and 14 on the respect for the responsibilities, rights and duties of parents in the general implementation of the rights in the treaty and freedom of thought, conscience and religion respectively.

the child" in taking into account the child's views.[29] However, the CRC does not define the term. Lansdown holds that the evolving capacities premise allows children's protection needs and their position as "active agents" entitled to participation to coexist.[30] As the capacities of the child evolve, the child is a more active participant in the exercise of their rights and up until then, the parents and the family are recognized as intermediaries.

Outside the two major theories of rights, the civil rights approach has emerged as a third strand in modern times.[31] The civil rights approach to children's rights carries further the flag of social liberation movements that have hitherto given a social voice to excluded or oppressed groups. As children are considered among these excluded and marginalized groups, the civil rights approach seeks to give them "a public voice, agency, and participation."[32] A central characteristic of civil rights approaches is a rejection of and resistance to top-down impositions of power structures. Within this framework, children's rights are therefore not a means to protect interests or enable choices but a means to challenge marginalization and discrimination, and to achieve inclusion. In many ways, the civil rights approach envisions achieving empowerment. Wall argues that this approach is not without its limitations, as children's experience of being denied power on the basis of age transcends the socio-political realm and may be rooted in legal and institutional structures. Children's ability to "take political action, express public views, organize grassroots movements, hold positions of influence and press for new political agendas" is affected by their age,[33] necessitating their reliance on the initiative of adults to a very large extent to overcome legal and political impediments on their participation in decision making.

The apparent disconnect between different theoretical approaches to children's rights has led John Wall to argue for what he calls a "postmodernist ethicist" view of children's and human rights. Because any one theory is not sufficient individually to explain the different facets of children's rights, Wall allows the three different approaches (choice, interest and civil rights) to converge. He argues: "[C]hildren show that human rights ethics can and should involve

[29] CRC, Art. 12.

[30] Lansdown, *Evolving Capacities of the Child*, p. 3.

[31] Wall, "Human Rights in Light of Childhood," p. 532.

[32] Wall, *Ethics in Light of Childhood*, p. 120.

[33] Ibid.

a robust combination of all three traditional groundings. Children will suffer in one form or another so long as their developmental, top-down, and bottom-up rights are not intertwined with one another."[34]

Sociological approaches to childhood have also had a bearing on the way children's rights have been codified. The child, from a sociological perspective, is a social actor. Drawing on Freud's terminology on the phases of psychosexual development, Parsons and Bale described socialization as a "series of phases."[35] "[L]ikened to a pebble 'thrown' by the fact of birth into the social 'pond',"[36] the child starts out in the family and participates in wider social circles – akin to ripples – while growing and acquiring capacity (or "fulfill[s] certain of the conditions of full participation in the narrower ones").[37] In this configuration, childhood is deemed a "period" during which transition into adulthood takes place.[38] The CRC echoes the ideas of acquisition of capacity within ripples of social circles, when it refers to

> the responsibilities, rights and duties of parents or, where applicable, the members of the extended family or community as provided for by local custom, legal guardians or other persons legally responsible for the child, to provide, in a manner consistent with the evolving capacities of the child, appropriate direction and guidance.
>
> (Article 5 CRC)

The more recent sociology of childhood approach challenges the underlying assumptions about the universality of childhood and of children's experience as 'becomings.' Accordingly, "childhood (but also any identity) is a historically and culturally contingent construction, not an essential, transhistorical or transcultural continuity, predetermined by inherent biological or physiological factors."[39] Children, in turn, are not dependent beings but meaningful social actors. Mayall argues that the recognition of children as beings in their own right will be instrumental in changing the way we think about child-related issues. Children will

[34] Wall, "Human Rights in Light of Childhood," 536.

[35] Talcott Parsons and Robert F. Bales, *Family, Socialization and Interaction Process* (Routledge, 2002), p. 40.

[36] Ibid., p. 36.

[37] Ibid., p. 37.

[38] Jens Qvortrup, "Childhood as a Structural Form," in Jens Qvortrup, William A. Corsaro, Michael-Sebastian Honig (eds.), *The Palgrave Handbook of Childhood Studies* (1st ed.) (Palgrave Macmillan, 2009), pp. 23–24.

[39] Karin Lesnik-Oberstein, "Introduction: Voice, Agency and the Child," in Karin Lesnik-Oberstein (ed.), *Children in Culture, Revisited: Further Approaches to Childhood* (Palgrave Macmillan, 2011) p. 1.

thus be viewed as "competent, contributing social actors" who "intersect [. . .] with the structures surrounding their lives," whose "own wishes and expressed needs are relevant to the construction and implementation of social policies and practices."[40] Mayall further contends that understanding children "not just as individuals but as members of a social group" necessitates a reflection on "that group's rights to participate in constructing the social order, social policies and practices."[41] According to McGillivray, rights cannot be divorced from relationships an individual has with others based on the interdependence of individuals making up collectivities. She argues that rights are needed to overcome exclusion, which is "a declaration of subordination and an invitation to exploit."[42] Such insights are pivotal for thinking about the obligations of businesses in relation to children's rights and the need for having a conversation on why children's rights are relevant for private entities such as businesses.

1.1.2 The Premises for a Children's Rights Focus for Business Obligations

The overall perspective of both legal scholarship and of international efforts in view of conceptualizing the human rights obligations of actors other than the domestic state has remained largely fragmented. Debates on the extraterritorial human rights obligations of states, the human rights obligations of businesses and of financial actors remain by and large unlinked.[43] It is clear that a reconceptualization needs to take place in order to advance beyond traditional constrictive understandings. The relatively recent interest in children's human rights and business as a specialized area is indicative of a growing recognition that children and their rights merit particular attention in undertaking this reconceptualization. The premises warranting this particular attention include the status of childhood as a special period of development causing violations to have long-lasting and even transgenerational impacts, children being politically voiceless, experiencing difficulties in accessing information,

[40] Berry Mayall, "The Sociology of Childhood in Relation to Children's Rights" (2000) 8 *The International Journal of Children's Rights* 243–259 at 248.

[41] Ibid., 256.

[42] Anne McGillivray, "Why Children Do Have Equal Rights: In Reply to Laura Purdy" (1994) 2 *International Journal of Children's Rights* 243–258 at 257–258.

[43] Wouter Vandenhole, Gamze Erdem Türkelli and Rachel Hammonds, "New Human Rights Duty-Bearers: Towards a Re-conceptualisation of the Human Rights Duty-Bearer Dimension," in Anja Mihr and Mark Gibney (eds.), *The SAGE Handbook of Human Rights* (Sage, 2014).

not being consulted and facing challenges in accessing remedies.[44] These premises are based on an amalgamation of concepts from physiological and psychological developmental approaches, sociological frames and empowerment perspectives.

Childhood as a Stage of Rapid Development

The first premise for focusing on children's rights in the context of transnational human rights obligations, including those of businesses, is that childhood is a period of rapid development with physiological, psychological and social aspects. The heightened survival and development needs of children are linked to the nature of childhood as a period when the human organism develops holistically. During this period, deprivations ("of food, clean water, care and affection"), abuse and exploitation may have disproportionate impacts on the physical and psychological development of a child.[45]

Research on young children in developing countries shows first and foremost that "stunting, inadequate cognitive stimulation, iodine deficiency, and iron deficiency anaemia" and subsequently "malaria, intrauterine growth restriction, maternal depression, exposure to violence, and exposure to heavy metals" are important risk factors for children, determining negative outcomes in terms of biological and cognitive development.[46] Likewise, children born in iodine-deficient communities may reportedly lose on average as much as 13.5 IQ points when compared with children born in communities that do not suffer from an iodine deficiency.[47] While one might argue over whether IQ rates are the most appropriate measure of human capacity, such a difference remains statistically significant in terms of cognitive ability. Negative effects of material deprivations in childhood may also be decisive in determining adult outcomes. Indicators such as the prevalence of early childhood stunting and the number of people living in absolute poverty in a country are found to be intricately linked with low

[44] CRC Committee, GC 16 on state obligations regarding the impact of the business sector on children's rights, CRC/C/GC/16, 17 April 2013, para 4; UNICEF, *Children Are Everyone's Business: A Practical Workbook to Help Companies Understand and Address Their Impact on Children's Rights* (UNICEF, 2012), p. 15.

[45] UNICEF, *Children Are Everyone's Business*, p. 15.

[46] Susan P. Walker, Theodore D. Wachs et al., "Child Development: Risk Factors for Adverse Outcomes in Developing Countries" (2007) 369 *The Lancet* 145–157 at 145.

[47] UNICEF, *Tracking Progress on Child and Maternal Nutrition: A Survival and Development Priority* (UNICEF, 2009), p. 14.

levels of cognitive and educational performance in children.[48] These children are found to perform poorly because they receive fewer years of schooling and learn less during the school year, reducing drastically their productivity in adulthood. It has been argued that with lower levels of education for children, higher fertility rates and lower earnings, poverty is transmitted between generations.[49]

Emotional deprivation, abuse and exploitation in childhood may affect future physical and psychological health, educational outcomes and social relationships. Emerging patterns from medical research suggest that the greater the number of negative childhood experiences, both physiological and psychological, the greater the likelihood of health issues later on in life.[50] Research such as the Adverse Childhood Experiences (ACE) Study has uncovered that "multiple instances of traumatic or abusive childhood events" (those that are considered either physically or psychologically toxic) are linked to conditions like "cardiovascular disease, chronic lung disease, cancer, depression, alcoholism, and drug abuse."[51]

The first five years of childhood are believed to be the period when the seeds affecting social competence are sown and thus bear on the "emotional well-being and . . . later ability to functionally adapt in school and to form successful relationships throughout life."[52] Furthermore, these first years are also when the brain is most sensitive to the acquisition of skills critical for later in life, such as language, numeracy, vision, hearing, responding, peer social skills and emotional control.[53] Empirical research points to the pivotal nature of early childhood in the process of rapid development more so than any other part of childhood. Research on brain plasticity has uncovered so-called "sensitive periods" in early brain development. In fact, the physical and mental capacity of children to acquire vision, hearing, emotional control, habitual ways of responding,

[48] Sally Gratham-McGregor, Yin Bun Cheung et al., "Developmental Potential in the First 5 Years for Children in Developing Countries" (2007) 369 *The Lancet* 60–70 at 60.

[49] Ibid., 60–66.

[50] National Scientific Council on the Developing Child (NSCDC) and the National Forum on Early Childhood Policy and Programs (NFECPP), *The Foundations of Lifelong Health Are Built in Early Childhood* (Center on the Developing Child – Harvard University, 2010), p. 6.

[51] Ibid., pp. 5–6.

[52] NSCDC, "Children's Emotional Development Is Built into the Architecture of Their Brains" (2004) Working Paper No. 2, 1.

[53] Council for Early Child Development, *The Science of Early Child Development* (Council for Early Child Development, 2010), cited in Sophie Naudeau et al., *Investing in Young Children: An Early Childhood Development Guide for Policy Dialogue and Project Preparation* (World Bank, 2011), p. 6.

conceptualization and language peak on average roughly between months six and twenty-four of a child's life and start declining afterwards. Peer social skills and number skills peak between two and three years of age, respectively. By the time a child is five years of age, the brain is still sensitive to acquiring some cognitive skills such as language, social skills and numbers acquisition albeit at a slower rate but acquisition of vision, the sensitivity for acquiring vision, hearing and emotional control have all but ceased.[54]

A number of studies also indicate that when children experience chronic and extreme hardship without having support systems to shield them or to mitigate the severity of the hardship, they develop a "toxic stress response," which may lead to changes in brain architecture.[55] A number of studies have documented troubles with cognitive development and learning linked to this toxic stress response.[56] Children from more disadvantaged socioeconomic backgrounds are found to be more prone to having higher stress responses.[57] Furthermore, research reveals that almost half of children who live in poverty are exposed to violence, either witnessing it or indirectly being victims of it.[58] The importance of preventing negative experiences and creating positive environments for children both physiologically and psychologically is all the more evident given that removing the impacted children from a harmful environment after initial trauma has already occurred is not sufficient to reverse the effects caused by that experience.[59]

Enhancing the debate that is almost at the exclusive purview of developmentalist approaches, John Eekelaar has argued from a moral point of view that "all children should have an equal opportunity to maximize the resources available to them during their childhood (including their own inherent abilities) so as to minimize the degree to which they enter adult life affected by avoidable prejudices incurred

[54] Gillian Doherty, *Zero to Six: The Basis for School Readiness* (Applied Research Branch R-97-3E) (Human Resources Development Canada, 1997); Margaret Norrie McCain and J. Fraser Mustard, *Early Years Study* (Publications Ontario, 1999); Jack Shonkoff (ed.), *From Neurons to Neighborhoods: The Science of Early Childhood Development* (National Academy Press, 2000).

[55] NSCDC and NFECPP, *The Foundations of Lifelong Health*, p. 6.

[56] NSCDC, "Persistent Fear and Anxiety Can Affect Young Children's Learning and Development" (2010) Working Paper No. 9, p. 5.

[57] NSCDC and NFECPP, *The Foundations of Lifelong Health*, p. 7.

[58] Ibid., p. 1.

[59] NSCDC, "Persistent Fear and Anxiety Can Affect Young Children's Learning and Development," p. 6.

during childhood."[60] Whether the debate is framed in developmental terms (stunting lowers cognitive performance), in pedagogic terms (stunting causes lower educational outcomes due to lower cognitive performance), in economic terms (lower educational outcomes caused by stunting result in lower earnings) or in moral terms (the conditions leading to stunting result in inequalities and injustice), it is clear that especially the earlier years of childhood are a critical period in human life, determining not just present but future outcomes.

Disproportionate and Different Effects of Harms

The argument that children are "differently and more severely" impacted by "everyday harms" rests on findings from medical research on the impacts of exposure to toxins in the environment as well as data from different disciplines on "economic, social and physical disruptions."[61] One may refer in particular to the effects of pollutants, inadequate nutrition or disruptive events such as forced migration and displacement. While the focus rests once more on the developmental aspects of childhood, the disproportionate and different ways harms affect children are as much about children's "being" as their "becoming." In this respect, the definition of "harm" comprises but cannot be reduced to exposure to chemicals or other dangerous substances.

The first major international study on the effects of chemicals was undertaken by the World Health Organization (WHO) and the International Program on Chemical Safety (IPCS). This 1986 report analyzed the differences between adults and young children when exposed to chemicals, based largely on findings from medical science.[62] The report concluded that physiological differences between adults and young children such as larger body surface area compared to weight, higher metabolic rates and oxygen consumption, and greater energy requirements caused chemicals to be "absorbed more readily by the infant than the adult" and to have delayed effects as well as "manifestations due to the disturbed maturation of organ systems and their altered response to other environmental influences."[63] The conclusions from this study and subsequent research that has validated and built on its

[60] John Eekelaar, "The Emergence of Children's Rights" (1986) 6 *Oxford Journal of Legal Studies* 161–182 at 170.

[61] UNICEF, *Children Are Everyone's Business*, p. 15.

[62] Germaine Buck Louis et al., *Principles for Evaluating Risks from Chemicals During Infancy and Early Childhood: The Need for a Special Approach* (WHO, 1986).

[63] Ibid.

findings[64] have informed the argument of disproportionate and different effects of harms in children as compared to adults and hence, of the need for a special focus on children's needs and interests. Medical science reveals that children's metabolisms are able to automatically increase the absorption of required nutrients in accordance with their biological developmental needs.[65] While clearly useful for biological growth, this mechanism may also present dangers when, for instance, beneficial nutrients are masked by the presence of harmful chemicals in the environment. This is the reason why research finds that "lead . . . is absorbed to a greater extent in children than in adults" and that it also "accumulates more rapidly in children's bones than in adult bones, doubling between infancy and the late teen years."[66]

Children's increased risk of exposure to harmful chemicals or toxins relates also to their habits such as "hand-to-mouth behavior" and their preference to play on the ground.[67] Exposure to toxins in childhood means that there is a longer period of time for chronic illnesses set off by such exposure to develop.[68] In addition, research seems to suggest that the damage from exposure to toxins may sometimes be irreversible. For instance, once exposed to lead and adversely affected by it, a child's impaired developmental functioning may not improve even after that substance is successfully removed with medications from the child's body.[69] Beyond biological, behavioral and developmental reasons for the disproportionate effects of harms from exposure, Lewit and Schuurmann Baker identify another reason for children being "inadequately protected from environmental hazards": "because no national research or policy agenda exists to address their unique vulnerabilities."[70]

[64] For an overview of why a special consideration must be accorded to children's risk of exposure to chemicals with more recent data, see: WHO, *Summary of Principles for Evaluating Health Risks in Children Associated with Exposure to Chemicals* (WHO, 2011), www.who.int/ceh/health_risk_children.pdf (accessed 15 April 2019).

[65] Cynthia F. Bearer, "Environmental Health Hazards: How Children Are Different from Adults" (1995) 5 *The Future of Children – Critical Issues for Children and Youths* 11–26 at 20.

[66] Bearer, "Environmental Health Hazards," 20.

[67] Philip J. Landrigan and Joy E. Carlson, "Environmental Policy and Children's Health" (1995) 5 *The Future of Children – Critical Issues for Children and Youths* 34–52 at 36.

[68] Landrigan and Carlson, "Environmental Policy and Children's Health."

[69] Patrice L. Engle, Maureen M. Black et al., "Child Strategies to Avoid the Loss of Developmental Potential in More Than 200 Million Children in the Developing World" (2007) 369 *The Lancet* 229–242 at 236.

[70] Eugene M. Lewit and Linda Schuurmann Baker, "Children's Health and the Environment" (1995) 5 *The Future of Children – Critical Issues for Children and Youths* 8–10 at 9.

Harms need not originate from exposure to chemicals or pollutants. Socioeconomic disruptions can also inflict disproportionate harm on children's lives compared to adults. Research on poverty rates of children compared to the overall population has shown that in many countries child poverty rates tend to be higher than those in the general population.[71] For every 1 percent increase in poverty rates among the general population, child poverty was measured to increase 1.5 to 2 percent in five of the countries studied.[72] The European Commission's 2010 report on child poverty compared the at-risk-of-poverty rates for the overall population and for children in the EU.[73] The findings indicated that in most EU states children's at-risk-of-poverty rates (20 percent) were higher than those of adults and that children were at a higher risk of poverty on average (by 3 percent) than the general population (17 percent). Child poverty risk rates could exceed those of the general population even among better-performing members. The at-risk-of-poverty rate for children in EU28 had risen to 26.4 percent in 2016, 3.1 percent higher than the average rate for the general population (23.5 percent).[74] More worryingly, in some member states such as Bulgaria and Romania, the percentage of children living in a household at risk of poverty or social exclusion was over forty-five.[75] Similarly, 2016 OECD data on child poverty confirm that even among most of the world's affluent countries, poverty rates of children continue to be slightly higher than the poverty rates for the total population.[76]

Data compiled from household surveys or income data may overlook "invisible children," children most at risk of poverty who do not live in households such as children living in institutions, children in the prison system, asylum seeker or refugee children, children living on the streets or children in mobile homes such as Roma

[71] Michael G. Wyness, *Childhood and Society: An Introduction to the Sociology of Childhood* (Palgrave Macmillan, 2006), p. 35.

[72] UNICEF, *Children at Risk in Central and Eastern Europe: Perils and Promises – A Summary* (UNICEF, 1997), p. 3.

[73] Tarki Social Research Institute and Applica, *Child Poverty and Child Well-Being in the European Union: Volume 1 – Main Report* (European Commission Directorate General [DG] Employment, Social Affairs and Equal Opportunities, 2010), pp. 24–25.

[74] Eurostat, "People at Risk of Poverty or Social Exclusion," May 2018, https://ec.europa.eu/eurostat/statistics-explained/index.php/People_at_risk_of_poverty_or_social_exclusion#Number_of_people_at_risk_of_poverty_or_social_exclusion (accessed 24 April 2019).

[75] Ibid.

[76] OECD, "CO2.2: Child Poverty – OECD Family Database," 13 July 2018, p. 1, www.oecd.org/els/CO_2_2_Child_Poverty.pdf (accessed 15 April 2019).

children.[77] Intersectionality with migration or minority status exacerbates the risk of poverty for children who are already at a higher risk of poverty than the general population.[78] The discrepancy between overall and child poverty rates even in most affluent societies suggests that issues of disproportionate effect are not limited to countries with lower levels of economic development.

Conflict situations and displacement also bear more heavily on children both young and older. It has been estimated that twenty-two million of the forty million people displaced (either as refugees or as internally displaced persons) due to conflict are below twenty-four years of age.[79] In most instances, displacement is a long-term condition with one estimate noting that it lasts on average seventeen years, which would mean that a child born into displacement could conceivably spend an entire childhood in that situation.[80] Conflict situations acutely threaten children's physical and emotional health as well as educational opportunities and "can have a devastating impact on human nutrition by threatening livelihoods and compromising food security, health and the ability of caregivers to provide for the young."[81] Malnutrition is a common problem under such conditions. Studies indicate that an overwhelming majority (98.5 million out of 143 million) of underweight children below five years of age in the developing world are in emergency situations.[82] In conflict situations, the toll of other problems caused by political and social instability and poverty may be more severe than the violence itself. A 2008 UN Security Council (UNSC) report for instance cited that twenty-five times more Afghans (about 40,000 persons) died annually of hunger and poverty than as a result of violence.[83] In conflict areas, diseases may become rampant due to poor water quality, inadequate infrastructures, lack of sanitation and contamination. For instance, diarrhea, one of the leading causes of under-five child mortality globally accounting for approximately one in

[77] UNICEF Innocenti Research Centre, *Measuring Child Poverty: New League Tables of Child Poverty in the World's Rich Countries* (UNICEF Innocenti Research Centre, 2012), p. 21.

[78] Tarki and Applica, *Child Poverty and Child Well-Being in the EU: Vol. 1*, pp. 102–107.

[79] Women's Refugee Commission, "Education for Refugee Children Fact Sheet," 2010.

[80] Ibid.

[81] Office of the SRSG for Children and Armed Conflict in collaboration with UNICEF, *Machel Study 10-Year Strategic Review: Children and Conflict in a Changing World* (Office of the SRSG for Children and Armed Conflict and UNICEF, 2009).

[82] Ibid.

[83] United Nations Security Council (UNSC), "Report of the Security Council Mission to Afghanistan," S/2008/782, 12 December 2008, para. 37.

five child deaths, becomes a life-threatening condition in humanitarian crises.[84] Children are at a higher risk of mortality due to diarrhea than adults as a greater proportion of their body weight is made up of water.[85] Young children are even more vulnerable because their higher metabolic rates require more water and their kidneys are less able than adults and older children to conserve water.[86]

The long-term effects of emotional trauma due to loss of family members or acts such as violence or rape during conflict situations are not easily quantifiable, yet remain very pertinent. Research on Afghan school children found that "exposure to multiple trauma and caregiver mental health" strongly predicted poor mental outcomes for the children studied[87] and concluded that "[t]he experience of five or more traumatic events trebled the risk of probable psychiatric disorders and post-traumatic stress, also increasing depression symptoms."[88]

According to UNICEF data, one out of three children is out of school in conflict- or disaster-affected countries, amounting to a total of 104 million children worldwide.[89] Children in conflict- or disaster-affected countries make up half of all children out of school at the primary level.[90] At the turn of the millennium, the Women's Refugee Commission conducted research into education in conflict situations, which uncovered that most displaced and refugee children in conflict situations are not schooled. Where educational opportunities exist, the quality of education may not be very high due to infrastructural inadequacies such as the lack of appropriate school materials or classrooms. Also, high student-to-teacher ratios have the possibility of adversely affecting the quality of education.[91] UNHCR's 2016 report attested that refugee children who are "five times more likely to be out of school than non-refugee children" continue to have diminishing educational opportunities as they get older.[92]

84 UNICEF and WHO, *Diarrhoea: Why Children Are Still Dying and What Can Be Done Globally?* (UNICEF and WHO 2009), pp. 5 and 9.

85 Ibid., p. 10.

86 Ibid.

87 Catherine Panter-Brick et al., "Violence, Suffering, and Mental Health in Afghanistan: A School-Based Survey" (2009) 374 *The Lancet* 807–816 at 813.

88 Ibid.

89 UNICEF, *A Future Stolen: Young and Out-of-School* (UNICEF, 2018), p. 5.

90 Ibid.

91 Women's Commission for Refugee Women and Children, *Global Survey of Education in Emergencies* (Women's Commission for Refugee Women and Children, 2004), p. 17.

92 United Nations High Commissioner for Refugees (UNHCR), *Missing Out: Refugee Education in Crisis* (UNHCR, 2016), p. 4.

The recognition that children may be differently and disproportionately affected by negative conditions such as those stemming from exposure to harmful substances, pollution, malnutrition and conflict situations is an important stepping-stone in acknowledging the contribution that a children's rights focus may make with a view of addressing, remedying and preventing their occurrence. Giving children's rights a special place in addition to general human rights concerns may urge policy makers, whether public or private, to consider how children may be differently affected by a given policy prior to its adoption.

Invisibility

Children "employed or affected by business are often unseen and uncounted,"[93] in particular children illegally employed in supply chains or as domestic workers, children of migrant workers, children detained by security services and children who experience intersectional discrimination. Of course, children do not remain "unseen and uncounted" only when employed by business or affected by business practices and decisions. Acts and practices of all actors (state or non-state) that hold power and operate in their environments can potentially affect children, without these effects being acknowledged. When children are indirectly affected by economic activities and decisions as opposed to being directly affected, their visibility tends to diminish even further. For instance, children's rights violations such as hazardous child labor in supply chains may be more visible than children's rights violations that result from the displacement of a community or the pollution of the environment due to a large-scale infrastructure project.

Even when human rights are being highlighted, human rights of children may be overlooked. Cantwell's account of the CRC drafting negotiations is a case in point. Cantwell, who led the NGO Group for the CRC during the negotiation of the treaty, recalls that some delegates in the Working Group had initially called into question the usefulness of repeating fundamental rights that were already featured in the ICCPR and the ICESCR and expressed support for only including rights specific to children.[94] Of course, it does not follow that children's fundamental human rights will be systematically disregarded and disrespected by

[93] UNICEF, *Children Are Everyone's Business*, p. 15.

[94] Nigel Cantwell, "Are Children's Rights Still Human?," in Invernizzi and Williams (eds.), *The Human Rights of Children* (Ashgate, 2011), p. 41.

business as such. Yet, there is a risk that they may be an afterthought in the business and human-rights nexus in the absence of special attention.

Lack of Public Voice and Consultation

Children are not allowed in most jurisdictions to vote, be elected or legally organize, thus creating barriers even for older children to having their voices heard. Children are not ordinarily considered social stakeholders, especially when political and economic decisions are concerned. As Qvortrup, Corsaro and Honig point out, children's participatory potential and contributions have been overlooked while they are distanced from decision-making centers.[95] The Introduction to the Children's Rights and Business Principles (CRBPs), a set of voluntary principles developed by UNICEF, Save the Children and UN Global Compact on children's rights and business in the wake of the adoption of UN Guiding Principles on Business and Human Rights (UNGPs), underlines that although children make up almost one third of the global population, "they are rarely given a say or consulted about how communities make decisions – even decisions affecting them directly, such as planning for schools and recreational areas."[96]

Preconceived notions of a child's immaturity or inadequate reasoning skills, which often underlie the systematic failure to include children in decision making, appear not to be backed by empirical evidence. Even very young children may be able to comprehend and exercise moral judgment on what seem to be highly complex and abstract concepts. Research shows, for instance, that children as young as six years old consider restrictions by institutions on freedom of speech and religion unacceptable.[97] Likewise, children between eight and eleven years of age have complex understandings of these freedoms, including their personal as well as sociocultural dimensions: young children view these rights as rights for "individual self-expression" while older children consider rights as societal tools for "fostering communication" or "rectify[ing] social injustices."[98] Hence, denying children a voice not only deprives

95 Jens Qvortrup, William A. Corsaro and Michael-Sebastian Honig, "Why Social Studies of Childhood: An Introduction to the Handbook," in Qvortrup, Corsaro and Honig (eds.), *The Palgrave Handbook of Childhood Studies* (1st ed.) (Palgrave Macmillan, 2009), p. 6.

96 UNICEF, Save the Children, UN Global Compact, "Children's Rights and Business Principles," 2012, 2.

97 Charles C. Helwig and Elliot Turiel, "Children's Social and Moral Reasoning," in Peter K. Smith and Craig H. Hart (eds.), *Wiley-Blackwell Handbook of Childhood Social Development* (2nd ed.) (Wiley-Blackwell, 2010), p. 576.

98 Ibid.

public debates on the valuable contributions children could make, but also creates unjust restrictions very clearly visible to children.

The children's rights-based approach, like any rights-based approach, "seeks to challenge, dismantle and reconfigure existing power relations and structures . . . by orienting the terms of the policy debates towards the language of rights" and empowering children as "active subjects" with individual entitlements.[99] Faced with children's lack of public voice and adult reluctance to consult their opinions, children's rights provide an avenue for children's empowerment. Recognizing the rights of the most powerless is a way to alter existing hierarchies, fight exclusion, push for equality, and offer access to legal processes.[100] Federle also emphasizes the "transformative aspect" of human rights of children and situates rights in the greater scheme of power relationships, whereby rights become enablers for children. For this reason, in order to achieve the best possible outcomes for children and to overcome the lack of public voice, children should be empowered by rights that "have the potential to reduce victimization and dependence by changing the rights holder into a powerful individual who commands the respect of those in the legal system."[101]

On Targeting and Mainstreaming

Children are members of societal structures and are affected by the same issues that affect the communities of which they are a part. Rights violations and deprivations create disadvantages for everyone. Issues like poverty, environmental hazards, displacement and conflict impact communities more generally and may result in human rights violations. Focusing on children's rights and their specific conditions does not substitute a children's rights perspective in the place of a broader human rights one but rather complements the broader human rights perspective by placing children in the spotlight. Achieving this requires "articulat[ing] right claims on behalf of children that promote children's legal interests without reference to capacity, protection, or dependence."[102]

[99] John Tobin, "Understanding a Human Rights Based Approach to Matters Involving Children: Conceptual Foundations and Strategic Considerations," in Invernizzi and Williams (eds.), *The Human Rights of Children* (Ashgate, 2011), p. 82.

[100] Federle, "Rights Flow Downhill," 345 and Van Bueren, *The International Law on the Rights of the Child*, p. 6.

[101] Federle, "Review Essay: Rights, Not Wrongs" (2009) 17 *International Journal of Children's Rights* 321–329 at 329.

[102] Ibid., 328.

A special children's rights approach allows for a critical assessment of how rights can create a more inclusive and enabling environment across the board, not only for some but for everyone, including children. The CRC Committee defines a child rights approach as:

> [O]ne which furthers the realization of the rights of all children as set out in the Convention by developing the capacity of duty bearers to meet their obligations to respect, protect and fulfil rights (art. 4) and the capacity of rights holders to claim their rights . . ., is holistic and places emphasis on supporting the strengths and resources of the child him/herself and all social systems of which the child is a part: family, school, community, institutions, religious and cultural systems.[103]

Accordingly, the two key components are compliance with obligations incumbent on duty-bearers and the empowerment of rights-holders in claiming their rights.

There are two major avenues for advancing subfields of human rights, such as women's rights, children's rights or the rights of the disabled: mainstreaming and targeting. The targeting approach denotes a special focus on a given subset of specialized rights whereas mainstreaming would necessitate that this subset of rights is a permanent concern in designing and implementing legislation, policies and programs that have the potential to impact on these rights. The "underlying rationale [in mainstreaming] is that certain policy issues are of such paramount importance that they need to inform all undertakings."[104] Although mainstreaming has now become a buzzword, it continues to present challenges because it requires knowledge of the mainstreamed set of rights and the capability to adequately integrate the mainstreamed perspective effectively and continuously in policies or normative responses to real world problems, legal or otherwise. A comparison of targeting versus mainstreaming in Sweden's and Norway's international cooperation on children's rights issues has led researchers to conclude that targeting produces "comparatively quick results" but suffers from "limited coverage, short duration and low sustainability" whereas mainstreaming is "slower in producing results and more resource-demanding, though with better prospects of long-term sustainability."[105] Thus, whether targeting or mainstreaming is a better approach may be dependent on a number

[103] CRC Committee, General Comment (GC) 13 on the right of the child to freedom from all forms of violence, CRC/C/GC/13, 18 April 2011, para 59.

[104] Arne Tostensen et al., *Supporting Child Rights: Synthesis of Lessons Learned in Four Countries* (Edita, 2011), p. 97.

[105] Ibid.

of factors and may benefit from a case-by-case appraisal. In the context of children's rights and business, whether children's rights should be mainstreamed in the broader business and human rights debates or specifically targeted is an interesting question. Of course, it may be wise to remember that targeting and mainstreaming are not mutually exclusive or antithetical exercises and may make up a "two-pronged strategy."[106] This "two-pronged strategy" allows for targeting to be used in the short to medium term to create awareness and a sense of urgency on an issue while mainstreaming denotes a long-term perspective to keep an active focus on the issue. Thus, focusing specifically on children's rights in the context of the business and human rights debates is important as a first step in bringing visibility to children's rights issues through targeting. Before children's rights can be mainstreamed in the broader transnational human rights obligations debate, there is a need to illuminate what children's rights mean in this context and how they can be contextualized.

1.1.3 The Characteristics of a Children's Rights Focus for Business Duties

What is it that distinguishes a children's rights focus from a general human rights approach when dealing with businesses as duty-bearers from both a conceptual and practical standpoint? A children's rights focus has a two-fold consequence. First, it entitles children to additional rights and entails corresponding additional duties. Second, it provides specific principles to guide the realization of these substantive rights by duty-bearers.

Children are entitled to their rights as human beings as well as special rights by virtue of being children. The Inter-American Court of Human Rights (IACtHR) recognized the distinctive nature of children's rights in *Girls Dilcia Yean and Violeta Bosico* v. *the Dominican Republic*, concluding that

> children . . . by virtue of that condition had special rights entailing special duties on the part of their family, society, and the state, and required special protection from the State, which should be understood as an additional, complementary right.[107]

[106] Ibid.

[107] *Girls Dilcia Yean and Violeta Bosico* v. *the Dominican Republic* (Judgment on the preliminary exceptions, merits and reparations) [2005] IACtHR para. 133.

Children's rights, as legalized in the CRC, are often characterized as being guided by four general principles based on Articles 2 (nondiscrimination), 3 (best interests), 6 (survival and development) and 12 (right to express views, also deemed participation).[108] The so-called general principles, initially addressed to states parties to guide their periodic reporting to the Committee, have enjoyed widespread recognition, owing to the work of the CRC Committee as well as their espousal by international organizations such as UNICEF.[109] These general principles are increasingly being conceptualized as core principles for other children's rights duty-bearers beyond the state. For example, the CRBPs place these principles at the heart of corporate duties for children's rights to "underpin any action concerning children, whether taken by governments, parents, communities or the private sector."[110]

The two principles of the best interests of the child and survival and development are related more intricately to the position of the child as a human being that progresses from a more dependent being to one that is increasingly independent and expressive. The CRC Committee has called best interests "a right, a principle and a rule of procedure."[111] The CRC Committee, GC 5 had already clarified that the application of the principle of best interests as a rule of procedure, which requires a systematic consideration of how children's rights and interests may be impacted by proposed decisions or actions not only when they affect children directly but also when they do so indirectly.[112] The CRC Committee itself has recognized that the concept of best interests is a complex one whose "content must be determined on a case-by-case basis."[113] The practical implications of a best interests approach in the context of business duties may not be clearly discernible. One important contribution of the CRC Committee's GC 16 on state obligations

[108] CRC Committee, GC 5 on general measures of implementation of the CRC, CRC/GC/2003/5, 27 November 2003.

[109] The so-called general principles have been criticized in literature on various grounds; see "Introduction," in Wouter Vandenhole, Gamze Erdem Türkelli and Sara Lembrechts, *A Commentary on the Convention on the Rights of the Child and Its Protocols* (Edward Elgar, forthcoming).

[110] CRBPs, Principle 1, p. 14.

[111] CRC Committee, GC 14 on the right of the child to have his or her best interests taken as a primary consideration, CRC/C/GC/14, 29 May 2013, para 6.c.

[112] CRC Committee, GC 5, para. 12.

[113] CRC Committee, GC 14, para. 32. (For a broader discussion of best interests and its case-by-case application, also see: Vandenhole and Erdem Türkelli, "Best Interests of the Child," in Jonathan Todres and Shani King [eds.], *The Oxford Handbook on Children's Rights* (Oxford University Press, forthcoming))

regarding the impact of the business sector on children's rights is the use of "Child-rights impact assessments" (CRIAs) as well as child impact evaluation as processes by which businesses and states can ascertain that best interests of children are in fact a primary consideration.[114] Impact assessments have the benefit of being a method already familiar to businesses by virtue of environmental and social impact assessments that are required by law in many jurisdictions prior to the approval of investment projects. In essence, when conducted continuously, CRIAs may be an effective way of "[e]nsuring that the best interests of the child are a primary consideration in business-related legislation and policy development and delivery at all levels of governments."[115]

The companion to best interests, the principle of survival and development, is not only a reiteration of the importance of a child's right to life but to the right to "physical, mental, spiritual, moral, psychological and social development."[116] As such, when legislations are drafted, when public or private policies are made, they should be done so to support the development of children in this extensive meaning of the term. In scholarship, the principle of survival and development has also been considered as giving meaning to the principle of best interests.[117]

The two other general principles, namely nondiscrimination and participation, are not specific to children's rights. Nondiscrimination is a key principle underlying many other human rights conventions, where the rights are designated for persons within a specific group that are disadvantaged by virtue of belonging to that group.[118] In fact, nondiscrimination is "a basic principle of any rights based approach."[119] Many groups have historically been portrayed as vulnerable or dependent through discourse constructed by those in positions of power. This constructed discourse of vulnerability and dependency has allowed

[114] The concept was first introduced in CRC Committee's GC 5, para. 45.

[115] CRC Committee, GC 16, para. 78.

[116] CRC Committee, GC 5, para. 12.

[117] Jean Zermatten, "Best Interests of the Child," in Saïd Mahmoudi et al., *Child-Friendly Justice: A Quarter Century of the UN Convention on the Rights of the Child* (Brill Nijhoff, 2015), p. 34.

[118] See Arts. 1, 2 and 5 Convention on the Elimination of All Forms of Racial Discrimination (CERD), Arts. 1 and 2 Convention on the Elimination of All Forms of Discrimination against Women (CEDAW), Art. 5 Convention on the Rights of Persons with Disabilities (CRPD) and Art. 7 International Convention on the Protection of the Rights of All Migrant Workers and Members of Their Families (CPRMW).

[119] Tobin, "Understanding a Human Rights Based Approach to Matters Involving Children," p. 70.

denying certain people equal social and legal status. Moreover, negative effects of rights violations perpetuate vulnerability and further disenfranchise those experiencing multiple and intersectional discrimination.[120] Often, being a child is sufficient to put an individual at a disadvantage compared to an adult with fully recognized legal participation rights. The disenfranchisement is compounded for children who belong to more than one disadvantaged or marginalized group, such as girl children, indigenous children or children with disabilities. The principle of participation is also a corrective to combat the created voicelessness of persons or groups experiencing marginalization and disadvantage as well as their absence from processes and decisions that affect them.[121] Often, disenfranchisement and lack of visibility come about as a result of discrimination. The principle of participation accompanies the principle of nondiscrimination in creating equality of opportunity or the so-called level playing field. While the two principles are not specific to children's rights, they are nonetheless critical to counterbalance the relative invisibility of children in standard setting on human rights obligations of business. As articulated by the Committee, the nondiscrimination principle also entails the active identification of "individual children and groups of children the recognition and realization of whose rights may demand special measures."[122]

Tobin argues that other general principles, due deference and evolving capacities both extracted from Article 5 CRC, should also inform a children's rights-based approach in addition to best interests and survival and development.[123] Tobin's due deference principle means that the role of parents and guardians should be respected in exercising their duties towards a child.[124] The second principle is that of evolving capacities, which means that children are to be given more power in the exercise of their rights as they mature. Evolving capacities have less to do with the rights themselves than their exercise: "All the rights in the [CRC] extend to all children irrespective of capacity. What is at issue is where responsibility for the exercise of the rights lies."[125] There is an inverse

[120] The seminal work on intersectionality is Kimberlé Williams Crenshaw, "Mapping the Margins: Intersectionality, Identity Politics, and Violence Against Women of Color," in Martha Albertson Fineman and Rixanne Mykitiuk (eds.), *The Public Nature of Private Violence* (Routledge, 1994), pp. 93–118.

[121] See Art. 5 CERD, Art. 11 CEDAW, Arts. 29 and 30 CRPD, Arts. 42 and 43 CPRMW, Art. 41 of the nonbinding UN Declaration on the Rights of Indigenous Peoples.

[122] CRC Committee, GC 5, para. 12.

[123] Tobin, "Understanding a Human Rights Based Approach," p. 72.

[124] Ibid.

[125] Lansdown, *Evolving Capacities of the Child*, p. ix.

relationship between due deference and evolving capacities: as children get older and mature, the deference to power exercised by parents or guardians declines. Evolving capacities thus underscores the need for "appropriate respect for children's agency without exposing them prematurely to the full responsibilities normally associated with adulthood."[126] Tobin's insights are valuable because, in this way, protection and participation aspects of children's rights may be brought to a better balance. The principle of due deference is material in the business and children's rights nexus, as it underscores the importance of respecting parents' rights and enabling them to provide and care for their children with repercussions for policies on maternity and paternity, wages, health and safety standards at work as well as interactions with communities housing business investments. Evolving capacities is, in turn, an important safeguard to ensure that children are consulted and involved in decision-making on issues that are of concern to them within business and human rights debates.

Any children's rights-focused exploration of the human rights obligations of businesses has to begin by exploring the broader transnational human rights obligations debate, given that most discussions and progress have taken place within that broader human rights debate. Yet, to be complete, that exploration cannot remain at a general human rights level. The two human rights principles of nondiscrimination and participation are key to ensuring that de facto constraints created on the bases of age, disability status, minority status and others do not hamper the discharge of human rights obligations by duty-bearers, including businesses. They have to be complemented by core principles underlying a children's rights approach. The most comprehensive vision of a children's rights perspective is served by embracing all important principles enshrined in the CRC, namely of best interests, survival and development as well as the role assigned to parents or other relevant caretakers (due deference) and evolving capacities.

1.1.4 The Need for a Children's Rights Specific Approach: An Intermediate Conclusion

Childhood and the particular situation of children in society have been captivating subjects of study across many disciplines. Because children are multifaceted beings, numerous disciplines have long explored the physical, psychological, social, economic and moral attributes of their lives.

[126] Ibid.

In most disciplines, there is no consensus on the nature of childhood and the characterization of the child. A historical review of the child from the perspective of moral philosophy is able to distinguish "top-down," "bottom-up" and "developmental" approaches simultaneously inhabiting the same disciplinary space.[127] The implicit lesson emerging from moral philosophy from antiquity through Enlightenment is that children may have rights with provision components to guide their transition from "becomings" to "beings" in their own right. On the other hand, a synthesis of the different modern theories of rights under moral philosophy, namely, choice theory, interest theory and the civil rights approach, demonstrates that each of them tends to favor one aspect of rights. Focusing on capacity and the exercise of rights, choice theory provides the premises for "top-down" protection. Interest theory, on the other hand, focuses on children's needs, which is correlated with a "developmental" provision approach. The civil rights approach is squarely about recognizing children as independent actors and therefore prioritizes rights fostering children's "bottom-up" participation. These three distinct approaches are in fact complementary in closing a "human rights circle," which in turn creates corresponding duties correlated to each of the protection, provision and participation aspects. Although substantive rights often have a stronger focus on either protection, provision or participation, each substantive right may also have protection, provision and participation dimensions. When businesses engage with children or are involved in ventures that have potential impacts on children, a specific focus on children's rights is important in ensuring that none of the three dimensions of children's rights is overlooked, especially for children experiencing multiple and intersectional discrimination.

Childhood is indisputably a stage of rapid development in human life. Both physiological and psychological (including psychosocial) approaches to childhood and to children's rights distinguish children's particular experiences from those of adults by virtue of the contextual importance and distinctiveness of childhood as a developmental stage. Although children's experience of development will be shaped by their circumstances and social space they share with others, the breadth, depth and speed of physiological and cognitive development that occurs in childhood remain unparalleled for all children. Perhaps more striking is the fact that children's capacities and the recognition of their agency are lowest when their physiological and psychosocial development is at

[127] Wall, "Human Rights in Light of Childhood."

its most rapid. As such, children most likely to be adversely and severely impacted by business activities and decisions may also be the ones that do not have any measure of recourse to public voice and remediation.

Lessons from different disciplines ranging from moral philosophy to psychology and sociology, when merged with medical, economic and social research, create a more holistic and comprehensive children's rights vision for conceptualizing business duties towards children. In this children's rights vision, children are capable of agency and have rights to participate. They also have interests that warrant protection and provision, not because of any permanent structural dependence but because of physiological and psychosocial developmental needs. There is no one linear developmental trajectory for all children and children participate in the creation and recreation of social structures within their specific conditions as social actors in their own right.

Research findings from various disciplines indicate that children are both more severely impacted by adverse physical, social, economic, environmental or psychological harm and more susceptible to being impacted. On the other hand, children from a very young age are able to form and express informed views and exercise agency. The development of a children's rights and business discourse should thus be based not only on the unique character of childhood as a developmental stage which necessitates enhanced protection from harm and a heightened duty for the provision of care and other services, but also on children's disadvantaged situation as regards participation, exemplified by children's lack of a formal public voice and exclusion from consultation processes. This relatively recent focus on children's rights within the broader business and human rights debates is a way in which children may become more visible, more active as agents and also be accorded the level of protection and provided with care and services necessary for their holistic development. A true children's rights focus for business obligations would be practically translated into the inclusion of the four children's rights-specific principles of best interests, survival and development, due deference and evolving capacities, as argued by Tobin, in addition to nondiscrimination and participation, both of which are important principles of international human rights law more generally.

1.2 Businesses as Human and Children's Rights Duty-Bearers

> One thing law does is to serve as a common metric. . . . As lawyers, we turn everything into rights and obligations. That's our common metric, our

common currency. It's almost like alchemy, where we take all these disparate things, complicated cases, and we reduce them to: "You have these obligations and you have these rights, and how do those work?"

Anne-Marie Slaughter[128]

The traditional reading of international law designates the domestic state as the primary and perhaps only duty-bearer for the realization of children's rights and the sole actor responsible for rights violations occurring in the country. This view, however, fails to acknowledge the socioeconomic interactions that underpin global production and consumption patterns. States, businesses and other economic entities interact in multiple ways while investments and finance routinely move across borders. Although they mostly remain unseen and unheard, children inhabit the universes of production and consumption simultaneously, impacted by the multiple and complex interactions of various economic actors, state and otherwise.

Various nonlegal approaches have been proposed to govern the interactions businesses have with human beings and their communities. For one, the concept of Corporate Social Responsibility (CSR), defined since the late 1970s along the lines of the "social responsibility of business encompass[ing] the economic, legal, ethical, and discretionary expectations that society has of organizations at a given point in time,"[129] is showcased as an alternative to legal regulation. Yet, as Anne-Marie Slaughter's words unequivocally illuminate, law can serve as a useful common metric to disentangle complex situations in the language of rights and obligations and to thus offer solutions. Of course, law does not exist in a vacuum nor is it best served in being conceptualized as such. Oscar Schachter once wrote that "international lawyers, both individually and as a group, play a role in the process of creating new law and in extending existing law to meet emerging needs."[130] This "international legislative task" requires analyzing existing binding rules under public international law as well as nonbinding norms that have been proliferating in the area of business and human rights during the last decade of the 20th century and more rapidly since the beginning of the 21st century. It also requires identifying trends and patterns of legalization, even if that

[128] Anne-Marie Slaughter, "Filling Power Vacuums in the New Global Legal Order" (2013) 54(3) *Boston College Law Review* 919–936 at 934.

[129] Archie B. Caroll, "A Three-Dimensional Conceptual Model of Corporate Social Performance" (1979) 4 *Academy of Management Review* 497–505 at 500.

[130] Oscar Schachter, "The Invisible College of International Lawyers" (1977–1978) 72(2) *Northwestern University Law Review* 217–226 at 223.

process of legalization does not happen in traditional treaty-making settings.

"[A]n increasing need to attach *public law duties to ostensibly private actors*"[131] underlies the preoccupation with conceptualizing duty-bearers beyond the state. As Koh eloquently puts it, this vocation "means using transnational law to help organize the activities and relations of myriad transnational players, not simply nation-states, with the goal not of reflecting parochial state [and private[132]] interests, but of advancing an enlightened global system dedicated to the promotion of human dignity."[133] Of course, the proliferation of human rights norms and their enforcement are not the only avenues for achieving human dignity and pursuing social justice.[134] Nonetheless, human rights law is and will remain an important and adequate component of public international law's response to the challenges posed by the changing global political and economic landscape.

The prominence of states in international lawmaking, including in the construction of the human rights legal regime in the aftermath of World War II, has also resulted in what might be called a statist fixation. The erroneous conclusion that since human rights treaties are concluded between states, human rights must be addressed exclusively or principally to states has all too often been voiced by despondent commentators in attempts to cast doubt on the reasonability of scholarly or policy-oriented initiatives seeking to broaden the scope of human rights duty-bearers. To counteract the statist bias specifically within children's rights, it is worth noting that although the CRC is an international human rights treaty negotiated and ratified by states parties, it sets out parameters for the relationship of children and their rights not just vis-à-vis states but also rights vis-à-vis and alongside the child's parents, extended family and community.[135] Hence, the argument that the provisions of the CRC on the human rights of children concern only states parties and no other

[131] Harold H. Koh, "Is There a 'New' New Haven School of International Law?" (2007) 32 *The Yale Journal of International Law* 559–573 at 569 (original emphasis).

[132] Author's addition.

[133] Koh, "Is There a 'New' New Haven School of International Law?," 572.

[134] See, for instance, the critique of David Kennedy, "Reassessing International Humanitarianism: The Dark Sides," 2005, www.law.harvard.edu/faculty/dkennedy/speeches/TheDarkSides.pdf, pp. 3–4 (accessed 24 April 2019).

[135] See Arts. 5 (responsibilities, rights and duties of parents or, where applicable, the members of the extended family or community), 18 (primary responsibility of parents/legal guardians for the upbringing and development of the child) and 27 (primary responsibility of parents and others to secure adequate conditions of living) CRC.

types of actors (be they private individuals such as parents, communities or business enterprises) is an apparent fallacy. At the intersection of business and children's rights, there is an evident need to "devise new and innovative approaches as well as to adapt existing approaches if NSAs are to be held properly to account under the CRC."[136]

Designating NSAs as human rights duty-bearers under international human rights law is often met with strong reluctance and sometimes even a certain degree of resistance. One reason is that states already have obligations under international law not only to respect human rights by not interfering with their enjoyment but also to protect human rights from incursions by private actors.[137] Arguably, if all states in the world were able and willing to regulate the activities of businesses operating within their borders effectively, there would be no pressing reasons to address actors beyond the domestic state as direct human rights duty-bearers under international law. The reality, however, is that many states are unable, and some states are unwilling, to protect or even respect the human rights of persons living on their territories. Human rights, which is "distinct from the current enforcement system of international human rights law," can be used to remedy the shortcomings of the existing enforcement system by focusing on the rights-holder and not the "identity of the violator."[138]

Accordingly, the inability of standing legal mechanisms to remedy situations where human rights are violated or remain unrealized, simply on the basis of the claim that their violator is not a traditionally agreed duty-bearer, does not nullify the existence of human rights obligations of that violator as such. Even more importantly, that certain actors such as private enterprises have not traditionally been deemed human rights duty-bearers under existing international legal mechanisms should not prejudice their consideration as such through the evolution of international law.

Existing inadequacies of human rights legal mechanisms at the international level in responding to "widening gaps between the scope and

[136] Alston and Tobin (with the assistance of Mac Darrow), *Laying the Foundations for Children's Rights: An Independent Study of Some Key Legal and Institutional Aspects of the Impact of the Convention on the Rights of the Child* (UNICEF, 2005), p. xii.

[137] John H. Knox, "The Ruggie Rules: Applying Human Rights Law to Corporations," in Radu Mares (ed.), *The UN Guiding Principles on Business and Human Rights – Foundations and Implementation* (Martinus Nijhoff Publishers, 2012), p. 55.

[138] McBeth, *International Economic Actors and Human Rights*, p. 7.

impact of economic forces and actors, and the capacity of societies to manage their adverse consequences"[139] should certainly not impede normative assessments of how law might better respond to existing realities and assist in better managing the adverse impacts of these actors. Notwithstanding the eventual outcome of *Kadi* in the Grand Chamber of the Court of Justice of the European Union (CJEU), the Court of First Instance's bold statement concerning the peremptory status of human rights based on the UN Charter[140] and its binding nature on the members of the UN and its bodies[141] is a welcome challenge to conventional legal thinking. Even if not all human rights norms can be considered non-derrogable *jus cogens* provisions, overcoming the misconception that human rights are merely contractual obligations creates space to reaffirm their fundamental and universal nature without prejudice to the identity of eventual violators.

Two issues have dominated the debate on direct human rights obligations of NSAs, especially businesses. The first issue is linked to the state-centricity of traditional human rights mechanisms and the near obsession to link human rights obligations to jurisdiction in its narrowest conception. The second issue is that of subjecthood under international law or international legal personality and the perceived difficulties arising from extending subjecthood to entities without recognized public functions. Yet, attributing human rights obligations exclusively on the basis of notions such as jurisdiction and constraining subjecthood in international law to a certain class of actors is problematic in achieving the fundamental motivation of human rights law, as outlined in the Preamble to the UDHR: "the recognition of the inherent dignity and of the equal and inalienable rights of all members of the human family [as] the foundation of freedom, justice and peace in the world."[142]

139 John G. Ruggie, *Just Business: Multinational Corporations and Human Rights* (W.W. Norton, 2013), p. xxiii.

140 The Court of First Instance held: "the [UN Charter] itself presupposes the existence of mandatory principles of international law, in particular, the protection of the fundamental rights of the human person. In the preamble to the Charter, the peoples of the United Nations declared themselves determined to 'reaffirm faith in fundamental human rights, in the dignity and worth of the human person" (*Yassin Abdullah Kadi* v. *Council of the European Union and Commission of the European Communities*, Judgment of the Court of First Instance (Second Chamber, extended composition) CJEU 21 September 2005, para. 228).

141 Ibid., para. 229.

142 UDHR, Preamble (para. 1).

1.2.1 Breaking Free from "Jurisdiction"

Jurisdiction is the habitual link used for determining whether a given state is to be or can be held responsible for the realization of human rights in a given context or as regards a certain person or group. Many meanings are given to the concept of jurisdiction in international law, including its use as "a synonym for words such as power, authority, or control, either over people or over territory, or as a synonym for the territory within which such power is exercised."[143] Jurisdiction has a dual-faceted nature: it may either be permissive (i.e. allowing for its exercise) or mandatory (i.e. requiring its exercise). In fact, the traditional "negative" understanding of jurisdiction in public international law (thus, what is permissible) and its "positive" understanding in human rights law (thus, what is required) may be distinguished by exactly this parameter.[144] The mandatory meaning of jurisdiction in human rights law sets it apart from jurisdiction under general public international law, given that human rights obligations may flow from effective control over persons or territory (mandatory jurisdiction) even when a state would not be considered to have (permissive) jurisdiction under public international law.[145] Notwithstanding this basic distinction between mandatory versus permissive jurisdiction, the exercise of jurisdiction under public international law is also increasingly assuming more "positive" characteristics in the form of obligations.[146] A way out of the permissive versus mandatory distinction might be to restyle the idea of state jurisdiction under public international law to include "a mixture of discretionary, mandatory and prohibitive elements."[147]

Judges Higgins, Kooijmans and Buergenthal argued that the "slow but steady shift to a more extensive application of extraterritorial jurisdiction by States reflects the emergence of values which enjoy an ever-increasing recognition in international society."[148] While extending

[143] Marko Milanovic, *Extraterritorial Application of Human Rights Treaties: Law, Principles, and Policy* (Oxford University Press, 2011), p. 39.

[144] Cedric Ryngaert, "The Concept of Jurisdiction in International Law," in Alexander Orakhelashvili (ed.), *Research Handbook on Jurisdiction and Immunities in International Law* (Edward Elgar, 2015), p. 54.

[145] Alex Mills, "Rethinking Jurisdiction in International Law" (2014) 84(1) *British Yearbook of International Law: 2013* 187–239 at 194, footnote 22.

[146] See Ryngaert, "The Concept of Jurisdiction in International Law," 54.

[147] Mills, "Rethinking Jurisdiction in International Law," 213.

[148] *Arrest Warrant of 11 April 2000* (*Democratic Republic of the Congo* v. *Belgium*) ICJ, Joint Separate Opinion of Judges Higgins, Kooijmans and Buergenthal, Judgment of 14 February 2002, para 73.

"non-territorially based grounds of national jurisdiction" for the most egregious crimes under international law is considered a welcome development in this vein,[149] the extension of nonterritorial jurisdiction has been a feature transcending international criminal law and crossing over into children's rights law. One example from children's rights is the consideration of the sale of children, child prostitution and child pornography as offenses that permit the extension of nonterritorial jurisdiction under the Optional Protocol on the Sale of Children, Child Prostitution and Child Pornography (Article 4.2 OPSC), in line with international criminal law approaches.

Nearly all global and regional human rights instruments reference jurisdiction as grounds on which a state's human rights obligations are to be invoked and its eventual responsibility engaged. The general obligation provision under Article 4 CRC, however, recognizes state obligation to "undertake all appropriate legislative, administrative, and other measures for the implementation of the rights" under the CRC but does not link these obligations to jurisdiction. On the other hand, the jurisdiction condition is included under Article 2.1 CRC, which notes that the States Parties to the CRC "shall respect and ensure the rights set forth in the [CRC] to each child within their jurisdiction without discrimination of any kind." In doing so, the provision links the obligation of respecting and ensuring children's rights without discrimination to jurisdiction but does not provide a general obligation specifically tying jurisdiction to territory. In fact, the CRC Committee has argued, in response to widespread child sexual abuse findings in Catholic places of worship and schools around the globe, that the jurisdiction of the Holy See extends to persons and institutions under its authority as per canon law even if these are beyond the territory of the Vatican.[150] This interpretation is nonconventional and bound to be controversial from a traditional public international law perspective, as was reflected in the Holy See's response to the Committee, which stated that it did not "have the capacity or legal obligation to impose [children's rights] principles upon the local Catholic churches and institutions present on the territory of other States and whose activities abide with national laws" and that such would violate the "principle of non-interference in the internal affairs of States."[151] Of

[149] Ibid.

[150] CRC Committee, "Concluding observations on the second periodic report of the Holy See," 31 January 2014, CRC/C/VAT/CO/2, para 8.

[151] The Holy See, "Comments of the Holy See on the Concluding Observations of the Committee on the Rights of the Child," 2014, www.vatican.va/roman_curia/secretariat_

course, the Vatican response confounds the notion of noninterference in domestic affairs, given that the ICJ pronounced as early as 1970 in its landmark *Barcelona Traction* case that the rights of the human person, thus including the human child, were *erga omnes* obligations:

> By their very nature, the [obligations of a State towards the international community as a whole] are the concern of all States. In view of the importance of the rights involved, all States can be held to have a legal interest in their protection; they are obligations *erga omnes*.
>
> Such obligations derive, for example, in contemporary international law [among others] . . . from the principles and rules concerning the basic rights of the human person . . . .[152]

Based on their children's rights obligations, states are also mandated to establish their jurisdiction in relation to certain situations. The Convention on the Rights of the Child requires that states take "national, bilateral and multilateral measures" to protect children from "all forms of sexual exploitation and sexual abuse" (Article 34 CRC) and from abduction and sale or trafficking (Article 35 CRC). In taking national measures, OPSC further allows states to establish their jurisdiction over these aforementioned offenses not only when they are committed on its territory (or a vessel registered in that state) but also extraterritorially, in accordance with both passive and active personality principles, based respectively on the nationality or habitual residence of the offender or the nationality of the victim (Article 4.2 OPSC). Furthermore, the offenses are to be "treated, for the purpose of extradition between States Parties, as if they had been committed not only in the place in which they occurred but also in the territories of the States required to establish their jurisdiction" (Article 5.4) in order to ensure that legal grounds for the establishment of jurisdiction and for extradition are not challenged on territorial limitations.

Notwithstanding the increasing visibility of human rights impacts transcending state borders, the imposing presence of jurisdiction has continued to serve as a legal straightjacket in cases where the wrongdoers or those contributing to harm are shielded from scrutiny simply on the basis of claims that they are either entities unable to exercise it such as NSAs or that the exercise of "extraterritorial jurisdiction" is exceptional

state/2014/documents/rc-seg-st-20140205_concluding-observations-rights-child_en.html (accessed 21 December 2018).

152 *Case Concerning Barcelona Traction, Light, and Power Company, Ltd (Belgium* v. *Spain)* ICJ 5 February 1970, paras. 33 and 34.

and highly conditional.[153] In *Bankovic*, the European Court of Human Rights (ECtHR) concluded that the exercise of extraterritorial jurisdiction had to be weighed against the sovereignty of another state over its territory and thus circumscribed.[154] In fact, jurisdiction was defined as an "ordinary and essentially territorial notion" while "other bases of jurisdiction [were considered] exceptional and requiring special justification in the particular circumstances of each case."[155] According to Milanovic, the Court's judgment that "the scope of application of human rights depends on the right of states to regulate certain types of conduct by their domestic law" amounted to a "category error."[156] One test for the aforementioned exceptional circumstances accepted by the ECtHR as allowing for extraterritorial jurisdiction was "effective control" over territory, persons or the situation in question. This converges considerably with the test used for the extraterritorial application of human rights within different legal systems and human rights regimes.[157] The ECtHR has relied on arguments of effective control over territory (for instance, *Loizidou* v. *Turkey* and the subsequent *Cyprus* v. *Turkey* cases), individuals (*Öcalan* v. *Turkey*, *Issa and Others* v. *Turkey*, *Al-Saadoon and Mufdhi* v. *the UK*, *Medvedyev and Others* v. *France* and later *Hassan* v. *the UK*) or situations (*Al-Skeini and Others* v. *the UK*).

In *Bankovic*, the ECtHR basically concluded that extraterritorial jurisdiction was made permissible in order to substitute one state party in lieu of another, based on the exercise of public powers in a given territory – once again underscoring its territorial nature.[158] The Court's restriction of jurisdiction to the "effective overall control" over a given territory "when violations of a negative obligation are at stake" is also in question.[159] On the basis of this constrained scope of jurisdiction, no issue of different types of duty-bearers can be raised. In *Al-Skeini*, in

[153] For an overview of arguments for and against the extraterritorial application of human rights treaties, see Karen da Costa, *The Extraterritorial Application of Selected Human Rights Treaties* (Martinus Nijhoff Publishers, 2013), pp. 9–14.

[154] *Banković and Others* v. *Belgium and Others* (Decision – Grand Chamber) Application No. 52207/99 ECtHR 12 December 2001, para. 59.

[155] Ibid., para. 61.

[156] Milanovic, *Extraterritorial Application of Human Rights Treaties*, p. 40.

[157] Oona A. Hathaway et al., "Human Rights Abroad: When Do Human Rights Treaty Obligations Apply Extraterritorially?" (2011) 43 *Arizona State Law Journal* 389–426 at 390.

[158] *Banković and Others* v. *Belgium and Others*, para. 71.

[159] Milanovic, *Extraterritorial Application of Human Rights Treaties*, p. 41.

a turn, ECtHR concluded that the decisive element of the exercise of jurisdiction was "the exercise of physical power and control over the person in question" and not solely the "control exercised ... over the buildings, aircraft or ship in which the individuals were held."[160] As the interpretation of the ECtHR in *Al-Skeini* stands, the "exceptional" exercise of extraterritorial jurisdiction under the meaning of ECHR Article 1 could be based on effective control over territory but also power and control over a person when a state party is found to be exercising elements of public power.[161]

Evidently, the ECtHR's conceptualization of jurisdiction surpasses territorial borders, even if the Court is nominally reluctant to accept the premise of obligations beyond territory. This reluctance, however, is not shared across the board. For instance, the Inter-American Commission on Human Rights (IACmHR) has construed the issue of control independently of territory by noting that "a state's human rights obligations are not dependent upon a person's nationality or presence within a particular geographic area, but rather extend to all persons subject to that state's authority and control" based on the fundamental principle that individuals are entitled to human rights protection not by virtue of being "the citizen of a particular state" but by being human beings.[162]

The European Court of Human Rights' territorial model has not impeded it from recognizing that overlapping obligations may be attributed to multiple states. In *Ilaşcu and Others* v. *Moldova and Russia*, the ECtHR found that both the government of Moldova and the government of Russia had obligations in the events in question.[163] Even though the government of Moldova did not exercise effective control over the territory in question, the Court held that Moldova had "a positive obligation ... to take the diplomatic, economic, judicial or other measures that it [was] in its power to take and are in accordance with international law to secure to the applicants the rights guaranteed by

160 *Al-Skeini and Others* v. *the UK*, para. 137.

161 Marko Milanovic finds that the public powers qualification is a "vaguely defined" one that creates an "entirely arbitrary" "limitation on the application of the personal conception of jurisdiction" (Marko Milanovic, "*Al-Skeini* and *Al-Jedda* in Strasbourg" [2012] 23[1] *The European Journal of International Law* 121–139 at 131).

162 Inter-American Commission on Human Rights (IACmHR), "What Is Terrorism? Report on Terrorism & Human Rights," OEA/Ser.L/V/II.116 Doc. 5 rev. 1 corr. 22 October 2002, para. 44.

163 *Ilaşcu and Others* v. *Moldova and Russia* (Application no. 48787/99) Judgment 8 July 2004 ECtHR, paras. 331–335 and paras. 384 and 394.

the Convention."[164] The Court distinguished positive obligations, not absolute but to be discharged by balancing "the general interest and the interest of the individual," giving governments the choice to set priorities and dispense resources accordingly.[165] The Court reaffirmed this assessment in subsequent judgments regarding Transnistria.[166] In this way, the Court found that the attribution of human rights obligations to multiple states – one with formal territorial sovereignty but no effective control and another with effective control – delimits the range of obligations assigned to the party without effective control. The ECtHR has made an overture in considering the involvement of multiple states and whether there is a possibility to engage multiple jurisdictions with *Jaloud* v. *the Netherlands,* where the Court found that the death of Mr. Jaloud through shots fired by a Dutch Lieutenant and several Iraqi Civil Defense Corps (ICDC) members in a British-controlled part of Iraq had "occurred within the 'jurisdiction' of the Netherlands."[167] The Court did not answer the question of whether there were grounds for a possible exercise of "concurrent jurisdiction" by the United Kingdom as it had not been asked to do so.[168] The "concurrent jurisdiction" notion is an interesting one from the point of view of multiple duty-bearers, especially if the future case law of the Court prompts it to sufficiently develop the notion independently of territoriality considerations.

An alternative proposal has been to reinvigorate or "revolutionise"[169] the concept of jurisdiction is contained in the Maastricht Principles on Extraterritorial Obligations of States in the area of Economic, Social and Cultural Rights. In addition to "authority or effective control,"[170] Article 9 of the Maastricht Principles expands the scope of jurisdiction to include

b) situations over which State acts or omissions bring about foreseeable effects on the enjoyment of economic, social and cultural rights, whether within or outside its territory;

[164] Ibid., para. 331.

[165] Ibid., para. 332.

[166] *Catan and Others* v. *Moldova and Russia* (Applications no. 43370/04, 8252/05 and 18454/06), Judgment 19 October 2012 ECtHR.

[167] *Jaloud* v. *the Netherlands* (Application no. 47708/08), Judgment 20 November 2014 ECtHR, para. 152.

[168] Ibid., para. 153.

[169] Vandenhole, "Obligations and Responsibility in a Plural and Diverse Duty-Bearer Human Rights Regime," in Vandenhole (ed.), *Challenging Territoriality in Human Rights Law*, p. 120.

[170] The Maastricht Principles on Extraterritorial Obligations of States in the area of Economic, Social and Cultural Rights, Art. 9(a).

c) situations in which the State, acting separately or jointly, whether through its executive, legislative or judicial branches, is in a position to exercise decisive influence or to take measures to realize economic, social and cultural rights extraterritorially, in accordance with international law.[171]

Accordingly, jurisdiction extends beyond the borders of a given state. In fact, a state is assigned extraterritorial obligations of respect through the extension of its jurisdiction to its acts/omissions with foreseeable effects as well as obligations to protect and fulfill through the exercise of decisive influence as well as through international cooperation and assistance.[172] This improved and enhanced concept of jurisdiction is helpful in conceptualizing extraterritorial obligations of states and, by extension, the parameters of regulation of businesses by their home states, but less so for an assessment of direct obligations transcending state borders, both literally and figuratively.[173]

Jurisdiction as a concept has routinely been applied to states and entities exercising public functions of state-like character. The inadequacy of styling jurisdiction in the image of territory as a basis for human rights obligations is never more apparent than when confronted with NSAs, including businesses.[174] Importing the concept of jurisdiction into the business and human rights debate, given its territorial baggage, at best creates confusion and tension. Businesses routinely operate in numerous territorial jurisdictions simultaneously, where they may be involved in activities with human rights impacts. When these impacts amount to violations, the requisite responsibility cannot be conceptualized through a jurisdictional inquiry. Even if the ECtHR case law stresses territorial underpinnings for the concept of jurisdiction, the Court's own assessment about the purpose of human rights law is on the mark. In *Cyprus v. Turkey*, the Court motivated its assessment by arguing that any other finding would result in "a regrettable vacuum in the system of human-

171 Ibid., Art. 9 (b) and (c).

172 Ibid.

173 Compare Arne Vandenbogaerde, *Towards Shared Accountability in International Human Rights Law: Law, Procedures and Principles* (Intersentia, 2016), pp. 254–255, 271 and 281.

174 International humanitarian law allows armed NSAs that may actually control territory, even if they cannot claim jurisdiction over the territory that they control to be brought within its scope by assigning obligations to these actors. (See: Daragh Murray, "How International Humanitarian Law Treaties Bind Non-State Armed Groups" (2015) 20(2) *Journal of Conflict & Security Law* 101–131.)

rights protection in the territory in question by removing from individuals there the benefit of the Convention's fundamental safeguards and their right to call a High Contracting Party to account for violation of their rights in proceedings before the Court."[175]

There is a need to break free from a territorial concept of jurisdiction, which is neither useful nor adequate in filling regrettable vacuums that exist in the protection of human rights, including those of children.

1.2.2 Moving Away from Personality to Participation

The second contested issue is whether NSAs can be considered subjects of international law or whether they are merely its objects.[176] The ICJ Reparation Advisory Opinion dating from 1949 may be the single most cited grounds on which subjecthood and international personality are postulated in international law.[177] The ICJ's assessment has been called largely "circular"[178]: in order for an entity to be considered a subject of international law, thus possess rights and duties, it needs to be attributed international personality. The Court, however, goes on to conclude that the rights enjoyed on the international plane are evidence of international personality. The UN's subjecthood as an international organization was pronounced early on in the ICJ Reparation Advisory Opinion by citing its exercise and enjoyment of functions and rights that "can only be explained on the basis of the possession of a large measure of international personality and the capacity to operate upon an international plane" as evidenced by its legal position, privileges and immunities as well as a political position separate from its member states.[179] The acceptance of an entity as a subject of international law with international legal personality does not mean it enjoys all the rights and duties on an equal footing with states, but does mean that it is able to enjoy rights and be held to obligations.[180] The extension of international legal personality and subjecthood under international law to private businesses is a heavily contentious matter.[181] In fact, it arguably necessitates a "radical

[175] *Cyprus* v. *Turkey*, para. 78.

[176] See Clapham, *Human Rights Obligations of Non-State Actors*, pp. 59-63 for a discussion about the "subject of subjects."

[177] *Reparation for Injuries Suffered in the Service of the United Nations Advisory Opinion*, 11 April 1949 ICJ, p. 8.

[178] McBeth, *International Economic Actors and Human Rights*, p. 57.

[179] *Reparation Advisory Opinion*, p. 9.

[180] Ibid.

[181] For an overview, see Clapham, *Human Rights Obligations of Non-State Actors*, pp. 76–80.

departure from the structure of legal orthodoxy."[182] Some scholars have argued the impossibility as well as the undesirability of such a move,[183] while others contend that private businesses already enjoy different degrees of legal personality.[184] In reality, where "no positive international law catalogue of legal persons exists,"[185] as is the case in the present day, it is possible to revisit the issue of subjecthood in international law. The determination of legal personality or subjecthood does not precede the attribution of obligations to a given actor. The development occurs in the opposite direction: "legal personality is created by international law by way of attribution of specific rights and/or duties to an actor."[186] Revamping the attribution of international legal personality and subjecthood is perhaps desirable[187] but a more effective approach may be to abandon the concepts altogether. After all, the dichotomy between subjecthood and objecthood is largely fictional and "an intellectual prison of our own choosing," which has come to be considered "an unalterable constraint."[188] To echo Higgins, the positivist view that inclusion into subjecthood in international law requires a specific rule permitting such a characterization is misleading.[189]

It is futile to begin the discussion of the attribution of human rights obligations to businesses by considering whether they are subjects of international law or not as evidenced by the attribution of international legal personality. As Klabber notes, personality is "but a descriptive notion: useful to describe a state of affairs, but normatively empty, as

[182] David Kinley and Junko Tadaki, "From Talk to Walk: The Emergence of Human Rights Responsibilities for Corporations at International Law" (2004) 44(4) *Virginia Journal of International Law* 931–1023 at 945.

[183] Antonio Casesse, *International Law in a Divided World* (Clarendon Press, 1987), p. 103 and Jose E. Alvarez, "Are Corporations 'Subjects' of International Law?" (2011) 9(1) *Santa Clara Journal of International Law* 1–36.

[184] Peter M. Muchlinski, "Human Rights and Multinationals: Is There a Problem?" (2001) 77(1) *International Affairs* 31–61 at 33; Nicola Jägers, *Corporate Human Rights Obligations*, p. 34.

[185] Janne E. Nijman, "Non-State Actors (NSAs) and the International Rule of Law: Revisiting the 'Realist Theory' of International Legal Personality," in Math Noortmann and Cedric Ryngaert (eds.), *Non-State Actor Dynamics in International Law: From Law-Takers to Law-Makers* (Routledge, 2010), p. 101.

[186] Ibid.

[187] Ibid., p. 116.

[188] Rosalyn Higgins, *Problems and Process: International Law and How We Use It* (Oxford University Press, 1994), p. 49.

[189] Although Higgins makes the point for individuals, the assessment remains true for other non-state entities (ibid).

neither rights nor obligations flow automatically from a grant of personality."[190] Thus, other notions such as capacity have been suggested to replace personality. As early as 1970, O'Donnell suggested that different actors on the international legal plane (from states to individuals) have capacities ranging from more limited to more comprehensive to perform different acts and that limiting personhood to the most comprehensive form of capacities was in fact erroneous.[191] More recently, Clapham has revisited the concept of capacity as a basis for a given actor's enjoyment of rights and obligations.[192]

International law should indeed undergo a much-needed revision and recognize "any international actor with factual (social, economic or political) power should also have legal visibility."[193] But this legal visibility need not be equated with legal personality.[194] This is not to say that international legal personality as a concept is irrelevant to NSAs. International legal personality, in whatever variant, may be a consideration in theorizing about the de jure lawmaking capacity of a given actor. It should be less of a concern in determining whether that actor has human rights duties commensurate with its impacts on human rights given the de jure and de facto power and rights it enjoys on the international plane. Even then, whether actors such as business enterprises are acknowledged across the board to have international legal personality that is required for them to participate in lawmaking may be inconsequential because they may be able to "enlist powerful states to create international public law that advances their interests," "independently create transnational private legal orders" or "export their internal standards globally through decentralized processes of diffusion."[195]

The discussion would be better served by an overhaul of the frame of reference for the recognition of international legal actors from persons to "participants" as designated by the founders of the New Haven School, Myres McDougall and Harold Lasswell.[196] In fact, there is a tension "between the dynamic idea of participation and the static concepts of subject, personality, rules and responsibility inherent in any legal

[190] Jan Klabbers, *An Introduction to International Law* (Cambridge University Press, 2002), p. 57.
[191] Daniel Patrick O'Connell, *International Law, Vol. 1* (2nd ed.) (Stevens and Sons, 1970), pp. 81–82.
[192] Clapham, *Human Rights Obligations of Non-State Actors*, pp. 70–71.
[193] Nijman, "NSAs and the International Rule of Law," p. 119.
[194] Ibid.
[195] Gregory C. Shaffer, "How Business Shapes Law: A Socio-Legal Framework" (2009) 42(1) *Connecticut Law Review* 147–183 at 172.
[196] Nijman, "NSAs and the International Rule of Law," 105.

system."[197] These static concepts too often create impediments for human rights accountability by portraying international law as it if were a club whose membership is exclusionary and exclusive to certain actors possessing certain qualities. Nijman affirms the usefulness of the constructivist underpinnings of the transnational legal process approach in moving away from the so-called fiction theory of international legal personality towards "legal personality that emerges from social interaction and actual influence on the transnational decision-making processes in which NSAs participate."[198] Even more boldly, Higgins holds that in understanding international law as a dynamic, authoritative decision-making process, "there are no 'subjects' and 'objects', but only *participants*."[199]

Abandoning static concepts for the benefit of dynamism, or trading personality for participation, would clearly allow the recognition of not only states, but also of international and regional organizations, NSAs such as armed military groups, corporations, NGOs, transnational advocacy networks as well as individuals as participants and thus, human rights duty-bearers, in the international legal arena. NGOs, transnational advocacy networks and epistemic communities already play important roles as participants in international lawmaking and implementation but would never qualify for international legal personality in the conventional sense of the term. Replacing subjecthood with participation would allow not just businesses but also other international and domestic entities and even individuals to be considered to have rights and duties on the international plane, including duties in the field of international human rights law. Furthermore, participation also presupposes capacity: in order to be able to participate, the actor has to have the capacity to participate. Just as importantly, participation also presupposes the intent to participate. For instance, by capitalizing on its participation in the international arena, an influential actor may give rise to "new patterns of behaviour ... with a bearing on the emergence or consolidation of international practices which may acquire the status of customary norms or general principles of international law."[200]As such,

[197] Jean d'Aspremont, "Introduction: Non-State Actors in International Law: Oscillating Between Concepts and Dynamics," in d'Aspremont (ed.), *Participants in the International Legal System: Multiple Perspectives on Non-State Actors in International Law* (Routledge, 2011), p. 1.

[198] Nijman, "NSAs and the International Rule of Law," p. 106.

[199] Higgins, *Problems and Process*, p. 50 (original emphasis).

[200] Mac Darrow, *Between Light and Shadow: The World Bank, the International Monetary Fund and International Human Rights Law* (Hart Publishing, 2003), pp. 145–146.

participation can best serve as the groundwork for both rights and duties. This view is also the most adept to any future response to the demands for broadening the scope of human rights duty-bearers.

1.3 Business and Children's Rights: A Story in the Margins

Much of the debate relevant to businesses as children's rights duty-bearers under international law has taken place in the broader business and human rights field. Legal processes underlying the attribution and distribution of human rights and children's rights obligations and of responsibility for violations are common at the normative level. Hence, normative frameworks seeking to shed light on corporate obligations for human rights are useful as an indication of the direction in which the current legal process and related norms are evolving. Furthermore, the broader human rights scholarship informs the discussions on human rights obligations extending beyond the domestic state. Various frameworks have emerged out of the discussion on how to directly regulate the human rights behavior of businesses since the 1970s. Only after four decades of developments in the business and human rights discussion did children's rights begin to receive special attention. The developments in that broader discussion, when viewed using a children's rights lens, allow for an accurate picture of the state of the art on business and children's rights to emerge. It permits an assessment of whether children's rights have been integrated into the business and human rights debate and if so, to what extent. It also allows one to evaluate to what extent the developments in the business and human rights area have culminated in the legalization of governance norms in this area.

Governance norms may be construed in a hard law–soft law continuum or in what has been called a "matrix of hard law, soft law, governance norms, rules applicable to states, municipal law and policy."[201] Ultimately, the hard- versus soft-law dichotomy may prove artificial, if not irrelevant, because "actors, working ex ante, use agreements having different characteristics to further particular aims" and these different agreement types "can have unpredicted effects, ex post, leading to new cycles of international

[201] Larry Catá Backer, "Rights and Accountability in Development ('Raid') V Das Air and Global Witness V Afrimex – Small Steps Towards an Autonomous Transnational Legal System for the Regulation of Multinational Corporations" (2009) 10 *Melbourne Journal of International Law* 258–307.

lawmaking."[202] For many legal scholars, the distinction between hard law and soft law emerges from the binding versus nonbinding dichotomy.[203] Yet, that black and white outlook is often too simplistic as it disregards the many nuances that underlie the process whereby law evolves, which may be termed "legalization."[204] According to Abbott et al., the matrix of legalization is made up of the three dimensions of obligation, precision and delegation. Accordingly, legalization need not be immediate and may occur overtime. A case in point is the international human rights regime, which evolved from the "only minimally legalized" UDHR into harder forms through the various international human rights conventions.[205] Echoing Shaffer and Pollack, "hard- and soft-law instruments serve as complements to each other in the progressive development of international law, leading to greater international cooperation and coordination over time."[206] Hard law and soft law are thus two end points on a "continuum" where fluidity and hybridization are possible.

The efforts to regulate business behavior at the international level date from almost half a century ago when the crosswinds of decolonization and development movements called into question the effects of business behavior on developing countries. The earlier attempts within and outside the United Nations (UN) focused on bringing clarity to the duties of multinational enterprises (MNEs) vis-à-vis nation states, particularly host states, and urging company behavior compliant with certain social norms. In the 1960s and 1970s, the UN General Assembly (UNGA), as a forum based on the principle of equal voice and vote for every state, was a key enabler for the leaders of newly decolonized or developing countries to set their own agenda, voice their grievances and set out their visions. In this period, the UNGA gave birth to various declarations which, despite their nonbinding nature, held important symbolic value. One such declaration, the Declaration on the Establishment of a New International Economic Order, became the forerunner of the efforts

[202] Gregory C. Shaffer and Mark A. Pollack, "Hard vs. Soft Law: Alternatives, Complements and Antagonists in International Governance" (2010) 94 *Minnesota Law Review* 706–799 at 714.

[203] Ibid., 712.

[204] Kenneth W. Abbott et al., "The Concept of Legalization" (2000) 54(3) *International Organization* 401–419.

[205] Abbott et al., "The Concept of Legalization," 405.

[206] Shaffer and Pollack, "Hard and Soft Law: What Have We Learned?" in Jeffrey L. Dunoff and Mark A. Pollack (eds.), *International Law and International Relations: Insights from Interdisciplinary Scholarship* (Cambridge University Press, 2012), p. 11.

within the UN for regulating international corporate behavior. The declaration enumerated the principles on which a "new international economic order" should be based. One of these principles stipulated the "regulation and supervision of the activities of transnational corporations by taking measures in the interest of the national economies of the countries where such transnational corporations operate on the basis of full sovereignty of those countries."[207] The early movement that followed led to the Tripartite Declaration of Principles concerning MNEs and Social Policy of the ILO (now revamped as the ILO MNE Declaration) and the OECD Guidelines for MNEs. Such early efforts were geared towards 'taming' MNEs in order to strengthen the position of developing country governments and did not in essence seek to protect human rights.

The shift away from company duties vis-à-vis states to their obligations towards individuals is, however, a more recent phenomenon which has led to the explicit inclusion of human rights concerns within the existing frameworks and the search for new frameworks that deal expressly with human rights. Examples include the earlier work on the Draft Code of Conduct on Transnational Corporations, the launch of the UN Global Compact, the Draft UN Norms exercise as well as the current frameworks in force such as the UN Framework and UNGPs, the revised OECD Guidelines for MNEs and the ILO MNE Declaration. Even more recent is the elaboration of a children's rights-specific agenda for businesses through the Children's Rights and Business Principles Initiative of UNICEF, UN Global Compact and Save the Children as well as the CRC Committee's GC 16.

1.3.1 *The Draft Code*

The UN ECOSOC requested the Group of Eminent Persons appointed by the UN Secretary General to prepare a report on "the role of multinational corporations and their impact on the process of development . . . and their implications for international relations" in 1974.[208] In addition to the creation of a "commission on multinational corporations" under the ECOSOC, recommendations issued included

[207] UN General Assembly (UNGA), "Declaration on the Establishment of a New International Economic Order," A/RES/S-6/3201, 1 May 1974.

[208] UN Department of Economic and Social Affairs Report of the Group of Eminent Persons, "The Impact of Multinational Corporations on Development and on International Relations," E/5500/Rev.1 ST/ESA/6, United Nations, 1974, 7.

the elaboration of principles to serve as codes of conduct for both governments and MNEs. The Group also recommended "explor[ing] the possibility of concluding a general agreement on multinational corporations, enforceable by appropriate machinery, to which participating countries would adhere by means of an international treaty."[209] The ongoing work within the UN on MNCs eventually culminated in the *Draft Code of Conduct on Transnational Corporations* in 1990, which the UN Commission on Transnational Corporations prepared per request of the UN ECOSOC in 1982.[210] Although the negotiations on the Draft Code took place during the same time period as the negotiations on the CRC, the Draft Code did not contain any references to children or to children's rights. There was, however, a paragraph dictating that multinational corporations "should/shall respect human rights and fundamental freedoms in the countries in which they operate."[211] The draft code was never adopted due to the contradicting positions of the developing and the developed countries.[212]

1.3.2 The UN Global Compact

The failure of the *Draft Code of Conduct* to garner enough support resulted in a change of strategy by the late UN Secretary General Kofi Annan, when he announced the "Global Compact" on 31 January 1999.[213] The UN Global Compact is a voluntary strategic policy initiative for businesses that are committed to aligning their operations and strategies with ten universally accepted principles in the areas of human rights, labor, environment and anti-corruption. It has been described as the "largest corporate citizenship and sustainability initiative in the world" with over 12,000 participants and stakeholders from 160 countries.[214] None of the UN Global Compact's ten principles explicitly refer to children or to children's rights. The first two principles

[209] Ibid.

[210] UN ECOSOC Resolution 1982/68, 27 October 1982.

[211] Draft UN Code of Conduct on Transnational Corporations, para. 13.

[212] Olivier de Schutter, "Transnational Corporations and Human Rights: An Introduction," Global Law Working Paper 01/05. Symposium – Transnational Corporations and Human Rights, NYU School of Law.

[213] UN Secretariat General, "Press Release: Secretary-General Proposes Global Compact on Human Rights, Labor, Environment, In Address to World Economic Forum in Davos," 1 February 1999.

[214] Website of the UN Global Compact, www.unglobalcompact.org/ParticipantsAndStakeholders/index.html (as of 10 January 2019).

state that businesses "should support and respect the protection of internationally proclaimed human rights," and that they should "make sure that they are not complicit in human rights abuses."[215] Children's rights are implicitly covered among internationally proclaimed human rights. Although the Global Compact has a human rights component, it is not a human rights-focused instrument. In addition, its principles do not go beyond "prevention" of abuse, "respect" and the avoidance of complicity. The UN Global Compact is "intended as a mutually reinforcing complement to, and not a substitute for, other approaches, including regulatory ones."[216] The Compact's lack of effective monitoring of signatory businesses to ensure that they live up to their commitments has been heavily criticized, some arguing that it is used as a public relations campaign or a cover-up tool for company misconduct and malpractice.[217] The work of the Global Compact has become more focused on Sustainable Development Goals (SDGs) following the adoption of the 2030 Agenda for Sustainable Development. On the human rights front, the UNGPs guide the work of the Global Compact, which offers businesses tools to implement the UNGPs including for developing human rights policies.[218] Its guide for businesses looking to develop a human rights policy notes that where companies have "significant interaction with a potentially vulnerable group, [they] may decide to prepare and refer to a separate, dedicated policy in relation to that group, e.g. an indigenous peoples' or children's rights policy."[219] In addition, the issues of child labor as well as its worst forms and minimum age for employment are

[215] The Ten Principles of the UN Global Compact, www.unglobalcompact.org/aboutthegc/thetenprinciples/index.html (accessed 24 April 2019).

[216] UN Global Compact, "Note on the UN Global Compact and Business and Human Rights," 13 January 2009.

[217] In a campaign against Nestlé for aggressive marketing of baby milks and foods and undermining breastfeeding, the NGO Baby Milk Action produced a report entitled *Nestlé's UN Global Compact Cover Up: How Nestlé's Shared Value Reports Cover Up Malpractice and Bring the UN Voluntary Initiative for Corporate Responsibility into Disrepute* (Baby Milk Action, 2009). The NGO then went on to lodge instances against the company at the Global Compact and the OECD UK and Swiss NCPs (Baby Milk Action, "Nestle, the UN Global Compact and OECD Guidelines – What Happened When Nestlé Was Reported for Violating the UN Global Compact and OECD Guidelines for Multinational Enterprises?," 21 May 2010).

[218] UN Global Compact, *A Guide for Business: How to Develop a Human Rights Policy Second Edition* (UN Global Compact, 2015), www.unglobalcompact.org/docs/issues_doc/human_rights/Resources/HR_Policy_Guide_2nd_Edition.pdf), an online tool to learn about business and human rights (http://human-rights-and-business-learning-tool.unglobalcompact.org) (accessed 24 April 2019).

[219] UN Global Compact, *A Guide for Business: How to Develop a Human Rights Policy*, p. 18.

listed as key issues to be addressed in the context of the human rights of workers.[220] The Global Compact is also an initiating party to the CRBP initiative.

1.3.3 The Draft UN Norms

The push for binding standards to regulate business enterprises did not completely die down, notwithstanding the rejection of the earlier *Draft Code of Conduct* and the acceptance of voluntary opt-in initiatives such as the UN Global Compact. In 2002, the UN Commission on Human Rights Sub-Commission on the Protection and Promotion of Human Rights prepared the UN Norms on the Responsibilities of Transnational Corporations and Other Business Enterprises with Regard to Human Rights (Draft UN Norms). It was dubbed the "first nonvoluntary initiative" designed to elucidate the human rights duties of transnational corporations (TNCs).[221] The Draft UN Norms adopted a more progressive reading of obligations, clearly noting that the obligation to *fulfil*/through provision and facilitation, as well as obligations to *respect* and *protect* may be demanded of TNCs. The draft recognized both the potential positive and negative impacts that TNCs have due to rapid globalization, and consequently reaffirmed that while states had the "primary responsibility for the promo[tion] and protect[ion of] HR," "TNCs and other business enterprises" also had responsibility "for promoting and securing the HR set forth in the UDHR."[222] The document stipulated a state duty to ensure the compliance of TNCs and other business enterprises and envisaged implementation, monitoring and reporting mechanisms as well as obligations for financial compensation enforceable by relevant adjudicatory bodies.

The text of the Draft UN Norms made one reference to children and one reference to children's rights. In the non-discrimination clause, TNCs and other businesses were required to eliminate all forms of discrimination, including on the basis of age, except for cases where children would be accorded greater protection.[223] Under the section on

220 Ibid.

221 David Weisbrodt and Muria Kruger, "Norms on the Responsibilities of Transnational Corporations and Other Business Enterprises with Regard to Human Rights" (2003) 97 (4) *The American Journal of International Law* 901–922 at 903.

222 Ibid.

223 UN Working Group on the Working Methods and Activities of Transnational Corporations (UNWG TNCs), "Draft Norms on the Responsibilities of Transnational Corporations and Other Business Enterprises with Regard to Human Rights," E/CN.4/Sub.2/2003/12, 2003, para. 2.

the Rights of Workers, the Draft UN Norms made a reference to the rights of children, with a focus on child labor.[224] The Draft UN Norms constituted the first instance that a detailed set of human rights provisions was proposed as direct human rights obligations for TNCs in what was coined their "spheres of activity and influence."[225] Although the Draft UN Norms were approved by the UN Sub-Commission, they incited vehement opposition from part of the global business community and were not approved by the then UN Commission on Human Rights.[226] The resistance by those lobbying against the Norms was both visible and strong[227] even without any prospect of them becoming a binding treaty-like mechanism given their recommendatory nature.

1.3.4 The UN Guiding Principles (UNGPs)

The OHCHR prepared a report in 2005 on the responsibilities of TNCs and related business enterprises with regard to human rights, which included a detailed comparative analysis of the scope and legal status of existing initiatives and standards and concluded that further studies were needed.[228] Professor John G. Ruggie, who was appointed Special Representative by the then UNSG Annan, with a mandate to "identify and clarify standards of corporate responsibility and accountability with regard to human rights,"[229] presented the UN Protect, Respect, Remedy Framework in his third report to the UN HR Council in June 2008.[230] Contrary to the previous UN initiatives, the UN Framework was

[224] Ibid., para. 6.

[225] Ibid., para. 6.

[226] The International Chamber of Commerce and the International Employers Organization were among those raised their voice against the UN Draft Norms; www.reports-and-materials.org/IOE-ICC-views-UN-norms-March-2004.doc (accessed 24 April 2019).

[227] The intense lobbying campaign against the Draft UN Norms by a number of states, companies and by business representatives ICC and the IOE are documented in Giovanni Mantilla, "Emerging International Human Rights Norms for Transnational Corporations" (2009) 15(2) *Global Governance* 279–298 at 287–288.

[228] UN ECOSOC, "Report of the Sub-Commission on the Promotion and Protection of Human Rights: Report of the UN High Commissioner on Human Rights on the Responsibilities of Transnational Corporations and Related Business Enterprises with Regard to Human Rights," E/CN.4/2005/91, 15 February 2005.

[229] UNSG, "Press Release: Secretary-General Appoints John Ruggie of United States Special Representative on Issue of Human Rights, Transnational Corporations, Other Business Enterprises," SG/A/934, 28/07/2005.

[230] UN HR Council, Protect, Respect and Remedy: A Framework for Business and Human Rights Report of the Special Representative of the Secretary-General on the Issue of

unanimously approved by the UN HR Council upon presentation.[231] The model, said to "rest on differentiated but complementary responsibilities," has three pillars: the state duty to protect against human rights abuses by third parties, including business (Protect), the corporate responsibility to respect human rights (Respect) and greater access by victims to effective remedy, both judicial and nonjudicial (Remedy).[232]

The notion of "differentiated but complementary" responsibilities is of interest, especially as regards the attribution and distribution of human rights obligations to various actors. It has, however, been construed very narrowly in the UN Framework, excluding the possibility that the complementary responsibilities – in addition to differentiated ones – of different actors may overlap in certain instances. With the UN Framework, Ruggie tried to steer clear of framing the business and human rights debate in legal terms, coining his approach "principled pragmatism."[233] Unanimously endorsed by the UN HR Council in June 2011, the "Guiding Principles on Business and Human Rights" (UNGPs) aimed to operationalize the UN Framework. UNGPs also refined the Framework's three pillars, recognizing a primary role for states as duty-bearers in protecting and promoting human rights, a duty for businesses "as specialized organs of society performing specialized functions . . . to comply with all applicable laws and meet societal expectation to not infringe on the human rights of others," as well as the need for the provision of effective remedies for breaches of duties.[234]

Protect

The UN Framework places the legal duty for protecting persons from corporate human rights abuse on States. The UN Framework defines state duty to protect in broad terms, ranging from administrative requirements, market-based processes, policy making, policy coordination and policy alignment to international technical and financial cooperation and

Human Rights and Transnational Corporations and Other Business Enterprises (UN Framework), John Ruggie, A/HCR/8/5, 7 April 2008.

231 UN HR Council, "Mandate of the SRSG on the Issue of Human Rights and Transnational Corporations and Other Business Enterprises," A/HRC/RES/8/7, 18 June 2008.

232 UN Framework, para. 9.

233 OHCHR, "Principled Pragmatism – The Way Forward for Business and Human Rights," 7 June 2010, www.ohchr.org/EN/NewsEvents/Pages/PrincipledpragmatismBusinessHR.aspx (accessed 24 April 2019).

234 UN HR Council, Guiding Principles on Business and Human Rights: Implementing the United Nations "Protect, Respect and Remedy" Framework (UNGPs), A/HRC/17/31, 2011.

preventive measures for conflict situations. The Framework envisages a more effective protection of human rights through practices similar to sustainability reporting, stakeholder notifications and similar market pressures to promote what may be called a human rights-friendly corporate culture. By tying a company's policies and practice to liability, the Framework hopes to deter abuses.[235] Of course, whether liability in civil or criminal law can be established depends on the legal system of individual domestic states. Also, *locus standi* requirements, procedures and grounds of permissibility depend on national jurisdictions. The Framework reiterates a legal duty on states that is already well established in international human rights law, while highlighting the governance aspect of protection on the local, national and international levels through vertical and horizontal domestic policy alignment. Ruggie has elsewhere argued the most pressing problems to be the failure to enforce existing laws as well as the lack of coordination between different parts of the government in charge of shaping business practices in areas such as trade, investment, insurance, export credit, securities and corporate law and those that work on the state's human rights obligations.[236] Thus, the Framework's focus has been to address the implementation and coordination gaps.

The UNGPs cover first and foremost the "state duty to protect against business-related human rights abuse" through prevention, investigation, punishment and remediation by using tools of policy, regulation and adjudication. There is an additional duty on the state "to encourage" business enterprises to respect human rights. In both cases, there is a territorial and jurisdictional condition: states must protect against abuse "within their territory and/or jurisdiction," should "encourage business enterprises domiciled in their territory and/or jurisdiction" and "set out clearly their expectations for all business enterprises operating or domiciled in their territory and/or jurisdiction."[237] The Framework rests on the premise that the domestic state is able and willing to enforce its laws vis-à-vis businesses. What recourse rights-holders have in cases where the domestic state fails – either through unwillingness or inability – to protect against business-related human rights abuses taking place within its territory remains unclear, especially when

[235] UN Framework, para. 31.

[236] Ruggie, "Prepared Remarks: Public Hearings on Business and Human Rights Sub-Committee on Human Rights," European Parliament, 16 April 2009.

[237] UNGPs, Principles 1 and 2.

there is no corresponding obligation for states where the businesses are domiciled.

Respect

The duty of business enterprises is described as a responsibility to respect human rights in their operations. Responsibility carries less binding force in colloquial use than obligations, especially in contrast with the ascribed state "duty" to protect. The distinction between duty and responsibility is explained by contrasting companies and states, by arguing "[w]hile corporations may be considered 'organs of society', they are specialized economic organs, not democratic public interest institutions," which is in turn interpreted as precluding the duties traditionally ascribed to states from being applied on equal footing to companies.[238] The nature of the "responsibility to respect" and the threshold that is expected of companies are differentiated from state obligations by their nature and not by their degree: the corporate responsibility to respect exists independently of states' duties. Importantly, the corporate responsibility to respect is considered the baseline and the failure to respect that baseline cannot be offset by the performance of philanthropy or similar beneficial acts in other contexts.[239]

The Framework clearly articulates that the corporate responsibility to respect applies to all companies in all situations for all internationally recognized human rights. The Framework and the UNGPs set the responsibility to respect as a minimum requirement stipulating "there are situations in which companies may have additional responsibilities."[240] The "do no harm" axiom is qualified, both in the Framework and the UNGPs, to include responsibilities that require action on the part of enterprises such as putting in place appropriate policies and processes,[241] operationalizing human rights due diligence at all levels of their supply chain,[242] carrying out human rights impact assessments,[243] tracking performance[244] and providing remediation.[245]

238 UN Framework, para. 16.
239 Ibid., para. 55.
240 The UN Framework gives two examples for such cases: first, when companies "perform certain public functions" and second "because they have undertaken additional commitments voluntarily" (UN Framework, 9.)
241 UNGPs, Principle 13.
242 Ibid., Principle 15.
243 Ibid., Principles 16 and 17.
244 Ibid., Principle 18.
245 Ibid., Principle 20.

Ruggie has summarized the four steps of a human rights due diligence process as "assessing actual and potential human rights impacts, integrating and acting on the findings, tracking responses, and communicating how impacts are addressed."[246] Yet, the specific content of human rights due diligence or a particular definition was not adopted in the UNGPs. A subsequent guide on the interpretation by the Office of the High Commissioner for Human Rights (OHCHR) defined due diligence as "a measure of prudence, activity, or assiduity, as is properly to be expected from, and ordinarily exercised by, a reasonable and prudent [person or enterprise] under the particular circumstances; not measured by any absolute standard, but depending on the relative facts of the special case."[247] Human rights due diligence was interpreted as "an ongoing management process that a reasonable and prudent enterprise needs to undertake, in light of its circumstances (including sector, operating context, size and similar factors) to meet its responsibility to respect human rights."[248]

The Framework also addresses issues of "spheres of influence" and "complicity" for businesses. On complicity, the Framework pointed to its "legal and non-legal pedigrees" and defined it as "indirect involvement by companies in human rights abuses – where the actual harm is committed by another party."[249] The reference to complicity is an important step but it lacks clarity. Complicity in the UNGPs is not qualified, although the concept has been used by Clapham, among others, with respect to criminal complicity in reference to businesses.[250] The birth of the notion of corporate complicity may be traced to a desire to attach a level of accountability to corporate behavior without nullifying state responsibility for human rights violations in the late 1990s.[251] From the viewpoint of responsibility for one state's complicity in the wrongdoing perpetrated

[246] Ruggie, "The Social Construction of the UN Guiding Principles on Business and Human Rights" Corporate Responsibility Initiative Working Paper No. 67 (John F. Kennedy School of Government – Harvard University, 2017), p. 14.

[247] Office of the UN High Commissioner for Human Rights (OHCHR), *The Corporate Responsibility to Respect Human Rights: An Interpretive Guide* (OHCHR, 2012), p. 4.

[248] Ibid.

[249] UN Framework, para. 73.

[250] See: Clapham, "On Complicity," in Marc Henzelin and Robert Roth (eds.), *Le droit pénal à l'épreuve de l'internationalisation* (LGDJ, 2002), pp. 241–275 and later, Clapham, "Corporations and Criminal Complicity," in Gro Nystuen, Andreas Follesdal and Ola Mestad (eds.), *Human Rights, Corporate Complicity and Disinvestment* (Cambridge University Press, 2010), pp. 222–239.

[251] Clapham, "Corporations and Criminal Complicity," pp. 225–228.

by another state, the concept comprises "different financial, technical, and military or other contributions" and is distinguished from coauthoring of an internationally wrongful act by virtue of its "degree and extent."[252] Complicity based on omission is also distinguished from the failure to comply with a due diligence obligation given that complicity requires actual knowledge of the circumstances while due diligence – for states – requires the exercise of a degree of effective control and is based on an assessment of the risk that the wrongdoing will occur.[253] Although the accent is on state complicity, the observations regarding the various forms contribution to a wrongdoing can take, and the distinction between the author and the complicit on the basis of the "degree and extent" of the contributions, remains equally relevant for other types of actors.

Corporate complicity has thus far been mainly explored with respect to international crimes, focusing on an MNE's potential "to significantly contribute to, or enhance the ability of, a state to perpetrate gross human rights abuses."[254] But, because human rights violations do not always amount to international crimes, "criminal standards for complicity ... represent a starting point but not the whole story."[255] In the UNGPs, there is no assessment of what complicity might mean when the violation in question does not amount to a nationally or internationally defined crime. Thus, the broader concept of corporate complicity beyond issues of criminality remains uncharted. It may be useful to integrate insights from the broader meaning of complicity in the law on responsibility in order to enhance our understanding of what corporate complicity not amounting to criminality may look like. Complicity in the context of state responsibility extends to circumstances that do not necessarily involve or amount to international crimes. One expression is provided in Article 16 of the Articles on the Responsibility of States for Internationally Wrongful Acts (ARSIWA), under the rubric of 'aid or assistance.' Complicity in this context would mean a contribution to the commission of an internationally wrongful act with the knowledge of the circumstances of this act, and if that act would be wrongful when committed by the aiding/assisting state itself.[256]

252 Vladyslav Lanovoy, "Complicity in an Internationally Wrongful Act," in Nollkaemper and Plakokefalos, *Principles of Shared Responsibility*, pp. 141, 143–144.

253 Ibid., pp. 146–147.

254 Markos Karavias, "Shared Responsibility and Multinational Enterprises" (2015) 62 *Netherlands International Law Review* 91–117 at 99.

255 Clapham, "Corporations and Criminal Complicity," p. 239.

256 ILC, Articles on the Responsibility of States for Internationally Wrongful Acts (ARSIWA) (Annex to General Assembly resolution 56/83 of 12 December 2001 and corrected by document A/56/49[Vol. I]/Corr.4), 2001, Article 16.

Contextually, complicity is not limited per se to those circumstances that fulfill the conditions under Article 16 ARSIWA but could extend to rules under specialized international legal regimes.[257] Although Article 16 ARSIWA does not refer to complicity as such, the ICJ concluded in 2007 that customary law on state responsibility also covered complicity and that Article 16 was a reflection of this customary rule.[258] But, while the principle that complicity gives rise to responsibility is widely accepted, what the constituent elements of that responsibility entail remains debated.[259] When wrongful acts that take place are in the form of human rights violations, a business that aids or assists another actor (state or non-state) in the commission of a violation (which is a demonstration of intent), with the knowledge that its aid/assistance will facilitate or make possible the violation, could incur responsibility based on complicity. As Lanovoy notes,

> Assuming that international law is designed for the benefit of peoples and not merely to justify the action of the most powerful actors, [footnote omitted] the duty not to knowingly facilitate the wrongful act is inherent to the respect of every international obligation, whether it is bilateral, multilateral or peremptory.[260]

As such, "[n]o actor [including a business] should be permitted to knowingly support another in breaching the latter's obligations."[261]

Remedy

The UN Framework stresses the importance of access to effective remedy to address grievances for wrongs caused by business activity. The framework distinguishes between different types of remedy mechanisms. State-based remedy mechanisms include both judicial and nonjudicial remedies. The framework encourages states to make available processes whereby corporations can be held accountable in civil as well as criminal law. There are also numerous nonjudicial mechanisms such as public agencies, publicly funded mediation services, national human rights

[257] Helmut Philipp Aust, *Complicity and the Law of State Responsibility* (Cambridge University Press, 2011), p. 10.

[258] *Application of the Convention on the Prevention and Punishment of the Crime of Genocide* (*Bosnia and Herzegovina* v. *Serbia and Montenegro*), judgment of 26 February 2007 ICJ, paras. 419–420.

[259] Vladyslav Lanovoy, *Complicity and Its Limits in the Law of International Responsibility* (Hart Publishing, 2016), p. 9.

[260] Ibid., p. 12.

[261] Ibid.

bodies and other soft-law mechanisms like the OECD National Contact Points (NCPs). Non-state remedy mechanisms may include arbitration, mediation or similar processes that are administered by industry-based or multi-industry associations or stakeholder groups.

UNGPs also define effectiveness criteria for nonjudicial mechanisms ("state based" or "non-state" based): they should be legitimate, accessible, predictable, equitable, rights-compatible and transparent, and should be based on dialogue and engagement.[262]

Children in the UN Framework and UNGPs

The UN Framework does not address children or children's rights explicitly. Paragraph 83, which notes that "[e]xpectations for States to take concrete steps to adjudicate corporate-related human rights harm are expanding" as evidenced in the work of the UN treaty bodies, contains a reference to children's issues in a footnote. This footnote refers to the CRC Committee's recommendation to states to take measures "to establish criminal, civil or administrative liability of legal persons for treaty offences" for violations enumerated in Article 3(4) of the Optional Protocol on the Sale of Children, Child Prostitution and Child Pornography (OPSC).[263]

Following the adoption of the Framework, the UN Human Rights Council (HRC) requested the SRSG to focus on persons belonging to vulnerable groups such as children and to integrate a gender perspective into the Framework. The UNGPs conclude that businesses have a heightened duty in their policies or actions vis-à-vis "individuals from groups or populations that may be at heightened risk of becoming vulnerable or marginalized,"[264] which by inference includes children. It is recognized that these individuals may require special attention in the implementation of the UNGPs as well as the adoption of additional standards.[265] The heightened duty is also incumbent upon states, under the duty to protect, by providing "guidance to business enterprises on respecting human rights, ... recognizing the specific challenges that may be faced by

[262] UNGPs, Principle 29.

[263] UN Framework, para. 83, footnote 49.

[264] These include indigenous peoples, women, national or ethnic minorities, religious and linguistic minorities, persons with disabilities, and migrant workers and their families (OHCHR, "UN Guiding Principles on Business and Human Rights," UN Doc. HR/PUB/11/04, 2011, p. 1).

[265] UNGPs, Principles 3 and 12, Commentary.

[...] children [among others]."[266] As such, other UN instruments on the rights of so-called vulnerable groups, such as the CRC, are implicitly invoked.[267] Nonetheless, the definition of internationally recognized human rights included in Article 12(a) UNGPs are to be understood, at a minimum, as the principles contained in the International Bill of Human Rights as well as the ILO's eight core conventions. In sum, the CRC is not explicitly referenced, although ILO Conventions 38 and 182 on Minimum Age and the Worst Forms of Child Labor, respectively, are included. The application of these principles "across a business enterprise's activities" as well as "to all enterprises regardless of their size and ownership structure and of how they distribute responsibilities" is also set out in Article 12(b) and (c).

Children in National Action Plans

The implementation of the UNGPs at the global level is overseen by the UN Working Group (UNWG) on the issue of human rights and transnational corporations and other business enterprises.[268] The principal means for the adoption of the UNGPs at the domestic level has been the development of National Action Plans (NAPs), based on the guidance published by the UNWG in December 2014 whereby four essential criteria for effective NAPs were identified as being: founded on the UNGPs, developed in an inclusive and transparent fashion, "context-specific and addressing the given country's actual and potential adverse corporate human rights impacts," and subject to regular revision.[269] Children are included in the guidance within the list of groups that are more vulnerable to human rights abuses and that should be consulted in the elaboration of the country's NAP as stakeholders.[270] In addition to consultation requirements, the guidance also recommends according equal footing in legal protection to these groups and their representatives in state-based judicial remedy mechanisms.[271] With regards specifically to children, the UNWG invites states to eliminate legal barriers to access

[266] Ibid., Principle 3 Commentary.
[267] Ibid., Principle 12 Commentary.
[268] UN HR Council, "Resolution 17/4 on Human Rights and Transnational Corporations and Other Business Enterprises," A/HRC/RES/17/4, 2001, para. 6 (a, b, c).
[269] UN WG on Business and Human Rights, "Guidance on NAPs on Business and Human Rights – Version 1.0," 2014, p. ii.
[270] Ibid., pp. 4, 6, 20, 27, 28 and 29.
[271] Ibid., p. 29.

to effective remedies, for instance, through providing "tailored assistance"[272] as well as to consider addressing gaps in domestic legal frameworks using, among others, the CRC Committee's GC 16 to "ensur[e] that the national legal framework requires business enterprises to respect children's rights."[273]

The uptake of the NAP preparation process has been rather slow.[274] Within existing NAPs, children are mentioned in the context of groups more vulnerable to violations and marginalization[275] or in the context of child labor.[276] The CRBPs are also listed among the different initiatives on business and human rights that may be incorporated into the state's broader human rights and business framework, beyond the UNGPs.[277] Children's rights are referenced in different NAPs in the context of international policy priorities,[278] reporting on the implementation to the CRC Committee,[279] and compliance with the CRC.[280] The duties of

272 Ibid., p. 30.

273 Ibid., p. 19.

274 As of January 2019, twenty-three states had published NAPs and thirteen states were in the process of preparing one (source: Danish Institute of Human Rights, "National Action Plans on Business and Human Rights," https://globalnaps.org/).

275 See: UK HM Government, "Good Business: Implementing the UN Guiding Principles on Business and Human Rights" (UK NAP), "New Actions Planned," 2013, vi; Government of Italy, "The Foundations of the Italian Action Plan on The United Nations' Guiding Principles on Business And Human Rights" (Italian NAP), 2014, 23; Gobierno de España, "Plan de Empresa y Derechos Humanos" (Spanish NAP), 2014, 14; Belgium – Commission Interdépartementale pour le Développement Durable, "Plan D'Action National Entreprises et Droits de l'Homme" (Belgian NAP), 2017, Action 24; República de Chile – Ministerio De Relaciones Exteriores, National Action Plan on Business and Human Rights Chile" (Chilean NAP), 2017; Germany, "German National Action Plan – Implementation of the UN Guiding Principles on Business and Human Rights 2016–2020" (German NAP), 2016, 20.

276 For example: The Netherlands, "NAP on Business and Human Rights" (Dutch NAP), 2013, 2, 4, 6, 7; Denmark, "Danish NAP – implementation of the UN Guiding Principles on Business and Human Rights" (Danish NAP), 26; Belgian NAP, Action 19; United States, "National Action Plan on Responsible Business Conduct" (US NAP), 2016, Outcomes 1.3, 2.1, 3.1 and 4.1.

277 UK NAP; Italian NAP Italy, 80; Government Offices of Sweden, "Action Plan for Business and Human Rights," 2015, 13; Belgian NAP, Action 24; Action 3.2; Colombia, "Plan Nacional de Acción sobre Derechos Humanos y Empresas," 2015, Action 4.7; Ireland, "National Plan on Business and Human Rights," 2017, 18;

278 Italian NAP, 31–32; Danish NAP, Introduction; République Française, "Plan National D'action Pour La Mise En Œuvre Des Principes Directeurs Des Nations Unies Relatifs Aux Droits De L'homme Et Aux Entreprises," 2017, Action 5, 16.

279 Finland, "NAP on the Implementation of the UN Guiding Principles on Business and Human Rights," 2014, 15.

280 Sweden, "Action Plan for Business and Human Rights," 15 and 17.

businesses vis-à-vis parents, including the provision of decent wages,[281] and the prevention of commercial sexual exploitation of children and adolescents[282] are among other children's rights issues invoked in the NAPs.

Notwithstanding UNWG Guidance, the content and the scope of the NAPs are ultimately left to the discretion of states and the inclusion of children's rights and children-related concerns are thus not guaranteed. In fact, there has been criticism of existing NAPs for "fail[ing] to provide children with the appropriate level of attention" and also disregarding the CRC as one of the fundamental international human rights treaties.[283]

1.3.5 OECD Guidelines for MNEs

The OECD's Guidelines for MNEs, originally adopted in 1976 and revised most recently in 2011, provide a voluntary and nonbinding code of conduct encompassing "principles and standards of good practice" addressed to MNEs "consistent with applicable laws and internationally recognized standards."[284] While the Guidelines progressively acquired a more extensive reach, the chapter on human rights was only added in 2011 in line with the UNGPs.[285]

OECD Guidelines make numerous references to children. The human rights chapter underscores that "enterprises can have an impact on virtually the entire spectrum of internationally recognized human rights" and that "some human rights may be at greater risk than others in particular industries or contexts, and therefore will be the focus of heightened attention."[286] The Guidelines refer, in these instances, to relevant UN instruments on indigenous peoples, minorities, women, children, people with disabilities and migrant workers and families.[287]

281 Belgium, "Plan D'Action National," Action 24.

282 Colombia, "Plan Nacional de Acción sobre Derechos Humanos y Empresas," 2015, Action 4.8; Poland, "Polish National Action Plan for the Implementation of the United Nations Guiding Principles on Business and Human Rights 2017–2020," 2017, 12; Switzerland, "Report on the Swiss Strategy for the Implementation of the UN Guiding Principles on Business and Human Rights," 2016, Pl14, 20–21.

283 Francis West, "Leadership and Being First Aren't the Same Things: An Assessment of the UK National Action Plan on Business and Human Rights," LSE Blogs, 3 June 2016, http://blogs.lse.ac.uk/businesshumanrights/2016/06/03/francis-west-leadership-and-being-first-arent-the-same-things/.

284 OECD Guidelines for MNEs, Chapter I. Concepts and Principles, para. 1.

285 Ibid., Chapter IV. Human Rights, 31.

286 Ibid., Chapter IV. Human Rights, para. 40.

287 Ibid.

The OECD Guidelines stipulate that for children as well as other "specific groups or populations that require particular attention," businesses may need to consider adopting supplementary standards, which is effectively another expression of a heightened duty when children's rights are at stake.[288]

The Guidelines contain a number of references to the abolition of child labor and elimination of the worst forms of child labor. Chapter V on Employment and Industrial Relations calls on enterprises to "contribute to the effective abolition of child labor, and take immediate and effective measures to secure the prohibition and elimination of the worst forms of child labor as a matter of urgency," referring to ILO Convention 182.[289] Within this context, education is prioritized as a means to eliminate child labor.

The OECD Guidelines do not explicitly mention children's rights as such but they do not limit the scope of children-related principles to child labor and children as vulnerable persons. In the Commentary to Chapter VIII on Consumer Interests, children are recognized as "becoming increasingly significant forces in the market" and business enterprises are called on to "apply fair business, marketing and advertising practices and to ensure the quality and reliability of the products that they provide."[290] Indirectly, the chapeau of Chapter VIII on Consumer Interests evokes the right to health of adult and child consumers alike.

The OECD Guidelines are intended for use by private enterprises in their daily business operations. In addition, the states adhering to the Guidelines are under an obligation to implement the Guidelines and encourage private enterprises to employ these Guidelines. Accordingly, the adherent states are required to set up National Contact Points (NCPs) to promote the Guidelines and act as a forum of discussion.[291] The work of the NCPs is explored under avenues for human rights responsibility.

1.3.6 ILO MNE Declaration

The ILO's Tripartite Declaration of Principles concerning MNEs and Social Policy was adopted on 16 November 1977 in response to "requests [since the mid-1960s] ... for ILO action in the field of multinational

[288] Ibid., para. 40, 34.
[289] Ibid., Chapter V, 35.
[290] Ibid., Chapter VIII, paras. 83–84.
[291] Ibid., Chapter I – Concepts and Principles, para. 11.

enterprises."[292] The Declaration undoubtedly has clear labor overtones and concerns itself not only with the relationship of companies with their employment base but also with the host and home states. The Declaration is important from a human rights point of view because it made an early reference to human rights when elaborating guidelines for companies in the domains of labor, employment and social policy. The Declaration calls upon parties concerned "[to] respect the [UDHR] and the corresponding International Covenants adopted by the [UNGA] as well as the Constitution of the [ILO] and its principles."[293] It is also interesting as a soft-law instrument resulting from a tripartite agreement between states, trade unions and business organizations. The Declaration, now dubbed the ILO MNE Declaration, was reviewed in March 2017 in line with the UNGPs as well as the Sustainable Development Goals (SDGs).

The 2017 version sets out the division of duties between states and business enterprises based on the UNGPs and the UN Framework. Accordingly, corporate responsibility to respect human rights in their places of operation amounts a requirement to exercise due diligence and:

> (i) avoid causing or contributing to adverse impacts through their own activities, and address such impacts when they occur; and (ii) seek to prevent or mitigate adverse human rights impacts that are directly linked to their operations, products or services by their business relationships, even if they have not contributed to those impacts.[294]

In addition, the Declaration states that MNEs "should use their leverage to encourage their business partners to provide effective means of enabling remediation for abuses of internationally recognized human rights."[295]

The Declaration calls on home states to "promote good social practice . . . having regard to the social and labor law, regulations and practices in host countries as well as to relevant international standards."[296] The Declaration entails a duty for MNEs as well as national

[292] Hans Guenter, "The Tripartite Declaration of Principles Concerning Multinational Enterprises and Social Policy (History, Contents, Follow-Up and Relationship with Relevant Instruments of Other Organizations)," ILO MNEs Programme Working Paper No. 18, ILO, 1981, p. 1.

[293] The ILO Tripartite Declaration of Principles Concerning MNEs and Social Policy (ILO MNE Declaration) 2017, para. 8.

[294] Ibid., para. 10(c).

[295] Ibid., para. 64.

[296] Ibid., para. 12.

enterprises to respect minimum age requirements or work towards the effective abolition of child labor and "take immediate and effective measures within their own competence to secure the prohibition and elimination of the worst forms of child labor as a matter of urgency."[297] In relation to the prohibition and elimination of the worst forms of child labor, the Declaration states that any worker with a grievance should be able to raise it at the company level and that "[t]his is particularly important whenever the [MNEs] operate in countries which do not abide by the principles of ILO Conventions pertaining [among others] ... to child labor and to forced labor."[298] The MNE Declaration, as limited also by the mandate of the ILO, does not mention or address children's rights beyond child labor issues.

The focus on the effective abolition of child labor is also found in the 1998 Declaration on Fundamental Principles and Rights at Work, which covers four fundamental principles and rights at work and which is referenced in the UNGPs.[299] This Declaration refers to children's rights in the context of combatting a "lack of awareness of children's rights" to enhance basic education as a panacea to child labor.[300]

1.3.7 Children's Rights and Business Principles

The Children's Rights and Business Principles (CRBPs) Initiative was unveiled by UNICEF, the UN Global Compact and Save the Children on 24 June 2010, following in the footsteps of the UN Framework. Similar to the process through which the UN Framework came to be developed, CRBPs were informed by a multi-stakeholder consultation process that lasted over three months, and involved not only businesses, civil society, experts and government representatives but also children. In addition, links between children's rights and business were elucidated in a mapping exercise. The multi-stakeholder consultation process and research culminated in the draft CRBPs, which were made public and opened up for written and online consultation. In addition, a number of consultation meetings were held in eleven different cities in Europe, Asia, Africa and South America.[301]

297 Ibid., para. 27.

298 Ibid., para. 66.

299 ILO Declaration on Fundamental Principles and Rights at Work.

300 Ibid.

301 UNICEF, The Global Compact and Save the Children, "The Children's Rights and Business Principles Initiative – Draft Principles Consultation Feedback Analysis & Report," August 2011, p. 3.

Children's participation in the process leading to the adoption of the CRBPs was ensured by a Child Participation Strategy developed by Save the Children and Plan International, whereby over 400 children between ages of seven and seventeen in nine countries were consulted.[302] A report published after the consultation period showed a number of fault lines among respondents, first on the adequacy of the strength of the responsibility as implicated by CRBPs and second on how they should apply to businesses of different sizes. On the first issue, there was a rift between those who believed that the scope was too far-reaching and the initiative too ambitious and others, who considered CRBPs to be too broad, based too large an extent on voluntary commitments and lacking strong wording. This divide reflected the different visions of business and NGO representatives on the direction that CRBPs should take. On the second issue of company size, a divide among similar business and nonprofit sector lines was visible: private sector representatives were pushing for a two-tier approach whereby small and medium-sized enterprises (SMEs) would be treated differently to larger companies. At the end, however, CRBPs defined a business enterprise as a 'for-profit enterprise.' Only one distinction was introduced in a footnote for human rights due diligence, where SMEs with limited human rights risks are allowed to "seek other independent external expert resources and insights . . . when direct consultation with affected stakeholders is not possible . . . due to legitimate financial, geographical or other constraints."[303]

Globally launched in 2012, the CRBPs draw heavily on the format and the content of the UN Framework. The Principles start out by underlining the (state) duty to protect, respect, and fulfill children's rights and go on to underscore that national law and relevant international standards on children's rights must be observed by all of society.[304] Children's rights and human rights of children are used as synonyms, while the CRC and the ILO Conventions 138 and 182 are referenced as key international documents outlining children's rights. The Principles organize business action with respect to children's rights in two

[302] UN Global Compact, "Development of the Children's Rights and Business Principles," www.unglobalcompact.org/Issues/human_rights/childrens_principles/development.html (accessed 24 April 2019).

[303] UNICEF, The Global Compact and Save the Children, *Children's Rights and Business Principles*, p. 8, footnote 2.

[304] Ibid., p. 13.

categories, corporate responsibility to respect and corporate commitment to support.

Corporate Responsibility to Respect

According to the CRBPs, businesses have, as a minimum, the responsibility to respect children's rights and human rights by avoiding infringement on the human rights of others, including children, and addressing any adverse impacts they might cause. This responsibility is applicable to a business's own activities as well as dealings with other parties regarding its operations, products or services. This is framed as a requirement by the CRBPs, echoing the UN Framework and the UNGPs.

Corporate Commitment to Support

Corporate commitment to support under the CRBPs relates to voluntary actions to support children's rights through "core business activities, strategic social investments and philanthropy, advocacy and public policy engagement, and working in partnership and other collective action," which "are strongly encouraged even if not required."[305] This aspect of the CRBPs does not advance business duties with regard to children and their rights given that it is framed as a 'commitment' and further qualified as being voluntary. The mention of philanthropy as one of the means through which children's rights may be supported is further distressing as it poses the danger of portraying rights as charity. Nonetheless, the notion of 'support' does go beyond the responsibility to respect and is a step further than the UN Framework and UNGPs.

In terms of substance, the CRBPs focus on diverse issues such as child labor, decent work, protection of children's rights and safety of children in business activities linked to delivering products and services, marketing and advertising as well as those with impacts on the environment and on land use. Further considerations are linked to children in security arrangements and in emergencies, including conflict situations.

The CRBPs have been conceptualized in a circle, which incorporates children's rights at the workplace, the marketplace, and within the community and environment. In this setting, the first principle relating to "children's rights integration" sits at the core of all business endeavors and entails a three-fold responsibility: policy commitment, due

[305] Ibid., p. 5.

diligence and remediation.[306] Under each principle, business action with respect to the two categories of 'responsibility to respect' and 'action to support' are enumerated. Business enterprises are called to make a policy commitment through a statement setting out the business's responsibility to respect rights, including children's rights, and to act with human rights due diligence. Accodingly, they are to identify and assess any actual or potential adverse impact on children's rights, integrate findings from their impact assessments across relevant internal functions and processes and take appropriate action, monitor and track the effectiveness of the business's responses, in accordance with the UNGPs.[307] The value added beyond the UNGPs is the focus on child-sensitive processes for remediation and the mainstreaming of children's rights throughout their activities and business relationships. Again, the CRBPs support the accent on a heightened duty when businesses engage with children, whether these children are the children of their employees, consumers, potential workers or part of the broader community in which businesses operate.

1.3.8 CRC Committee General Comment 16

The CRC Committee issued its GC 16 on state obligations regarding the impact of the business sector on children's rights on 17 April 2013. Previously, the Committee on Economic, Social and Cultural Rights (CESCR) had illuminated different aspects of the business–human rights relationship. In its 1999 GC 12 on the Right to Food, the CESCR had concluded that different NSAs including 'private business sector' are responsible for the realization of the right to adequate food alongside states. GC 12 also pointed to the duty of the national and transnational private business sector to "pursue its activities within the framework of a code of conduct conducive to respect of the right to adequate food."[308] In 2000, CESCR GC 14 on the right to the highest attainable standard of health, noted that "all members of society," including businesses had "responsibilities regarding the realization of the right to health."[309] This move was born out of the growing momentum in the human rights

[306] UNICEF, *Children are Everyone's Business: Workbook 2.0 – A guide for integrating children's rights into policies, impact assessments and sustainability reporting*, December 2013, www.unicef.org/eapro/Workbook_2.0_231213_Web.pdf.

[307] Ibid., pp. 15–16.

[308] CESCR, GC 12 on the right to adequate food, E/C.12/1999/5, 12 May 1999, para. 20.

[309] Ibid., para. 42.

movement to extend human rights duties to NSAs. The CRC Committee had already touched upon children's rights and responsibilities of NSAs at its 2002 General Day of Discussion, referring to CESCR GC 14 and concluding that "responsibilities to respect and ensure the rights of children extend beyond the State, including individuals, parents, legal guardians and other [NSAs]."[310]

CRC Committee's GC 16 on state obligations regarding the impact of the business sector on children's rights addresses the question of direct obligations of business enterprises by underlining that while there is no international legally binding instrument on human rights obligations of businesses as of the present, businesses nonetheless have duties to respect children's rights:

> At this juncture, there is no international legally binding instrument on the business sector's responsibilities vis-à-vis human rights. However, *the Committee recognizes that duties and responsibilities to respect the rights of children extend in practice beyond the State and State-controlled services and institutions and apply to private actors and business enterprises.* Therefore, all businesses must meet their responsibilities regarding children's rights and States must ensure they do so. In addition, business enterprises should not undermine the States' ability to meet their obligations towards children under the Convention and the Optional Protocols thereto.[311]

1.3.9 CoE Recommendation on Human Rights and Business

The Committee of Ministers of the Council of Europe (CoE) adopted its Recommendation on human rights and business in March 2016. The Recommendation contains provisions on the implementation of the UNGPs through general measures as well as NAPs, on states' duty to protect human rights, on how states can enable corporations to respect human rights and what access to remedy may mean in the context of business and human rights.[312] In terms of its normative grounds, the Recommendation is based on the premise of the UNGPs and their delineation of state duties to protect and corporate responsibility to respect. The Recommendation's section on additional protections for children addresses states in their host- and home-state capacity, in noting

[310] CRC Committee, General Day of Discussion 2002 on the Private Sector as Service Provider and its Role in Implementing Child Rights Recomm. 6, 20 September 2002, 8.

[311] CRC Committee, GC 16, para. 8 (emphasis added by the author).

[312] CoE, "Recommendation CM/Rec (2016)3 on Human Rights and Business," 2 March 2016.

that "Member States should require that business enterprises respect the rights of children when operating within their territorial jurisdiction and, as appropriate, throughout their operations abroad when domiciled in their jurisdiction."[313]

The Recommendation also asserts that states should give consideration to the CRC Committee's GC 16, to "reinforce efforts to meet obligations with regard to children" under the European Convention on Human Rights, the Revised European Social Charter and the ILO Conventions on child labor, as well as to the CRBPs.[314] In response to the challenges children experience in accessing information and enjoying the right to express their views, CoE member states are called to "encourage" companies to mainstream children's rights within human rights due diligence, remove barriers to access to remedy for children and to specifically address children's rights in NAPs.[315] The rather weak wording of "encourage[ment]" as regards whether States have an obligation to compel businesses to conduct children's rights due diligence or simply encourage it falls short of the "require" obligation the CRC Committee's GC 16 pronounces.[316] On the prohibition of child and forced labor, the Recommendation calls on states to meet their obligations.[317] Furthermore, the Recommendation underscores that business enterprises should "be held liable under their criminal law or other equivalent law" for the commission of offences covered under the CoE Convention on the Protection of Children against Sexual Exploitation and Sexual Abuse (the Lanzarote Convention) and the OPSC.[318]

The Recommendation includes a very detailed exposé of how civil liability including through home state regulation, criminal liability for serious human rights abuses, administrative remedies or nonjudicial mechanisms may be employed to ensure access to remedy.

1.3.10 CESCR General Comment 24

The CESCR issued its GC 24 on state obligations under the International Covenant on Economic, Social and Cultural Rights (ICESCR) in the context of business activities in 2017. This adds stronger normative

313 Ibid., para. 61.
314 Ibid., para. 62.
315 Ibid., para. 64.
316 CRC Committee, GC 16, para. 62.
317 CoE, "Recommendation on Human Rights and Business," para. 59.
318 Ibid., para. 44.

content to business duties as well as the obligations of home states, going further than the CRC Committee's GC 16.

First of all, although the GC is formally addressed to states parties, it makes business duties autonomous from host state obligations, reaffirming the approach taken by the UNGPs, noting that businesses "expected to respect Covenant rights regardless of whether domestic laws exist or are fully enforced in practice."[319] Furthermore, an expressed objective of GC 24 is "to assist the corporate sector in discharging their human rights obligations and assuming their responsibilities, thus mitigating any reputational risks that may be associated with violations of Covenant rights within their sphere of influence."[320] In this way, it breaks from the UNGPs, pronounces obligations for businesses and points to responsibility, in the public international law sense of the term, when these obligations are violated.

General Comment 24 considers children among the most disproportionately affected groups.[321]It also references the CRC Committee's GC 16 to support its assertion that a state party in a position to "influence situations located outside its territory, by controlling the activities of corporations domiciled in its territory and/or under its jurisdiction," incurs extraterritorial obligations as foreseen under international law and hence may make a positive contribution to the enjoyment of ESC rights abroad.[322] Accordingly, home-state extraterritorial obligations are triggered when they exercise control over businesses but other means "short of the direct imposition of obligations," such as the use of incentives, have been identified as approaches to induce businesses to put in place "robust and effective human rights due diligence mechanisms."[323] The UN Committee on Economic, Social and Cultural Rights also calls on states parties to use domestic regulation with extraterritorial effects to ensure due diligence on the part of businesses domiciled under their jurisdiction in the context of their obligation to protect. Accordingly, states should "require corporations to deploy their best efforts to ensure that entities whose conduct those corporations may influence, such as subsidiaries (including all business entities in which they have invested, whether registered under the State party's laws or under the laws of

[319] CESCR, GC 24, para. 5.
[320] Ibid., para. 5.
[321] Ibid., para. 8.
[322] Ibid., para. 28.
[323] Ibid., para. 31.

another State) or business partners (including suppliers, franchisees and subcontractors), respect Covenant rights."[324]

Although the issues are not linked to children and their rights, GC 24 underscores the protect obligations of states when they privatize important public goods and services such as education and healthcare as well as water and electricity, calling for the imposition of "public service obligations" on private providers.[325]

The right to an effective remedy is a prominent feature of GC 24, again in line with UNGPs. Unlike the UNGPs, however, CESCR's GC 24 challenges the use of legal doctrine of corporate veil by businesses that shields parent companies from liability when their subsidiaries are involved in human rights abuses, even when they are in a position to influence these subsidiaries as well as of the use of *forum non conveniens* by courts when it is unclear that "victims will have access to effective remedies in the alternative jurisdiction."[326] GC 24 notes that remedy mechanisms should be sensitive to the needs of indigenous peoples[327] but does not consider the specific needs of other groups such as children, people with disabilities or others.

1.3.11 A "Legally Binding Instrument"?

The UN Framework and UNGPs, unlike their predecessors, succeeded in garnering consensus among states within the UN HR Council on the minimum content and the scope of the regulation of corporate activities with regard to human rights.[328] This accomplishment does not preclude that further reflection and critique are needed, as Bilchitz and Deva note, for "putting in place a robust framework regarding the human rights obligations of companies."[329] In that vein, the Government of Ecuador proposed an internationally binding instrument on business and human rights at the 24th Session of the UN HR Council in September 2013, considering UNGPs to be "only a partial answer."[330] The premise was that

[324] Ibid., para. 33.

[325] Ibid., para. 21.

[326] Ibid., paras 42 and 43, respectively.

[327] Ibid., para. 46.

[328] Knox, "The Ruggie Rules," pp. 79–80.

[329] Deva and Bilchitz, "The Human Rights Obligations of Business: A Critical Framework for the Future," in Deva and Bilchitz (eds.), *Human Rights Obligations of Business: Beyond the Corporate Responsibility to Respect?* p. 4.

[330] UN HR Council, "Statement on behalf of a Group of Countries at the 24th Session of the HRC," September 2013, http://business-humanrights.org/sites/default/files/media/docu

> [a]n international legally binding instrument, concluded within the UN system, would clarify the obligations of transnational corporations in the field of human rights, as well as of corporations in relation to States, and provide for the establishment of effective remedies for victims in cases where domestic jurisdiction is clearly unable to prosecute effectively those companies.[331]

Ecuador and South Africa tabled a resolution at the UN HR Council's 26th Session for the elaboration of such an instrument through the establishment of an open-ended intergovernmental working group (OEIGWG).[332] Supported by a number of civil society organizations, the Resolution was accepted in a vote highly divided, largely along developed versus developing country lines.[333] Another resolution drafted by Norway was tabled and adopted by consensus at the same session, issuing a three-year extension of the mandate of the UN WG on Business and Human Rights and requesting it to focus on improving access to remedy for victims, which included exploring "the benefits and limitations of a legally binding instrument."[334]

The OEIGWG met for the first time in Geneva in July 2015 to start the groundwork for the binding instrument for businesses operating transnationally. A first draft of the treaty, dubbed the "Zero Draft" was tabled in July 2018 ahead of its fourth session.

The Zero Draft was entitled Legally Binding Instrument to Regulate, in International Human Rights Law, the Activities of Transnational Corporations and other Business Enterprises, making clear that the treaty is not about articulating direct human rights obligations for businesses but about the regulation of business activities under international human

ments/statement unhrc-legally-binding.pdf. (A number of NGOs supported this initiative with a petition: FIAN International et al. "Statement to the HRC in Support of the Initiative of a Group of States for a Legally Binding Instrument on Transnational Corporations," 13 September 2013, www.stopcorporateimpunity.org/?p=3830.)

331 Statement on behalf of a Group of Countries at the 24th Session of the HRC, General Debate – Item 3: "Transnational Corporations and Human Rights," September 2013, https://business-humanrights.org/sites/default/files/media/documents/statement-unhrc-legally-binding.pdf.

332 UN HR Council, draft resolution, "Elaboration of an International Legally Binding Instrument on Transnational Corporations and Other Business Enterprises with Respect to Human Rights," A/HRC/26/L.22/Rev.1, 24 June 2014.

333 Business and Human Rights Resource Centre, "UN Human Rights Council 26th Session (Geneva, 10–27 June 2014)," http://business-humanrights.org/en/binding-treaty/un-human-rights-council-sessions#twenty_six_session.

334 UN HR Council, Draft resolution, "Human Rights and Transnational Corporations and Other Business Enterprises," para. 8.

rights law. A revised draft of the proposed treaty was released in July 2019.

In the Zero Draft, an expression of business obligations was confined to the preamble, where it was "underlined" that "all business enterprises, regardless of their size, sector, operational context, ownership and structure shall respect all human rights, including by avoiding causing or contributing to adverse human rights impacts through their own activities and addressing such impacts when they occur." [335] In the Revised Draft, the reference to a hard obligation as denoted by the word "shall" was considerably softened and replaced by business enterprises having "the responsibility to respect all human rights" in line with previously adopted language in the UNGPs and other subsequent frameworks.[336] In both the Zero Draft and the Revised Draft, the preamble first and foremost underscores the primary responsibility of states in promoting, respecting, protecting and fulfilling human rights.

While the Zero Draft limited the stated purposes of the draft Convention to strengthening "the respect, promotion, protection and fulfilment of human rights in the context of business activities of transnational character," the Revised Draft covers business activities without restricting it to those of a transnational character (Article 2.1[a]). The definition of a "business activity" in Article 1 of the Revised Draft covers but is not limited to "productive or commercial activities" that may be undertaken by a natural or legal person and also covers electronic activities. The proposed instrument is applicable, as outlined in the Revised Draft, to human rights violations resulting from all business activities, "including particularly but not limited to those of a transnational character" (Article 3.1). The definition of "business activity of a transnational character" was made in the Revised Draft as an activity that takes places in more than one national jurisdiction or state (Article 3.2[a]), that takes place contractually in one state but "a substantial part of its preparation, planning, direction, control, designing, processing or manufacturing takes place in another State" (Article 3.2[b]), or that takes place in one state but has "substantial effect" in another (Article 3.2[c]).

[335] Open-Ended Intergovernmental Working Group on Transnational Corporations and Other Business Enterprises with Respect to Human Rights (OEIGWG), "Zero Draft," July 2018, Art. 1, Preamble.

[336] OEIGWG, "OEIGWG CHAIRMANSHIP REVISED DRAFT 16.7.2019," July 2019, Preamble.

Another aim of the proposed legally binding instrument is to prevent human rights abuses and violations resulting from business activities and to ensure that victims have effective access to justice and remedy (Article 2.1[b]). The Revised Draft has replaced the aim of enhancing international cooperation for the realization of human rights with that of international cooperation for the prevention of abuses and violations and for the provision of access to justice and remedy (Article 2.1[c]).

The Revised Draft covers all human rights (Article 3.3), changed from "international human rights as well as rights recognized domestically" in the Zero Draft. The definition of human rights violations or abuses as made in Article 1 of the Revised Draft covers violations or abuses resulting from "acts or omissions in the context of business activities" against individuals or groups "individually or collectively." The basis for the violation or abuse may be "physical or mental injury, emotional suffering, economic loss or substantial impairment of their human rights, including environmental rights" (Article 1.2). The Revised Draft encompasses environmental rights as well as collective rights, which may be particularly important in the case of indigenous peoples or other groups that experience difficulties in accessing their collective rights. The specific article on the Rights of Victims (Article 4) includes procedural rights for victims, including "the right to fair, effective, prompt and non-discriminatory access to justice and adequate, effective and prompt remedies" (Article 4.5). The Revised Draft includes strong wording on remediation, at least from the procedural perspective: "[v]ictims shall be guaranteed the right to submit claims to the courts and State-based non-judicial grievance mechanisms of the State Parties" (Article 4.8) and states parties "shall provide effective mechanisms for the enforcement of remedies for violations of human rights" (Article 4.14).

Children are mentioned in the Revised Draft first in the Preamble within the context of "the distinctive and disproportionate impact of certain business-related human rights abuses" on certain persons or groups such as "women and girls, children, indigenous peoples, persons with disabilities, migrants and refugees." Attention to the needs of these specific persons or groups, including children, is again recognized when businesses consult groups that their activities might affect in the context of due diligence (Article 5.3[b]) and when states implement the proposed binding instrument (Article 14.4). In addition, the use of child soldiers is listed as a crime for which state parties shall ensure legal liability either through criminal, civil or administrative law sanctions (Article 6.7[f]).

Due diligence is a central tenet of the proposed binding instrument. Under the heading of Prevention, the Revised Draft first requires states to regulate the activities of businesses within their territory or jurisdiction, which is already well established under international law. Second, states "shall adopt measures necessary to ensure that all persons conducting business activities, including those of transnational character, to undertake human rights due diligence" (Article 5.2).

The Zero Draft had been closely based on the conceptualization of due diligence in the "duty of vigilance" (*devoir de vigilance*) featured in France's pioneering Law No. 2017–399 of 27 March 2017 on the corporate duty of vigilance for parent and instructing companies. This law requires all companies established in France with at least 5,000 employees within their parent and direct or indirect subsidiaries with their statutory seat on French territory or those that have at least 10,000 employees in their parent or direct or indirect subsidiaries with their statutory seat on French territory or abroad, to establish and effectively implement a vigilance plan.[337] This plan consists of "reasonable vigilance measures adequate to identify risks and to prevent serious harms against human rights and fundamental freedoms, to the health and security of individuals and the environment" that result from the activities of the parent company, of the subsidiaries that it directly or indirectly controls as well as activities of subcontractors and suppliers with whom it has "an established commercial relationship, in so far as these activities are linked to this relationship."[338] The vigilance plans should be elaborated in concertation with relevant stakeholders and also made public. They are required to include the following elements: an assessment of risks, procedures for continuous and systematic evaluation of supply chain relations, measures for risk mitigation and prevention of human rights violations, an alert mechanism for risks that materialize and, finally, a follow-up system for implemented measures to assess their effectiveness. Failure to abide by the duty of vigilance obligations under the law carries legal sanctions. In the Revised Draft, human rights due diligence includes the identification of potential impacts (impact assessment), taking action to prevent violations, monitoring and reporting to stakeholders (Article 5.2). In a departure from the French "duty of vigilance" law, there is no longer a mention of sanctions in the case of failure to

[337] Republic of France, Loi n° 2017-399 du 27 mars 2017 relative au devoir de vigilance des sociétés mères et des entreprises donneuses d'ordre, Art. 1.

[338] Ibid.

implement due diligence in the Revised Draft. On the other hand, a business failure to prevent human rights violations continues to give rise to liability (Article 6), including when the business fails to prevent actors it has a contractual relationship with from causing harm in cases of sufficient control, supervision or foreseeable risks (Article 6.6).

Legal liability under the Revised Draft is designed to respond to human rights violations or abuses with "effective, proportionate, and dissuasive sanctions and reparations" (Article 6.4).

While the Zero Draft had foreseen civil liability for harms in general and criminal liability for violations amounting to domestic or international crimes under either domestic law or international criminal law, the Revised Draft requires that states parties "shall ensure that their domestic legislation provides for criminal, civil, or administrative liability of legal persons" for crimes that include war crimes, crimes against humanity, genocide, torture and degrading treatment, enforced disappearance, extrajudicial execution, forced labor, use of child soldiers, forced eviction, slavery, forced displacement, human trafficking (including sexual exploitation), sexual and gender-based violence (Article 6.7). In this context, corporate criminal liability for crimes resulting from commercial child sexual exploitation and sale of children as covered under the Revised Draft's Article 6.7(j) are also dealt with under Articles 3 and 4 CRC OPSC and Article 26 of the CoE Lanzarote Convention on corporate liability.

The Revised Draft requires civil liability to be applied autonomously from criminal liability, stating the obligation that it "shall not be made contingent upon finding of criminal liability or its equivalent for the same actor" (Article 6.3).

The broader article on jurisdiction in the Zero Draft was replaced by the article on "adjudicative jurisdiction" in the Revised Draft. In the Zero Draft, a business was considered to be domiciled in the place it has its seat, central administration as well as "substantial business interest" or "subsidiary, agency, instrumentality, branch, representative office or the like" but the Revised Draft limits this to where the business is incorporated, has its statutory seat, central administration or "substantial business interests" (Article 7.2), thereby discounting subsidiaries or branches. The result is that the proposed legally binding instrument would allow victims to seek remedies "independently of their nationality or place of domicile," in "the courts of the State where" violations have occurred

(Article 7.1[1]), where "victims are domiciled" (Article 7.1[2]) or where the businesses are domiciled (Article 7.1[3]), meaning that there would not be much novelty to the existing situation where victims indeed have recourse to these three channels when the legal basis exists in that specific domestic jurisdiction.

Alongside the Zero Draft, the text of a draft Optional Protocol (OP) to the proposed convention on the establishment of a "National Implementation Mechanism" was also released in 2018.[339] The proposed mechanism would serve to make the legally binding instrument known to the public, including businesses and victims (Article 2) and cooperate with national institutions, their international counterparts and civil society to raise awareness of the implementation of the instrument (Article 3). More importantly, it would be mandated to request information from a state party on the implementation of the due diligence obligations at a minimum (Article 4) and to "conduct reviews on the implementation of due diligence obligations" and provide recommendations (Article 5). In addition, where states allow for this, the mechanism may be fashioned as a complaints mechanism (and named a "Committee") (Article 6) that is to provide good offices akin to the OECD National Contact Points (NCPs) to reach an amicable settlement, without prejudice to the rights of victims to seek remedies under formal legal systems (Article 7). In addition, this committee will have the mandate to request information from states parties, intergovernmental and nongovernmental organizations or other sources, receive testimony (Article 6.3[a] and [b]), conduct visits or inspections (Article 6.3[c]) and request interim measures from the state party (Article 6.3[d]). The draft OP also sets out some procedural measures such as inadmissibility criteria, confidentiality and the complaint resolution process for this opt-in communications mechanism (Articles 8–11). Finally, the draft OP foresees the possibility of regional integration organizations with competence in the area of the legally binding instrument to accede to the OP, which could in practice be used by the European Union. There is no clear indication in the draft of what specific accommodations will be provided for individuals and groups that have traditionally been

[339] OEIGWG, Draft Optional Protocol to the Legally Binding Instrument to Regulate, in International Human Rights Law, the Activities of Transnational Corporations and Other Business Enterprises, Annex, October 2018. (A revised draft of the optional protocol was not yet available at the time of writing in August 2019.)

marginalized and therefore faced difficulties in accessing remedies for violations. Consequently, it is also unclear how children could use the opt-in communications mechanisms and whether there would be child-friendly procedures put in place.

1.4 Legalization of Business Duties

1.4.1 Business and Human Rights: A Legalization Process Set in Motion

The chronological survey of developments in the business and human rights field is indicative of a legalization process of obligations set in motion. In fact, the involvement of various stakeholders with different priorities and agendas, the ensuing bargaining and milestone agreements that serve to define the applicable norms (even if they are not binding) in the interim, and the continuation of bargaining on these interim norms are best explained in such a legal process perspective, borrowing insights from the discipline of International Relations (IR) on how norms are born or constructed, and how they evolve in global contexts as well as in global governance.

The preoccupation with moral progress in international law's response to contemporary human rights challenges[340] necessarily implies a process-based transformation of the existing conventional outlook on international law. The idea of process as the vehicle of transformation is based on the premise that interests and identities are not given or fixed, in line with constructivist insights from IR theory.

Constructivists Insights on Norms and Transformation

One of the most important insights regarding process that Constructivist IR research has produced is on the trajectory of norms in international life. Norms are generally defined as "standard[s] of appropriate behavior for actors with a given identity."[341] Finnemore and Sikkink underline the commonly drawn distinction between "regulative norms, which order and constrain behavior, and constitutive norms, which create new actors, interests, or categories of action."[342] In either form, "[n]orms channel

340 Richard M. Price, "Moral Limit and Possibility in World Politics" (2008) 62(2) *International Organization* 191–220 at 210.

341 Martha Finnemore and Kathryn Sikkink, "International Norm Dynamics and Political Change" (1998) 52(4) *International Organization* 887–917 at 891.

342 Ibid., 891.

and regularize behavior,"[343] often on a moral basis for action or nonaction. Finnemore and Sikkink argue that norms become widespread through a three-stage process: norm emergence, norm cascade and internalization. Norms emerge on the international stage through the efforts of norm entrepreneurs, who "frame" issues in various ways to draw attention to them.[344] These norm entrepreneurs are then able to persuade a critical mass of states to adopt the norm, culminating in a "tipping point" and resulting in a "norm cascade" or more plainly put, acceptance of the norm.[345] In a third stage, those performing different societal functions internalize the norms.

Finnemore and Sikkink, despite their state-centric assessment of how tipping points come about (by the adoption of the norms by a critical number of *states*), recognize other "agents of socialization" capable of exerting pressure on "targeted actors to adopt new policies and laws" and capable of "monitoring compliance with international standards."[346] As a specific argument on international law norms, they contend: "the power or persuasiveness of a normative claim in law is explicitly tied to the 'fit' of that claim within existing normative frameworks."[347] In addition, this "logic of appropriateness" may lead to "notions of duty, responsibility, identity, and obligation (all social constructions) . . . [to] drive behavior as well as self-interest and gain."[348]

Constructivism argues that even interests are not completely materially or rationally based. Interests are also constructed and shaped by identities through an interactive and interactional process. Through the "creation, interpretation, and implementation of law," which bridges interests and identities, a sufficiently widespread "predisposition towards compliance" is created.[349] Once the internalization of legal norms happens at a broader scale through cooperative action of those rallying for these norms, the norms take their place within the system of rules "embedded in bureaucratic routine and legal structures."[350] As such,

343 Ibid., 894.

344 Ibid., 897.

345 Ibid., 895. Even though they accept and even herald the role of actors beyond the state, Finnemore and Sikkink remain highly state-centric in their analysis of how norms become accepted and internalized.

346 Ibid., 902.

347 Ibid., 908.

348 Ibid., 913.

349 Ian Johnstone, "The Power of Interpretive Communities," in Barnett and Duvall (eds.), *Power in Global Governance* (Cambridge University Press, 2005), p. 189.

350 Ibid.

"the *practice* of law serves to blur the distinction between calculations of interest and a sense of feeling bound."[351]

Wendt, in his seminal article "Anarchy is what states make of it," outlines what the transformation at the global systemic level from competitive to cooperative would look like in four stages. In stage one, the consensus about identity commitments of the given actor (in Wendt's case, a state actor) collapses. In stage two, the collapsing consensus leads to a reevaluation of the self and the other as well as the structures governing their interaction. As a result, a new or modified identity formation is launched. In stage three, the new/modified identity is exhibited through practice that is aimed at bringing about a transformation of interactions. In the fourth and final stage, the changed behavior of the given actor is rewarded by other actors, resulting in a fresh basis for the formation of new identities and interests.[352] Although Wendt is concerned mainly with states and is silent on the matter of "law" as either the transformative object or the transformation's subject, his four-stage model is nonetheless relevant to illustrate the assumptions made when surveying the business and human rights field, as it moves from competitive (between businesses, states and individuals or communities) to more collaborative, all the while oscillating in between through bargaining around interests and identities in a legal process.

Although "understanding which norms will become law ('soft' law as well as 'hard' law) and how, exactly, compliance with those laws comes about"[353] are not always clear, Bederman argues for a compelling trajectory of what may be called norm solidification. He contends that even when "standards of conduct" developed by international actors are aspirational or informal, "the inevitable trend is that soft law hardens into legal obligation."[354] There is an "asymmetric dynamic at work" in that "[r]ules rarely dissolve into standards, but standards . . . will usually solidify into legal rules."[355] Whether norm solidification is inevitable

[351] Ibid., p. 188.

[352] Wendt specifically considers the example of a transformation from a competitive security system to a cooperative security system for states in the existing state of anarchy. Yet, these stages would also be applicable, with some modifications to other actors as well. (Wendt, "Anarchy Is What States Make of It," 420–422).

[353] Finnemore and Sikkink, "International Norm Dynamics and Political Change," 916.

[354] David Bederman, "Constructivism, Positivism, and Empiricism in International Law" (2001) 89(2) *Georgetown Law Journal* 469–499 at 484.

[355] Ibid. (Bederman notes that he uses "standards" as a surrogate for "soft law in an international context".)

remains open to question but the possibility for norms to transform into more authoritative rules and the process through which such a transformation occurs remain ever more relevant in the business and human rights debates, given the push of certain norm entrepreneurs for the solidification of various norms into legally binding international rules. These norm entrepreneurs are attempting to fulfil the features of legalization through the proposed legally binding instrument by increasing "the degree to which rules are obligatory, the precision of those rules, and [achieving] the delegation of some functions of interpretation, monitoring, and implementation to a third party."[356] In fact, the Revised Draft of the proposed legally binding instrument on business and human rights recognizes in its Preamble that it desires "to contribute to the development of international law, international humanitarian law and international human rights law in this field."[357]

Regulation of MNEs: A Story of Social Construction and Contestation

Wendt's insights on the transformation of identities at the global systemic level can easily be transposed to how norms regulating behavior and consequently shaping identities are invented and reinvented overtime. Taking the regulation of MNEs as a case in point, starting with the 1960s and intensifying throughout the next two decades, the consensus about the operation of MNEs in the developing world free from the pressures of external regulation collapsed. At first, this collapse marked the recognition that developing states were well within their rights to regulate MNEs operating in their territory, while it also signaled to MNEs themselves and their home states that 'business as usual' was on its way to changing.

In stage two, this collapsing consensus gave rise to international efforts under the auspices of the ILO, OECD and the UN, reevaluating the position of state actors and international bodies in the regulation of MNE activities, at first in relation to their impacts on developing host states and consequently, but more significantly, their impacts on individuals and groups populating these host states. This second stage has been particularly prolific in giving rise to a number of normative frameworks with varying degrees of acceptance in modifying the

[356] Judith Goldstein et al., "Introduction: Legalization and World Politics" (2000) 54(3) *International Organization* 385–399 at 387.

[357] OEIGWG, "OEIGWG CHAIRMANSHIP REVISED DRAFT 16.7.2019," Preamble.

structures governing MNE regulation globally, namely the ILO Tripartite Declaration, the OECD Guidelines on MNEs and the proposed UN Draft Code, UN Global Compact and the Draft Norms. Finally, the formation of a new consensus has culminated in the development and the adoption of the UN Framework and UNGPs as the last step of stage two.

The UN Framework and UNGPs constitute the basis of a new structure governing the interactions of MNEs, on the one hand, and host states and their populations, on the other. This new consensus mostly among developed states and business enterprises themselves has come about through MNEs as actors being restyled as working under host state laws and regulations but also under societal expectations to respect human rights. The newly constructed consensus, which has been called the "current globally agreed baseline in the field of business and human rights,"[358] has played a role in shaping or reshaping other soft-law normative frameworks such as the OECD Guidelines, the CRBPs and most recently, the ILO MNE Declaration.

The business and human rights landscape is currently at the third stage of identity transformation that Wendt describes: the new consensus is being put to test through states' NAPs, the CoE's 2016 Recommendation, the implementation of the OECD Guidelines, including through the work of the NCPs, the ILO MNE Declaration, as well as through initiatives attempting to put specialized standards such as the CRBPs or industry-based efforts into action. Whether the operationalization of the new consensus will become the basis for cooperative action as regards the human rights duties of businesses operating transnationally and thus culminate in the formation of new identities or interests on the basis of this cooperative action is uncertain. This is because those not completely satisfied with the current consensus, including some developing states, civil society actors and academics, are seeking to challenge its premises and build another, based on norms that are formally legalized in hard law, such as through the proposed legally binding instrument. The proposed legally binding instrument itself is a venue of contestation as exemplified by the negative reaction of the business sector to the Zero Draft[359] and the subsequent revision of the text, which accommodates

[358] CoE, "Recommendation on Human Rights and Business."

[359] International Organization of Employers, International Chamber of Commerce, Business at OECD and Business Europe, "Business Response to the Zero Draft Legally Binding Instrument to Regulate, in International Human Rights Law, the Activities of

many of the business concerns by limiting overtures on extraterritorial jurisdiction and delinking failures to conduct effective due diligence from legal liability.

The implementation process of the UNGPs and the ongoing work on a legally binding instrument demonstrate that the business and human rights landscape is one populated by competing norm entrepreneurs. On one side are those norm entrepreneurs content with nonbinding standards espoused by the UNGPs, refashioned by other nonbinding frameworks such as the OECD Guidelines, the CRBPs or the ILO MNE Declaration and implemented through voluntary regulatory schemes at the public and the private levels. On the other side are the proponents of a binding international instrument on the regulation of business enterprises. The fact that proponents of the treaty process include not only civil society and academics but also a number of developing states points to a contestation of the normative status quo as defined by the UNGPs also at the state level.

The proponents of the binding instrument consider that the UN Framework "underestimates (... intentionally or not) what is required to push corporate responsibility for human rights beyond due diligence processes and the redress of individual grievances."[360] The challenge to the former SRSG's "principled pragmatism"[361] in the form of the instigated treaty process signals that the process within the UN for legalizing the human rights obligations of business into some form of hard law is well at work and far from over. Many proponents of a binding instrument believe, as Simons has argued, that "transnational corporate actors and their home states will remain opposed to binding legal obligations as long as they are allowed to do so."[362] The underlying suggestion is that these powerful businesses and their home states should not be allowed to oppose binding obligations indefinitely.

Transnational Corporations and Other Business Enterprises ('Zero Draft Treaty') and the Draft Optional Protocol to the Legally Binding Instrument ('Draft Optional Protocol') Annex," October 2018.

360 Christine Parker and John Howe, "Ruggie's Diplomatic Project and Its Missing Regulatory Infrastructure," in Mares, *The UN Guiding Principles on Business and Human Rights – Foundations and Implementation* (Martinus Nijhoff Publishers, 2011), p. 274.

361 OHCHR, "Principled Pragmatism."

362 Penelope Simons, "International Law's Invisible Hand and the Future of Corporate Accountability for Violations of Human Rights" (2012) 3(1) *Journal of Human Rights and the Environment* 5–43 at 41.

From a process perspective, the ongoing competition between binding and voluntary norms and their respective proponents indicates that despite the continued resistance to recognizing the need for human rights obligations that legally bind businesses, norm entrepreneurs are working to push the boundaries of the law towards a more expansive definition of recognized human rights duty-bearers. Ruggie contests the usefulness of the legally binding approach in legalization by contending that "further international legalization has a role to play through carefully crafted precision tools intended to reinforce this dynamic, not by means of some overarching treaty that tries to encompass the entirety of the complex, diverse and contested issues that make up business and human rights as a subject of concern and action."[363]

Whether the process of legalization to create a clear and strong normative framework around human rights obligations of businesses operating transnationally is best served by a human rights convention at the international level is an open question. Nevertheless, skeptics of direct obligations might be too hasty to discount what the proliferation of nonbinding norms and standards might mean for the evolution of the normative legal framework as regards direct human rights obligations of corporations by pointing out their current limits and repeating the adage that corporations are not assigned human rights obligations under international law.[364] In fact, we are most likely moving closer to a setting where increased human rights scrutiny over companies under international law will become more legalized.[365] The evolution of the proposed legally binding instrument at the UN indicates that the content of that scrutiny will also be a battlefield between different norm entrepreneurs.

A clear and strong normative legal framework that takes into account the rights of individuals and groups at risk of marginalization, such as children, might prevent UNGPs becoming "the basis for a lukewarm, ever counter-productive, set of practices around business and human

[363] Ruggie, "The Social Construction of the UNGPs" 16.

[364] Eric de Brabandere, "Non-State Actors and Human Rights: Corporate Responsibility and the Attempts to Formalize the Role of Corporations as Participants in the International Legal System," in Jean d'Aspremont (ed.), *Participants in the International Legal System: Multiple Perspectives on Non-State Actors in International Law* (Routledge, 2011), p. 276.

[365] Robert McCorquodale, "Human Rights and Business: Is International Law Relevant?," *OUPblog* (blog.oup.com), 19 December 2016, https://blog.oup.com/2016/12/human-rights-business-law/ (accessed 24 April 2019).

rights."[366] In addition, the hard-to-swallow truth is that simply strengthening existing human rights enforcement mechanisms as de Brabandere suggests,[367] is likely not a solution.

Case law of the ECtHR demonstrates, for instance, that in claims related to human rights violations as a result of corporate activities or decisions, the Court has consistently emphasized the domestic state party's obligation to protect, without addressing the impact of the corporate entity or its duties. In two separate cases concerning gold mining, *Taşkın and Others* v. *Turkey* and *Tatar* v. *Romania*, the Court found violations of Article 8 ECHR on the right to respect for private and family life in the domestic state's failure to protect the rights of those that may be adversely affected by mining activities without pronouncing what obligations the mining company was expected to comply with.[368] The ECtHR has stayed true to its previous case law in the more recent *Özel* v. *Turkey* judgment as well, particularly missing the opportunity to elucidate the "interplay between different liability regimes – state versus private actor liability, criminal versus civil liability and corporate versus individual liability."[369]

The European experience may not necessarily be replicated universally, as the 2015 *Kaliña and Lokono Peoples* v. *Suriname* judgment of the IACtHR on human rights violations linked also to mining demonstrates. In this case, the IACtHR focused not only on the state obligation to protect from damage caused by third parties but also on what the business obligations amounted to:

> [Observing that the mining activities resulting in adverse impacts on the environment and indigenous peoples were carried out by private companies], the Court takes note of the [UNGPs], which establish that businesses must respect and protect human rights, as well as prevent, mitigate, and accept responsibility for the adverse human rights impacts directly linked to their activities. Hence, as reiterated by these principles, 'States must protect against human rights abuse within their territory and/or jurisdiction by third parties, including

366 Parker and Howe, "Ruggie's Diplomatic Project and Its Missing Regulatory Infrastructure."

367 De Brabandere, "Non-State Actors and Human Rights: Corporate Responsibility and the Attempts to Formalize the Role of Corporations as Participants in the International Legal System," p. 280.

368 *Taşkın and Others* v. *Turkey* (Application No. 46117/99) Judgment (FINAL), 30 March 2005 ECtHR; *Tatar* v. *Romania* (Application No. 67021/01) Judgment, 27 January 2009 ECtHR.

369 Lieselot Verdonck, "How the European Court of Human Rights Evaded the Business and Human Rights Debate in *Özel* v. *Turkey*" (2016) 2(1) *The Turkish Commercial Law Review* 111–118 at 118.

> business enterprises. This requires taking appropriate steps to prevent, investigate, punish and redress such abuse through effective policies, legislation, regulations and adjudication.' [footnotes omitted][370]

Hence, the Court interpreted the UNGPs as establishing not only the obligation to respect human rights but also obligations to protect, prevent, mitigate and accept responsibility for violations. The enforceability of these obligations had to take place through a discharge of state obligations to protect taking all appropriate measures. In this way, even though the IACtHR did not have *ratione personae* jurisdiction over the two companies in question, it linked a company's failure to comply with its obligations to a domestic state's failure to carry out its protect obligations to "prevent, investigate, punish and redress" such harm resulting from the behavior of private agents. As a matter of law, it is clear that Suriname has the obligation to protect indigenous peoples and the environment from detrimental actions of third parties. The state was in breach of this obligation when it did not require social and environmental impact assessments prior to the launch of mineral extraction activities, did not ensure prior and informed consent of the indigenous peoples and did not supervise or monitor impact assessments undertaken after the start of the mineral exploitation.[371] What is in fact missing in the IACtHR decision is how obligations of corporate entities will be upheld if Suriname is either unwilling or incapable of carrying out this obligation to protect. The private agents in question in the *Kaliña and Lokono Peoples* v. *Suriname* case were subsidiaries of MNEs set up and operating in the United States as well as in Australia and the United Kingdom, having entered a joint venture to exploit minerals in Suriname. When a domestic state fails to live up to its protect obligations, as happened in Suriname, there is continued need for a fail-safe to ensure that rights-holders are not left without recourse. The contestation between norm entrepreneurs pushing for more comprehensive and effective implementation of adopted norms and those pushing for stronger norms that are enshrined in hard law is in fact caused by this continued need for a fail-safe.

370 *Kaliña and Lokono Peoples* v. *Suriname* (Merits, Reparations and Costs) 25 November 2015 IACtHR, para. 224.

371 Ibid., para. 216.

Norms En Route to Internalization and Legalization: Human Rights Due Diligence and Remediation

A survey of the development of the business and human rights field yields several observations. First, the normative debates on business and human rights have produced a relatively substantial set of standards or "norms," even if the implementation of such standards have remained by and large voluntary. Second, while these standards as included in the UNGPs and later replicated in other instruments such as the OECD Guidelines or the ILO MNE Declaration have not revolutionized the human rights field in any major way or drastically improved respect for, protection or fulfillment of rights, they have been adopted by a critical number of state and non-state stakeholders and are increasingly being used as benchmarks. Third, the willingness of stakeholders to engage with and implement these human rights standards on business behavior has served as a catalyzer for the push to elaborate binding norms as well as the extension of the reach of such standards to specific groups of rights holders such as children.

The notion of corporate 'responsibility' to respect human rights as a complement to state obligations to protect from corporate-related human rights abuse is the extent to which duties for businesses have been espoused by the UN Framework and UNGPs. The OECD Guidelines, the ILO MNE Declaration and the CoE Recommendation all echo the differentiation of duties between businesses and states where they operate based both on the extent of the duty (respect versus respect, protect and fulfill) as well as on the nature of the duty (softer worded 'responsibility' versus legally binding 'obligation'). What is important and also relatively positive is the recognition that corporate 'responsibility' exists independent of state obligations; as such, businesses cannot hide behind a host state's failure as a duty-bearer for their failure to discharge their duties.

The attribution of complementary but independent human rights duties to businesses has resulted in the two particular norms of human rights due diligence and remediation gaining widespread acceptance with the adoption of the UNGPs. The Former SRSG Ruggie also agrees that the norm of human rights due diligence is being internalized, having passed the tipping point and entered the norm cascade stage.[372] Human rights due diligence and remediation as recognized standards were consequently taken up by all nonbinding frameworks seeking to regulate

[372] John Ruggie, *Just Business*, pp. 128–129.

business behavior, including specific frameworks on children's rights and business. The norm of human rights due diligence entails a distinct and specific duty for businesses. Its key components have crystallized as human rights policy statements, human rights impact assessments and reporting. Remediation or the requirement to ensure access to remedy for rights holders is diffused, creating a less specific duty on businesses as it also applies to states. Due diligence and remediation have in fact become norms denoting common standards for all business activity and operations. In fact, they featured prominently in the Zero Draft and still do so in the Revised Draft, which seeks to give obligatory force to these norms by binding home states to regulate the activities of businesses domiciled in their jurisdiction not only within their borders but also when they operate transnationally.

Internalized Norms on Children's Rights and Business

Children's rights are only implicitly incorporated into the UNGPs alongside the rights of 'vulnerable' groups susceptible to marginalization, entailing a heightened general duty correlated with marginalization and disadvantage. The OECD Guidelines, the CoE Recommendation, ILO MNE Declaration, CESCR's GC 24 and the Revised Draft of the proposed legally binding instrument all share the UNGP's premise that the rights of children entail a higher risk of negative impacts and therefore require a heightened duty of due diligence, particular attention as well as the possible application of additional standards. The heightened duty for rights that are at a higher risk of being negatively impacted is based on the identity of their rights-holders as traditionally marginalized and disadvantaged. This heightened duty is not a norm in and of itself, it is a qualifier for the due diligence norm in human rights.

Children's rights-specific frameworks on businesses build on the application of the general norms of human rights due diligence and remediation to the particular situation of children when they are directly or indirectly concerned by business activity. Both the CRBP and CRC Committee's GC 16 therefore stress the importance of children's rights due diligence including through children's rights impact assessments, and of child-friendly access to effective remedy.

While the heightened duty for children's rights is recognized under the numerous governance frameworks, it is still both conceptually and practically unclear how responsibility for violations is to be attributed when this heightened duty is breached by a business enterprise. In fact, public international law has still not provided an adequate formulation of the law of responsibility in today's world of "plural and diverse duty-bearers."[373] In this respect, one specific children's rights norm that has passed the tipping point in the business and children's rights arena is related to the prohibition of the worst forms of child labor and hazardous child labor which are covered under various soft-law normative frameworks on business and human rights and in frameworks specific to children's rights alike, including the OECD Guidelines, the ILO MNE Declaration, the CoE Recommendation, the CRBPs and the CRC Committee's GC 16. The Revised Draft particularly focuses on child labor giving rise to criminal responsibility such as child soldiering explicitly and arguably also includes within the broader headings of forced labor and sexual exploitation, child forced labor and child sexual exploitation. Other provisions of children's rights have not reached such universal uptake. While child labor is the first and sometimes only aspect of the business–children's rights relationship that consistently attracts scrutiny, OECD Guidelines, the CoE Recommendation, the CRBPs and the CRC Committee's GC 16 all recognize the broader relevance of business activity for children and their rights beyond the limited scope of child labor.

1.5 Business Responsibility for Wrongdoings

1.5.1 Legal Considerations of Responsibility for Multiple Duty-Bearers

In the business and human rights nexus, the words "obligations" and "responsibility" are often used to denote a scale of legal duties: binding norms and nonbinding norms, respectively. Under public international law, however, the concepts are fundamentally different. As Vandenhole neatly sums it up: "the notion of 'obligations' refers to substantive human rights obligations (primary norms), responsibility refers to responsibility for human rights violations (secondary norms)."[374]

The often-disregarded reality is that children's rights violations as with other human rights violations, especially if they are the violations of economic, social and cultural rights, may not be confined to a single act or omission by a single actor. They may also be set in motion through a process comprising multiple acts/omissions by multiple actors.

[373] The expression is borrowed from Vandenhole (ed.), *Challenging Territoriality in Human Rights Law.*

[374] Wouter Vandenhole and Willem van Genugten, "Introduction: An Emerging Multi-Duty-Bearer Human Rights Regime?," in Vandenhole (ed.), *Challenging Territoriality in Human Rights Law*, p. 5.

Furthermore, each actor may contribute to the process in a different way and at a different rate. In addition, these actors may not always be traditionally recognized subjects of international law. When multiple actors separately or jointly contribute to a harm or a violation, three overarching matters need to be addressed: attribution of obligations to different actors, attribution of responsibility to duty-bearers and the distribution of the responsibility for the violation between the various duty-bearers.

1.5.2 International Law on Responsibility

Norms on the attribution of obligations, or the primary norms, are both conceptually and practically important for the attribution and distribution of responsibility, or the secondary norms. The primary norms, however, do not automatically prescribe the nature of the secondary norms as to how responsibility should be envisaged in relation to situations involving multiple duty-bearers. The traditional account of international law on responsibility would dictate that any endeavor to attribute responsibility to an actor (usually a state) would commence invariably with the attribution of conduct for the wrongdoing to that actor. The Articles on the Responsibility of States for Internationally Wrongful Acts reduces this attributable conduct to the conduct of state organs, defined as "any person or entity which has that status in accordance with the internal law of the State."[375] The function of the state organ is of no importance.[376] If this conduct of a state organ "is not in conformity with what is required of it by that obligation" at the time of the conduct, a breach is concluded to have taken place.[377] According to the ARSIWA, the breach of obligations through a conduct or an "act" that has a continuing character results in the extension of the breach over the entire period of its wrongfulness.[378] Expert opinion expressed in the Maastricht Principles, on the other hand, links state responsibility not only to state conduct in breach of international human rights obligations but to the conduct (acts or omissions) of NSAs controlled by the state as well as of persons or entities "empowered by the State to exercise elements of governmental authority."[379] For international organizations,

[375] ILC, ARSIWA, Art. 4.2.
[376] Ibid., Art. 4.1.
[377] Ibid., Arts. 12 and 13.
[378] Ibid., Art. 14.
[379] The Maastricht Principles, Principles 11 and 12 respectively.

the Articles on Responsibility of International Organizations (ARIO) echo ARSIWA and link the attribution of responsibility to two grounds: the attribution of the conduct to a given organization and the characterization of that conduct as an internationally wrongful act.[380] The Articles on Responsibility of International Organizations, as noted in the Commentary by the ILC, contain only secondary rules and do not speak to "the existence or otherwise of any particular primary rule binding on international organizations."[381]

Both ARSIWA and ARIO have assigned responsibility to a state or international organization for "aid or assistance in the commission of an internationally wrongful act" (or complicity) when that actor "(a) . . . does so with knowledge of the circumstances of the internationally wrongful act; and (b) the act would be internationally wrongful if committed by that [actor]."[382] Regrettably, the test for attribution of responsibility habitually stops at the point of the attribution of conduct. In real-life situations, however, there is often no clear single internationally wrongful act to attribute to a single actor. Often, there is a series of wrongful acts that come about through the involvement and contribution of several actors, which may be of different nature. Even when this is the case, there is often a strong pull to attempt to reconceptualize these scenarios to fit the conventional frameworks. Karavias considers, for instance, home and host states may be held responsible for wrongful corporate action based on the breach of their obligation of due diligence to regulate the conduct of corporate nationals or corporations operating within their jurisdiction, respectively.[383]

Public international law debates on responsibility (of states and international organizations), as evidenced by ARSIWA and ARIO, build on the premises that states are primary actors on the international plane and that other actors (namely, international organizations or corporations) can be addressed by international law only on the condition of being recognized as international legal persons.[384] The Articles on Responsibility of International Organizations and ARSIWA are

380 ILC, Articles on the Responsibility of International Organizations (ARIO), 2011, Art. 4.

381 ILC, "General Commentary to the DARIO," Draft articles on the responsibility of international organizations, with commentaries, 2011, http://legal.un.org/docs/?path=../ilc/texts/instruments/english/commentaries/9_11_2011.pdf&lang=EF, para. 3 (accessed 15 April 2019).

382 ILC, ARSIWA, Art. 16 and ILC, ARIO, Art. 14, respectively.

383 Karavias, "Shared Responsibility and Multinational Enterprises," 99.

384 Even in discussions of how responsibility may be shared between a state and a non-state actor, the discussion first and almost requisitely centers on whether a given actor may be

insufficient for dealing with responsibility when wrongfulness results from the acts or omissions of several actors, especially when businesses are involved. Their insistence on the condition of international legal personality, a notion demonstrably based on legal fiction, is particularly constricting. This failure of the ILC's principles to incorporate other types of actors such as individuals and NSAs is also recognized by Nollkaemper and his coauthors in their examination of the state of the art of shared responsibility in international law.[385]

Human rights responsibility may also be theorized on the basis of alternative conceptions that do not restrict responsibility to causality based on conduct and its attribution. Public international law frameworks on responsibility such as ARIO and ARSIWA are not frameworks on human rights responsibility. Therefore, their focus on the attribution of conduct and the resulting liability for damages does not cover the entire spectrum of what human rights responsibility commonly entails. In fact, responsibility based exclusively on direct causality is a very limited aspect of human rights responsibility. In *Munaf* v. *Romania*, the Human Rights Committee concluded that when the "necessary and foreseeable consequence" of state conduct creates a risk for extraterritorial violations and this risk is known to the state party at the time, that "State party may be responsible for extraterritorial violations of the Covenant, if it is a link in the causal chain that would make possible violations in another jurisdiction."[386] The Committee's reference to "links" in the causal chain is a recognition that causality may be understood in less strict terms, covering a broader range of actions, decisions or omissions with foreseeable consequences. In *Velásquez-Rodríguez* v. *Honduras*, the IACtHR concluded that a state's international responsibility may be engaged in the case of violations caused by private entities or by unknown authors on a number of bases: "the lack of due diligence to prevent the violation or to respond to it as required by the Convention" and by failing to carry out the duty to investigate these violations in a serious and thorough manner.[387] As such, even if the conduct itself is not attributable to an actor (directly or indirectly,

considered a subject, which would allow it to incur obligations under international law. (See: Karavias, "Shared Responsibility and Multinational Enterprises," 100–102.)

[385] Nollkaemper and Plakokefalos, "Conclusions: Beyond the ILC Legacy," in Nollkaemper and Plakokefalos, *Principles of Shared Responsibility*, pp. 359–361.

[386] *Munaf* v. *Romania*, CCPR/C/96/D/1539/2006, 21 August 2009 HRC, para. 14.2.

[387] *Case of Velásquez-Rodríguez* v. *Honduras* (Judgment), Series C No. 4. Case 7.615, 29 July 1988 IACtHR, paras. 172 and 177, respectively.

through its agents), responsibility of that actor may still be engaged for failing to carry out its obligations to prevent and respond to the violation. Of course, the content of the "standard of 'due diligence'" is critical given that it "is becoming the accepted benchmark against which state actions to prevent or respond to human rights and other violations originating in the acts of third parties are to be judged."[388] The effectiveness of secondary rules about the attribution of responsibility also depends on the clarity of primary rules about obligations.[389]

What is needed is to "mak[e] human rights law relevant to the nature of contemporary human rights violations,"[390] which may defy traditional patterns of causality that directly link a perpetrator with a violation (conduct). One such effort by Salomon in her work on global justice and poverty contends that responsibility for violations of a systemic or structural nature such as those resulting from world poverty may be attributed not on the basis of conduct or "establishment of a *direct causal* relationship" but on the basis of the failure to carry out due diligence and conform to the standard of care.[391] Salomon's alternative responsibility model rests on the "principle of common but differentiated responsibilities" for structural global problems such as world poverty and proposes four yardsticks for determining responsibility that may be summarized as contribution to the "emergence of the problem," control or "relative power" that gives the actor "influence over the direction of finance, trade, and development," capability to assist, and interest or benefit derived from "the existing distribution of global wealth and resources."[392]

Clearly, responsibility for human rights violations may be theorized on different grounds than other internationally wrongful acts even if these conceptualizations are not mainstream. Here, Clapham's views on the applicability of the "complementarity" concept from physics to human rights responsibility allows to remove the "jurisdiction filter of an international or national court" from the analysis of human rights violations,

[388] Anne T. Gallagher, "The Practice of Shared Responsibility in Relation to Human Rights and Human Trafficking," in André Nollkaemper and Ilias Plakokefalos (eds.), *The Practice of Shared Responsibility in International Law* (Cambridge University Press, 2016), p. 565.

[389] Ibid.

[390] Margot E. Salomon, *Global Responsibility for Human Rights: World Poverty and the Development of International Law* (Oxford University Press, 2007), p. 182.

[391] Ibid., pp. 186–187 (original emphasis).

[392] Ibid., p. 193 (footnotes omitted).

underscoring that "the observation of an event depends on both the observer and the viewing apparatus."[393] When the jurisdiction filter is lifted, "multiple overlapping layers of responsibility" become visible.[394]

Nollkaemper's model of shared responsibility rests on contribution, insofar as "contributions to a harmful outcome trigger the legal responsibility of the authors of such contributions" wherein "causal contribution is only a necessary and not a sufficient condition."[395] He also recognizes that many instances may fall beyond the scope of international law for the time being.[396] For instance, Nollkaemper and Jacobs refer to the notion of "shared accountability" for situations where a multiplicity of actors have accountability for breaking international rules that may not involve responsibility under international law in its formal meaning.[397]

The proliferation of multilateral governance structures and the complex nature of economic transactions across the globe increasingly amount to situations where multiple duty-bearers are implicated in wrongdoing. On the ground, both states (in their territorial capacity or extraterritorially) as well as businesses may be involved in the commission of a violation to varying degrees. Existing guidelines provided through ARSIWA and ARIO address neither the responsibilities of private businesses, for instance, nor the nature of responsibility when indirect involvement or contribution to the wrongdoing and not the particular conduct is attributable to a given actor. It has even been suggested that ARSIWA and ARIO do not cover the consequences of breaches with regard to individuals.[398] In addition, the question of how multiple and diverse duty-bearers are to be

[393] Andrew Clapham, "The Subject of Subjects and the Attribution of Attribution," in L. Boisson de Chazournes and M. Kohen (eds.), *International Law and the Quest for its Implementation: Liber Amicorum Vera Gowlland-Debbas* (Brill, 2010), p. 56.

[394] Ibid.

[395] Nollkaemper, "Introduction" in Nollkaemper and Plakokefalos, *Principles of Shared Responsibility*, p. 9.

[396] Ibid., p. 11.

[397] André Nollkaemper and Dov Jacobs, "Shared Responsibility in International Law: A Conceptual Framework" (2013) 34 *Michigan Journal of International Law* 359–438 at 369.

[398] Mirka Möldner, "Responsibility of International Organizations – Introducing ILC's DARIO" (2012) 16 *Max Planck Yearbook of United Nations Law* at 309 and Armin Von Bogdandy and Mateja Steinbruck Platise, "ARIO and Human Rights Protection: Leaving the Individual in the Cold" (2012) 9 *International Organizations Law Review* 67–76.

assigned responsibility in a given situation where each duty-bearer contributes to the violation in a different way (some directly, others indirectly or through proxy) remains unanswered by the two sets of "Articles."

From a rights-holder perspective, the complete picture of responsibility for violations can only be drawn when multiple duty-bearers implicated in a violation can be held distinctly accountable. The existence or construction of accountability structures for multiple duty-bearers is all the more crucial for rights holders such as children who may not be visible when their rights are breached or who are unable to exercise their agency directly in seeking redress for these breaches due to social or legal constraints. Children often face serious impediments to having a public voice and accessing *ex ante* as well as *ex post* processes aimed at assessing, preventing or mitigating the impact of any given decision or action on their lives. When multiple actors negatively affect children's rights in a given situation, either in a concerted or independent fashion, the lack of conceptual and practical clarity in how they will be held to account creates an additional layer of complexity. Finding the addressees of their rights claims in situations of multiple wrongdoers, places an insurmountable burden on children, who are often considered to lack legal competence.

1.5.3 Responsibility of Private Business: Attribution

The CRC Committee's GC 16 notes that given the complexities arising especially from global supply chains and contractual business operations, the impact of businesses "on children's rights, whether positive or negative, is rarely the result of the action or omission of a single business unit."[399] In fact, different business units in various territorial jurisdictions may contribute to these impacts. There are two important issues to address in devising parameters for attributing responsibility to private business for children's rights violations. The first issue is linked to the complexities arising from supply and value chains, creating physical and legal distances between duty-bearers and rights holders. The second issue is that of the incorporation structure of a business enterprise, which may legally obscure the links between the violation and duty-bearers downstream. In practice, these two issues are intertwined.

[399] CRC Committee, GC 16, para. 38.

Corporate Structures and Responsibility

Attributing responsibility directly to a business enterprise under international law is itself not straightforward. The outlook is further complicated when this business enterprise that is made up of several different legal entities in different territorial jurisdictions and the wrongdoing is linked to the activities/acts or omissions of one of these entities (subsidiaries) most likely incorporated and operating in a different territorial jurisdiction than its parent. Most complexities arise from two inherently related concepts: limited liability and the so-called corporate veil.

The doctrine of limited liability in domestic law amounts to the capping of the liability of a company's shareholders commensurate with their investment or contribution in that company. In other words, "shareholders in a corporation may not be held liable for the debts of that corporation beyond the level of their investment."[400] Accordingly, each self-standing business enterprise can be said to exist behind the "corporate veil," meaning that it exists separately as a legal person in its own right and that its shareholders are separated from the legal entity by this so-called veil. In reality, however, parent companies as shareholders may and do exercise different degrees of influence over their subsidiaries. In fact, many TNCs operate as one large corporate tree with a trunk, branches and leaves, where each branch and even each leaf might be a separate legal entity in different domestic jurisdictions.

The doctrine of limited liability may become problematic from the point of view of responsibility for human rights violations, particularly if it is used to shield parent companies from responsibility for violations committed or contributed to by their subsidiaries/affiliates. Here, the incorporation structure of a group of companies may create different self-standing legal persons recognized in different jurisdictions with no direct control by the parent company from a legal perspective. When human rights are breached by the actions/omissions of a subsidiary, parent companies may be contributing to the harm or simply be associated with the subsidiary.[401] As corporate veil is the general rule in

[400] De Schutter, "Corporations and Positive Duties in the Area of Economic and Social Rights," Université Catholique de Louvain, CRIDHO Working Paper 2013/7, 2013, p. 15.

[401] Radu Mares, "Responsibility to Respect: Why the Core Company Should Act When Its Affiliates Infringe Human Rights," in Radu Mares (ed.), *The UN Guiding Principles on Business and Human Rights – Foundations and Implementation* (Martinus Nijhoff Publishers, 2011), p. 169.

corporate law, 'piercing or lifting' the corporate veil is only confined to exceptional circumstances. According to the ICJ, these include the prevention of "misuse of the privileges of legal personality" as well as the "prevent[ion] of evasion of legal requirements or of obligations."[402] In *Barcelona Traction*, the ICJ also noted a general consideration about the evolution of law in the face of "economic realities" in order to "provide protective measures and remedies in the interests of those within the corporate entity as well as of those outside who have dealings with it."[403] Given this need for evolution to accommodate current realities, "the independent existence of the legal entity cannot be treated as an absolute."[404] In practice, however, both domestic and international courts have been hesitant to lift the proverbial corporate veil.

The cases against Royal Dutch Shell in the Netherlands for oil spills in the Niger Delta brought by Nigerian farmers and environmental NGOs demonstrate that although courts may traditionally be reluctant to lift the corporate veil, the legal process in a constructivist sense may play out differently over time. In one of the original cases against Shell, *Oguru et al* v. *Shell PLC*, for instance, the District Court of The Hague dismissed the claim against parent company Shell PLC.[405] The Court listed three criteria based on tort law from a 1990 ruling of the English House of Lords (*Caparo Industries PLC* v. *Dickman*) on the duty of care:

(i) the foreseeability for the defendant that the plaintiff would suffer damage;
(ii) the proximity between the plaintiff and the defendant;
(iii) whether it is fair, just and reasonable to assume that a duty of care exists in a specific situation.[406]

The Court concluded on the basis of these three criteria that in the case "a duty of care on the part of the parent companies of the Shell Group" could not be "fair[ly], … quick[ly] and reasonabl[y]" argued.[407] While the foreseeability of damage should be an important consideration in the

[402] *Case Concerning The Barcelona Traction, Light and Power Company, Limited (Belgium* v. *Spain)*, Second Phase, Judgment, 5 February 1970 ICJ, p. 39, para. 56.
[403] Ibid.
[404] Ibid.
[405] District Court of The Hague, Commercial team, Judgment dated 30 January 2013 in the matter with case number/docket number: C/09/330891 / HA ZA 09-057, para. 4.36.
[406] Judgment dated 30 January 2013 – C/09/330891 / HA ZA 09-057 District Court of the Hague, para. 4.20.
[407] Ibid., para. 4.36.

attribution of responsibility, the proximity criterion is no longer in line with current economic realities given that the "activities [of businesses] can equally affect the right of people far away from the source" and that proximity is not an accurate reflection of "whether or not a human rights impact falls within" a given company's obligations.[408] This lower court delivered similar judgments in other cases on the oil spills in 2013.

In *Akpan*, the only case in which the district court found grounds for liability for tort of negligence was related to Shell's wholly owned subsidiary Shell Petroleum Development Company of Nigeria Ltd (SPDC), based on a violation of its duty of care.[409] Significantly, even if the liability of the parent company was eventually not established, the court reasoned that claims against both the Dutch parent company and its foreign subsidiary could be brought before a Dutch court as long as "the claims against the parent company and its subsidiary [were] . . . connected and . . . based at least in part on the same legal claim."[410] A Dutch appeals court overturned the dismissal of claims against the parent company Royal Dutch Shell PLC for the oil spills on 18 December 2015, concluding that the Dutch court had international jurisdiction to hear claims against both the parent company and the subsidiary and ordering Royal Dutch Shell to provide access to documents for the Court and the plaintiffs to assess the causes of the oil spills and whether the parent company's high-level management had knowledge of the events in question.[411] The appeals court noted that the duty of care on the part of Shell as the parent company could not be ruled out in light of the "foreseeable serious consequences of oil spills to the local environment from a potential spill source" and the fact that Shell was actively engaged in managing the business operations of its subsidiaries.[412]

[408] UN HR Council, "Protect, Respect, Remedy: A Framework for Business and Human Rights," UN Doc A/HRC/8/16, 2008, para. 71.

[409] *Friday Alfred Akpan and Vereniging Milieudefensie* v. *Royal Dutch Shell PLC and Shell Petroleum Development of Nigeria Ltd* (LJN BY 9854), 30 January 2013 District Court of the Hague (in Dutch).

[410] Nicola Jägers, Katinka Jesse and Jonathan Verschuuren, "The Future of Corporate Liability for Extraterritorial Human Rights Abuses: The Dutch Case Against Shell" (2014) *American Journal of International Law Unbound* e-40.

[411] *Eric Barizaa Dooh and Vereniging Milieudefensie* v. *Royal Dutch Shell Plc and Shell Petroleum Development of Nigeria Ltd.* (Case c – 200.126.843) and v. *Shell Petroleum N. V. and the "Shell" Transport and Trading Company Ltd.* (Case d – 200.126.848) (translated from Dutch) Court of Appeal at The Hague (Den Haag), paras 8 and 6.9–6.10, respectively.

[412] Ibid.

On 10 April 2019, the UK Supreme Court ruled on a procedural appeal in *Vedanta Resources PLC and another* v. *Lungowe and others* and unanimously upheld that English courts could have jurisdiction in relation to a group tort claim based on common law negligence and breach of statutory duty regarding the allegations by 1,826 Zambian nationals around toxic emissions from Nchanga Copper Mine in Zambia from 2005 onwards.[413] The decision was a procedural one on admissibility and not on the substance of the claims, which were raised against the owner of the mine, Konkola Copper Mines PLC, a Zambian company and a 79.4 percent owned subsidiary of the UK incorporated and domiciled Vedanta Resources PLC.[414] The Court noted that even though the Zambian government had owned a minority share in Vedanta's subsidiary, Vedanta's own published materials had claimed that Vedanta had practically full ownership level of control.[415] The UK Supreme Court's lead judgment penned by Lord Briggs noted on the most appropriate forum question

> [e]ven if the court concludes (as I would have in the present case) that a foreign jurisdiction is the proper place in which the case should be tried, the court may nonetheless permit (or refuse to set aside) service of English proceedings on the foreign defendant if satisfied, by cogent evidence, that there is a real risk that substantial justice will not be obtainable in that foreign jurisdiction. ... If there is a real risk of the denial of substantial justice in a particular jurisdiction, then it seems to me obvious that it is unlikely to be a forum in which the case can be tried most suitably for the interests of the parties and the ends of justice.[416]

On the substance of how parent companies may be opened up to responsibility for the wrongdoings of their subsidiaries, the judgment noted that while adopting group-wide policies such as those "about minimising the environmental impact of inherently dangerous activities, such as mining" may not automatically constitute a basis for the duty of care of parent companies, "tak[ing] active steps, by training, supervision and enforcement, to see that they are implemented by relevant subsidiaries" may in fact do so.[417]

413 *Vedanta Resources PLC and another (Appellants)* v. *Lungowe and others (Respondents)* Judgment date, 10 April 2019 [2019] UKSC 20.

414 Vedanta Resources, "Copper," www.vedantaresources.com/Pages/Copper.aspx (accessed 26 April 2019).

415 *Vedanta Resources PLC and another (Appellants)* v. *Lungowe and others (Respondents)*, para. 2.

416 Ibid., para. 88.

417 Ibid., paras. 52–53.

Beyond the duty of care, in cases where the parent corporation retains a considerable degree of control over the decision and policy-making processes of a subsidiary, the corporate veil may no longer shield the parent from direct responsibility for the wrongdoings of the subsidiary by virtue of its 'contribution' to this wrongdoing. Even when a parent company sets up its subsidiary as a separate entity in its decision and policy-making capacity, this may be problematic from a human rights angle.

1.5.4 Distribution of Responsibility Among Duty-Bearers

The attribution of responsibility answers the question of whether a given actor or 'participant' is responsible for a given children's rights violation. When, however, more than one participant bears legal responsibility for a given violation, the attribution of responsibility does not automatically provide guidance on how that responsibility is to be apportioned between these participants. Parameters for allocating responsibility to multiple actors of diverse nature need to respond to the differences between the actors (such as state versus non-state) as well as to the differences in circumstances around the attribution of responsibility (such as direct versus indirect links). When the responsibility of more than one actor is engaged, this responsibility may be engaged either on the basis of independent individual responsibility of each actor or on the basis of joint/shared responsibility in the case of inseparable responsibility of the different actors involved. The independent individual responsibility of different actors is often termed 'concurrent responsibility,' while inseparable responsibility of multiple actors is termed 'joint or shared responsibility.'

Taking the ILC's ARIO and ARSIWA as starting points would require the attribution of conduct as a first step in assigning responsibility. But "from the perspective of the injured party" it might often be unclear whether a conduct can be attributed to a given actor, i.e. if that actor has "the capacity to commit the wrongful act in question, based on control over his her own conduct."[418] In order to place the burden of proof on the duty-bearer that is a potential wrongdoer and not the injured right-holder, the use of joint and several liability has been suggested.[419]

[418] Christiane Ahlborn, "To Share or Not to Share? The Allocation of Responsibility between International Organizations and their Member States" (2013) 28 *SHARES Research Paper* 17–18.

[419] Ibid., 20.

However, for both analytical and practical reasons, the use of a shared responsibility model for human rights violations based on joint and several liability as a distributional principle is fraught with difficulty.

The principle of joint and several liability is essentially imported from tort law. As a principle, it is linked not to the distribution of responsibility as such but to the distribution of damages, once this responsibility (or in tort law terms, liability) is ascertained as belonging to several tortfeasors. The three possible bases for the attribution of damages to a given actor, according to the Principles of European Tort Law (PETL), are the causation of the fault through conduct, causation of the fault through abnormally dangerous activity or the causation of the fault by an auxiliary "within the scope of his functions."[420] Causation is defined in the PETL as "an activity or conduct . . . in the absence of [which], the damage would not have occurred."[421] Once an actor is attributed the damage, liability of that actor for compensation of the damage is engaged. As a synonym for joint and several liability, the PETL refer to "solidary and several liability."[422] In this configuration, the victim is able to claim the full compensation from any of the multiple tortfeasors[423] and each of the tortfeasors will be able to seek to recover the damages paid to the victim from other tortfeasors in return.[424]

Analytically, the notion of responsibility for violations under human rights law is linked to accountability, which is a broader concept than damages or reparations. In fact, accountability goes beyond responsibility, which is corrective, to espouse a preventive function in society.[425] The characterization of responsibility for human rights violations – inspired by tort law – as joint and several does not directly enhance accountability for human rights violations. Furthermore, "in the decentralized international legal system," it is practically unclear how the duty-bearer held responsible for the entire violation could then demand other duty-bearers to share that responsibility.[426]

420 European Group on Tort Law, "Principles of European Tort Law" (PETL), 2 September 2005, Chapter 1, Article 1:101 (2).

421 PETL, Chapter 3:101.

422 PETL, Chapter 9, Art. 9:101.

423 PETL, Chapter 9, Art. 9:101(2).

424 PETL, Chapter 9, Art. 9:102(1).

425 OHCHR and Center for Economic and Social Rights, "Who Will Be Accountable? Human Rights and the Post-2015 Development Agenda," 2013, ix.

426 Ahlborn, "To Share or Not to Share?," 23.

Seeking to assess the normative grounds for the distribution of shared responsibility, Nollkaemper and Jacobs have concluded that different scenarios may be applicable to the contribution of multiple actors (in their case, states) to a harmful outcome and that the corresponding responsibility may be conceptualized both through legal and nonlegal notions.[427] One distinction they draw is between cumulative and cooperative responsibility. In the case of cumulative responsibility, each actor's individual action or omission results in the harmful outcome but this outcome is cumulated when several actors engage in the same type of action or omission, without engaging in a concerted act or omission. In cooperative responsibility, "two or more actors stand in some relationship to each other, and the conduct or omission of one influences the conduct or omission of the other(s)."[428] Of course, in either case, it is not entirely clear how responsibility would be allocated. Nollkaemper and Jacobs sketch out a number of different considerations that might have a bearing on how a distributive normative framework may be set for shared responsibility. These include the strength or degree of the obligations, causation, the degree and nature of contributions to the harm, the role of power in terms of ability to influence or control others and fairness or equity.[429] Ultimately, these five proposed bases on which the distribution of responsibility may be designed – at least from a theoretical perspective – do not resolve the question of what the secondary norms for distribution ought to be. They do provide useful tools to think about distribution and to road test the applicability of these legal and nonlegal notions to real life situations.

The distribution of responsibility is in fact another beast altogether, especially as regards its practice. Although bases for attributing responsibility may be set out and recognized in theory, their translation into practice through interpretation and application is not guaranteed.[430] For instance, despite the normative recognition of "the plurality of obligations and the probability of multiple contributors" to a wrongdoing, the practice of attributing responsibility in the field of human trafficking

[427] Nollkaemper and Jacobs, "Introduction: Mapping the Normative Framework for the Distribution of Shared Responsibility," in Nollkaemper and Jacobs, *Distribution of Responsibilities in International Law* (Cambridge University Press, 2015), pp. 3–7.

[428] Ibid., p. 14.

[429] Ibid., pp. 22–27.

[430] Gallagher, "The Practice of Shared Responsibility in Relation to Human Rights and Human Trafficking," p. 565.

remains afflicted by discrepancies in interpretation, implementation and fragmentation of compliance mechanisms and processes.[431]

The issue of attributing and distributing responsibility for wrongdoings in relation to the business impact on human rights is quite possibly one of the areas where discrepancy between normative frameworks and their application is greatest. The possible ripple effects of global transactions by MNEs may lead to a multiplicity of wrongdoings by multiple actors.[432] Yet, questions of legal personality and subjecthood under traditional conceptions of public international law often allow MNEs to escape an assessment of responsibility in adjudicatory forums when domestic courts prove ineffective in providing accountability. Amao concludes, for instance, that with no binding secondary rules of responsibility applicable to MNEs at the international level and a lack of an international adjudication body overseeing MNE responsibility for violations of international law, the only foreseeable option remains the soft-law frameworks such as the UN Framework and UNGPs, and OECD Guidelines.[433] These soft-law frameworks, however, lack clarity as regards how they are to be translated into rules that govern the attribution and distribution of responsibility for violations when they take place on the ground.

1.5.5 Governing the Children's Rights Responsibility of Businesses in Practice

The attribution and distribution of children's rights (and human rights) responsibility for business-related harms in practice is as fraught with complications as the theoretical considerations behind the efforts to link business responsibility to parameters used for the responsibility of states and international organizations. One essential feature of alternative avenues in seeking responsibility for business-related human rights violations is the quest for a 'failsafe' when the domestic state cannot or will not demand corporate accountability. In this regard, three options have emerged with the possibility of providing that failsafe: home or third state, proxy avenues and private sector governance.

431 Ibid., p. 581.

432 Olufemi Amao, "The Practice of Shared Responsibility in Relation to Multinational Corporations," in Nollkaemper and Plakokefalos (eds.), *The Practice of Shared Responsibility in International Law*, p. 799.

433 Ibid., pp. 819–821.

Home States: Extraterritoriality in Action

The use of home- or third-state avenues has historically comprised the use of home or third–state-based judicial or quasi-judicial mechanisms for business-related wrongdoings abroad but the use of domestic regulations with extraterritorial effects is also gaining in importance.

Home- and Third-State Judicial and Quasi-Judicial Mechanisms

Home- and third-state judicial and quasi-judicial mechanisms include domestic courts that may be mandated to use criminal law, tort law or administrative law provisions, ombudspersons and specialized bodies of mediation, compliance or good offices mandated to deal with corporate responsibility for alleged wrongdoings, such as the OECD MNE Guidelines National Contact Points (NCPs).

Home-State Domestic Courts Home-state courts have been used by victims of business-related human rights violations in situations where the host state avenues have proved ineffectual. Plaintiffs have used home-state domestic courts in France, Germany, Italy, the Netherlands, Sweden and the United Kingdom with varying degrees of success to bring claims against large enterprises in sectors including mining, consumer goods, retail, agribusiness, petroleum, energy and textiles.[434] The claims have included allegations of complicity in human rights abuses or war crimes in conflict situations and fragile zones of governance, violations of labor rights, environmental damage and pollution, land grabbing and involuntary displacement. Applicants have sought to make use of domestic tort law, criminal law and administrative law in their claims. Most of the cases have not directly included children's rights-related claims, although NGOs Sherpa and ActionAid France launched a second civil party lawsuit against Samsung and its French subsidiary in 2018 in France alleging misleading advertising made using the company's code of conduct when in reality, the working conditions in the company's factories were allegedly in violation of the code, including evidence of employment of children under the age of sixteen.[435]

[434] Axel Marx and Claire Bright (in collaboration with Nina Pineau), "Access to Legal Remedies for Victims of Corporate Human Rights Abuses in Third Countries" (European Parliament Sub-Committee on Human Rights – European Union, 2019), pp. 18–30.

[435] Sherpa, "SAMSUNG: Sherpa and ActionAid France File A Second Lawsuit Following the Closing of the Case by the Public Prosecutor," 25 June 2018, www.asso-sherpa.org

Third-State Domestic Courts Through the Use of Tort Law The use of the Alien Tort Statute (ATS) in the United States against egregious human rights abuses abroad since the landmark *Filartiga* v. *Pena Irala* case in 1980 has been well studied and problematized in literature. The Alien Tort Statute may no longer provide the same extensive opportunities for the litigation of extraterritorial human rights abuses in the United States after the 2013 opinion of the Supreme Court of the United States (SCOTUS) in *Kiobel* v. *Royal Dutch Shell*, when it found that the presumption against extraterritoriality applied to claims brought under the ATS.[436] The SCOTUS articulated two exceptional grounds for waiving the presumption against extraterritoriality of a statute enacted in the United States: if there is an indication in the statute that rebuts the presumption against extraterritoriality, or if the "claims touch and concern the territory of the United States . . . with sufficient force to displace the presumption against extraterritorial application."[437] The SCOTUS, however, did not rule on the issue of corporate liability for breaches of international law at the time.[438] More recent experience demonstrates that lower-level US courts and US judges are less willing to dismiss ATS completely as a basis for litigation of extraterritorial human rights violations in the United States, relying on the exceptional grounds for waiving the presumption against extraterritoriality.[439] For instance, in the previously dismissed *Doe* v. *Nestle SA* case about the use of child slavery in Ivory Coast's cocoa fields, the US Court of Appeals in San Francisco overturned the dismissal of the case and granted the plaintiffs the opportunity to amend their complaint to show that the claims fulfilled the sufficient force of "touch and concern" condition as articulated by the SCOTUS in *Kiobel*.[440] The defendant companies (Nestlé,

/samsung-sherpa-and-actionaid-france-file-a-second-lawsuit-following-the-closing-of-the-case-by-the-public-prosecutor (accessed 15 April 2019).

[436] David P. Stewart and Ingrid Wuerth, "*Kiobel v. Royal Dutch Petroleum Co.*: The Supreme Court and the Alien Tort Statute" (2013) 107(3) *The American Journal of International Law* 601–621.

[437] *Kiobel v. Royal Dutch Petroleum Co.*, 569 U.S. 108 (2013), pp. 13–14.

[438] Joel Slawotsky, "Corporate Liability for Violating International Law Under the Alien Tort Statute: The Corporation Through the Lens of Globalization and Privatization" (2013) 6 *International Review of Law* at 12.

[439] Michael D. Goldhaber, "The Global Lawyer: The 'Zombie' Alien Tort, Three Years After Kiobel," *The American Lawyer*, 12 May 2016.

[440] *John Doe I* v. *Nestle, USA*, No. 10-56739 (9th Cir. 2014); Edvard Pettersson, "Child Slavery Claims Against Nestle, Cargill Get One More Chance," Bloomberg.com, 9 January 2017, www.bloomberg.com/news/articles/2017-01-09/child-slavery-claims-against-nestle-cargill-get-one-more-chance (accessed 15 April 2019).

Archer-Daniels-Midland, Cargill) petitioned for a *certiorari* with the SCOTUS, arguing that this decision conflicted with *Kiobel* as well as subsequent decisions of other circuit courts, causing a circuit split and asked the case to be thrown out.[441] The SCOTUS rejected that writ.[442] On 24 April 2018, the SCOTUS rendered its opinion in the case *Jesner et al.* v. *Arab Bank, PLC*, concluding that foreign corporations may not be defendants in suits brought under the ATS.[443] The SCOTUS found that notwithstanding major developments in the human rights arena since the end of World War II, the international community had shown a "conscious decision" to thus far exclude corporate entities from being subject to the jurisdiction of international criminal tribunals. According to the SCOTUS, this fact "counseled against a broad holding that there is a specific, universal, and obligatory norm of corporate liability under currently prevailing international law" as required by the ATS in *Sosa* v. *Alvarez-Machain*.[444]

In her dissenting opinion, Justice Sotomayor, joined by Justices Ginsburg, Breyer and Kagan, noted the quicksand of the majority's reliance upon the practice of international criminal enforcement:

> It cannot be persuasive evidence for purposes of ascertaining the availability of corporate civil liability under the ATS, then, that the jurisdiction of the handful of international criminal tribunals that states have seen fit to create in the last 75 years has not extended to corporate defendants.
>
> Ultimately, the evidence on which the plurality relies does not prove that international law distinguishes between corporations and natural persons as a categorical matter. To the contrary, it proves only that states' collective efforts to enforce various international-law norms have, to date, often focused on natural rather than corporate defendants.[445]

Justice Sotomayor's jurisprudential argument rested on the reading of accountability for law of nations violations as being in the US interest not only in remedying harms suffered by the actions of US citizens but also in preventing third-country citizens from using the United States as safe

[441] *Nestle U.S.A., Inc., et al., Petitioners* v. *John Doe I, et al.*, No. 10-56739 (9th Cir. 2015).

[442] Olivier Nieburg, "Nestlé Bid to Throw Out Cocoa Child Labor Lawsuit in SCOTUS Rejected," *Confectionerynews.com*, 12 January 2016, www.confectionerynews.com/Commodities/Supreme-court-rejects-Nestle-child-labor-lawsuit-dismissal-attempts (accessed 15 April 2019).

[443] *Jesner* v. *Arab Bank, PLC*, 584 U. S. ___ (2018).

[444] Ibid.

[445] Justice Sotomayor, with whom Justice Ginsburg, Justice Breyer and Justice Kagan join, "Dissenting," in *Jesner et al.* v. *Arab Bank*, p. 1423.

harbor when they violate the law of nations.[446] A more fundamental criticism is that although "[n]othing about the corporate form in itself justifies categorically foreclosing corporate liability in all ATS actions,"[447] the majority decision "categorically bar[s] all suits against foreign corporations under the ATS . . . [allowing them to] remain immune from liability for human rights abuses, however egregious they may be."[448]

While the majority's main argument centered on their reading of the original intent of the ATS when it was enacted, at least some of the other reasons cited were a desire to prevent the souring of US foreign relations with allies and to avoid scenarios where other countries would also take US corporations to their domestic courts for alleged violations of international law in response, which may have had a chilling effect on investments of US companies in developing countries.[449] In short, by the SCOTUS overturning this decision in *Jesner* v. *Arab Bank*, the road for future ATS claims concerning foreign corporations seems to have been foreclosed for the time being.

Ombudspersons In January 2018, the Canadian government announced that it would create the Canadian Ombudsperson for Responsible Enterprise (CORE) as well as a multistakeholder Advisory Body to advise CORE and the government on extraterritorial responsible business conduct. The CORE is envisaged as a multi-sectoral, independent body that can investigate, report publicly, recommend remedies and track implementation related to allegations of human rights abuses linked to the practices of Canadian companies abroad. Priority sectors in relation to the CORE's mandate were identified as mining, oil and gas, and garment.[450] Although the specifics of the CORE's mandate have yet to be defined, one crucial novelty is the possibility to sanction noncooperation of companies by recommending "denial or withdrawal of trade advocacy and future Export Development Canada financial support, as an interim measure or as a final recommendation."[451]

446 Ibid., p. 1428.

447 Ibid., p. 1429.

448 Ibid., p. 1436.

449 *Jesner et al.* v. *Arab Bank*, pp. 1405–1406.

450 Government of Canada, "The Government of Canada Brings Leadership to Responsible Business Conduct Abroad," www.canada.ca/en/global-affairs/news/2018/01/the_government_ofcanadabringsleadershiptoresponsiblebusinesscond.html (accessed 15 April 2019).

451 Global Affairs Canada, "Responsible Business Conduct Abroad – Questions and Answers," www.international.gc.ca/trade-agreements-accords-commerciaux/topics-domaines/other-autre/faq.aspx?lang=eng (accessed 15 April 2019).

Previously, Canada had a Corporate Social Responsibility (CSR) Counsellor on the extractive sector but the work of the counsellor involved a confidential informal dialogue.[452] The mandate of the CSR Counsellor ended and was subsumed into the CORE. In line with the work of the CSR Counsellor, a working group led by the Government of Canada joined by UNICEF, UNICEF Canada and Barrick Gold Corp. had developed a Child Rights and Security Checklist as a part of the multistakeholder initiative, Voluntary Principles on Security and Human Rights, that was adopted in 2000. Substantively, the Child Rights and Security Checklist focuses on the worst forms of child labor and gender-based violence, as well as abuses that may result from private and public security arrangements.[453]

Specialized Bodies: National Contact Points for OECD Guidelines The OECD NCPs have been named by the UN Framework and UNGPs as possible nonjudicial state-based remedy mechanisms to provide remedies to rights holders in cases of harm. The OECD Guidelines acquired more teeth with the establishment of the NCPs, which are government offices responsible for encouraging observance of the Guidelines in national contexts. NCPs are tasked with "undertaking promotional activities, handling enquiries and contributing to the resolution of issues that arise relating to the implementation of the Guidelines in specific instances."[454] NCPs, acting as a grievance mechanism to the OECD Guidelines, can receive complaints, called 'specific instances' relating to issues covered by the Guidelines. While their decisions are not binding, they serve as a platform to bring grievances forward and to draw both public and corporate attention to practices that run contrary to the Guidelines. International cooperation among different NCPs is also foreseen in case need arises. NCPs have to report to the OECD Investment Committee and hold regular meetings with one another. Adhering states have been given flexibility in the way they wish to set up their NCPs but the OECD expects all NCPs to be impartial and functionally equivalent.[455] According to the NGO OECD Watch, however, "the structure and location of an NCP can influence how it handles

[452] Global Affairs Canada, "Responsible Business Conduct Abroad – Q&A."
[453] Government of Canada et al. "Child Rights and Security Checklist," 2017.
[454] OECD, Amendment of the Decision of the Council on the OECD Guidelines for MNEs, I. National Contact Points, 25 May 2011, para. 1.
[455] Website of the OECD Guidelines for MNEs, Specific Instances, http://mneguidelines.oecd.org/specificinstances.htm (accessed 20 April 2019).

instances."[456] Therefore, the NGO recommends that "NCPs not be housed in a single government department to avoid conflicts of interest (real or perceived) with the goals of the Guidelines."[457] NCPs do not play a judicial role and do not formally accept cases. The emphasis is on problem solving through good offices, conciliation or mediation. The various NCPs set up under the Guidelines have thus far examined over 400 specific instances and approximately 32 percent of these have been related to human rights.[458]

Given the close integration of the UNGPs in the 2011 OECD Guidelines, the conclusions and decisions of NCPs will likely strengthen the stress on the concepts of due diligence and leverage. In fact, even prior to the revision of the OECD Guidelines in 2011, concepts such as "sphere of influence" from the Draft UN Norms and "due diligence" from the UN Framework were utilized by NCPs in children's rights-related cases. For example, in an instance against Bayer CropScience on allegations of the use of child labor in its supply chain in India, the German NCP's 30 August 2007 final statement featured a declaration of voluntary commitment issued by Bayer CropScience whereby the company pledged to continue to actively combat child labor, protect and support children within its "sphere of influence" with a view to schooling, contribute to the productivity of Indian farmers, disclose seasonal reports to the NCP and other interested parties and build links with the ILO on these issues.[459] In another instance against Vedanta Resources PLC, the UK NCP made the recommendation to implement a practical "due diligence" policy, the practical details and requirements of which had been set forth by the UN SRSG Ruggie in the UN Framework, again before this concept had become a part of the revised OECD Guidelines.[460]

OECD Guidelines and NCPs arguably have deficiencies including the nonbinding nature of the Guidelines and the outcome of complaints, the

[456] OECD Watch Website, "NCPs," http://oecdwatch.org/oecd-guidelines/ncps (accessed 15 April 2019).

[457] Ibid.

[458] As of 15 April 2019.

[459] German NCP, "Statement by the German NCP for the 'OECD Guidelines for MNEs' on the Instance Filed against Bayer CropScience by German Watch, Global March, and Coordination gegen Bayer-Gefahren," 30 August 2007, p. 2.

[460] UK NCP, "Articles 76, 77, 78 and 79, Final Statement by the UK NCP for the OECD Guidelines for MNEs – Instance from Survival International against Vedanta Resources PLC," 25 September 2009, www.oecd.org/dataoecd/49/16/43884129.pdf (accessed 15 April 2019).

closed nature of the mediation procedure, and the procedural ambiguities in the functioning of certain NCPs.[461] The OECD Guidelines and similar voluntary and nonbinding mechanisms have also been criticized for their underlying weaknesses linked to a lack of forcible enforcement.[462]

An OECD report from 2016 indicates that in order to improve their effectiveness, nineteen countries have created advisory bodies for NCPs in the form of multi-stakeholder platforms where businesses, NGOs, trade unions or academia are represented. In addition, six countries have created oversight bodies that also include representatives of different departments from the government.[463]

Domestic Regulation with Extraterritorial Effects

Regulatory measures with extraterritorial effects may include regulation under administrative or criminal law. Such domestic measures seeking to regulate corporate behavior to protect human rights extraterritorially are becoming more common. In the specific area of children's rights, the criminalization of business activities linked to the sexual exploitation and abuse of children abroad through the production of abuse images or media and procurement of children for prostitution purposes has been one of the clear areas where the extraterritorial misconduct of legal persons, including companies, is made subject to liability under criminal or penal regimes in a number of states.

In the broader area of business and human rights, examples of measures targeting supply-chain practices are reporting regulations, supply-chain management measures or transparency and disclosure regulations. Some recent examples include the US Dodd-Frank Bill Section 1502 and EU Supply Chain Due Diligence Regulation on the so-called conflict minerals; other efforts seek to offer labor protections to workers abroad, including children, such as the UK Modern Slavery Act of 2015, the EU's public procurement legislation[464] and EU legislation on disclosure of nonfinancial information.

[461] ECCHR, *Forced Labor of Children and Adults in Uzbekistan: How Effective Is the OECD Complaint Mechanism?* (ECCHR, 2013), p. 6.

[462] Global Witness, *"Faced with a Gun, What Can You Do?," War and the Militarisation of Mining in Eastern Congo* (Global Witness, 2009), p. 69.

[463] OECD, *Implementing the OECD Guidelines for Multinational Enterprises: The National Contact Points from 2000 to 2015* (OECD, 2016), p. 7.

[464] Directive 2014/24/EU of the European Parliament and of the Council of 26 February 2014 on public procurement and repealing Directive 2004/18/EC Text with EEA relevance, 28 March 2014.

Child Sexual Abuse and Exploitation Abroad Domestic legislation looking to establish extraterritorial jurisdiction over businesses for offenses relating to the sexual exploitation of children abroad have been enacted by a number of countries. For instance, Australia's 1994 Crimes (Child Sex Tourism) Amendment Act establishes Australia's jurisdiction over alleged crimes committed overseas not only by Australian citizens and residents but also by businesses incorporated in Australia or one that "carries on its activities principally in Australia" as well as over the corporate entities benefiting from or encouraging the commission of such crimes.[465] The 1999 Japanese Act on Punishment of Activities Relating to Child Prostitution and Child Pornography, and the Protection of Children foresees dual liability for the crimes of child prostitution and pornography for legal persons alongside individuals "[w]hen a representative of a juridical person or a proxy, employee or any other staff member of a juridical person or of an individual has committed [the said crimes] with regard to the business of said juridical person or individual."[466] The US Protect Act of 2003 also foresees fines and/or imprisonment of those that "arrange[...], induce[...], procure [...] or facilitate[...] the travel of a person" for "commercial advantage or private financial gain" with the knowledge of this person's intent to commit criminal acts (sexual abuse of children) at the destination.[467] As such, a business enterprise engaged in arranging or facilitating travel for sexual abuse and exploitation of children abroad is covered under this provision.

Conflict Minerals Using domestic legislation to induce extraterritorial behavior change to remedy supply-chain-related human rights abuses aims to put pressure on end users, who will then exercise their influence or use their leverage on those players further down the supply chain to

[465] Australian Government, Crimes (Child Sex Tourism) Amendment Act 1994 No. 105, 1994, Art. 50AD(c) and (d).

[466] Japan, Act on Punishment of Activities Relating to Child Prostitution and Child Pornography, and the Protection of Children (Act No. 52 of 26 May 1999), Art. 11 (Unofficial English translation), www.unodc.org/res/cld/document/jpn/act-on-punishment-of-activities-relating-to-child-prostitution-and-child-pornography-and-the-protection-of-children_html/Act_on_Punishment_of_Activities_Relating_to_Child_Prostitution_and_Child_Pornography.pdf (accessed 12 March 2019).

[467] United States Government, PROTECT Act of 2003 (Prosecutorial Remedies and Other Tools to End the Exploitation of Children Today Act), Public Law 108–21, 30 April 2003, Sec. 105(d) "Ancillary Offenses," 151.

stop and/or prevent actions or omissions resulting in adverse human rights impacts. Pressuring end-user companies was at the heart of the conflict minerals strategy of many international conflict mineral advocacy groups, including the Enough Project, when they advocated for legal pressure to be exerted primarily but not exclusively on the electronics industry operating in industrialized countries that use tin, tungsten and tantalum (now known as the "3Ts") in their end products.[468] Section 1502 of the mammoth Dodd-Frank Reform Bill of 2010 (otherwise geared towards reforming the activities of the financial sector in the United States in the aftermath of the collapse of capital markets following the 2008 crisis) came about as a result of intensive lobbying of a number of human rights NGOs in the United States.[469] The conflict minerals part of the legislation was based on the position of the US Congress that:

> [T]he exploitation and trade of conflict minerals originating in the [DRC] is helping to finance conflict characterized by extreme levels of violence in the eastern [DRC], particularly sexual- and gender-based violence, and contributing to an emergency humanitarian situation therein, warranting the provisions of section 13(p) of the Securities Exchange Act of 1934, as added by subsection (b).[470]

Dodd-Frank Bill Section 1502 requires publicly traded companies in the United States to annually disclose information on whether their supply chains contain conflict minerals originating in the DRC or its neighboring countries and if they do, on what due diligence measures are being taken by the company.[471] This report to be submitted to the SEC is required to have undergone an independent private sector audit.[472] The designation of "DRC conflict free" is accorded to products that do not "contain conflict minerals that directly or indirectly finance or benefit armed groups in the [DRC] or an adjoining country."[473] For products that a company produces or contracts to be manufactured found not to be "DRC conflict-free", there is the requirement of disclosure of the product description, identity of the entity that has conducted the

[468] The Enough Project, "A Comprehensive Approach to Congo's Conflict Minerals," p. 9.

[469] Laura E. Seay, "What's Wrong with Dodd-Frank 1502? Conflict Minerals, Civilian Livelihoods, and the Unintended Consequences of Western Advocacy," CGD Working Paper 284, Center for Global Development, January 2012.

[470] US Congress, Dodd-Frank Wall Street Reform and Consumer Protection Act, Section 1502.

[471] Ibid., Section 1502, A (i).

[472] Ibid., 1502, A (i).

[473] Ibid., 1502, D.

independent private sector audit, "facilities used to process the conflict minerals, the country of origin of the conflict minerals, and the efforts to determine the mine or location of origin with the greatest possible specificity."[474] As a further requirement, information pertaining to the supply-chain due diligence report on conflict minerals from the DRC should be made publicly available on the website of the given company.[475] The Final Rule that the SEC adopted in 2012 linked to Section 1502 envisaged a phase-in process, during which the companies unable to determine the origin of the minerals going into their supply chain and to conclusively determine that these minerals do not originate from the DRC or neighboring locations are accorded a grace period.[476]

Dodd-Frank Bill Section 1502 defines a 'conflict mineral' as coltan, gold, wolframite or their derivatives as well as any other mineral or derivatives "determined by the Secretary of State to be financing conflict in the DRC or an adjoining country."[477] A mining venture is considered to be "under the control of armed groups" not only if armed groups physically control a mine and force civilians to work in these mines but also when they "tax, extort, or control any part of the trade routes for conflict minerals . . . [or] trading facilities."[478]

Dodd-Frank Bill Section 1502 is not the only one of its kind, as both the United States and other countries have habitually enacted legislation aimed at producing extraterritorial effects, for instance, in efforts to enforce politically motivated trade embargoes. An example of similar legislation is the Foreign Corrupt Practices Act of 1977, which made it illegal for any US exchange-listed company and any person (real or legal) acting on behalf of it or as its agent to give bribes to non-US/foreign officials for the facilitation of business transactions.[479] The driving force behind this 1970s legislation included the numerous investigations by the Office of the Special Prosecutor and consequently the SEC, revealing that some publicly listed companies had committed fraudulent practices such as falsifying their corporate records in order to "disguise or conceal the source and application of corporate funds misused for illegal purposes, as well as the existence of secret 'slush funds' disbursed outside the normal

[474] Ibid., Section 1502, A (ii).

[475] Ibid., Section 1502, E.

[476] US SEC, "Final Rule (Rule 13p-1)," 77 Fed. Reg. at 56, 22 August 2012.

[477] Dodd-Frank Act, Section 1502.

[478] Ibid.

[479] US Congress, Foreign Corrupt Practices Act, 1977 (Anti-Bribery Provision §30A of the Securities Exchange Act of 1934 [15 U.S.C. §78dd-1]).

financial system . . . used for . . . in some instances, questionable or illegal foreign payments."[480]

The resulting Foreign Corrupt Practices Act was a reaction to the ongoing practices of overseas bribery of foreign officials, just as Section 1502 of the Dodd-Frank Reform Bill was a reaction to the involvement of US companies in the ongoing conflict in eastern DRC indirectly through their supply chains. In both cases, the US Congress enacted a domestic legislation with the policy objective of effectively creating change in the extraterritorial behavior of domestically incorporated business actors, namely of curtailing corruption and bribery by US firms overseas and exerting pressure on private US companies to cease sourcing from conflict zones in the DRC. While effective enforcement of enacted legislation remains the single most reliable method of eliciting such behavior change, the introduction of reporting and disclosure requirements, audits and certification schemes adequately serves as a deterrent to knowingly sourcing conflict minerals.

Dodd-Frank Bill Section 1502 has not gone unchallenged. The National Association of Manufacturers, US Chamber of Commerce and Business Roundtable brought a civil lawsuit against the US Securities and Exchange Commission in 2012, alleging the measures enacted to be "arbitrary and capricious."[481] The District Court went on to uphold Section 1502 and the disclosure and reporting requirements it brings, noting that there was a "reasonable fit" between the bill and the objectives of the US Congress "in promoting peace and security in and around the DRC" as exemplified by Congress's previous actions and decisions on the DRC.[482] The Court noted that the Final Ruling of the SEC had made sufficient accommodations, allowing companies a transitional period in their due diligence efforts to ascertain the provenance of minerals used in their supply chains.[483] In 2014, however, the US Court of Appeals for the DC Circuit upheld Section 1502 but found that the requirement for companies to publicly declare that their products have not been determined "DRC conflict-free" constituted a violation of the First Amendment of the US Constitution.[484] The challenge to the appellate

[480] US SEC, "Report of the Securities and Exchange Commission on Questionable and Illegal Corporate Payments and Practices," May 1976, p. 3.

[481] *Nat'l Ass'n of Mfrs. v. SEC,* 956 F. Supp. 2d 43, 77 (D.D.C. 2013), pp. 1–2.

[482] Ibid., p. 63.

[483] Ibid.

[484] *National Association of Manufacturers (NAM)* v. *SEC,* No. 13- 5252, 748 F.3d 359 (D.C. Cir. 2014).

decision and the request for review undertaken by the appeals court resulted in upholding this ruling of a First Amendment violation, while a further challenge by the SEC was struck down without a rehearing of the case.[485]

The uptake and implementation of Dodd-Frank Bill Section 1502 by US companies has not been uniform. A 2015 study by Amnesty International and Global Witness concluded that only a very small fraction of the reports submitted under the legislation they analyzed met the legislation's minimum requirements.[486]

Domestic legislation with extraterritorial effects such as the Dodd-Frank Bill Section 1502 is able to permeate territorial borders with the objective of delivering human rights protection to individuals and communities. Although the routine exercise of extraterritorial jurisdiction by states and the concept of extraterritorial human rights obligations remain hotly debated, states are by and large at liberty to use domestic legislation for extraterritorial policy reasons, including the protection and promotion of human rights beyond their borders. The immediate impact of these measures and their eventual potential to achieve human rights objectives, on the other hand, is another matter entirely.

The European Parliament (EP) and the EU Council reached an agreement on the "EU system for supply chain due diligence self-certification of responsible importers of tin, tantalum and tungsten, their ores, and gold originating in conflict-affected and high-risk areas" legislation in June 2016 after a long debate.[487] In fact, diverging positions of the EP calling for mandatory certification on the one hand and EU member states largely supporting voluntary opt-in due diligence legislation on the other had resulted in a gridlock.[488] According to the legislation approved by the EP and EU Council in March 2017, all EU firms save the smallest ones that import 3T and gold (collectively called 3TG) and their ores from conflict-affected or high-risk areas are required to conduct due diligence audits on their suppliers in accordance with the OECD's due diligence guidelines.[489] Refiners and smelters as well as users of recycled materials are also covered

485 Ibid.

486 AI and Global Witness, "Digging for Transparency: How U.S. Companies Are Only Scratching the Surface of Conflict Minerals Reporting," April 2015, 5.

487 European Parliament (EP), "Press Release: Conflict Minerals: MEPs Secure Mandatory Due Diligence for Importers," 16 June 2016.

488 Cécile Barbière, "EU Institutions Still Divided over Conflict Minerals," *EurActiv.fr*, 3 February 2016.

489 Council of the EU (EU Council), "Press Release – Conflict Minerals: Council Adopts New Rules to Reduce Financing of Armed Groups," 181/17, 3 April 2017.

under the mandatory due diligence requirement.[490] In addition, companies with more than 500 employees that are covered under the EU's nonfinancial disclosure legislation and that produce goods using 3TG in their supply chain will be given the opportunity to voluntarily report on their due diligence policies and practices by joining a registry.[491]

The EU agreement has a fail-safe review clause, possibly as a means to respond to controversy surrounding the Dodd-Frank legislation, allowing the EU Commission to monitor the effects of the regulation on the ground and to track compliance. The review clause will enable the Commission to table new mandatory measures in case the regulation does not succeed in creating the desired impact.[492] One major difference between the Dodd-Frank Act Section 1502 and the EU's responsible sourcing legislation is that the EU legislation does not limit the geographical scope of the sourcing activity subject to due diligence to the DRC and neighboring countries but broadens it more generally to conflict zones and high-risk areas. A second difference is that the legislation requires mandatory due diligence, which will have to be implemented by almost all EU companies.

Labor Protections Declaring practices of slavery (including servitude and forced or compulsory labor) and human trafficking (including exploitation) offenses under UK law, the UK Modern Slavery Act of 2015 introduces transparency and reporting requirements for corporate entities in the form of "slavery and human trafficking statements." The Act extends to the activities of businesses ("commercial Organization[s]"), defined as a corporation or a partnership "which carries on a business, or part of a business, in any part of the [UK]" regardless of the place of incorporation or formation of partnership.[493] Thus, the Act covers not only businesses of which the United Kingdom is the home state but also all businesses that have business activities in the United Kingdom. In the Netherlands, the proposed Dutch Child Labor Due Diligence Bill, yet to be approved in the Dutch Senate, would require

[490] EU Council, Proposal for a Regulation of the European Parliament and of the Council setting up a Union system for supply chain due diligence self-certification of responsible importers of tin, tantalum and tungsten, their ores, and gold originating in conflict-affected and high-risk areas, 7239/17, 20 March 2017, para. 16.

[491] Ibid., Statement 3.

[492] Ibid., para. 24.

[493] UK Government, The Modern Slavery Act, "Part 6 – Transparency in Supply Chains etc," Art. 54(12), 2015.

companies to conduct mandatory due diligence in the supply chain on child labor risks and to develop action plans.[494]

The EU Directive on the disclosure of nonfinancial information requires large public-interest corporations with more than 500 employees to prepare a nonfinancial statement outlining, among other things, the corporate action taken in line with respect for human rights, which may include "information on the prevention of human rights abuses."[495] The statement is required to include:

> [A] description of the policies, outcomes and risks related to [at least environmental matters, social and employee-related matters, respect for human rights, anti-corruption and bribery matters] [as well as] . . . information on the due diligence processes implemented by the undertaking, also regarding, where relevant and proportionate, its supply and subcontracting chains, in order to identify, prevent and mitigate existing and potential adverse impacts.[496]

The reporting guidelines are limited to the prevention of human rights violations by focusing on due diligence and risk mitigation but do have the potential to extend to the entire supply chain and circle of subcontractors.

The EU's 2014 public procurement directives revamp its public procurement processes to ensure that noneconomic considerations, including environmental, social and labor considerations can be taken into account at each and every stage of public procurement as necessary.[497] One of the grounds on which companies may be excluded from public procurement processes is a conviction on the use of child labor by that company.[498] Furthermore, EU member states are required to guarantee the compliance of companies with "applicable obligations in the fields of environmental, social and labour law established by Union law, national law, collective agreements or by the international environmental, social and labour law

[494] The Government of the Netherlands, "Proposal: Wet Zorgplicht Kinderarbeid/Child Labour Due Diligence Law," https://zoek.officielebekendmakingen.nl/kst-34506-A.html (accessed 24 April 2019).

[495] Directive 2014/95/EU of the EP and of the Council of 22 October 2014 amending Directive 2013/34/EU as regards disclosure of non-financial and diversity information by certain large undertakings and groups, para. 7 and Art. 19(a).1.

[496] Ibid., para. 6.

[497] Directive 2014/24/EU of the EP and of the Council of 26 February 2014 on public procurement and repealing Directive 2004/18/EC, para. 40.

[498] Ibid., Art. 57.1(f); Directive 2014/23/EU of the EP and of the Council of 26 February 2014 on the award of concession contracts, Art. 38.4(f).

provisions" in carrying out public contracts.[499] In this respect, ILO Conventions 138 and 182 on Minimum Age and the Worst Forms of Child Labour, respectively, are listed among the applicable international law instruments.[500] The rules governing EU public procurement would be applicable beyond the territory of EU member states in cases where public procurement is conducted for works and services to be undertaken outside of the EU and include "compliance with obligations in the fields of environmental, social and labour law that apply at the place where the works are executed or the services provided and result from laws, regulations, decrees and decisions, at both national and Union level."[501] In this respect, obligations under ILO Conventions and other international agreements expressly listed in the EU Directives on public procurement are to be applied throughout the contract performance.[502]

Outside of the EU, the US Federal Acquisition Regulation (FAR) also interdicts the acquisition of products "mined, produced, or manufactured wholly or in part by forced or indentured child labor."[503] According to FAR, US DoL's List of Products Requiring Contractor Certification as to Forced or Indentured Child Labor should serve as guidance in contracting processes, and Certification Regarding Knowledge of Child Labor for Listed End Products should be required.[504] In cases where the prohibition of acquisition of products using forced child labor is violated, FAR foresees possible legal investigations or remedies such as the termination of the contract, suspension or debarment of the contractor.[505]

Multilateral Proxy Avenues

The use of regional human rights courts as well as international criminal courts has been curtailed by the fact that most international courts do not have *rationae personae* over businesses. As a proxy, when business-related

[499] Directive 2014/24/EU, Art. 18.2; Directive 2014/25/EU of the EP and of the Council of 26 February 2014 on procurement by entities operating in the water, energy, transport and postal services sectors and repealing Directive 2004/17/EC, Art. 36.2; Directive 2014/23/EU, Art. 30.3.

[500] Directive 2014/24/EU, Annex X; Directive 2014/25/EU, Annex XIV; Directive 2014/23/EU, Annex X.

[501] Ibid., para. 37.

[502] Ibid.

[503] US Government, Federal Acquisition Regulation (FAR), 2005-94, 2005-95, 19 January 2017, Subpart 22.15, 22.1502.

[504] Ibid., 22.1503.

[505] Ibid., 22.1504.

human rights harms have involved multilateral financiers such as multilateral development banks (MDBs), claimants have taken their human rights abuse allegations to the compliance and monitoring bodies of these institutions. The compliance mechanisms of leading MDBs such as the World Bank (WB) African Development Bank (AfDB) and Asian Development Bank (ADB) appraise compliance of the institutions with their internal regulations. One compliance mechanism where claims may be directly brought also against companies is the International Finance Corporation's (IFC) Office of the Compliance Advisor Ombudsman (CAO). The IFC's Performance Standards (PS) on Environmental and Social Sustainability place a due diligence requirement on clients to respect human rights (PS1) in line with the parameters set out in the UNGPs and prohibit exploitative, hazardous and harmful child labor by clients as well as require clients to continuously monitor the issue in their primary supply chain (PS2).[506] The IFC also applies the IFC Exclusion list both to its clients and to financial intermediaries. The IFC Exclusion List and the exclusion of products or activities involving harmful child labor (and harmful or exploitative forms of forced labor) are replicated in the safeguard policies of many regional and national financial institutions.[507] Affected persons and communities have taken their grievances to the IFC with respect to concerns over involuntary resettlement, indigenous people's rights, consultation requirements, labor and compensation conditions, environmental damage and pollution as well as the use of harmful and hazardous child labor.[508] Proxy avenues such as the IFC CAO have been used in the absence of international courts to achieve remedies such as compensation but also to bring visibility to alleged violations at the international level.

Sector-Based Reporting and Certification

Sector-based reporting and certification schemes are linked closely with Corporate Social Responsibility (CSR) approaches. There are various such schemes in the retail sector such as eco-labeling, fairtrade certification, cruelty-free certification and sustainability certification (for fish,

[506] IFC, "Performance Standard 2: Labor and Working Conditions," in IFC, "IFC Sustainability Framework: Policy and Performance Standards on Environmental and Social Sustainability and Access to Information Policy," 1 January 2012, paras 21 and 27.

[507] See: ADB, "Safeguard Policy Statement," June 2009, in Annex 5: ADB Prohibited Investment Activities List, and AfDB, "Private Sector Development Policy of the AfDB Group," May 2013, Section 2.9, respectively.

[508] IFC CAO, "CAO Cases," www.cao-ombudsman.org/cases/ (accessed 24 April 2019).

palm oil, paper and others). Although these certification schemes have been called into question,[509] they have continued to multiply. In areas linked to children's rights, sector-based reporting and certification schemes have concentrated on child sexual abuse and exploitation abroad as well as conflict minerals.

Child Sexual Abuse and Exploitation Abroad Many companies in the travel, tourism and hospitality sectors have joined the Code of Conduct for the Protection of Children from Sexual Exploitation in Travel and Tourism (The Code), an initiative led by the NGO coalition ECPAT. The Code entails several commitments: adopting a company policy against commercial sexual exploitation of children, providing training to personnel both in origin and destination countries, raising awareness of travelers as well as key persons at destination countries and annual reporting. Another commitment, which is very interesting from a compliance perspective, is the introduction of obligations for suppliers through clauses in contracts to commit to repudiation of sexual exploitation of children and a zero tolerance policy.[510] Although The Code started out as a multi-stakeholder initiative against the exploitation of children in prostitution, production of abuse materials, sale and trafficking in tourism and hospitality sectors more narrowly defined, it now deals with issues such as "voluntourism, orphanage tourism and mega sporting events."[511] The Code has members from different sectors including transport (airlines and ferry lines), hospitality (hotels, bars and restaurants), tourism (tour companies, travel agencies, associations and agencies) as well as tourism schools and nonprofits. Some of the biggest multinational corporations in these sectors such as AccorHotels, Carlston, Hilton, Hyatt, Jetair, Orbitz, Thomas Cook and TUI Group are members. The Code website has an E-Learning tool for staff training by members as well as a list of contact points to report abuse. Although The Code has more than three hundred members, it has introduced the distinction of "Top Members," to distinguish the adherent institutions that have been effectively implementing the commitments, which may also signal the willingness of certain companies to sign up to

[509] Changing Markets Foundation, *The False Promise of Certification: How Certification Is Hindering Sustainability in the Textiles, Palm Oil and Fisheries Industries* (Changing Markets Foundation, 2018) and OECD, *Environmental Labelling and Information Schemes: Policy Perspectives* (OECD, 2016).

[510] The Code of Conduct for the Protection of Children from Sexual Exploitation in Travel and Tourism (The Code), "About," www.thecode.org/about/ (accessed 24 April 2019).

[511] The Code, "About."

voluntary initiatives without intending to continuously implement the commitments.[512]

Conflict Minerals Private and industry-led certification and traceability schemes have been developed simultaneously with conflict mineral regulation under the Dodd-Frank Bill.[513] The most notable of these include the Certified Trading Chains (CTC) scheme of the German Federal Institute for Geosciences and Natural Resources (BGR), the Conflict-Free Sourcing Initiative (CFSI) of the US Electronic Industry Citizenship Coalition (EICC) and Global e-Sustainability Initiative (GeSI) that has merged with the Responsible Minerals Initiative through the Responsible Business Alliance (RBA).[514] The BGR's CTC was developed in the period 2007–2008, later utilized as a pilot in Rwanda and adapted to the responsible mining of 3TGs in the DRC from 2009 to 2016. The certification scheme focused on traceability and transparency as well as the prohibition of child labor, fair remuneration, good working conditions, respect for human rights in security arrangements, consultation with communities and effective environmental protection.[515]

The EICC and GeSI's CFSI was launched in 2013 as a multi-sector, multi-stakeholder platform encompassing automotive, electronics, information technologies and retail sectors among others in response to the legislative developments on conflict minerals. The CFSI also adheres to the guidelines developed by the Responsible Business Minerals Initiative of GeSI and RBA, founded in 2008. The initiative features a "Responsible Minerals Assurance Process," based on a Conflict Minerals Reporting Template (CMRT).[516] The CMRT has become an industry-standard for companies required to issue a Conflict Minerals Report under Section 1502 of the Dodd-Frank Bill and includes a global list of smelters of the

512 The Code, "Members of the Code," www.thecode.org/who-have-signed/intro/ (accessed 15 April 2019).

513 An excellent detailed analysis is available by Mary E Footer, "Human Rights Due Diligence and the Responsible Supply of Minerals from Conflict-Affected Areas: Towards a Normative Framework?" in Jernej Letnar Černič and Tara Van Ho (eds.), *Human Rights and Business: Direct Corporate Accountability for Human Rights* (Wolf Legal Publishers, 2015).

514 Matthysen and Montejano, "Conflict Minerals Initiatives in DRC," pp. 8–9.

515 German Federal Institute for Geosciences and Natural Resources (BGR), "Certified Trading Chains (CTC)," www.bgr.bund.de/EN/Themen/Min_rohstoffe/CTC/Concept_MC/CTC-Standards-Principles/ctc_standards-principles_node_en.html (accessed 15 April 2019).

516 GeSI, "The Value of Membership" (gesi.org, 2018). https://gesi.org/uploads/pdf/GeSI_membership_value_document_2018.pdf (accessed 15 April 2019).

3TGs. The smelters have to be audited by an independent third party to be certified as conflict-free. As of 2019, over "350 companies and associations from over 10 industries" were participating in the Responsible Minerals Initiative (RMI).[517]

Operational-Level Grievance Mechanisms

Operational-level grievance mechanisms have been hailed as a possible effective remedy to human rights violations by directly putting rights holders in touch with companies about their claims. The UNGPs pointed to such mechanisms as a venue for remediation and as a way to "support the identification of adverse human rights impacts as a part of an enterprise's ongoing human rights due diligence."[518] The work of SRSG Ruggie identified seven principles for operational-level grievance mechanisms: being legitimate, accessible, predictable, equitable, right-compatible, transparent and based on dialogue and engagement,[519] as also featured in UNGP 31. The piloting study from 2011, however, noted that "the extensive time . . . [devoted to] the process of design or revisi[on]" of these principles left "little time to monitor their operation in practice."[520] There is limited research into the state of operations of company-level grievance mechanisms but three stages in the process include the registration of complaints and proposed solution, "mediation/conciliation, or negotiation," and as needed, arbitration/mediation/conciliation with third-party involvement.[521] There is also usually an ex post reporting requirement following the process. A UNICEF discussion paper on operational-level grievance mechanisms calls for a child-sensitive approach, which includes a clear commitment to and incorporation of children's rights principles and expertise in dealing with these, engagement with children and communities both in the design and implementation phases, accessibility for children directly or through representatives, prompt resolution of grievances and swift provision of remedies, and

[517] Responsible Mining Initiative, "What is the Responsible Mining Initiative (RMI)?," www.responsiblemineralsinitiative.org/about/faq/general-questions/what-is-the-conflict-free-sourcing-initiative-(cfsi)/ (accessed 15 April 2019).

[518] Caroline Rees, *Piloting Principles for Effective Company-Stakeholder Grievance Mechanisms: A Report of Lessons Learned* (Harvard Kennedy School Corporate Social Responsibility Initiative, 2011), p. 8.

[519] Ibid., p. 9.

[520] Ibid., p. 5.

[521] Christina Cedillo, *Better Access to Remedy in Company-Community Conflicts in the Field of CSR: A Model for Company-Based Grievance Mechanisms* (Institute for Environment Security, 2011), p. 12.

assessment of children's rights performance as a part of the company's overall human rights due diligence.[522] This children's rights perspective on operational-level mechanisms is fairly new and further empirical research is needed to evaluate the promise of these mechanisms as effective remedies for human and children's rights violations linked to businesses.

[522] UNICEF, "Discussion Paper: Operational-Level Grievance Mechanisms Fit for Children," 2018.

PART II

Case Illustrations: A Brief Introduction

Children and their rights may be affected by business-related issues in different ways, directly or indirectly. The two main avenues where businesses come into relationship with children and may affect children's enjoyment of their rights are global supply chains and investment projects, especially when these are large scale. The following section focuses on four case illustrations of how business-related harms may befall children. Two cases are linked to global supply chains and two to investment projects. All have been chosen to showcase different aspects of the business-children's rights nexus. They demonstrate the multifaceted nature of that nexus: child labor in global supply chains, indirect effects of business sourcing decisions on children in conflict-affected zones, the impact of involuntary resettlement on children and the specific vulnerabilities of children to violence and exploitation in large-scale investment settings.

The chosen cases are among those best-documented in detail by civil society actors as well as through official documentation from multilateral financiers and documents emerging from various grievance mechanisms such as the OECD NCPs, the World Bank Inspection Panel and the Compliance Advisor/Ombudsman of the International Finance Corporation (IFC).

They have also been chosen to illustrate the difficulties in assigning and apportioning responsibility for children's rights violations when they involve multiple state and non-state actors. They also demonstrate the variety in responses from the international community and international institutions in the face of different children's rights issues and the significance of the direct versus indirect impact distinction when those responses are formulated. These case illustrations are the use of forced child labor in Uzbekistan's cotton sector, the impact of the extraction of so-called conflict minerals in eastern Democratic Republic of Congo (DRC), the impacts of the Bujagali Hydropower Project on children and the children's rights violations linked to the Uganda Transport Sector Development Project, in that order.

2

Children's Rights in Supply Chains

In today's world, many businesses, in particular larger enterprises, either operate across national borders or have supply and value relationships that transcend territorial jurisdictions. In addition, businesses routinely set up a network of subsidiaries in different countries and enter into joint ventures with other businesses. Many human rights and children's rights violations linked to supply or value relationships occur outside of the territorial jurisdictions (home states) where such multinational business enterprises are incorporated or headquartered. In fact, supply chains of end-user products are often made up of various business enterprises which may operate in different sectors. Supply chains comprise "all parties involved in the provision of services and the manufacturing of goods, from raw material to finished product, including packaging and transportation," meaning that due diligence should involve all steps and connections within that supply chain.[1] The supply chain structures of different goods and services will inevitably look different and businesses thus need to map their supply chains accordingly to uncover human rights risks.[2] From human rights risk assessments to the implementation of a human rights policy, due diligence is considered the cornerstone of responsible global supply chain management.

Human rights violations may occur in any step of the supply chain, from the upstream production of agricultural crops such as cotton or cocoa or the extraction of minerals such as gold to the manufacturing of intermediate goods or final goods in subcontractor settings. While child labor is considered the focus *par excellence* of the business relationship to children in supply chains, it is not the only one. Businesses employ children's parents or other caregivers. Business sourcing practices may have impacts on the livelihoods and the rights of communities of which

[1] IEH – Ethical Trading Initiative Norway (with funding from the Norwegian Ministry of Foreign Affairs), *A Guide to Human Rights Due Diligence in Global Supply Chains* (IEH, 2013), p. 7.

[2] Ibid., p. 10.

children are part. Moreover, businesses may operate in weak governance zones or zones of armed conflict where risks of children's rights violations are compounded by the effects of conflict and deprivations resulting from weak governance.

Two issues are vital in supply chain management and regulation in order to prevent adverse human and children's rights impacts: traceability and what will be termed 'impactability.'

2.1 Supply Chain Management and Regulation: Key Issues

Traceability

Traceability is the most salient concern for retailers regarding human rights issues arising from supply chains. Traceability is the one essential factor for a company in being able to ascertain that raw materials or intermediate goods linked to human rights violations during their production do not get into the supply chain. Ensuring traceability is considered a key element of sustainable supply chain management. The International Organization for Standardization's (ISO) widely used definition of traceability is "the ability to identify and trace the history, distribution, location, and application of products, parts, and materials."[3] Qualifying this definition, UN Global Compact and BSR's *A Guide to Traceability* defines traceability as "[t]he ability to identify and trace the history, distribution, location and application of products, parts and materials, to ensure the reliability of sustainability claims, in the areas of human rights, labor . . ., the environment and anti-corruption."[4] Traceability is essential to ensure that materials sourced do not come from places where human rights violations are known to be systematic. Traceability is a central issue in many supply chains, especially when the businesses selling end products are several steps removed from the upstream raw materials or services used in manufacturing the products. Traceability (or chain of custody) has become an important consideration in international regulatory guidelines such as the OECD Due Diligence Guidance for Responsible Supply Chains of Minerals from Conflict-Affected and High-Risk Areas (2016), the OECD-FAO Guidance for Responsible Agricultural Supply Chains (2016) and the

[3] UN Global Compact and BSR, *A Guide to Traceability: A Practical Approach to Advance Sustainability in Global Supply Chains* (UN Global Compact, 2014), p. 7, www.bsr.org/reports/BSR_UNGC_Guide_to_Traceability.pdf (accessed 24 April 2019).

[4] Ibid.

OECD Due Diligence Guidance for Responsible Supply Chains in the Garment and Footwear Sector (2018).

Impactability

The second important challenge in ensuring that global supply chains act in accordance with the entire range of internationally recognized human rights standards is the ability for businesses at the end of the supply chain, such as retailers, to impact the behavior and modes of operation of other businesses upstream.[5] This may be termed 'impactability.' At present, the debate about Corporate Social Responsibility (CSR) and business obligations concerns the entire supply chain.[6] As such, "upstream CSR demands go beyond the direct suppliers to include the complete production process from resource extraction to product assembly."[7] Guidance from the Shift Project, founded by the former SRSG Ruggie, points out two related difficulties: first, many issues in the supply chains with regard to human rights have root causes that may be due to "structural or systemic issues, beyond the direct control of individual suppliers, requiring systemic responses – including social context, regulatory environments, and the broader labour relations context in the country."[8] Second, companies often overlook their own contributions that further exacerbate adverse impacts, for instance, in terms of purchasing practices that "undercut their stated commitments to better social performance in their supply chains and contribute directly to the impacts they are intent on preventing."[9]

Locke, Amengual and Mangla have linked the limited success of a traditional private, voluntary compliance model to its "misguided theoretical and empirical assumptions concerning the power of multinational corporations in global supply chains."[10] They argue that there

[5] For an overview of developments in upstream and downstream Corporate Social Responsibility (CSR), see: Judith Schrempf-Stirling, Guido Palazzo and Robert A. Phillips, "Ever Expanding Responsibilities: Upstream and Downstream Corporate Social Responsibility," in Adam Lindgreen, et al. (eds.), *Sustainable Value Chain Management: Analyzing, Designing, Implementing, and Monitoring for Social and Environmental Responsibility* (Ashgate, 2012), pp. 353–368.

[6] Ibid., p. 354.

[7] Ibid., p. 356.

[8] Shift, *From Audit to Innovation: Advancing Human Rights in Global Supply Chains* (Shift, 2013), p. 6.

[9] Ibid.

[10] Rick Locke, Matthew Amengual and Akshay Mangla, "'Virtue out of Necessity?': Compliance, Commitment and the Improvement of Labor Conditions in Global Supply

are misconceptions about the incentives needed to alter behavior and improve standards throughout production networks. Accordingly, it is not always the case that global retail brands are powerful enough to foster compliance with codes of conduct and labor standards.[11] They argue that power relations within supply chains in different sectors, including for instance apparel supply chains, are not asymmetrical as has hitherto been assumed and are much more complex and intricate. Because apparel suppliers work with a large number of brands and each brand comprises a limited portion of their business volumes, these brands may not have the leverage to compel suppliers to introduce improvements to wages, working hours and conditions.[12] A retailer's decision not to use a particular factory is also no antidote to the issues at supplier level since retailers thus "lose any leverage they once had if the factory finds other, less demanding clients."[13] Their conclusion is that it is a fiction that willing global brands are able to 'force' suppliers to comply with codes of conduct. The proposed remedy for the vices of the traditional compliance model is offered in the form of a "commitment-oriented approach based upon joint problem-solving, information exchange, and the diffusion of best-practices."[14] In fact, Locke, Amengual and Mangla have pinpointed the inherent difficulty surrounding voluntary supply chain management:

> Power relations among the key actors in the supply chains are far from unidirectional or unambiguous and thus render simple responses (e.g., comply or else) unrealistic. Given the complex and interdependent nature of relations among the different actors in the supply chain, it is not clear whose behavior . . . should be induced to change.[15]

Although the authors view this difficulty as the prime reason for abandoning the compliance approach for a commitment-based approach, they are premature in their assessment. Notwithstanding the merits of a commitment-oriented supply chain management, it is not a turn exclusively to commitment but to more effective models of compliance that is badly needed from a human rights standpoint. From retailers to raw material procurement, effective and adequate regulation

Chains," MIT Sloan Working Paper No. 4719-08, October 2008, updated March 2009, p. 1.

11 Ibid., pp. 8–9.

12 Ibid., p. 12.

13 Locke, Amengual and Mangla, "Virtue out of Necessity?," p. 13.

14 Ibid., p. 1.

15 Ibid., p. 16.

at all levels of the supply chain across the globe is crucial squarely for overcoming the inherent complexities and ensuring that the burdens of compliance and reporting are distributed evenly and equitably. In essence, there is nothing that renders regulation and commitment-oriented approaches incompatible. As such, businesses along the supply chain can continue to engage in joint problem-solving, exchange of information and best practices in undertaking their duties set out in regulations.

Commitment-oriented methods are more effective when backed up with more teeth through measures for noncompliance. The introduction of new regulatory initiatives to implement existing international legal standards often happens in the wake of crises or tragedies. Such was also the context for the 2013 Accord on Fire and Building Safety in Bangladesh, a legally binding agreement signed between global unions and global brands sourcing from Bangladesh. The accord came about to prevent a repetition of tragedies such as the collapse of the Rana Plaza building which claimed the lives of 1,134 Bangladeshi garment workers.[16] The Accord provided for the arbitration of disputes under its Article 5. In 2016, two trade union signatories of the accord, IndustriALL Global Union and UNI Global Unionm initiated two separate arbitration proceedings under the Accord and 2010 UN Commission on International Trade Law (UNCITRAL) Arbitration Rules against two signatory global fashion brands. The Permanent Court of Arbitration (PCA) administered the two arbitrations, which were terminated after the parties reached settlements.[17] The names of the fashion brands were kept confidential during the proceedings. It was reported, however, that one of these arbitration proceedings resulted in a 2.3 million USD settlement: 2 million USD to remedy fire and building safety problems at Bangladeshi factories and 300,000 USD for the two trade unions brining the cases to fund their joint "supply chain worker support fund."[18] Having expired after five years on 15 May 2018, the Accord has been replaced by a Transition Accord which extends the protections until May 2021.[19]

[16] Paul M. Barrett, Dorothée Baumann-Pauly and April Gu, "Five Years After Rana Plaza: The Way Forward," NYU Stern Center for Business and Human Rights, April 2018.

[17] Permanent Court of Arbitration, "2016–36 Termination Order (Redacted)," 17 July 2018 and "2016–37 Termination Order (Redacted)," 17 July 2018.

[18] Dominic Rushe, "Unions Reach $2.3m Settlement on Bangladesh Textile Factory Safety," *Guardian*, 22 January 2018.

[19] Accord on Fire and Building Safety in Bangladesh, "Accord Continuation Beyond May 2018," https://bangladeshaccord.org/updates/2017/10/26/accord-continuation-beyond-may-2018 (accessed 15 April 2019).

The prevention of adverse impacts, their mitigation and remediation in cases where prevention and mitigation fail are also essential elements of a children's rights approach to business practices. The various frameworks spearheaded by the UNGPs focus on these respect and remedy duties. It is nonetheless instructive to look at how these norms play out in real-life situations and to conduct a reality check. The following two case illustrations on the production of cotton in Uzbekistan, using forced child labor, and the impact of artisanal mineral exploitation in the eastern DRC serve to illustrate the most salient issues around children in supply chains, child labor in one of its worst forms and children's rights in conflict situations, as well as the variety of global response through various legal and policy instruments.

2.2 Case 1: Child Labor and Cotton Production in Uzbekistan

The regulation of child labor has a century-long history as one of the issues that the ILO tackled after its establishment in 1919 through minimum age conventions.[20] Over the last three decades, the focus on the economic exploitation of children as a children's rights violation has been strengthened, first with the adoption of the CRC in 1989 and later the ILO Convention 182 on the Worst Forms of Child Labor in 1999. In 2002, the ILO created the International Programme on the Elimination of Child Labor (IPEC) to combat and progressively eliminate child labor globally by working to raise awareness and build capacity. In the context of the 2030 Agenda for Sustainable Development, Sustainable Development Goal (SDG) 8 on Decent Work and Economic Growth includes a target linked to child labor, among others. Target 8.7 calls on states to "take immediate and effective measures to eradicate forced labor, end modern slavery and human trafficking and secure the prohibition and elimination of the worst forms of child labor, including recruitment and use of child soldiers, and by 2025 end child labor in all its forms."[21] The linked indicator 8.7.1 will measure the "proportion and number of children aged 5–17 years engaged in child labor" disaggregated by sex and age.

International Labour Organization data from 2017 indicates that 152 million children are in child labor globally, 73 million of whom are

[20] ILO Website, "ILO: Origins and History," www.ilo.org/global/about-the-ilo/history/lang–en/index.htm (accessed 24 April 2019).

[21] UNGA, "Transforming Our World: The 2030 Agenda for Sustainable Development," A/RES/70/1, 21 October 2015, Goal 8.7.

engaged in hazardous labor. Child labor is most prevalent in Africa with 19.6 percent of African children in child labor, followed by 7.4 percent of children in Asia and the Pacific. In addition, there is great variance across sectors: 11.9 percent of children in child labor are in industry, 17.2 percent are in services and a striking 70.9 percent are in the agriculture sector.[22]

2.2.1 *Cotton Production: Facts and Processes*

Early autumn is the season for cotton harvest in Uzbekistan. Uzbekistan is the world's seventh leading cotton producer and the world's sixth leading cotton exporter.[23] Uzbekistan's share of world cotton production and its share of world cotton exports have been in continuous decline since peaking in the late 1970s and have averaged at just under 3.5 percent between 2014 and 2018.[24] Since its independence after the dissolution of the USSR, Uzbekistan has espoused a state-controlled import substitution economic system, coupled with an export-oriented agricultural sector to maximize earnings from global markets and generate a current account surplus. Cotton is reportedly cultivated on more than half of the country's total cropland by state requirements. Land ownership resides exclusively with the state and farmers are able to obtain lease contracts to gain usufruct rights. The size and the location of the fields for cotton cultivation, the selection of dates for ploughing, seeding, irrigation, fertilizer application and harvesting are all regulated heavily by the state.[25]

The production of cotton follows a centrally determined quota system implemented at the regional and local level through district cotton production targets, enforced by regional governors (*khokims*).[26] The production cycle of cotton from cultivation to harvesting has relied heavily, and at some locations, completely, on manual labor. During the Soviet era, the policies for cotton self-sufficiency had dictated the "intensive use of machinery, fertilizers, and pesticides."[27] After independence, cotton remained the major cash crop of Uzbekistan but the

22 ILO, *Global Estimates of Child Labour: Results and Trends, 2012–2016* (ILO, 2017), p. 5.

23 Kai Hughes, "The Cotton Report: Cotton Production & Trade Trends," International Cotton Advisory Committee, November 2017.

24 Data extracted from the US Department of Agriculture, Foreign Agriculture Service, Cotton: World Markets and Trade, December 2018.

25 Nodir Djanibekov et al., *Pros and Cons of Cotton Production in Uzbekistan – Case Study # 7–9 of the Program: Food Policy for Developing Countries: The Role of Government in the Global Food System* (Cornell University, 2010), pp. 1–4.

26 EJF, *White Gold: The True Cost of Cotton* (EJF, 2005), pp. 15–16.

27 Djanibekov et al., *Pros and Cons of Cotton Production in Uzbekistan*, p. 2.

machinery-intensive production strategies were replaced by a turn to manual labor.[28] In October 2013, in a sharp departure from the two-decade-long manual labor policy, the then Prime Minister announced that the Tashkent Tractor Plan would be manufacturing new cotton picker machines, with the objective of 80 to 90 percent of Uzbek cotton being machine-harvested by 2016.[29] The complexities of undertaking such a massive overhaul of the production system and "its potential impact on rural employment" were already recognized by December 2014 in the government's talks with the WB Inspection Panel and a 2016 WB report.[30]

2.2.2 Impacts on Children

The issue of forced child and adult labor in Uzbekistan's cotton farms started making its way to the global agenda at the turn of the new millennium with increasing civil society scrutiny. A 2005 report by the NGO Environmental Justice Foundation (EJF), based on field visits, contained allegations regarding forced child labor on cotton fields with schools remaining closed during the three-month autumn harvest period (September to November).[31] Reportedly, regional authorities turned to organized forced child labor when the best part of the cotton had been picked and adult workers were no longer enticed by earnings from the remaining cotton.[32] The exact number of children mobilized through the cotton production cycle was unknown but estimates were as high as 2.7 million children (grades 5 through 11) annually.[33] A 2006 study by

[28] Richard Pomfret, "State-Directed Diffusion of Technology: The Mechanization of Cotton-Harvesting in Soviet Central Asia" (2002) 62(1) *The Journal of Economic History* 170–188 at 186 and 173 (footnote 7), respectively.

[29] Fibre 2 Fashion, "Uzbekistan to machine-harvest 90% of cotton by 2016," 17 October 2013, www.fibre2fashion.com/news/textile-news/newsdetails.aspx?news_id=154101 (accessed 15 April 2019).

[30] WB Inspection Panel, "Final Eligibility Report and Recommendation on a Request for Inspection – Republic of Uzbekistan: Second Rural Enterprise Support Project (P109126) and Additional Financing for the Second Rural Enterprise Support Project (P126962) – Report No. 93222-UZ," para. 28, and Rob Swinkels, Ekaterina Romanova and Evgeny Kochkin, "Assessing the Social Impact of Cotton Harvest Mechanization in Uzbekistan," The World Bank, June 2016.

[31] EJF, *White Gold*, pp. 19–21.

[32] Tahlil and Save the Children, "Child Labor in Uzbekistan," 2002, cited in EJF, *White Gold*, p. 21 (footnote 32).

[33] SOAS, *Invisible to the World? The Dynamics of Forced Child Labour in the Cotton Sector of Uzbekistan* (SOAS, 2009), p. 26.

the School of Oriental and African Studies (SOAS) concluded that "practically all [10 to 15 year old] school children" in cotton-producing rural areas and small towns were recruited.[34] Each child was designated a daily cotton-picking requirement ranging from 40 to 60 kilograms.[35] The NGO Uzbek-German Forum for Human Rights (UGFHR) alleged that *khokims* utilized the services of the prosecutor's office and law enforcement in order to mobilize the population for cotton picking.[36] The follow-up 2007 SOAS study concluded that the mass scale of mobilization of school children could "only be achieved under directives or tacit consent of the central government."[37] The Uzbek case has thus been called a "rare instance of state-sanctioned mass mobilization of children's labour."[38] The pay rate was based on the amount and grade of cotton and reportedly between 100 and 125 Uzbek soums (approximately 3 cents) per kilogram (2009 to 2011).[39] In 2011, UNICEF observation visits in twelve regions during that year's cotton harvest confirmed NGO reports, adding that children were found to be working full days in extremely hot weather, missing classes, exposed to pesticides, not "allowed to seek medical attention even though they were sick."[40]

Alleged Children's Rights Violations

An Alternative Report submitted by EJF to the 42nd Session of the CRC Committee in 2006 alleged "the systematic use of State-orchestrated forced child labour" with "substantial negative impact on both the health and education of th[e] children involved."[41] Allegations concerned violations of the freedom from economic exploitation (Article 32), right to adequate standard of living (Article 27), right to health (Article 24) and right to education (Articles 28–29) as contained in the CRC.[42] In addition, a lack of access to clean water, adequate nutrition, sanitation and

34 Ibid., p. 19.
35 Uzbek-German Forum for Human Rights (UGFHR), *Cotton – "It's Not a Plant, It's Politics" – The System of Forced Labour in Uzbekistan's Cotton Sector: Evidence from the 2011 Cotton Harvest* (UGFHR, 2012), p. 23.
36 Ibid., p. 18.
37 SOAS, *Invisible to the World?*, p. 20.
38 Ibid., p. iv, para. 6.
39 UGFHR, *Cotton – It's Not a Plant, It's Politics*, p. 24.
40 ILO CEACR, "Observation – Worst Forms of Child Labor Convention, 1999 (No. 182) – Uzbekistan, Adopted 2012, Published 102nd Session of the International Labor Conference," 2013.
41 EJF, "Alternative Report Child Labour in Cotton Production in Uzbekistan for the 42nd Session of the Committee on the Rights of the Child," 2006, p. 4.
42 Ibid.

suitable accommodations for children in cotton fields as well as dangers from pesticide exposure were noted.[43] The Committee in turn noted its concern about the involvement of school-age children in the cotton harvest, exposing them to "serious health problems such as intestinal and respiratory infections, meningitis and hepatitis."[44] The 2007 SOAS study also pointed to minimal provisions for hygiene, sanitation and health on the fields. In addition, the work performed by children would be considered heavy work, especially when it consisted of carrying heavy bales of cotton and working without weekend breaks as the reports have suggested.[45] The findings also indicated the use of chemicals for fertilization and defoliation: nitrates were being used during the spring and summer seasons as fertilizers, and defoliants were applied to the cotton in August and September during the ripening period,[46] although this allegation was denied.[47]

The report by UGFHR from the 2011 harvest stated that "the forced mobilization of students and employees of state enterprises, medical personnel and teachers, and even merchants and employees from the private sector" was commonplace in many parts of the country during the cotton harvest.[48] The report alleged that teachers from all levels of schooling as well as doctors were being forcefully mobilized for the cotton harvest. Human Rights Watch (HRW) argued accordingly that the right to education and right to health in the country's cotton-producing regions were jeopardized, if not violated, in the absence of teachers and medical personnel.[49] A teacher was quoted as saying that missed lessons were taught in an accelerated fashion, greatly sacrificing the quality of education.[50] From 2005 onwards, photographic evidence of child labor as well as very few written documents addressed to older children and adults were provided.[51] Basing estimations on the civil

[43] Ibid., p. 8.

[44] CRC Committee, "Concluding Observations 2006: Uzbekistan," para. 64.

[45] SOAS, *Invisible to the World?*, p. 21.

[46] Ibid.

[47] Terry P. Townsend on behalf of International Cotton Advisory Committee (ICAC), Letter: 30 November 2007, www.reports-and-materials.org/sites/default/files/reports-and-materials/Intl-Cotton-Advisory-Committee-letter-30-Nov-2007.pdf (accessed 15 April 2019).

[48] UGFHR, *Cotton – It's Not a Plant, It's Politics*, p. 18.

[49] HRW, "Press Release – Uzbekistan: Forced Labor Widespread in Cotton Harvest – More Adults, Older Children Required to Work, Abuses Persist," 25 January 2013.

[50] UGFHR, *Cotton – It's Not a Plant, It's Politics*, p. 26.

[51] Ibid.

society accounts of children, a child forced to work in the cotton harvests for a period of six weeks to two months every year from the age of ten until the age of eighteen would have hypothetically worked a total of twelve to sixteen months in the cotton sector under the described conditions over an eight-year period. Because the harvest falls on school months, this said child would have lost these twelve to sixteen months of education, roughly 22 percent of schooling time lost over an eight-year period. Even for older children who are recruited to work from fifteen years of age onwards, assuming that they were not recruited when they were younger, the loss of schooling time would be equal to four and a half to six months over three years. Evidently, the younger the children are recruited, the greater the educational losses both in terms of time spent without schooling and in terms of the cumulative effect of these losses on learning outcomes.

Domestic Legislation and International Commitments

Uzbekistan is a party to the CRC (since 29 June 1994), OPAC and the OPSC (both since 23 December 2008) as well as ILO Conventions 29 on Forced Labor, 182 on the Worst Forms of Child Labor (since 24 June 2008) and 138 on Minimum Age (since 6 March 2009).

The ILO Convention 138 underlines a commitment on the part of states parties "to pursue a national policy designed to ensure the effective abolition of child labor and to raise progressively the minimum age for admission to employment or work to a level consistent with the fullest physical and mental development of young persons" (Article 1). Article 3.1 further qualifies the commitment by setting the "minimum age for admission to any type of employment or work which by its nature or the circumstances in which it is carried out is likely to jeopardize the health, safety or morals of young persons" to at least eighteen. The ILO Convention 138 allows states parties to restrict the scope of application of the Convention on the basis of inadequate economic and administrative facilities. This flexibility is, however, not unlimited and cannot be applied to certain sectors including "plantations and other agricultural undertakings mainly producing for commercial purposes" such as cotton cultivation (Article 5[3]).

The definition of the worst forms of child labor under ILO Convention 182 includes both forced or compulsory labor and hazardous work. Furthermore, forced or compulsory labor is deemed one of the unconditional worst forms of child labor. Hazardous work can include "work ... which involves the manual handling or transport of heavy loads," "work in an unhealthy environment which may . . . expose children to hazardous substances, agents or processes, or to temperatures," "work under particularly difficult conditions such as work for long hours or during the night or work where the child is unreasonably confined to the premises of the employer."[52]

Uzbek domestic legislation formally prohibits forced labor and the worst forms of child labor. The country's Labor Code and the Law on the Guarantees of the Rights of the Child, which were amended in 2009, set the minimum age for work at sixteen,[53] and prohibited hazardous work for those under the age of eighteen. Manual harvesting of cotton is included in the list of hazardous activities that are prohibited for children but this prohibition reportedly "does not include protections for children aged 15 to 17 from the worst forms of child labor."[54] Overall, with the amendments in 2009 and the Ministerial Decree of 2012, Uzbekistan's domestic legislation on minimum age for employment and on child labor, including the list of hazardous occupations prohibited for children, have been brought in line with international standards.

The implementation and enforcement of these standards, however, have been called into question. A 2013 assessment by the US Department of Labor (US DoL) found that the Uzbekistan government's cotton policies acted as an incentive for local administrators to use forced child and adult labor.[55] Over the years, several UN treaty bodies noted their distress over the use of child forced labor in the cotton harvest.[56] The ILO Committee of Experts (CEACR) repeatedly called on the Uzbek government to accept "a high-level ILO tripartite observer mission" during the harvest period[57] but these calls were rejected until 2013.[58]

[52] ILO, "Time-Bound Programme Manual for Action Planning – TBP MAP Guidebook II: Time-Bound Programmes for Eliminating the Worst Forms of Child Labour – An Introduction," 2003, p. 17.

[53] US Department of Labor (DoL), Bureau of International Labor Affairs, "2013 Findings on the Worst Forms of Child Labor – Uzbekistan," www.dol.gov/ilab/reports/child-labor/findings/2013TDA/uzbekistan.pdf (accessed 15 April 2019).

[54] Ibid., p. 5.

[55] Ibid.

[56] These include the Committee on Economic, Social and Cultural Rights (CESCR), the CRC Committee, the Committee on the Elimination of Discrimination Against Women (CEDAW) and the Human Rights Committee (HRC).

[57] ILO CEACR, "Observation – Worst Forms of Child Labor Convention, 1999."

[58] Ibid.

2.2.3 *Uzbek Cotton Supply Chains*

The Uzbek cotton sector was run at all stages by state-controlled institutions or corporations until very recently. A majority (51 percent) state-owned company, Uzpakthasanoat, formerly Uzkhlopkoprom,[59] purchased the country's entire cotton production delivered by farmers through the network of district cotton gins[60] at a third of the market price, according to 2012 reports.[61] There were three state-owned companies lying at the heart of the cotton exports and that also coordinated the Uzbek Commodity Exchange (UzEx): Uzprommashimpex, Uzmarkazimpex and Uzterimpex.[62] Cotton not designated for export was used in local textile production, mostly through joint ventures established between the Uzbek state and foreign investors.[63] In January 2005, the Uzbek Cabinet of Ministers launched a program to increase the cotton processing capacity of Uzbekistan to 50 percent by attracting foreign investment totaling 1.2 billion USD.[64] The government offered projects exemption from income tax and all other budgetary taxes, with the exception of VAT until 1 January 2009.[65] Some of these projects include joint ventures with large multinationals such as Daewoo.[66] One such joint venture, Indorama Kokand Textile, was given a 40 million USD loan in December 2015 by the World Bank's private sector financing arm the International Finance Corporation (IFC) to expand its cotton yarn production plant in Uzbekistan's Fergana Valley.[67] The loan is aimed at increasing exports and "availability of good quality raw material for the local weaving and

[59] Assel Rustemova, "Rent Seeking and Authoritarian Consolidation in Kazakhstan and Uzbekistan," in Rachel Vanderhill and Michael E. Aleprete Jr. (eds.), *International Dimensions of Authoritarian Persistence. Lessons from Post-Soviet States* (Lexington Books, 2013), p. 72.

[60] EJF, *White Gold*, p. 14.

[61] RSN, "From the Field: Travels of Uzbek Cotton Through the Value Chain," 2012, p. 2.

[62] Bakhodyr Muradov and Alisher Ilkhamov, *Uzbekistan's Cotton Sector: Financial Flows and Distribution of Resources* (Open Society Foundations, 2014), p. 31.

[63] EJF, *White Gold*, p. 15.

[64] Jozef de Coster, "Uzbekistan textiles appeal to foreign investors," www.just-style.com, 24 October 2005, www.just-style.com/analysis/uzbekistan-textiles-appeal-to-foreign-investors_id92504.aspx (accessed 15 April 2019).

[65] De Coster, "Uzbekistan Textiles Appeal to Foreign Investors.'

[66] The joint ventures include Daewoo Textile Ferghana, FE Daewoo Textile Bukhara, FE LLC BF Production, FE LLC Osborn Textile, FE Daka Tex, JV LLC Mili Guliston Textile, JV LLC Baht Textile.

[67] IFC, "IFC Project Information Portal: Indorama Kokand," https://disclosures.ifc.org/#/projectDetailSII/5133 (accessed 15 April 2019).

knitting industry, thus enhancing the growth of local textile industry and increasing industrial employment."[68]

A 2007 SOAS study claimed that the main beneficiaries of the use of child labor in the cotton fields were the state-owned trading companies, which operated with little or no transparency and no popular oversight.[69] The report alleged that the disparity between international market prices of cotton and the domestic prices paid to farmers had allowed these trading companies to acquire large profits, "giv[ing] them a stake in the maintenance of the current procurement and labour control regime."[70] This cotton then found its way to the high street through complex global supply chains.

Global cotton supply chains require meticulous due diligence and tracking of origin in order to ensure that products of child labor or forced labor do not end up in a company's supply portfolio. Retail companies that are most susceptible to consumer pressure and risks regarding their brands often do not directly buy cotton as a raw material to produce fabric. Cotton sold by Uzbek joint-stock companies at global market prices was mostly purchased by Asian companies. According to one account, China and Bangladesh were the destination for around 70 percent of the harvest.[71] In these countries, the cotton was woven and made into fabrics. Cotton supply chains across the globe have a similar structure, even if the specific players involved may differ. As such, "the vast majority of the world's cotton is traded through commodity exchanges and undergoes several stages of exchange, processing and manufacture between the cotton field and final consumer."[72]

The apparent complexity of global cotton supply chains and the baffling number of intermediaries involved in the various steps – from cultivation to retail – have too often resulted in the misconception that it may be practically impossible for retailers to ascertain the origin of the cotton they purchase. At the level of the yarn spinners and cotton mills, cotton from different origins and different qualities may be mixed. Garment manufacturers routinely use subcontractors "to dye, launder

[68] IFC, "Indorama Kokand."

[69] SOAS, *Invisible to the World?*, p. 37.

[70] Ibid., p. iv, para. 6.

[71] Raveena Aulakh, "Uzbekistan Shuts Down High Schools, Universities in Forced Cotton Harvest," *Toronto Star*, 30 September 2014, www.caionline.in/articles/uzbekistan-shuts-down-high-schools-universities-in-forced-cotton-harvest-september-30-2014 (accessed 17 August 2019).

[72] EJF, *Somebody Knows Where Your Cotton Comes From: Unravelling the Supply Chain* (EJF, 2009), p. 7.

or embellish their product."[73] In addition, the same garment may be produced for the same retailer by different garment manufacturers. Generally, retailers do not have direct relationships further down the supply chain than the fabric mills.[74]

The Uzbek cotton supply chain differs from other cotton supply chains in one important aspect: cultivation, harvesting, ginning and export of cotton are completely regulated by the Uzbek State. As such, cotton of Uzbek origin should be more readily identifiable at the level of cotton trading companies as they will have purchasing contracts with one of the three Uzbek government-owned cotton export companies.

Traceability of Uzbek Cotton

Organic and fair-trade cotton is differentiated at the source, certified and its supply chains segregated using the identity preservation model.[75] Non-organic, non-fairtrade cotton, which makes up the majority of the world cotton trade, on the other hand, is traded in commodity exchanges. For this conventional cotton, traceability necessitates diligent record keeping of supplier relationships at all levels of the cotton supply chain, from the gins to the retailers.[76] Traceability can be ensured because all internationally traded cotton is required to travel with a country of origin certificate in order to be cleared through international customs.[77] When retailers purchase cotton, the cotton they purchase may come from different origins or may have been mixed. Thus, cotton origin which is "known and is of great importance in trading and the first textile process-spinning" becomes obscured in later stages unless "origin is synonymous with quality."[78] While consumer pressure is high on retailers, it is much lower up the chain where traceability must be first ensured. It is thus crucial to ensure traceability at the raw cotton commodity trade stage of the supply chain.

The global raw cotton trade is a highly concentrated market with a very small number of very large players. In fact, the cotton trade makes up a part of the global commodities trade, where many of the larger traders such as Cargill and Louis Dreyfus play dominant roles. In 2009 the global cotton trade was dominated by thirteen

[73] Ibid., p. 6.
[74] Ibid., p. 7.
[75] UN Global Compact and BSR, *A Guide to Traceability*, p. 11.
[76] Ibid., p. 12.
[77] EJF, *Somebody Knows*, p. 7.
[78] Ibid.

companies, four of which were government-owned (including the three cotton-trading companies of the Uzbek government).[79] Of the world's leading ten private cotton trading companies, nine had offices in Tashkent during the period when forced labor allegations were rampant.[80] In the specific case of Uzbek cotton, the crucial stage for ensuring cotton produced by forced child labor does not enter supply chains is again at the cotton trade stage (after the gin and before spinners). The entry of Uzbek cotton into global apparel supply chains occurs at this stage when private traders purchase Uzbek cotton from state-owned trading companies.

2.2.4 *Corporate Responses to Supply Chain Issues*

The Boycott

The civil society reaction in the face of reports about children's rights and human rights violations through the use of forced labor has resulted in a number of voluntary ad hoc initiatives in the absence of mandatory regulatory frameworks. For instance, the Cotton Campaign was initiated in 2007 as a "global coalition of human rights, labor, investor and business organizations dedicated to eradicating child labor and forced labor in cotton production."[81] In November 2007, a group of self-proclaimed civil society activists from Uzbekistan sent an open letter to a number of governments, the EU, EBRD, the WB, UNICEF and ILO calling for a boycott of Uzbek cotton.[82] In what followed, international retailers such as H&M (Sweden), Marimekko (Finland), Krenholm (Estonia), Tesco (UK) and Marks and Spencer (UK) announced that they would stop sourcing Uzbek cotton.[83] The reactions to the call were not uniform, however, including one from the International Cotton Advisory Committee (ICAC) characterizing a boycott as "highly impractical because of the nature of commodity markets."[84] What the ICAC

[79] ICAC, "Structure of the World Cotton Trade."

[80] RSN, "From the Field," p. 13.

[81] The Cotton Campaign, www.cottoncampaign.org (accessed 15 April 2019).

[82] Civil Society Activists of Uzbekistan, "Purge the Uzbek Cotton of the Stains of Forced Child Labor!," 15 November 2007, www.reports-and-materials.org/sites/default/files/reports-and-materials/Call-for-Uzbekistan-cotton-boycott-15-Nov-2007.pdf (accessed 15 April 2019).

[83] Gulnoza Saidazimova, "Uzbekistan: Cotton Industry Targeted by Child-Labor Activists," Radio Free Europe – Radio Liberty, 19 January 2008, www.rferl.org/content/article/1079375.html (accessed 15 April 2019).

[84] Townsend/ICAC, "Letter: 30 November 2007."

tacitly referred to in the form of the nature of commodity markets in essence means the realities of global supply chains.

Another civil society initiative, called the Cotton Pledge, of the Responsible Sourcing Network (RSN), brings together 274 companies/brands worldwide in a commitment "to not knowingly source Uzbek cotton for the manufacturing of any … products until the Government of Uzbekistan ends the practice of forced child and adult labour in its cotton sector."[85] Most Cotton Pledge signatories are companies from North America and Europe, including some of the largest brands in apparel and retail. The signatories to the Cotton Pledge are expected to take five steps in implementing their commitment:

1. Align Business Practices with the Commitment
2. Collect Country of Origin (COO) Documentation for all Cotton Products and Textiles
3. Involve Yarn and Textile Mills
4. Engage the Uzbek Government
5. Join Responsible Sourcing Network's Economic Leverage Working Group on Uzbek Cotton.[86]

Although many American and European retailers have announced that they will not knowingly source Uzbek cotton on account of forced child labor being used in cotton cultivation in the country, some companies have argued that it is very difficult to ascertain that no Uzbek cotton ends up in the supply chain.[87] The effectiveness of the Cotton Pledge campaign remains controversial as ensuring traceability remains at the core of the boycott and as most of the cotton from the Uzbek fields is purchased by Asian markets as opposed to European or American.[88]

[85] Responsible Sourcing Network (RSN), "The Cotton Pledge," www.sourcingnetwork.org/storage/cotton-pledge-intro-package-2013/RSN%20Pledge%20Agreement2013.pdf (accessed 15 April 2019).

[86] RSN, The Cotton Pledge Package 2013, www.sourcingnetwork.org/storage/cotton-pledge-intro-package-2013/Pledge_Packet_2013.pdf (accessed 15 April 2019).

[87] Jamie Doward, "H&M Comes Under Pressure to Act on Child-Labour Cotton," *Guardian*, 15 December 2012, www.theguardian.com/business/2012/dec/15/cotton-child-labour-uzbekistan-fashion (accessed 15 April 2019).

[88] SOAS, "What Has Changed? Progress in Eliminating the Use of Forced Child Labour in the Cotton Harvests of Uzbekistan and Tajikistan," November 2010, p. 11, www.soas.ac.uk/cccac/centres-publications/file64329.pdf (accessed 15 April 2019).

Attempts at Accountability Through the OECD National Contact Points

The NGOs ECCHR, Association SHERPA and UGFHR jointly brought instances to the OECD NCPs targeting cotton-trading companies on account that cotton production in Uzbekistan relied on the "systematical use of state-organized forced child labour" and these companies knowingly engaged in the trade for profit-making purposes.[89] The instances were filed against the major cotton traders Otto Stadtlander, Paul Reinhart, ECOM, Devcot, Louis Dreyfus, Cargill Cotton and ICT Cotton at NCPs in France, Germany, the United Kingdom and Switzerland. These instances were filed in 2010, before the 2011 Revision of the OECD Guidelines, which also led to the inclusion of a chapter on human rights in the Guidelines as well as the incorporation of the duty of human rights due diligence in line with the UNGPs. The 2011 Revision crystalized the duty to conduct risk-based due diligence, to avoid causing or contributing to adverse impacts, including human rights impacts and to prevent or mitigate such adverse impacts "directly linked to their operations, products or services by a business relationship," including business partners, entities in the supply chain and all those actors directly linked to business operations, goods or services.[90] Furthermore, the chapter on human rights has also introduced a requirement to provide remediation to those negatively affected by human rights impacts, which the enterprise caused or to which it contributed. No such requirements existed in the previous version of the Guidelines. The claims concerned the role of cotton trading companies in the prevention of the use of forced child labor in Uzbekistan, therefore, on the so-called protect obligations that these companies may have as a result of their business dealings in Uzbek cotton.

Swiss NCP The three instances at the Swiss NCP against Ecom Agroindustrial, Louis Dreyfus and Paul Reinhart by ECCHR, filed on 22 October 2010, were considered to merit further engagement. The instance against Ecom Agroindustrial resulted in conciliation through the NCP's good offices. The agreement highlighted the importance of both engagement and disengagement in dealing with the issue as well as

[89] ECCHR, "Case Up-Date Agreement with Cargill and ICT in OECD-Proceeding," 26 July 2011, p. 1.

[90] OECD, "2011 Update of the OECD Guidelines for Multinational Enterprises – Comparative Table of Changes Made to the 2000 Text," 2012, www.oecd.org/corporate/mne/49744860.pdf (accessed 15 April 2019).

the "different and complimentary roles of companies, NGOs and governments."[91] On the other hand, *ECCHR* v. *Louis Dreyfus* resulted in the company accepting that a significant problem of forced child labor existed in Uzbekistan and that it would continue its engagement with Uzbek public authorities to voice concerns over these practices.[92] The agreement included provisions for further consultations between ECCHR and the company to discuss future directions in case this engagement and participation in other initiatives did not lead to desired changes.[93] In *ECCHR* v. *Paul Reinhart*, the NCP made confidential initial assessments that the instances merited further consideration and offered its good offices to the parties.[94] The agreement stipulated the desirability of having the allegations assessed by an international body such as the ILO and that traders would have a role in addressing the issue.[95]

German NCP The German NCP used a different procedure in assessing the claim against Otto Stadtlander, requesting the parties to submit written views and holding talks with both parties. It noted that the Federal Government considered child labor an important concern in the Uzbek cotton sector and called on Uzbek authorities to "take effective steps to abolish this practice."[96] The request was found sufficiently relevant for an in-depth assessment "[d]espite the absence of an investment nexus."[97] The NCP concluded that Otto Stadtlander had not been supplied directly by Uzbek State-owned Enterprises (SOEs) in the last sixteen years but "purchas[ed] central Asian cotton exclusively from wholesalers" and that only 5 percent of Uzbek cotton indirectly entered the company's supply chain.[98] The NCP also relied on the absence of a national import ban on Uzbek cotton to conclude that the call to the company for a boycott was unwarranted. Furthermore, the

[91] Swiss NCP, "Closing Statement – Specific Instance Regarding Cotton Trade by Ecom Agroindustrial Corp. Ltd. in Uzbekistan," 22 December 2011, para. 13. (Although the Closing Statement mentions complimentary roles, seemingly a misprint of the word "complementary.")

[92] Swiss NCP, "Closing Statement: Specific Instance Regarding Cotton Trading by Louis Dreyfus Suisse SA in Uzbekistan," 17 February 2012, para. 13.

[93] Ibid., para. 13.

[94] Swiss NCP, "Closing Statement: Specific Instance Regarding Cotton Trading by Paul Reinhart AG in Uzbekistan," 7 March 2012, para. 8.

[95] Ibid., para. 13.

[96] German NCP, "Joint Final Statement by the German NCP for the OECD Guidelines for MNEs, ECCHR and Otto Stadtlander GmbH Regarding a Complaint by the ECCHR against Otto Stadtlander GmbH/Bremen," 17 November 2011.

[97] Ibid.

[98] Ibid.

NCP held that it was unrealistic for the company to engage with the Uzbek government directly given the indirect and limited nature of the business relationship. The NCP then qualified the cotton market situation at that moment as being a "seller's market, with cotton in short supply," making it "very difficult to influence those responsible for Uzbekistan's cotton trade from the buyer side."[99] The German NCP, housed in the Ministry of Economy and Technology, proved a challenging forum for strategic litigation. In fact, as a result of the final agreement, the NGO "pledge[d] to refrain from publicly criticizing the respondent's previous corporate policies as regards the trading of Uzbek cotton ... not includ[ing] the expression of opinions relating to human rights violations in Uzbekistan that have no discernible link with the respondent or its corporate policies" and "make clear in a press statement that their assertion that the respondent purchases large amounts of Uzbek cotton direct from state-owned companies in Uzbekistan ha[d] proven to be erroneous."[100]

The German NCP used a two-tier test in this instance: direct business link through direct purchase from Uzbek SOEs and relatively large volumes of purchase as a percentage of the total supply chain. Using this test, the German NCP concluded that Otto Stadtlander could not be presumed to have protect duties in the prevention of forced child labor. In addition, Germany's trade policy (whether there was a ban on the product in question) was used to determine whether the company was under an obligation to refrain from purchasing Uzbek cotton. In the absence of such domestic regulation with extraterritorial implications, the NCP concluded that the company could not be expected to cease trading in Uzbek cotton and would not be considered in violation of the Guidelines.

UK NCP The UK NCP decided to accept the two separate instances filed on 7 December 2010 on behalf of ECCHR against ICT Cotton and Cargill Cotton relating to the "Employment and Industrial Relations" and "General Policies" of the Guidelines.[101] The UK NCP issued an initial statement in the *ECCHR* v. *ICT Cotton* instance on

[99] Ibid.

[100] Ibid.

[101] UK NCP, "Final Statement by the UK NCP for the OECD Guidelines for MNEs – Complaint from the ECCHR against ICT Cotton Ltd (in Uzbekistan)," 11 July 2011, para. 6, and UK NCP, "Final Statement by the UK NCP for the OECD Guidelines for MNEs – Complaint from the ECCHR against Cargill Cotton Ltd (in Uzbekistan)," 11 July 2011, para. 6.

8 March 2011, declining ICT Cotton's claims that the instance should be rejected for the "lack of an 'investment nexus' between ICT Cotton and Uzbekistan, or between ICT Cotton and [Uzbek government owned] companies."[102] The UK NCP used an external conciliator-mediator for a conciliation process between the parties, whereby an agreement was reached.[103] During the process ICT Cotton declined ECCHR's request to cease trading in Uzbek cotton, noting disagreement with ECCHR's allegations that systematic abuses of forced child labor in cotton harvest were taking place.[104] Nonetheless, ICT Cotton recognized that

> [B]usinesses have a responsibility to take active steps to help to prevent such practices in their industry and to investigate the concerns properly (. . .). ICT is prepared to take appropriate actions as agreed with ECCHR and ECCHR is prepared to drop the request for cessation of trading for the time being. (. . .) ICT (. . .) would immediately suspend business relations with any supplier who will, beyond reasonable doubt, be found to have used such practices. (. . .)[105]

The agreement stipulated that the ECCHR and ICT would engage in a regular exchange of views and information process within the next year, to further discuss lessons learned and the way forward.[106] A similar process took place in the instance *ECCHR* v. *Cargill*, whereby Cargill recognized the "serious allegations about the systematic use of forced child labour in Uzbekistan" but an agreement through conciliation was possible only with ECCHR's agreement to temporarily withdraw its request to Cargill Cotton to cease trading in Uzbek cotton although this was still considered a backup measure by ECCHR if other efforts failed.[107] The process led to an agreement on the basis of the exchange of views and information, as had been decided in the agreement with ICT Cotton. The conclusion of both instances by agreement meant that the NCP would not investigate the allegations or determine whether the Guidelines had been breached or not.

French NCP The instance at the French NCP against Devcot was handled through the provision of good offices. The NCP concluded that the trade in

102 UK NCP, "Initial Assessment by the UK NCP for the OECD Guidelines for MNEs – Complaint from the ECCHR Against ICT Cotton Ltd (in Uzbekistan)," 8 March 2011.
103 Ibid., para. 11.
104 Ibid., para. 10.
105 Ibid.
106 ECCHR, "Case Up-Date Agreement with Cargill and ICT in OECD-Proceeding."
107 UK NCP, "Final Statement – ECCHR Against Cargill Cotton," para. 10.

goods produced from forced child labor was a violation of the Guidelines but that Devcot had declared that it had not purchased any Uzbek cotton in recent years and did not intend to trade in Uzbekistan until child labor had ended and conditions were ameliorated for children.[108] The French NCP reminded Devcot of the importance of the Guidelines and of its responsibilities in the supply chain of the cotton trade and called on the management of the company to ensure that they are in fact in compliance with the OECD Guidelines by undertaking a due diligence effort within the company.[109] In addition, the NCP found both the use of child labor and forced labor as well as the trade of goods manufactured using such labor "regardless of where it occurs, ... a serious and blatant violation of the OECD's Guidelines."[110]

In six out of the seven cases brought before NCPs, ECCHR and the cotton traders had agreed that companies should take action to specifically influence the situation of cotton production in Uzbekistan and that ECCHR should monitor the implementation of these measures.[111] According to an analysis, the outcome of the implementation process had been rather disappointing: "due to disagreements between ECCHR and the traders over the commitment required to address the situation in Uzbekistan" as a result of ECCHR's continued "request to companies to stop trade relations with Uzbekistan if the measures undertaken should not prove effective," the parties were no longer engaging in cooperation.[112] The report credited strong media attention to the situation at the time of the complaints with moving the companies in question to take concrete steps and contended that once the closed mediation procedures commenced and media attention waned, the companies were less inclined to continue their commitments.[113]

The NCPs of Italy and France have both since elaborated reports on the application of OECD Guidelines in textile and apparel sectors following the collapse of the Rana Plaza building. The French NCP was requested by the then Minister of Foreign Trade, Nicole Bricq, to inspect what the concept of "business relationship" meant for MNEs and to identify due diligence measures to be taken in response "with regard to security, working conditions and trade

[108] French NCP, "Communiqué du Point de contact national français chargé du suivi des principes directeurs de l'OCDE à l'intention des entreprises multinationals," 21 September 2012, available in French at: www.tresor.economie.gouv.fr/File/375194.

[109] Ibid.

[110] Ibid.

[111] ECCHR, *Forced Labor of Children and Adults in Uzbekistan*, p. 2.

[112] Ibid.

[113] Ibid., p. 3.

union rights."[114] In its response, the French NCP characterized the textile and apparel sector as one geared towards mass consumption and therefore price-sensitive, low value-added and highly labor-intensive.[115] The textile and apparel sector is one where subcontracting is the norm rather than the exception and subcontracting carries the risk of "recourse to informal labour and hidden subcontracting."[116] The French NCP clarified that outsourcing of production by means of subcontracting does not shield a company from responsibility and that responsibility is commensurate with the leverage a company wields through its business relationships.[117] Accordingly, the "activities" of a business enterprise encompass both actions and omissions that might lead to contributing to "an adverse impact actively by causing, facilitating or incentivizing another entity to cause an adverse impact ... [or] passively, through negligence."[118]

The report of the French NCP, however, qualifies responsibility as coming into existence only when there is a "direct link" between the company and the adverse impact that has come about or more clearly, if the company has substantially contributed to this adverse impact.[119] The Italian NCP's report, on the other hand, adopts a more extensive approach to a company's responsibility to use its leverage that is not limited to when the company is or has the risk of contributing directly to an adverse impact. Accordingly, if a company

> identifies a risk of an adverse impact directly linked to the operations, products, and services of an enterprise with which it has a business relationship, and even though it has not caused or contributed to the adverse impact, then it should – on its own or in cooperation with other entities – use its leverage to induce the entity that cause[s] the negative impact to prevent or mitigate it.[120]

According to the recommendations of the Italian NCP, MNEs should first map the structure of their supply chain from their suppliers upstream to their

[114] French NCP, "NCP Report on Implementation of the OECD Guidelines in the Textile and Clothing Sector" (Following a Referral from Nicole Bricq, Minister of Foreign Trade), 2 December 2013, p. 2.

[115] Ibid., p. 17.

[116] Ibid., p. 11.

[117] Ibid., p. 25.

[118] Ibid., p. 26.

[119] Ibid., pp. 20 and 25.

[120] Italian NCP, "Report on Responsible Business Conduct in the Textile and Garment Supply Chain: Recommendations of the Italian NCP on Implementation of the OECD Guidelines for MNEs," 2014, p. 16.

clients downstream in the chain.[121] Within the textile and apparel industry, the Italian NCP pointed to a heightened risk of human rights violations especially of the rights of children and workers as well as to risks of adverse environmental impacts.[122] Because retailers that use subcontractors are aware of the labor-intensive nature of the industry, the French NCP contends that they must also "analyse the regulatory environment, so as to identify risks of non-compliance with OECD Guidelines, international human rights standards and basic ILO norms in the country in question."[123] When subcontracting, these companies need to be mindful of the social context such as standards of living, living costs and other social parameters such as poverty and literacy levels, the political climate of the country and social movements.[124] The two different interpretations of how responsibility may be generated through business relationships demonstrate that there may be considerable divergence in the meaning and content of concepts like "leverage," "business relationship" or "business activity" and the way in which they are applied. Given that the NCPs are left to their own discretion in procedural matters and in giving meaning to the content of the OECD Guidelines in a domestic context, it would not be surprising for companies to be held to different due diligence and responsible business standards in the appraisal of their activities. While the OECD Guidelines themselves do not confine the business responsibility (in the ordinary and non-legal sense) to its direct relationships, the instances demonstrate that their implementation may be subject to more lenient interpretations. As a result, the legal responsibility of cotton trading companies or retailers downstream for knowingly sourcing from a country using forced child labor was not discerned with any consistency by NCPs.

2.2.5 Involvement of Development Finance Institutions and Introduction of International Monitoring

The WB – Rural Enterprise Support Project (RESP)

The WB started funding the Rural Enterprise Support Project Phase II[125] (RESP II) for Uzbekistan in 2008 with the objective "to increase the productivity and financial and environmental sustainability of

[121] Ibid., p. 22.
[122] Ibid., p. 24.
[123] French NCP, "Report on Implementation in the Textile and Clothing Sector," p. 14.
[124] Ibid.
[125] The first phase of the project as the Rural Enterprise Support Project ran between 2001 and 2008 and cost a total of 43.45 million USD. (WB, "Projects & Operations,"

agriculture and the profitability of agribusiness in the project area."[126] The first credit line of approximately 68 million USD was complemented in September 2012 with an additional financing of 40 million USD.[127] On 7 February 2014, WB and Uzbekistan signed an agreement for a 40 million USD loan to be disbursed from the IDA under RESP II.[128]

An April 2013 NGO report pointed to the need for child impact assessments for WBG funded projects.[129] By September 2012, the WB had extended loans totaling USD 25.7 million to 317 agribusinesses in Uzbekistan.[130] The aim of RESP II was to diversify agricultural production to reduce the reliance on cotton as a cash crop by increasing the share of fruits, vegetables and livestock in the country's agriculture sector, and while there was no conclusive evidence to contend that WB funds had been directly used in supporting the practice of forced child labor, NGOs contended that the WB had failed to carry out sufficient due diligence in the planning and approval stages of RESP II.[131] The 2008 Project Appraisal by the WB was based on the Social Assessment undertaken by the Uzbek government, which claimed that children were "not exploited for cotton production" and that the worst forms of child labor were of no concern in rural Uzbekistan.[132] Yet, the appraisal recognized that the labor of children ages twelve to eighteen was used in cotton picking "when districts/provinces [could not] fulfil their plan of cotton picking."[133] The contradictory statements were not scrutinized and the risks arising from forced child labor were not problematized beyond

www.worldbank.org/projects/P046043/rural-enterprise-support-project?lang=en) (accessed 15 April 2019).

126 WB, "Projects & Operations: Project P126962, Abstract," www.worldbank.org/projects/P126962/additional-financing-second rural-enterprise-support-project?lang=en (accessed 15 April 2019).

127 WB Inspection Panel, "Report and Recommendation – Republic of Uzbekistan: Second Rural Enterprise Support Project (P109126) and Additional Financing for Second Rural Enterprise Support Project (P126962), Report No. 83254-UZ," 9 December 2013, p. 2, para. 5.

128 WB, "Press Release – WB Continues Supporting Agricultural Diversification in Uzbekistan," 7 February 2014.

129 BIC and the Human Rights Society of Uzbekistan (Ezgulik), "The Need for Child Impact Assessments: A Case Study of the International Development Association Funded Uzbekistan Rural Enterprise Support Project-Phase II," April 2013.

130 WB, "Press Release – WB Continues Supporting Productivity and Sustainability of Agriculture in Uzbekistan," 11 September 2012.

131 BIC and Ezgulik, "The Need for Child Impact Assessments," p. 4.

132 Ibid., p. 7.

133 Ibid.

a proposal to finance public awareness campaigns to sensitize cotton farmers and the public to the issue of child labor.[134]

Asian Development Bank (ADB) – Amu Bukhara Irrigation System Rehabilitation Project

Amidst concerns about the WB – RESP II, the ADB launched the Modernization and Improved Performance of the Amu Bukhara Irrigation System (ABIS) Rehabilitation Project in Uzbekistan in 2013. The ABIS Rehabilitation Project aimed at upgrading irrigation and water supply infrastructure in Bukhara and two districts in Navoi and was expected to provide irrigation to 6,500 farms as well as drinking water to 725,000 persons.[135]

The project's Concept Note categorized the project safeguards as B for Environment with few site-specific impacts but did not look into any possible links with cotton cultivation, even though the document dates from 2011 when the reports on the use of forced child and adult labor in Uzbekistan's cotton production sector were widely available in media outlets.[136] The due-diligence reporting for the project proposal inspected the "Household and poverty reduction impacts" and "Gender impacts" of the projects in addition to the project's economic, financial and governance aspects.[137] The possible contribution of the project to the on going use of forced labor and child labor in the region was not explicitly explored. Prior to the approval of the project proposal by the ADB Board, civil society called on the ADB to refrain from funding until all concerns about forced and child labor had been adequately addressed.[138] The 220 million USD loan for the six-year long ABIS Rehabilitation Project was approved by the ADB on 25 September 2013. The ADB claimed it had "strong and comprehensive loan covenants to enforce the government's compliance with core labour standards in relation to the project's implementation" as well as the government's firm assurances to respect international labor

[134] Ibid., p. 8.

[135] ADB, "Press Release – ADB $220 Loan to Help Uzbekistan," 25 September 2013.

[136] ADB, Concept Note – Uzbekistan: Amu Bukhara Irrigation System Rehabilitation, 4 November 2011.

[137] ADB, "Proposed Loans – Republic of Uzbekistan: Amu Bukhara Irrigation System Rehabilitation Project, Project Number: 44458-013," August 2013.

[138] HRW, "Letter to the ADB President Mr. Takehiko Nakao: Concerns Regarding Forced Labor in the Modernization and Improved Performance of the Amu Bukhara Irrigation System (ABIS) Project in Uzbekistan," 3 September 2013 and The Cotton Campaign, "Letter to the ADB President Mr. Takehiko Nakao," 11 September 2013.

norms.[139] Civil society continues to be critical of the ADB arguing that the ADB "has only tried to prevent labor abuses in the irrigation project while ignoring forced labor in the fields they water."[140]

Complaint to the WB Inspection Panel and Third-Party Monitoring

A request for inspection of RESP II was filed on 5 September 2013 on several grounds, including lack of due diligence in identifying issues of forced labor in its assessment and in instating adequate measures against WB funds being utilized in lands where forced labor was used.[141]

The Preliminary Observations of the Inspection Panel, released after the Panel carried out a field visit to Uzbekistan, acknowledged that Project documents dating from the Project's early years "appear[ed] to envision more direct support for cotton production" during a period of wide use of forced and child labor and that this support may have been "contributing to the perpetuation of [the] alleged harm."[142] In substantiating the lack of adequate safeguards, the Panel noted that the Social Assessment included only one paragraph on child labor and completely neglected the issue of forced labor.[143] Overall, "significant issues of policy compliance" were raised by the request, including "insufficient due diligence" in the early years of the project.[144]

Prior to the Panel's Final Eligibility Report, WB Management prepared a Progress Report outlining the changes that had been made in response to the request, including the amendment of project documents to "require compliance with the applicable national and international laws and regulations against forced labour, in addition to child labour" and the inclusion of "prohibition of forced labour, in addition to child labour" in the training materials to be

[139] ADB, "ADB $220 Loan to Help Uzbekistan."

[140] Jessica Evans, "Asian Development Bank's Money vs. Its Mouth," *The Huffington Post*, 13 May 2016, www.huffingtonpost.com/jessica-evans/asian-development-banks-m_b_9961464.html (accessed 15 April 2019).

[141] WB Inspection Panel, "Report and Recommendation – Republic of Uzbekistan: Second Rural Enterprise Support Project (P109126) and Additional Financing for Second Rural Enterprise Support Project (P126962), Report No. 83254-UZ," 9 December 2013, paras. 13–15.

[142] Ibid., paras. 79–80.

[143] Ibid., para. 83.

[144] Ibid., para. 93.

provided to farmers.[145] In addition, the Third Party Monitoring (TPM) process had been set up in January 2014 and the task for child labor TPM had been delegated to the ILO. An Inspection Panel delegation conducted a field visit to Uzbekistan on 1–5 December 2014 and met with Uzbek government officials, the requesters, civil society, ILO and UNICEF representatives in the country among others.[146] The Panel found that the government had become more attuned to the issue of child labor in cotton production due, among other things, to the recognition of reputational risks.[147] The Panel had an overwhelming affirmation from different stakeholders that the 2014 harvest was not characterized by a regular use of forced child labor but development partners and civil society representatives stressed that child labor had been replaced by forced adult labor.[148] In conclusion, the Panel determined that the WB Management had taken all reasonable steps to ensure that concerns about child labor and forced labor had been incorporated into the project evaluation and monitoring activities.[149] Overall, the Panel contented itself with an assessment of the progress made after the complaint and chose not to investigate whether the Management had in fact acted negligently or without due diligence in initiating the project.[150] Although the Board of Executive Directors approved the Panel's final recommendation, the US representative issued a separate statement underlining the desirability of a full investigation given that important components of the proposed action plan had not as of yet been assured and were not all under the Management's control.[151] In introducing additional safeguards for upcoming projects, WB only made a reference to Uzbekistan's domestic legislation without referring either to Uzbekistan's commitments under international law, arising from its ratification of numerous human rights and labor conventions, or to Uzbekistan's duty to act in accordance with the aims of the UN, as outlined in the UN Charter Article 55, including the promotion of universal respect and protection of human rights.

[145] Ibid., para. 17.

[146] Ibid., para. 27.

[147] Ibid., para. 27.

[148] WB Inspection Panel, Report No. 93222-UZ, para. 26.

[149] Ibid., para. 36.

[150] Ibid., para. 37.

[151] US Treasury, "US Position: WB Inspection Panel's Report and Recommendation Uzbekistan – Rural Enterprise Support Project Phase II and Additional Financing for the Second Rural Enterprise Support Project," 23 January 2015.

Complaint to the IFC/MIGA Compliance Advisor/ Ombudsman (CAO)

The IFC's investment in the Indorama Kokand Textile company and Hamkor Bank also gave rise to a complaint at the IFC/MIGA CAO, alleging that due diligence to prevent IFC financing from contributing to forced labor had not been adequately undertaken.[152] One of the complainants had allegedly been a forced child laborer from the age of sixteen to eighteen (2013 to 2015), and feared being forced to pick cotton again during the 2016 harvest.[153] The CAO released its assessment report in March 2018, outlining a list of common goals for all stakeholders which included the elimination of the risk of child and forced labor in Uzbekistan's cotton sector, dialogue between the government, IFC, the companies and civil society, and the implementation of the IFC's relevant safeguards.[154] The CAO launched a voluntary dialogue between the claimants and the IFC management based on its dispute resolution function. Results from a first meeting indicated that a risk index developed by the IFC on child and forced labor had begun to be used by the clients in sourcing and portfolio decisions.[155]

The Post-2013 Situation

Faced with the severity of the allegations from international human rights groups and NGOs and struck by the international boycott of Uzbek Cotton, the Uzbek government introduced important legislative changes in 2012–2013 on combating forced labor and the worst forms of child labor and allowed joint ILO-Uzbek monitoring of the cotton harvest in 2013. It also agreed with the resumption of ILO IPEC activities in the domains of capacity building, advocacy, technical assistance and monitoring in Uzbekistan. The ILO-Uzbek joint monitoring mission (11 September–31 October 2013) concluded that child labor only took place to a "limited extent" and forced child labor was not systematically used in the 2013 harvest. Yet, the mission's findings included some

[152] CAO, "Complaint: Uzbekistan: Indorama Kokand/Hamkor Bank-01/Uzbekistan," 30 June 2016, p. 4, www.cottoncampaign.org/uploads/3/9/4/7/39474145/160630cao_submission_ifc-indorama_public_version.pdf (accessed 15 April 2019).

[153] Ibid.

[154] CAO, "CAO Assessment Report: Regarding Complaint in Relation to IFC's Indorama Kokand, Hamkor Equity/SL, Hamkorbank RIs, Hamkorbank SL, GTFP Hamkor," March 2018, p. 10.

[155] CAO, "Meeting Communique: Indorama Kokand/Hamkor Bank-01/Uzbekistan," July 2018.

suspect practices such as deficiencies in "school record keeping, in particular concerning school attendance, the work study programmes, and class schedules."[156] Reports after 2013 pointed to a shift away from using young children as laborers.[157] Instead, the government appeared to have moved the labor burden to secondary school students aged sixteen to eighteen, university students and employees of state-funded organizations and agencies and private businesses.[158] The ILO monitoring mission's scope was limited to the implementation of Convention 182 and could neither "establish or deny reported practices of forced labor of adults."[159]

The CESCR 2014 Concluding Observations raised continuing concern about children's continued involvement in the cotton harvest under hazardous working conditions and the loss of schooling up to two months per year.[160] The Committee pointed to enjoyment of just and favorable conditions of work, protection of children and young persons without discrimination and the right to education.[161] In 2015, the UN Human Rights Committee (HRC) called on Uzbekistan to "put an end to forced labor in the cotton and silk sectors" through enforcement of related legislation, improvement of working and living conditions and the rigorous prosecution of human rights violators.[162] The 2019 monitoring report from the ILO noted that the use of forced and child labor in Uzbekistan had come to an end.[163]

Issues Linked to Ongoing Violations

The use of forced child labor in the Uzbek cotton sector seems, at first glance, a straightforward case where violations can be traced to the

[156] ILO CEACR, "Observation – Worst Forms of Child Labor Convention, 1999 (No. 182) – Uzbekistan, adopted 2013, published 103rd Session of the International Labor Conference – Follow-up to the Conclusions of the Committee on the Application of Standards, International Labor Conference, 102nd Session, June 2013," 2014.

[157] HRW, "Press Release – Uzbekistan: Forced Labor Widespread in Cotton Harvest."

[158] UGFHR, "Executive Summary," in UGFHR, Human Rights Due Diligence and World Bank Funding in Uzbekistan's Agricultural Sector, June 2014, p. 7.

[159] ILO CEACR, "Application of International Labour Standards 2014 (I) Report III (Part IA), International Labour Conference 103rd Session," p. 172.

[160] CESCR, "Concluding Observations on the Second Periodic Report of Uzbekistan," E/C.12/UZB/CO/2, 13 June 2014, para. 19.

[161] Ibid., para. 19.

[162] HR Committee, "Concluding Observations 2015: Uzbekistan," CCPR/C/UZB/CO/4, 8–9 July 2015, para. 19.

[163] ILO, "Third-Party Monitoring of Measures Against Child Labour and Forced Labour During the 2018 Cotton Harvest in Uzbekistan," 2019.

conduct of the domestic state. In fact, the state's conduct has played both a necessary and a sufficient role in the wrongdoing. Whether it has tacitly encouraged, outright permitted or turned a blind eye to the use of forced child labor in cotton cultivation, the Uzbek State has breached its obligations under ILO Conventions 138 and 182 as well as under the CRC to protect children in addition to failing to uphold its own domestic laws and regulations. Exercising effective control in its territory and keeping a tight grip on the centrally organized export-oriented domestic cotton market, Uzbekistan is the primary duty-bearer as regards children's rights in its cotton sector. Yet, it is also a case of state unwillingness to comply with its obligations. There are a number of other influential actors whose actions or failures to act bore heavily on whether children's rights violations continued to take place as well as on whether the unwilling domestic state could have been encouraged or compelled to live up to its obligations under international human rights and labor law.

In the Uzbek case, the decision of textile retailers to boycott Uzbek cotton, persistent civil society criticism of the development financing extended to the agricultural sector as well as the media attention have resulted in children being pulled off the fields in the face of mounting pressure and further reputational risks for Uzbekistan. Accordingly, businesses involved down the supply chain may effectively play roles in protecting children's rights in countries where they operate, even from the state itself. It is, of course, hotly debated whether they are under a legal obligation to do so based fundamentally on the fact that they have the capacity and leverage to do so.

The questions about responsibility are even more complex. Businesses sourcing Uzbek cotton do not directly have a causal effect on the commission of the children's rights violations. They might have played necessary but insufficient roles individually in the continuation of the practice of forced child labor over the years. Yet, there was no concerted action on the part of these various actors in facilitating the wrongdoing. In summary, the decision of various companies to continue trading in or sourcing from Uzbekistan has contributed to the Uzbek State's continuing or ongoing violation of children's rights. Both ARSIWA Article 14 and its sister provision in ARIO (Article 12) refer to "Extension in time of the breach of an international obligation" and distinguish continuing violations from completed ones.[164] Accordingly, it is not the ongoing

[164] ILC, ARSIWA, Art. 14 Commentary, para. 2 and Art. 12.

effects of a violation but the ongoing nature of the violating conduct (act or omission) that defines a violation as continuing.

The notion of "continuing violation" has featured in the jurisprudence of regional courts such as the ECtHR and the IACtHR as well as that of the HRC. The European Court used the doctrine of "continuing violations" in *Papamichalopoulos, Agrotexim and Loizidou* to overcome *rationae temporis* restrictions that would have otherwise impeded it from rendering a judgment, given that the initial events in question had taken place during a period when the competence of the Court had either not been accepted or was contested.[165] United States Courts have also frequently referred to "continuing violations" in overriding the statute of limitations, particularly in discrimination cases based among others on allegations of a "persistent ongoing pattern" of conduct.[166] The characterization of a continuing violation as a persistent ongoing pattern fits squarely with how forced labor was mobilized annually in the Uzbek cotton harvest.

2.3 Case 2: Mineral Extraction and Trade in the Democratic Republic of Congo

2.3.1 Democratic Republic of Congo (DRC): Mineral Extraction, Conflict and Children

The issue of children's rights in mineral supply chains is a complex but important one. Depending on the local context, mining activities may also be linked to armed conflict, involuntary resettlement, environmental degradation, employment of children in hazardous work under conditions harmful to their wellbeing or sexual exploitation. Especially when mineral extraction takes place in conflict-affected zones, it is difficult to distinguish the effects of mining from those of conflict on children and their rights. Even when armed groups do not control or are not present in mining sites, the broader effects of the conflict in areas surrounding mining sites may mean that children have limited or no access to educational opportunities, healthcare services or childcare.

[165] ECtHR, *Papamichalopoulos and Others* v. *Greece*, Application no.14556/89, Judgment, 24 June 1993, para. 40; ECtHR, *Agrotexim and Others* v. *Greece*, no. 14807/89, Judgment (Merits), 24 October 1995, paras. 57–58, ECtHR, *Loizidou* v. *Turkey*, para. 41.

[166] Joseph C. O'Keefe and Daniel L. Saperstein, "Third Circuit 'Clarifies' Continuing Violation Doctrine," *Proskauer Client Alert*, 22 February 2013, www.proskauer.com/publications/client-alert/third-circuit-clarifies-continuing-violation-doctrine/ (accessed 15 April 2019).

A study was commissioned by UNICEF on children's rights and the mining sector in the wake of the launch of the CRBPs.[167] The empirical part of the study was confined to the formal and large-scale mining sector and several potential impacts, either direct or indirect, of mining activities on children were identified, including issues related to conflict, environmental degradation, labor-related impacts, safety and security around mining areas, migration into the mining region as well as land tenure and involuntary resettlement issues.[168] Artisanal and small-scale mining (ASM) activities were seen as correlated to large-scale mining as the introduction of mining activities in a region was in general a precursor to ASM, which occupied abandoned mining sites as well as nonoperational downstream areas.[169] The risks that ASM poses to children were identified as the use of child labor and corresponding loss of education, health and safety risks, risks of sexual exploitation and violence, and recruitment into armed conflict in conflict zones.[170]

The DRC is often cited as a traditional case for the so-called resource curse,[171] being stage to what is called the "world's bloodiest conflict since World War II" with more than five million casualties as well as millions of women and girls reportedly sexually abused.[172] Eastern DRC, where the internal conflict involving the state and numerous NSAs is fervently ongoing, is a hotbed for the mining of a number of commercially important minerals, including the 3 TG (tin, tantalum and tungsten and gold). The DRC is also rich in other deposits, including copper, manganese, lead, zinc as well as diamonds and semi-precious stones such as tourmaline. While some minerals such as copper are mined industrially,[173] so-called conflict minerals of 3TG are exploited largely through informal artisanal mining.[174]

[167] UNICEF, "Children's Rights and the Mining Sector: UNICEF Extractive Pilot," March 2015.

[168] Ibid., p. 7.

[169] Ibid., p. 16.

[170] Ibid.

[171] Nadira Lalji, "The Resource Curse Revised: Conflict and Coltan in the Congo," *Harvard International Review*, Fall 2007, 34; www.globalpolicy.org/the-dark-side-of-natural-resources-st/water-in-conflict/40150.html (accessed 15 April 2019).

[172] BBC Website, "DR Congo: Cursed by Its Natural Wealth," 9 October 2013, www.bbc.com/news/magazine-24396390 (accessed 15 April 2019).

[173] For an overview of major players in DRC's copper sector, see: Mbendi Information Services, "Copper Mining in Democratic Republic of The Congo," www.mbendi.com/indy/ming/cppr/af/zr/p0005.htm (accessed 15 April 2019).

[174] Ken Matthysen and Andres Zaragoza Montejano, "Conflict Minerals Initiatives in DR Congo: Perceptions of Local Mining Communities," IPIS, November 2013, p. 8.

The trade in minerals from eastern DRC is long documented to have provided fighting parties with the rationale and financial resources to continue threatening violence in sight of lucrative earnings from the exploitation of mineral resources.[175] Of course, the conflict in the DRC had started long before the utilization of minerals from the region for economic profits. An ethnographic study from 2000 to 2002 concluded that the stalemate in the conflict in eastern DRC resulted in the "commoditisation of war" through a "war economy."[176] Some features of this war economy included the domination of mineral extraction by the military as well as other armed actors, a sustained conflict in eastern DRC on the back of mineral exploitation profits, forced and prisoner labor in mines controlled by armed actors (state and non-state), while other effects included adverse impacts on agricultural production and animal husbandry, destruction of infrastructure and increased sexual violence.[177] The resulting militarization of mineral mining in eastern DRC is allegedly thwarting efforts to end the armed conflict through a security system reform, including by integrating both pro- and anti-government armed groups into the regular Congolese army.[178]

Portraying the links between mineral exploitation and armed groups as direct and unitary in their rationale may distort the reality where a plethora of motivations and relationships exist.[179] Accordingly, "activities that relate to the production, mobilisation and allocation of economic resources aimed at waging and sustaining war" should be distinguished from labor or trading activities taking place in the informal sector.[180] In addition, armed groups may use wildly different tactics of resource exploitation. The inexistence of effective governance mechanisms in eastern DRC creates fertile ground for non-state

[175] UN Panel of Experts on the Illegal Exploitation of Natural Resources and Other Forms of Wealth of the DRC, "2002 Report," S/2002/1146, 8 October 2002, pp. 6–7.

[176] Stephen Jackson, "Fortunes of War: The Coltan Trade in the Kivus," Background research for HPG Report 13, Overseas Development Institute, February 2003, pp. 3–4.

[177] Jackson, "Fortunes of War: The Coltan Trade in the Kivus," p. 4.

[178] Jeroen Cuvelier, "Introduction" in Jeroen Cuvelier (ed.), *The Complexity of Resource Governance in a Context of State Fragility: The Case of Eastern DRC, IPIS and International Alert*, November 2010, p. 10.

[179] Rachel Perks and Koen Vlassenroot, "From Discourse to Practice: A Sharper Perspective on the Relationship Between Minerals and Violence in DR Congo," Cuvelier (ed.), *The Complexity of Resource Governance in a Context of State Fragility: The Case of Eastern DRC*, IPIS and International Alert, November 2010, p. 65.

[180] Ibid., pp. 65–66.

armed groups as well as "rogue" groups from Congolese armed forces to run exploitative mechanisms.[181] There is thus a dual impact on children: the impact of mineral extraction as an industry and the impact of armed conflict.

2.3.2 *Children's Rights in Eastern DRC*

Impact of Mining on Children

The presence of children in the mining sector in the DRC is a well-recognized and widespread phenomenon. In 2008, the WB estimated that 40 percent of the population at mining sites were children either working as miners themselves or present as family members of miners.[182] These children were usually unable to access schooling either because schools did not exist or because they were not in the proximity and families did not have childcare options as all family members were working.[183] Later confirmed by a 2011 International Trade Union Confederation (ITUC) report, children were involved in mining sites in mining, picking, sorting, processing, transportation and trading of minerals in hazardous or harmful conditions, trading of other goods in mines and providing services in mines, including in prostitution.[184] According to the ITUC, although the domestic legislation foresees penalties ranging from ten to twenty years of imprisonment for trafficking or sexual exploitation of children, there was no evidence that these laws are effectively enforced.[185] Again, despite legislation in place against child labor in line with ILO standards, the ILO Committee of Experts noted that hazardous child labor in mines has remained an issue of concern.[186] A 2016 NGO report on cobalt trade in the DRC noted that because the government of the DRC restricted artisanal mining in most mining sites with the 2002 Mining Code and made these available to industrial and semi-industrial mining, "most artisanal miners end[ed] up working in unauthorized and unregulated areas or trespassing on land controlled

[181] Ibid., p. 66.

[182] WB, "DRC Growth with Governance in the Mining Sector," Report No. 43402-ZR, May 2008, p. 58.

[183] Ibid.

[184] PACT, "PROMINES Study: Artisanal Mining in the DRC," June 2010, pp. 90–91 and ITUC, "Violence Against Women in Eastern DRC: Whose Responsibility? Whose Complicity?," November 2011, p. 20.

[185] ILO CEACR, "Report of the Committee of Experts on the Application of Conventions and Recommendations," 100th Session, 2011, p. 313.

[186] Ibid., p. 314.

by industrial mining companies."[187] Although laborers in cobalt mines were mostly adult men, children went through the tailings discarded from industrial mines, washed and sorted the ore.[188] Some of the interviewed children had also been working in the mines carrying loads (during weekends and school holidays for those attending school and all year round for others).[189] For children whose parents did not have formal employment and could not afford school fees, working in mines was the only option.[190] Adult workers were not forthcoming with information about children working in the mining sector as most were under the impression that it was illegal for children to do so, even though the Congolese mining law of 2002 allows children over the age of fifteen to work in jobs that are not physically harmful. According to the report by Harvard Humanitarian Initiative and the WB, this led to children being marginalized alongside women in "underpaid secondary employment."[191] There were also accounts of children who worked in mines to extract cassiterite being cheated out of their pay by adults who impounded these minerals.[192]

The presence of armed groups in mining sites is an additional issue that puts children's rights in and around mining sites in peril. This is especially true for areas in DRC where the ores of 3TG are located. Field research undertaken in eastern DRC by International Peace Information Service (IPIS) mapping different mining sites has shown that the presence of armed groups (either units from within the Congolese Army [FARDC] ranks lacking discipline or non-state armed groups) was stronger in gold mining sites followed by cassiterite (chief ore of tin) mining sites than in others but tended to be occasional.[193] The most salient issues linked to an armed group presence included illegal taxation, purchasing of minerals, forced labor and pillaging.

[187] African Resources Watch (Afrewatch) and Amnesty International, "'This Is What We Die For': Human Rights Abuses in the Democratic Republic of the Congo Power the Global Trade in Cobalt," 2016, p. 5.

[188] Ibid.

[189] Ibid., p. 6.

[190] Ibid.

[191] Harvard Humanitarian Initiative and WBG, "Ressources et ingéniosité: genre, droits de l'homme, et resilience dans certaines centres miniers artisanales a l'est de la République Démocratique du Congo," July 2015, p. 38.

[192] Ibid., p. 16.

[193] IPIS, "Infographic – Mapping Mining Areas in Eastern DRC," www.ipisresearch.be/mapping/webmapping/drcongo/v5/#-3/28/5/2/1/ (accessed 15 April 2019).

Impact of Conflict on Children

The human rights situation in eastern DRC remains very precarious with a number of ongoing systematic human rights violations clearly and consistently documented. The UNSC's Group of Experts on the DRC reported in 2018 that the major human rights violations continued in the areas of recruitment and use of child soldiers in human rights violations and sexual violence.[194]

Children in eastern DRC are both directly and indirectly affected by the violent conflict between numerous armed groups. In fact, DRC has been a site of the "Six Grave Violations" of children's rights in conflict, which include killing and maiming of children, recruitment or use of children as soldiers, sexual violence against children, attacks against schools or hospitals, denial of humanitarian access for children and abduction of children.[195] The report of the UN Secretary General on children and armed conflict found that from 2016 to 2018, the "verified cases of the recruitment and use of children" in the armed conflict in the DRC had doubled to 1,049 children, more than half of which were recruited in the mineral-rich region of North Kivu and another third in the Kasais. In addition, attacks in schools and hospitals had increased approximately eightfold due to an outbreak of violence in the region of Kasai. In 2017, verified accounts pointed to 156 children killed, 178 children maimed, 181 children (179 girls and 2 boys) victims of rape and sexual violence and 420 children (143 girls and 277 boys) abducted. Also reported were 396 attacks on schools and 119 attacks on hospitals as well as 8 cases of denial of humanitarian access.[196]

Children's Rights Violations Linked to Mining in Eastern DRC

The most evident connection of mining activities to children's rights is the presence of children in mining sites and the use of child labor, resulting in economic exploitation. Mining activities in the DRC have been linked to breaches of children's other rights, including the right to education and health. The ongoing conflict has additionally created

194 UNSC Group of Experts on the DRC, "Midterm Report of the Group of Experts on the Democratic Republic of the Congo," 18 December 2018, published on 31 December 2018, S/2018/1133, pp. 8, 14–16.

195 Office of the SRSG for Children and Armed Conflict, "The Six Grave Violations Against Children During Armed Conflict: The Legal Foundation," Working Paper No. 1, October 2009 (updated November 2013).

196 UNGA/UNSC, "Children and Armed Conflict: Report of the SG," A/72/865–S/2018/465, 16 May 2018, paras. 6, 62–68.

conditions detrimental to the right to life, survival and development of the child, while exacerbating difficulties in accessing education, healthcare and conditions favorable to a child's mental and physical development.

The CRC Committee's 2009 Concluding Observations noted that "child workers as young as five years old" had been found "working in dangerous conditions in the mining industry, particularly in the Katanga region."[197] The 2015 findings of the US DoL concerning the worst forms of child labor indicated that children continued to be engaged in the "mining of gold, cassiterite (tin ore), coltan (tantalum ore), and wolframite (tungsten ore)."[198] Although the DRC's mining legislation prohibits young children from engaging in artisanal mining as workers, as many as 19,000–30,000 children under the age of fifteen were reported as participating in mining in the DRC's Copperbelt, making up almost a third of the workforce.[199] Engaging in artisanal mining activities were linked to the motivation to pay school fees, with children using time before or after school and on the weekends and holidays.[200] The CRC Committee's 2017 Concluding Observations indicated that not much had changed with respect to the exploitation of children in hazardous labor in the mining sector, particularly in the east of the country and called on the DRC to "take measures to investigate, prosecute and punish those who are responsible, as well as raise public awareness of the harmful effects" of child labor.[201] Additionally, sexual exploitation and abuse, especially of girl children, were reported in and around mining sites, where girl children were induced into involuntary prostitution.[202] Reports have pointed to the commercial sexual abuse of girl children taking place in conditions akin to sex slavery.[203]

[197] CRC Committee, "Concluding Observations 2009: DRC," para. 80.

[198] US DoL, 2015 Findings on the Worst Forms of Child Labor: Democratic Republic of the Congo, www.dol.gov/sites/default/files/images/ilab/child-labor/CongoDemocraticRepublic.pdf (accessed 15 April 2019).

[199] Nicolas Tsurukawa, Siddharth Prakash and Andreas Manhart, "Social Impacts of Artisanal Cobalt Mining in Katanga, DRC," November 2011, 31–32, www.oeko.de/oekodoc/1294/2011-419-en.pdf (accessed 15 April 2019).

[200] PACT, "PROMINES Study: Artisanal Mining in the DRC," p. 92.

[201] CRC Committee, "Concluding Observations on the Combined Third to Fifth Periodic Reports of the Democratic Republic of the Congo," CRC/C/COD/CO/3-5, 28 February 2017, para. 42.

[202] ITUC, "Violence Against Women in Eastern DRC," p. 21.

[203] Free the Slaves, "The Congo Report: Slavery in Conflict Minerals," June 2011, pp. 17–18.

The impact of the ongoing conflict on children in the DRC, especially in the eastern provinces, is most drastically observed in the violations to children's right to life, survival and development. The CRC Committee's 2017 Concluding Observations noted that grave violations against children, including killing, maiming and abduction, continued to be committed both by state armed forces and non-state armed groups.[204] In addition to these grave violations alongside "violence, rape, sexual and commercial exploitation," the continued conflict had also been further limiting the "already weak [education, healthcare and social care] services."[205] Both the DRC's armed forces FARDC and non-state armed groups are implicated in the violations of the right to life, survival and development of children.

The most pressing problems surrounding the right to education in mining regions of eastern DRC include availability and accessibility. Field research based on interviews has shown there to be a link between work in the mines and school attendance with many children working in the mines having dropped out of school and others going to school working at least part-time in the mines. Many children cited inability to afford school fees as an obstacle for attending school although the causal relationship between "working in mines, school attendance and inability to pay school fees could not be determined with certainty."[206] The CRC Committee's 2017 Concluding Observations noted that the children suffered from low primary school attendance rates as primary education in the country was not "genuinely free," and school drop-out rates were high "due to excessive costs, early marriage and fear of violence, especially in conflict affected areas of the country."[207] In addition, attacks against schools, students and teachers as well as the use of schools for military purposes continue to take place in conflict-affected areas in the DRC.

The environmental impacts of the mining practices result in the pollution of water, soil and air. There are also health and safety dangers to children working or being present in mining sites, particularly through exposure to dust and chemicals.[208] In addition, access to even most basic healthcare services is heavily crippled in eastern DRC due to the effects of

[204] CRC Committee, "Concluding Observations 2017: DRC," para. 17(a).
[205] Ibid.
[206] World Vision RDC, "Les enfants travaillant dans les mines s'expriment," pp. 5–6.
[207] CRC Committee, "Concluding Observations 2017: DRC," para. 39.
[208] UNICEF, "Children's Rights and the Mining Sector," p. 13.

the conflict.[209] The CRC Committee's 2017 Concluding Observations expressed grave concern with regard to the situation of healthcare services and access to healthcare in the country due to poor infrastructure, poor quality of services and lack of qualified medical personnel, resulting in high levels of malnutrition and insufficient vaccination among other issues. To remedy the situation, the CRC Committee called on the state to "[i]ncrease its allocation of resources for primary health care to make it both accessible and affordable" and to "[s]eek financial and technical assistance" from UNICEF and WHO.[210]

The CRC prohibits the recruitment of children under the age of fifteen into a state's armed forces and requires all states parties to "take all feasible measures" to ensure that children under that age "do not take a direct part in hostilities."[211] Moreover, CRC-OPAC increases the age threshold of direct involvement in hostilities and compulsory recruitment to eighteen.[212] In addition, state parties are required to take measures to protect children affected by armed conflict, even if they are not linked to armed groups.[213] In 2009, the DRC government enacted a law criminalizing the recruitment and use of children (defined as persons below the age of eighteen) in armed conflict with a penalty of ten to twenty years of imprisonment.[214] An action plan was signed with the UN in October 2012 to prohibit and prevent the recruitment and use of children in armed conflict and sexual violence against children by state armed forces FARDC.[215] In September 2015, a roadmap for the implementation of this action plan was adopted.[216] However, the UN Organization Stabilization Mission in the DRC (MONUSCO) documented that, despite this law, 9,276 children were recruited into

[209] Chris Bird, "The Hard Road to Healthcare for Eastern Congo's Poor," *Guardian*, 10 April 2012, www.theguardian.com/global-development/poverty-matters/2012/apr/10/hard-road-healthcare-congo-poor (accessed 15 April 2019); Luc Malemo Kalisya et al., "The State of Emergency Care in Democratic Republic of Congo" (2015) 5(4) *African Journal of Emergency Medicine* 153–158.

[210] CRC Committee, "Concluding Observations 2017: DRC," para. 35(a) and (f).

[211] CRC, Art., 38.3 and 38.2, respectively.

[212] CRC-OPAC, Arts. 1–2 and 4.

[213] CRC, Art. 38.4.

[214] DRC, "Loi No. 09/001 du 10 Janvier 2009 Portant Protection de l'Enfant," Arts. 71 and 187, respectively.

[215] Office of the SRSG for Children and Armed Conflict, "DRC Factsheet 2016," September 2016, https://childrenandarmedconflict.un.org/wp-content/uploads/2016/02/DRC-Fact-Sheet-September-2016.pdf.

[216] Office of the SRSG for Children and Armed Conflict, "DRC Factsheet 2016."

armed groups in the DRC between 2008 and 2014.[217] Although denied by DRC authorities, UN sources have consistently confirmed the recruitment of children by the DRC's armed forces as well.[218] In addition, sexual abuse, sexual exploitation and forced marriages of girl children both by members of the armed forces, police or state intelligence agencies and by members of different non-state armed groups constitute serious violations of children's rights. The CRC Committee's 2012 Concluding Observations on OPAC highlighted "[t]he use of children as human shields, as bodyguards for army commanders, as sexual slaves and for committing the most serious human rights abuses, including massacres and mass rapes" alongside "deliberate attacks of schools and hospitals" among the worst children's rights violations taking place in eastern DRC.[219] The CRC Committee noted that "little priority ha[d] been given to the establishment of effective law enforcement mechanisms to investigate, convict or sanction those responsible for grave violations against children."[220] Although the provisions of the Child Protection Code are in line with the relevant protections under the CRC, their implementation is another matter entirely.

The indirect results of the ongoing armed conflict in eastern DRC include one of the world's lowest life expectancy rates, lack of access to most basic healthcare, outbreaks of disease and epidemics, increase in infant and maternal mortality rates[221] as well as loss of livelihoods and lack of access to education.[222] The direct impact of mining activities has further jeopardized the right to health and education of children, while resulting in violations of protection from economic and sexual exploitation. The CRC Committee's GC 15 notes that "States should regulate and monitor the environmental impact of business activities that may compromise children's right to health, food security and access to safe drinking water and to

[217] UNSC, "Midterm Report of the Group of Experts on the DRC," S/2015/797, 16 October 2015, para. 104.

[218] CRC Committee, "Concluding Observations – OPAC: DRC," paras. 30–32.

[219] Ibid., para. 8.

[220] Ibid., para. 34.

[221] Medecins Sans Frontières, "DRC: Condition Still Critical," 18 November 2011, www.msf.org/en/article/democratic-republic-congo-condition-still-critical (accessed 15 April 2019).

[222] WBG, "Rebuilding Lives and Infrastructure in Eastern DRC," 11 February 2014, www.worldbank.org/en/news/feature/2014/02/11/rebuilding-lives-and-infrastructure-in-eastern-drc (accessed 15 April 2019).

sanitation."[223] In practice, however, the fragility of the political and security situation in eastern DRC and the lack of capacity on the part of the central government create de facto impediments, render rights moot unless human rights obligations (for both the rights of children and of adults) are also incumbent upon other relevant actors perpetrating or contributing to violations. This is a broader issue beyond the situation of eastern DRC, in all cases where the domestic state is either unable or unwilling to live up to its human rights obligations. In this regard, businesses have a due diligence obligation to respect human rights, which extends to "identify[ing], prevent[ing] and mitigate[ing] their negative impact on children's right to health including across their business relationships and within any global operations."[224] Furthermore, respecting children's right to health means that businesses should not employ children under hazardous labor conditions and respect minimum age standards.[225]

Businesses involved in the mining sector in DRC are usually not directly involved in the violations of children's right to life, survival and development. Many businesses sourcing 3TG from artisanal mines do not have a direct relationship to children as laborers nor do they directly cause the pollution in and around mining sites. Yet, the supply chain relationships would have to be subject to scrutiny under a business's due diligence duty. In addition, if sourcing from conflict-affected artisanal mines in the DRC does in fact perpetuate the conflict by providing rationale and resources for continued fighting, serious questions about complicity are raised.

Domestic Legislation and International Commitments

The DRC is party to the CRC, OPAC and OPSC as well as ILO Conventions 138 and 182. Over time, domestic legislation regarding children's rights has been brought largely in line with international standards.

The DRC's Constitution, Child Protection Code and Labor Code are the most important legislative frameworks containing protections for children's rights. Article 41 of the Constitution of the DRC prohibits all mistreatment of and violence against children and declares child exploitation punishable by law. In this respect, public authorities have an

[223] CRC Committee, GC 15, para. 49.
[224] Ibid., para. 80.
[225] Ibid., para. 81.

obligation to ensure the protection of children that find themselves in difficult conditions and to bring those responsible for or complicit in violence against children before the law.[226] According to Article 42 of the Constitution, public authorities have an obligation to protect youth from all infringements to health, education and full development.[227] The Constitution also guarantees the right to education through schooling and designates primary education as compulsory and free of charge in public institutions.[228] The child's right to education and the provision of compulsory free primary education are reiterated in the Child Protection Code.[229] The National Education Law further designates primary education and general secondary education (the first two years of secondary school) as fundamental education.[230] In order to achieve the goal of fundamental education for all, National Education Law places a threefold obligation on the state to "[g]uarantee compulsory and free primary education" including by dedicating adequate resources, to "[e]nsure the democratization of education" by making it accessible to all, and to promote holistic education including physical, non-formal education, fight against sexual violence, diseases such as HIV/AIDS and use of national/local languages.[231]

The DRC's Child Protection Code sets the minimum age of employment at sixteen and prohibits the worst forms of child labor, defined in line with ILO Convention 182.[232] The Code accords children protection from all forms of violence and exploitation, including economic exploitation[233] as well as from all forms of sexual abuse, sexual exploitation and violence.[234] The Child Protection Code also protects the child's right to a healthy environment that is favorable to thriving, including rights to sporting, cultural, manual and recreational activities.[235] After the DRC's ratification of ILO Conventions 138 and 182 in 2001, the 2002 Labor Code was instated to increase the minimum age for entry into

226 Constitution of the DRC, Kinshasa, February 2006, Art. 41.
227 Ibid., Art. 42.
228 Ibid., Art. 43.
229 DRC, "Loi n° 09/001 du 10 janvier 2009 portant protection de l'enfant," Art. 38 (translated from original text in French).
230 DRC, "Loi-Cadre n° 14/004 du 11 Février 2014 de L'Enseignement National," Preamble and Art. 10.
231 Ibid., Art. 12.
232 DRC, "Loi n° 09/001," Arts. 50 and 53, respectively.
233 Ibid., Arts. 57–58.
234 Ibid., Arts. 60–61.
235 Ibid., Art. 44.

employment to sixteen years of age and to address issues of the worst forms of child labor, including through the creation of a National Committee to this end.[236] In 2017, the DRC's Ministry of Mining published the 2017–2025 National Sectorial Strategy to Fight against Child Labor in artisanal and the areas around artisanal mines in the DRC.[237]

2.3.3 Involvement of Businesses in Mineral Extraction and Trade

There are several levels at which businesses are involved in the mining sector in the DRC: industrial mining, smelting, processing, manufacturing of intermediate parts and sourcing of intermediate mineral goods to produce consumer goods. Usually, only mining and smelting companies operate within the DRC, whereas companies that buy to trade minerals and those down the supply chain using minerals in their manufacturing processes operate from and are headquartered in other states. In many cases, the links between the mining process and the smelting, trading or manufacturing processes are not direct or clear. In fact, the structure of supply chains depends on the mineral. Minerals used in consumer electronics such as the 3Ts or cobalt have more tiered supply chains whereas gold supply chains may or may not involve as many levels, depending on whether the gold is used in the manufacturing of electric circuits or jewelry.

Mineral Supply Chains and Traceability

The 3T supply chains are complex. The minerals move through many territorial jurisdictions, handled by different business enterprises incorporated in various countries. According to the Enough Project, the minerals that are mined in eastern DRC are first transported or smuggled into bordering countries of Rwanda, Uganda and Burundi.[238] From there, they are sold to smelters and refiners in East Asia, particularly to Malaysia, Thailand and China to be processed into metals. Using the processed metals, manufacturers in East Asia and Europe produce plates, capacitors and solders, which are then used in circuit boards of modern

236 CRC Committee, "Concluding Observations 2009: DRC," CRC/C/COD/CO/2, 10 February 2009, para. 80.

237 DRC, "Strategie Nationale Sectorielle de Lutte Contre Le Travail des Enfants dans les Mines Artisanales et sur les Sites Minières Artisanaux en République Démocratique du Congo 2017–2025," Kinshasa, August 2017.

238 The Enough Project, "A Comprehensive Approach to Congo's Conflict Minerals," April 2009, p. 4.

electronics.[239] For gold, the most obvious destination is the United Arab Emirates' (UAE) trade center Dubai. As Dubai Multi Commodities Centre (DMCC) boasts, Dubai is nicknamed the City of Gold where approximately 25 percent of the global gold trade takes place.[240] According to one NGO account, despite the stricter import requirements that have been put in place in the UAE, gold from the DRC and neighboring countries continues to enter the inventories of audited DMCC gold refiners "misrepresented as scrap gold or as mined gold from another country" and this gold is more likely to be used in the jewelry sector or exported to trading partners such as India.[241] In fact, even though the international certification and traceability schemes and reporting regulation have helped curb the militarization of 3T mines, the situation is seen less promising in the case of artisanal gold mining.[242] Because gold is very high in value and easy to smuggle across borders, it has reportedly become a preferred mineral for the exploitation of the informal sector. The 2015 UN Group of Experts report noted the lack of effective due diligence and traceability mechanisms for the gold sector, allowing gold mined in eastern DRC to make its way to international supply chains through Uganda and the UAE.[243]

Various sectors in manufacturing use 3TG, including consumer goods (electronics, leisure goods, food, jewelry), healthcare, automotive, aerospace and chemicals.[244] Technology companies are the last link down the supply chain and purchase treated minerals from trading companies as intermediate goods to produce final goods sold directly to consumers. These companies are those most susceptible to pressure from end-users who are usually retail customers. Smelting or trading companies, on the other hand, may escape the same level of scrutiny even if their profits from mining are much larger and their links to hazardous mining practices more direct. An account of the mineral supply chains from

239 Ibid.

240 DMCC Website, "Gold," www.dmcc.ae/gateway-to-trade/commodities/gold (accessed 19 February 2019).

241 Partnership Africa Canada, "All that Glitters Is Not Gold: Dubai, Congo and the Illicit Trade of Conflict Minerals," May 2014, p. 15.

242 OECD, "Mineral Supply Chains and Conflict Links in Eastern DRC: Five Years of Implementing Supply Chain Due Diligence," 2015, pp. 21–22.

243 UNSC Group of Experts on the DRC, "Final report," p. 39, para. 190.

244 Michael Strohmer, "Conflict Minerals: Yet Another Supply Chain Challenge," A.T. Kearney, June 2012, www.atkearney.com/metals-mining/featured-article/-/asset_publisher/S5UkO0zy0vnu/content/conflict-minerals-yet-another-supply-chain-challenge/10192 (accessed 15 April 2019).

the viewpoint of companies selling to end users demonstrates the complexities:

> [A] company would need to sift through 35 manufacturers, 60 to 80 parts suppliers, more than 1,000 commodity parts suppliers, and an unknown number of distributors to get to all of its sources. Because only very small quantities of conflict minerals are typically integrated into any given product, traceability is even more difficult. For example, a 2-kilogram (4.5 pound) laptop contains 10 grams of tin, 0.6 grams of tantalum, 0.3 grams of gold, and 0.0009 grams of tungsten. Smelters, where metals of diverse origins come together to be processed, have been identified as the crucial traceability point. Fortunately, the number of smelters within the overall supply network is still manageable.[245]

The critical point in the supply chain is arguably the smelters, from which point onwards it becomes more difficult to ensure complete traceability.

2.3.4 *Children's Rights and Business in the DRC Case*

The children's rights obligations that are construed in relation to mineral extraction and trade in conflict-affected zones such as the extraction of the 3TG in eastern DRC stem not only from the so-called soft-law normative frameworks on business and human rights but also from harder legal obligations in the form of home state regulation with extra-territorial effects. In addition, businesses operating in weak governance zones may incur duties beyond simply complying with the domestic law in the context of avoiding complicity.[246]

Applicable Soft Norms and Standards

Avoiding Complicity The debate about business activity in weak governance zones or conflict-affected areas inevitably extends to considerations of complicity. The issue of complicity has been treated in the UNGPs in relation to business responsibility with respect to action regarding conflict zones. The UNGPs use the avoidance of complicity as a benchmark to guide businesses in their activities or operations taking place in conflict-affected zones. The UNGPs refer both to risk management and to complicity issues with regard to due diligence when companies are engaged in practices that may result in potential human rights violations in all situations.[247] In addition, when businesses are unable to

245 Ibid.

246 Backer, "Corporate Social Responsibility in Weak Governance Zones," pp. 300–301.

247 UNGPs, Principle 17 "Commentary."

discharge of their respect duties fully due to the domestic context, there is an expectation on businesses to respect international human rights standards to the "greatest extent possible in the circumstances" and make demonstrable efforts in doing so.[248] Accordingly,

> Business enterprises should treat th[e] risk [of complicity in gross human rights abuses] as a legal compliance issue, given the expanding web of potential corporate legal liability arising from extraterritorial civil claims, and from the incorporation of the provisions of the Rome Statute of the International Criminal Court in jurisdictions that provide for corporate criminal responsibility.
>
> (Commentary, Guiding Principle 23)

The heightened risk of human rights abuses in conflict-affected zones means that states are under an obligation to assist business enterprises in "identify[ing], prevent[ing] and mitigat[ing] the human rights related risks of their activities and business relationships" as well as assess heightened risks of abuses.[249] In addition, when businesses are "involved with gross human rights abuses" and do not demonstrate intent to address such situations, states are to deny public support and services to such businesses.[250] The UNGPs also recognize an additional role for home states and neighboring states to play in conflict-affected zones where the domestic state may be unable to provide an adequate level of human rights protection with respect to the activities of TNCs.[251] This role is described as "assisting both those corporations and host states to ensure that businesses are not involved with human rights abuse," although the question of what this assistance should consist of at a minimum has not been clarified.[252] Likewise, the OECD Guidelines stress that corporate entities "should respect the standards of international humanitarian law" in order to guide them to address and avoid risks that may result in negative human rights impacts.[253] The accent on risk assessment also underlies efforts to create traceability systems, which is a way to allow businesses to decrease risks of human rights violations taking place down the supply chain, either due to labor or sourcing practices.[254]

248 UNGPs, Principle 23 "Commentary."
249 Ibid., Principle 7 (a) and (b).
250 Ibid., Principle 7 (c).
251 Ibid., Principle 7 "Commentary."
252 Ibid.
253 OECD Guidelines for MNEs, "Chapter IV: Human Rights," para. 40.
254 UN Global Compact and BSR, *A Guide to Traceability*, p. 20.

Due Diligence

The OECD's Due Diligence Guidance for Responsible Supply Chains of Minerals from Conflict-Affected and High-Risk Areas is the main international toolkit through which the private sector has been assessing its risks and managing its sourcing practices. The guidance defines "conflict-affected" areas as areas where "armed conflict, widespread violence or other risks of harm to people" are present, regardless of the particularities of the armed conflict. "High-risk areas," on the other hand, are "areas of political instability or repression, institutional weakness, insecurity, collapse of civil infrastructure and widespread violence" resulting in violations of human rights as well as of domestic and international law.[255] This broad term goes beyond targeting some of the most prolific sites of armed conflict such as eastern DRC but lacks a coherent definition for assessing whether a given area fits within the term par excellence.

The Guidance establishes a five-step risk-based due diligence framework for responsible sourcing from conflict-affected and high-risk areas. The first step is to develop and communicate to both suppliers and the general public a mineral supply chain policy for minerals originating from conflict-affected and high-risk zones and to ensure that company management is structured in a way to support mineral supply chain due diligence. Additionally, the company should set up a traceability or a chain of custody system to establish control over its mineral supply chain, engage more effectively with its suppliers and establish a grievance mechanism either at the company or the industry level.[256] The second stage consists of identifying and assessing risks in the minerals supply chain with a view to then responding to these risks through the design and implementation of a strategy. The final two steps include engaging independent third-party audit of the supply chain due diligence, and reporting on the entire due diligence process.[257]

The model supply chain policy provided by the Guidance includes an explicit policy commitment to "not profit from, contribute to, assist with or facilitate the commission" of the most serious human rights abuses, including torture and degrading treatment, forced or compulsory labor, the worst forms of child labor, gross human rights violations, i.e. sexual violence, war crimes, crimes against humanity and genocide, and to

[255] OECD, *OECD Due Diligence Guidance for Responsible Supply Chains of Minerals from Conflict-Affected and High-Risk Areas* (2nd Ed.) (OECD, 2013), p. 13.

[256] Ibid., p. 17.

[257] Ibid., p. 19.

discontinue engagement with suppliers if such risks are identified in their activities.[258] The model also includes suspension or disengagement with suppliers in cases where the "extraction, transport, trade, handling or export of minerals" is found to risk supporting non-state armed groups.[259] When public and/or private security forces are found to be benefiting illegally from mineral extraction or trade, on the other hand, the procedure is much softer and requires the company to "immediately devise, adopt and implement a risk management plan with upstream suppliers and other stakeholders to prevent or mitigate the risk of direct or indirect support to public or private security forces" and move to disengagement or suspension only in case of failure.[260] This softer mitigation procedure also applies to bribery, fraud or misrepresentation, money-laundering and nonpayment by suppliers of taxes, royalties and fees to the government.[261]

An examination of the impact of OECD Due Diligence Guidance and other supply chain due diligence measures in eastern DRC demonstrates that, although armed presence in mining sites remains a challenge, there is a strong interest in sourcing from mines considered conflict-free through certification schemes, especially in the case of the 3Ts.[262] A noticeable move away from artisanal mining in the 3Ts to gold has happened in recent years due to world market prices as well as mounting pressure to source conflict-free 3Ts, aided by foreign regulations, numerous traceability schemes and assistance at local or provincial level in regulating mining practices and flows.[263] In the case of gold, militarization of the mines remains an important challenge. Furthermore, gold is widely available throughout the country including in hard-to-access areas, creating a fertile ground for armed group involvement in its extraction and trade, especially given that "the country's artisanal gold production is exported almost entirely unrecorded."[264]

Sectoral commercial actors in the UAE and in China have taken the OECD Due Diligence Guidance on board, demonstrating that there is a recognized need on the part of major trade and commerce players to at

[258] Ibid., pp. 20–21.
[259] Ibid., p. 21.
[260] Ibid., p. 23.
[261] Ibid., p. 24.
[262] OECD, *Mineral Supply Chains and Conflict Links in Eastern DRC: Five Years of Implementing Supply Chain Due Diligence* (OECD, 2015), pp. 7–8.
[263] Ibid., p. 9.
[264] Ibid., p. 16.

least formally introduce requirements for responsible sourcing even when these are not backed by effective implementation or oversight mechanisms. Dubai's DMCC, as the global leader in gold trade, released the DMCC Rules for Risk Based Due Diligence in the Gold and Precious Metals Supply Chain (DMCC Rules for RBD-GPM) based on the OECD Due Diligence Guidance and its Supplement on Gold. The implementation of DMCC Rules is overseen by the Independent Governance Committee for Responsible Sourcing, which is designed as a multistakeholder committee that currently represents mostly private sector actors from different segments of the gold sector.[265] The Chinese Chamber of Commerce of Metals, Minerals and Chemicals Importers and Exporters (CCCMC), supervised by China's Ministry of Commerce, also introduced responsible mineral sourcing guidelines in 2015.[266] Both guidelines are based on the five-step risk-based supply chain due diligence process, and while Dubai's DMCC Rules are focused on gold trade and apply to companies wishing to trade on the Dubai gold exchange, the Chinese CCCMC Guidelines are much more expansive in their reach and scope of application. According to the Guidelines, they apply to all upstream and downstream Chinese companies engaged at some point in their supply chain or production with minerals, defined as all those that are "extracting, trading, processing, transporting, and/or otherwise using mineral resources and their related products."[267] The definition of a Chinese company is also both broad and progressive, as it includes not only for-profit legal entities registered in China but also "overseas companies (including subsidiaries) which are wholly- or majority-owned or controlled by a Chinese entity or individual,"[268] thereby overcoming corporate veil restrictions that may hamper their applicability. While the guidelines prioritize due diligence around the 3TG, they are explicitly set to apply to all mineral resources such as ores, concentrates as well as derivates and by-products. Another distinction of the Chinese guidelines is that they invoke both host country and Chinese laws, regulations and standards.[269]

[265] DMCC, "Responsible Sourcing of Gold and Precious Metals," www.dmcc.ae/gold-responsible-sourcing-precious-metals (accessed 15 April 2019).
[266] CCCMC, "Chinese Due Diligence Guidelines for Responsible Mineral Supply Chains," 2015.
[267] Ibid., p. 10.
[268] Ibid.
[269] Ibid., p. 18.

The introduction of responsible sourcing guidelines or rules is of course not translated into an automatic implementation of such standards by the industry. For instance, an NGO report has alleged, based on a whistleblower account, that the findings from the first responsible gold sourcing audit of Dubai's largest refining company Kaloti, that raised important concerns of compliance with the DMCC Rules for RBD-GPM, were buried.[270] The initial concerns of compliance included a lack of proper checks on what the company itself deemed high-risk gold, the classification of new gold as scrap gold and important volume of purchases in 2012 from a company that was identified as linked to DRC conflict gold by the UN.[271] It was further contended that a clean compliance report was issued by the audit firm Ernst & Young once the DMC introduced changes to its Audit Review Protocol, reportedly after the "audit team had shared their findings with the DMCC."[272] The DMCC, on the other hand, rejected the allegations that it had altered its rules to benefit any member refinery or that it had concealed any findings of noncompliance.[273] It is difficult to determine how genuine the allegations and the responses are without an independent examination of the facts but the possibility of using voluntary industry schemes as whitewashing opportunities is a veritable concern.

Heightened Duties to Protect Children

Although the UNGPs and OECD Guidelines are not vocal on the issue, the CRBPs note that the protection of children affected by emergencies notes the "heightened risk of human rights violations in situations of armed conflict and other emergencies," underscoring the disproportionate risks on groups of children who may be more vulnerable, including displaced, migrant, separated or unaccompanied children, indigenous children or children with disabilities.[274] In eastern DRC, revenues from artisanal mining activities generated as a result of the failure of businesses to source minerals responsibly have played a key role in fueling the conflict. Businesses engaged in ventures in the DRC, especially in ventures linked to mining in the conflict-affected regions of eastern DRC,

270 Global Witness, "City of Gold: Why Dubai's First Conflict Gold Audit Never Saw the Light of Day," February 2014, pp. 2–3.
271 Ibid., pp. 6–7.
272 Ibid.
273 DMCC, "DMCC Response to 'City of Gold' 24.03.2014," 24 March 2014.
274 CRBPs, Principle 9.

conduct business aware of the exacerbated risks presented directly or indirectly by armed conflict in addition to the risks posed by the impact of the mining sector itself. The knowledge of exacerbated risks translates into the foreseeability of adverse impacts of these risks on children and businesses are required to avoid "causing or contributing to" children's rights violations in emergencies.[275]

The CRC Committee's GC 16 reminds that obligations under the CRC and its OPs continue to apply through emergency situations, including "conflict, disaster or breakdown of social or legal order."[276] The duties of home states with regard to business activities in conflict-affected or emergency zones include strong children's rights due diligence requirements, domestic legislation to address "for foreseeable children's rights risks for transnational businesses" as well as the provision of information and guidance to companies on the situation of children and their rights in places where they operate.[277] In addition, both home and host states should adopt and implement domestic legislation that prohibits the recruitment of children by private security companies and lays out "requirements for effective measures to protect children from violence and exploitation; and mechanisms for holding personnel accountable for abuses of children's rights."[278]

The difficult task for home states lies in the act of balancing the best interests of children in conflict-affected zones and the prevention of children's rights abuses by businesses. While violations of children's rights by businesses ought to be prevented, mitigated, remedied and even punished, an excessive accent on the prevention of violations and culpability may result in complete corporate disengagement from the area, which may in turn be detrimental to the wellbeing of children (and adults) more generally.

Attempts at Corporate Accountability

A number of civil society actors have tried to employ the OECD Guidelines in home state NCPs against companies trading in minerals originating from the DRC. Many of these instances were brought before the 2011 revision of the Guidelines and the inclusion of a human rights chapter therein and two of the most notable are *RAID* v. *DAS Air* and *Global Witness* v. *Afrimex*.

[275] Ibid.
[276] CRC Committee, GC 16, para. 49.
[277] Ibid., paras. 50–51.
[278] Ibid., para. 52.

RAID* v. *DAS Air In 2004, NGO Rights and Accountability in Development (RAID) initiated an instance in the UK NCP against DAS Air, a private air transport company registered in the United Kingdom with operations in Africa, Europe and the Middle East based on allegations that the company was transporting coltan, a conflict mineral, out of the conflict zones in the DRC.[279] In fact, the company was listed by the UN Panel of Experts on the Illegal Exploitation of Natural Resources and Other Forms of Wealth as one of the companies engaged directly or indirectly in the illegal exploitation of the DRC's mineral resources in violation of the OECD Guidelines.[280] By the time the NCP had issued its final assessment, DAS Air was in the process of liquidation, after "failing to recover from a ban on flights operating into and out of European Community (EC) that was imposed on 16 October 2006."[281] The UK NCP's findings noted that DAS Air had been flying between Entebbe and eastern DRC, which at the time was under the occupation of the Ugandan army, in contravention of the Convention on International Civil Aviation (CICA) prohibiting civilian flights in conflict zones.[282] The NCP underscored the requirement of "heightened care . . . by companies when investing and trading in weak governance zones."[283]

The NCP concluded that DAS Air had failed to take sufficient due diligence on the supply chain, in violation of the OECD Guidelines as it "did not try to establish the source of the minerals they were transporting from Kigali and Entebbe."[284] It also noted: "The NCP finds it difficult to accept that an airline with a significant presence in Africa including a base in Entebbe would not have been aware of the conflict and the potential for the minerals to be sourced from Eastern DRC."[285] Accordingly, the NCP declared that DAS Air did not "[r]espect the human rights of those affected by their activities consistent with the host government's international obligations and commitments."[286] The implication was that given its

[279] Rights and Accountability in Development (RAID), "Letter to the Rt Hon Patricia Hewitt MP, Minister of Trade and Industry," 28 June 2004, www.oecdwatch.org/cases/Case_41/124/at_download/file (accessed 15 April 2019).

[280] UN Panel of Experts, "2002 Report," Annex III.

[281] UK NCP, "Statement by the United Kingdom National Contact Point (NCP) for OECD Guidelines for Multinational Enterprises: DAS Air," 17 July 2008, para. 8, www.oecd.org/daf/inv/mnc/44479531.pdf (accessed 24 April 2019).

[282] Ibid., para. 47

[283] Ibid., para. 43.

[284] Ibid., para. 49.

[285] Ibid.

[286] Ibid., para. 50(II.2).

knowledge of the conflict in the region and the contention that the trade of minerals from conflict-affected regions was fueling the conflict, DAS Air was required to take measures to ascertain that it did not transport minerals sourced from eastern DRC to fulfill its due diligence duty. As DAS Air was being liquidated at the time, the final report and assessment of the violations did not have specific impacts on the company's operations.

Global Witness* v. *Afrimex The UK-based NGO Global Witness brought a claim in July 2007 against Afrimex, a mineral trading company registered in the United Kingdom, which was alleged to be trading with and paying taxes to armed rebel groups controlling the eastern provinces of the DRC and sourcing minerals from mines using child labor and forced labor. In August 2008, the UK NCP concluded that Global Witness's allegations were in fact substantiated as Afrimex had "initiated the demand for minerals sourced from a conflict zone" through its associated company SOCOMI and independent comptoires "who paid taxes and mineral licences to RCD-Goma," the armed group occupying the area.[287] The NCP appraised that these payments had "contributed to the ongoing conflict" and concluded that Afrimex had failed to contribute to sustainable development in the DRC, to "respect human rights" as well as to "take steps to influence the supply chain and to explore options with its suppliers" on how to source from child and forced labor-free mines.[288] This phrasing constituted an indirect reference to the due diligence concept featured in the UN Framework and UNGPs, which at the time had not yet been incorporated in the OECD Guidelines. A Global Witness report published almost one year after the NCP decision on Afrimex raised questions about the implementation of the NCP recommendations by the company.[289]

Impacts of Home State and Domestic Regulation

The US Congress's adoption of the Dodd-Frank Bill Section 1502 on conflict minerals and its entry into force in 2012 alongside pronouncement of the SEC's Final Rule on the question of conflict minerals from the DRC and neighboring locations coincided with a number of other developments. After the Dodd-Frank Bill was signed into federal law on

[287] UK NCP, "Final Statement by the UK NCP for the OECD Guidelines for MNEs: Afrimex (UK) Ltd," 28 August 2008, p.13, para. 62.

[288] Ibid., p.13, para. 1 and para. 62.

[289] Global Witness, *"Faced with a Gun, What Can You Do?"*

21 July 2010, a presidential mining ban suspending artisanal mining activities in Kivu provinces and Maniema in eastern DRC in order to de-link armed groups and mining activities was issued (11 September 2010).[290] Although the ban was lifted in March 2011, it is claimed to have resulted in the deterioration of socioeconomic conditions for local communities and further insecurity as international mineral trading companies did not resume their activities following the end of the ban, while also creating the unintended consequence of increasing the Congolese army's involvement in the mining sector.[291]

The legal requirements introduced by the Dodd-Frank Bill Section 1502 are argued to have resulted in a de facto embargo on minerals coming from the DRC, driving artisanal mining further into the informal sector.[292] Some companies reportedly pulled out or pushed their suppliers to pull out of the region covered by the bill instead of engaging with upstream practices through continuous responsible supply chain management practices.[293] Of course the Dodd-Frank Bill Section 1502 was not a precursor to other mineral conflict initiatives, it was rather a result of existing mineral conflict advocacy that followed the reports of the UN Panel of Experts starting in the early 2000s. Most civil society initiatives have in fact been calling for a responsible approach to sourcing that does not lead to complete disengagement.

A measure may be deemed successful if it attains the specific policy objectives it was designed to fulfill. From this vantage point, the Dodd-Frank Bill's Section 1502 has been successful in compelling many large companies to take closer looks at their supply chains and sourcing decisions. The value of Dodd-Frank Bill's Section 1502 lies in the opportunities it provides for curtailing the funding in the reach of armed groups through mineral exploitation and trading, with the knowledge that this in itself will not bring the conflict in eastern DRC to an end.[294] There has been, however, equally strong criticism of this US measure, arguing that the de facto embargo resulting from the DRC central government's decision to ban mining activities has led to the clear deterioration of living conditions of local artisanal miners and their

[290] Matthysen and Montejano, "Conflict Minerals' Initiatives in DRC," p. 41.

[291] Ibid., p. 8.

[292] Ibid., pp. 35–36.

[293] RSN, "Mining the Disclosures 2015: An Investor's Guide to Conflict Minerals Reporting in Year Two," 2015, p. 21.

[294] AI and Global Witness, "Digging for Transparency," p. 32.

families,[295] as well as rendering the supervision of working conditions in the mines including health, safety and the employment of children more problematic.[296] In fact, as early as 2003 research had found that pursuing a strategy of improving the governance of the DRC's mining sector would be preferable to a boycott, because although it was a tool for armed groups to extract profits, mining as an activity had become significant for sustaining local livelihoods.[297] Dodd-Frank has impacted an estimated five to twelve million Congolese, once the figures of artisanal miners left unemployed are extrapolated to reflect the number of their dependents.[298] The resulting situation has reportedly been detrimental for children, whose parents cannot provide them with adequate nutrition, tuition fees to attend school or medical treatment when needed.[299]

Proponents of Dodd-Frank type domestic supply chain measures with extraterritorial reach note that the purpose is not to purge supply chains of given minerals but to ensure that the use of these minerals happens in a transparent and responsible way, benefiting local populations without resulting in human rights abuses.[300] Whether there are longer-term human rights benefits to be gained from dissuading the trade in so-called conflict minerals and whether that longer-term benefit will outweigh the adverse short-term impacts remains unclear. In addition to demonstrating the difficulties of fostering more effective supply chain due diligence in conflict-affected areas, the legal responses to exploitation of mineral resources in eastern DRC also demonstrate the difficulties linked with achieving human rights results through legislation motivated by other objectives, in this case ending financial flows to armed groups. First, competing human rights claims of different groups may not all be accommodated through a single policy objective. Second, the broader policy concern of the third country enacting the domestic legislation with extraterritorial reach may not lend itself to offering the most adequate protection of the interests of local populations where extraterritorial effects of that legislation are felt. As such, curbing the profits of armed groups from mineral trade may not be the best objective to pursue if the legislation is intended also to secure the human rights of those involved in artisanal mining as well as their families, including children. Third, the

[295] Matthysen and Montejano, "Conflict Minerals Initiatives in DRC," p. 36.
[296] Lauren Wolfe, "How Dodd-Frank Is Failing Congo," *Foreign Policy*, 2 February 2015.
[297] Jackson, "Fortunes of War: The Coltan Trade in the Kivus," p. 18.
[298] Seay, "What's Wrong with Dodd-Frank 1502?"
[299] Ibid.
[300] AI and Global Witness, "Digging for Transparency," p. 32.

results of the extraterritorial reach of the enacted domestic measures may not always be foreseeable, especially in zones of conflict or weak governance. In this regard, the Presidential Mining Ban put into place after the adoption of the Dodd-Frank Bill in the United States has in fact exacerbated the precarious conditions under which artisanal miners and their families live.

On the other hand, if softer requirements such as due diligence or voluntary certification regimes are to be embraced in lieu of home-state regulation, there is no guarantee they will create the desired change. What is not evident from the focus on due diligence and risk management is whether having undertaken steps towards risk assessment and management absolves a business of failure of human rights compliance. A further critical question, from the viewpoint of responsibility for violations, is whether companies can simply rely on risk-based due diligence to comply with their obligations or whether they continue to incur responsibilities for human rights violations after having conducted risk-based due diligence if they continue to be engaged in the conflict-affected area with full knowledge of high risks and without mitigation strategies. This is all the more crucial in light of the calls to the private sector from both local actors and civil society to avoid complete disengagement from conflict-affected zones such as eastern DRC in order to avoid liability or responsibility. In fact, because the livelihoods of artisanal miners as well as their families, amounting to millions of people, depend on their ability to benefit from the mining sector, a complete disengagement in the form of a boycott may amount to an irresponsible management of supply chains. While this prospect is difficult to reconcile with a wrongdoing-based conceptualization of responsibility under international human rights law, whether complete disengagement from the region gives grounds for responsibility and whether responsibility for violations may be avoided solely on the basis of due diligence efforts are important considerations.

2.4 Intermediate Conclusions on Supply Chains: Extending the Coverage of Due Diligence Norms and Assessing Home State Regulation

Business and human rights frameworks posit due diligence as a remedy to human rights violations occurring in supply chains. The human rights due diligence requirement in the UNGPs is extended to adverse human rights impacts "which may be directly linked to its operations, products or services by its business relationships" in addition to a company's own activities.[301] This accent on direct business relationships was echoed in the test applied in the reasoning of the German NCP in the *ECCHR* v. *Otto Stadtlander* instance in addition to that business relationship being one of considerable magnitude. This test sidesteps a number of important issues. First, it fails to take into account the power and influence that a company may wield in its indirect business relationships. Second, the threshold imposed through a direct business relationship is so high that it would effectively absolve those actors downstream in the supply chain from any responsibility although they would continue to make considerable profits from the final products and services. In fact, even in the absence of direct supply-demand relationships, measures such as boycotts or industry-wide certification standards by companies in indirect business relationships have demonstrated promise, when coupled with other compliance approaches. Third, even if a business relationship is not one of considerable magnitude for a large company, it may be a significant one to its supplier. Accordingly, the company may be able to exert decisive influence over its supplier as long as its business is of significant value to the supplier.

The "direct business relationship of considerable magnitude" test also runs the risk of prompting companies downstream to find "creative legal solutions" to get around incurring responsibility by resorting to practices akin to offshore financial transactions, such as involving more intermediaries in their sourcing practices (thus, circumventing the direct relationship condition) or sourcing smaller volumes from a greater number of suppliers (thus, sidestepping the "considerable magnitude" test). These questions become even more pertinent in the case of minerals sourced from conflict-affected zones, which face more difficult traceability burdens.

With respect to specific children's rights, human rights due diligence requirements would entail enacting relevant policies and processes within the business enterprise, including a policy commitment and a children's rights impact assessment process, integration of the findings from this process to evaluate any activities or policies with adverse impacts and appropriately "cease or prevent the activity, or its contribution to it, and use its leverage to mitigate any remaining impact."[302]

[301] UNGPs, Principle 17(a).

[302] CRBPs, Principle 1, p. 15.

The supply chain issues highlighted in the two cases on Uzbek cotton and 3TG from eastern DRC also bring up interesting questions with respect to the role of home states in regulating business behavior linked to supply chains. According to the CRC Committee's GC 16, home states of business enterprises may be inferred to have a role in "reaching" the businesses with which they have a reasonable link, comprising where a business enterprise is "registered or domiciled or has its main place of business or substantial business activities in the state concerned"[303] to ensure compliance with children's rights standards in extraterritorial contexts. As the CRC enjoys almost universal ratification, the CRC Committee contends that the realization of its provisions should concern host and home states equally, with both "establish[ing] institutional and legal frameworks that enable businesses to respect children's rights across their global operations,"[304] which would also extend to global supply chains. The UNGPs, on the other hand, curtail the application of the state duty to protect human rights extraterritorially by arguing that "states are not generally required under international human rights law to regulate the extraterritorial activities of businesses domiciled in their territory and/or jurisdiction" although they are not "generally prohibited from doing so."[305] The ILO MNE Declaration is also rather weakly worded in calling on home states to simply promote (and not compel) "good social practice" among their MNEs operating extraterritorially as opposed to compliance with domestic laws and regulations and international standards.[306] More adequate treatment of state obligations with respect to territorial and extraterritorial activities of businesses may be found in the Maastricht Principles, which stipulate that home states have obligations to regulate the activities of private actors, exercise influence over those actors they are not in a position to regulate and create an enabling international environment for the realization of human rights globally.[307]

[303] CRC Committee, GC 16, para. 43.
[304] Ibid., paras. 41 and 46.
[305] UNGPs, Principle 2, "Commentary."
[306] ILO MNE Declaration, para. 12.
[307] The Maastricht Principles, Principles 24 and 25, 26 and 29, respectively.

3

Children's Rights in Investment Projects

Investment is at the core of business activities. In fact, facilitating investment opportunities for the private sector and incentivizing investment through the use of public funds, among others, is at the core of the 2030 Agenda for Sustainable Development. The use of public and private financing together in investment projects has been a key feature of the economic development agenda in the last three decades, especially when investment projects have required the mobilization of important financial sums. Particularly in developing countries, such large-scale investment projects often involve the construction of infrastructure facilities that are seen as essential to the economic development of the country.[1] Examples include the construction of transport infrastructure such as roads or ports, electrification projects for electricity generation and distribution or urbanization projects. Large-scale projects often involve a variety of actors: private companies that act as sponsors of the project itself, subcontractors that may play various roles in the project, financiers that may range from private banks to the host state and third state institutions as well as global or regional multilateral development finance institutions. In addition, the project financing in the form of loans or equity may be guaranteed through various private or public guarantees. Many large-scale infrastructure projects require important physical and environmental changes. These may include the physical displacement and resettlement of local populations as well as impacts on physical and/or environmental assets such as erosion, deforestation and inundation as well as risks to the local communities resulting from the influx of machinery, vehicles and workers for the construction or operation of the new investment.

To give an example, the construction of hydropower facilities and linked dam construction have been documented to cause displacement, inundation of physical, cultural or environmental assets, and loss of

[1] See: César Calderon and Luis Servén, "Infrastructure and Economic Development in Sub-Saharan Africa" (2010) 19(1) *Journal of African Economies* 113–187.

livelihoods. As early as 2000, the World Commission on Dams found that "40 to 80 million" people were estimated to be physically displaced as a result of large dams, with an estimated twenty-six to fifty-eight million people physically displaced (lower and higher ends of estimates) between 1950 and 1990 in China and India alone,[2] not including people whose livelihoods were affected as a result of the large hydroelectric projects, interconnection projects or other auxiliary construction as well as those impacted downstream or upstream due to dam construction.[3] The specific effects of large infrastructure projects on children and what these effects are translated into in terms of children's rights outcomes have neither been systematically documented nor analyzed. The limited documentation that does exist comes largely from civil society reports and analyses as well as from reporting and opinion pieces in the press.

Large hydroelectric dams have been opposed not only by civil society but also by a number of governments. For instance, the 2014 budget bill passed by the US Congress during the Obama Administration precluded US support of any large hydroelectric projects within international financial institutions.[4] In addition, the US government mandated its Executive Directors to "ensure" an adequate response by International Financial Institution (IFI) management to decisions from IFI accountability mechanisms, such as the WB Inspection Panel, by "providing just compensation or other appropriate redress to individuals and communities" when their human rights are violated, including through displacement as a result of IFI loans, grants, policies or strategies.[5]

Large investment projects also have "hidden" impacts on children, caused by the sudden influx of workers into a region that may strain local resources available for healthcare and education as well as increased risk for transmittable diseases. In addition, employment opportunities in and around the project may result in the development of informal working arrangements that pose an exploitation risk to children both in labor and sexual terms.[6]

[2] World Commission on Dams, "Dams and Development: A New Framework for Decision-Making," November 2000, p. 104.

[3] Ibid., p. 34, Chapter 1, footnote 44.

[4] US Congress, "Consolidated Appropriations Act, 2014," 13 January 2014, p. 1240.

[5] Ibid., pp. 1361–1362.

[6] Margaret Wachenfeld, "The hidden impacts of large infrastructure projects on children," *Guardian*, 3 May 2012, www.theguardian.com/sustainable-business/children-large-infrastructure-honeypot-effect (accessed 15 April 2019).

The following section analyzes two investment projects in Uganda, first the Bujagali Hydropower Project and second, the now cancelled Uganda Transport Sector Development Project (TSDP). Both projects were undertaken by private investors but received development financing from multilateral development banks (MDBs), including the World Bank and others as well as national development finance institutions. Both projects brought to the forefront allegations about violations of children's rights. These cases focus on the impacts of large-scale infrastructure projects on children and showcase the complexity with respect to the attribution and distribution of human rights obligations brought about by the involvement of numerous legally distinct types of actors in the financing and undertaking of a project, especially when that involvement results in adverse impacts. The cases allow an inspection of accountability mechanisms and self-regulatory frameworks at various institutions, including the WB, European Investment Bank (EIB) and African Development Bank (AfDB) as well as the International Finance Corporation (IFC) that govern to varying degrees the legal responsibility for corporate wrongdoings.

3.1 Key Issues for Investment Projects

There are three key issues in investment projects recognized across the board as relevant from a social and environmental perspective: issues around environmental and social impact assessments (ESIA); consultation and consent; and land acquisition, which may lead to involuntary resettlement and require restoration of livelihoods and related compensation.

Environmental and Social Impact Assessment (ESIA)

Any investment project, whether it is a greenfield investment or the expansion of an existing investment, has the potential to cause adverse environmental and social impacts, especially if it is a large-scale endeavor. Environmental and social impact assessments (ESIAs) may be required for certain types of investment as a matter of domestic law in host states. Moreover, many projects are only possible owing to the involvement of financial institutions providing project finance, advisory services and loans to either governments or businesses. Multilateral development banks (MDBs), organized as international organizations, apply their own safeguard policies and environmental and social frameworks to funding. In addition, many of the large private financial institutions have signed up to the Equator Principles, a risk-management framework developed and adopted by financial institutions, that is intended as the "financial industry benchmark for determining, assessing and managing environmental and social risk in projects."[7] All these institutions and their frameworks require borrowers to undertake environmental and social impact assessments (ESIA) prior to the disbursement of funds. The Equator Principles are applied by private businesses (that are financial institutions) in their project-related financial transactions with other private businesses. The safeguards of MDBs apply to borrower countries as well as to private businesses, when these are directly funded as project sponsors.

The Environmental and Social Framework (ESF) of the WB, in application since October 2018, for instance, requires ESIAs that assess "in an integrated way, all relevant direct, indirect and cumulative environmental and social risks and impacts throughout the project life cycle."[8] The social risks and impacts that ESIAs are required to account for include threats to human security, risks of discrimination in accessing development resources and project benefits, negative impacts from restrictions to land and natural resource tenure and use as well as impacts on health, safety and wellbeing linked to labor conditions or impacts on local communities. While there is no mention of specific impacts on children in the WB ESF, risks of disproportionate impacts on individuals or groups that may be disadvantaged or vulnerable should be included in an ESIA.[9] The WB Directive on Addressing Risks and Impacts on Disadvantaged or Vulnerable Individuals or Groups, which establishes WB due diligence obligations in this regard, requires WB project teams to review borrower ESIAs to ascertain that risks to disadvantaged or vulnerable individuals or groups are properly identified and mitigated.[10]

The social issues to be addressed in ESIAs, according to the Equator Principles, include "respect of human rights by acting with due diligence to prevent, mitigate and manage adverse human rights impacts," labor issues, impacts on affected peoples as well as vulnerable or disadvantaged

[7] The Equator Principles, June 2013.

[8] WB, Environmental and Social Framework, Environmental and Social Standard (ESS) 1: Assessment and Management of Environmental and Social Risks and Impacts, para. 23 (references omitted).

[9] Ibid., para. 28.

[10] WB, "Bank Directive Addressing Risks and Impacts on Disadvantaged or Vulnerable Individuals or Groups," 4 August 2016.

individuals and groups, socioeconomic impacts, gender impacts, land acquisition and involuntary resettlement, impact on indigenous peoples and community health, safety and security.[11]

With respect to children, the CRC Committee references children's rights due diligence through the identification, prevention and mitigation of child-related impacts either in the form of a children's rights impact assessment or through rendering "special consideration for the differentiated impact on children" in the context of a general human rights due diligence process.[12]

Consultation and Consent

Consultation and consent are two related but distinct issues linked to investment projects. The consultation requirement means that local populations must be consulted as stakeholders in decisions that may affect their living conditions, such as in investment projects.

The Food and Agriculture Organization (FAO) defines consultation as "engaging with and seeking the support of those who, having legitimate tenure rights, could be affected by decisions, prior to decisions being taken, and responding to their contributions," being mindful of power imbalances and fostering participation in the process.[13] Consent, often termed Free, Prior and Informed Consent (FPIC), is a condition embodied in the sparsely ratified ILO Convention 169 concerning Indigenous and Tribal Peoples as well as in the UN Declaration on the Rights of Indigenous Peoples. Consent has to be sought through "good faith consultations," "organized without intimidation" prior to "initiating any project or before adopting and implementing legislative or administrative measures" affecting indigenous community resources.[14] Differing from consultation, it implies agreement with the activity subject to consultation, meaning that indigenous peoples "also have the prerogative to withhold consent or to offer it with conditions."[15] While the FPIC norm for indigenous peoples is being incorporated into the safeguard frameworks of multilateral financiers, such as the WB with its new

[11] The Equator Principles, "Exhibit II: Illustrative List of Potential Environmental and Social Issues to be Addressed in the Environmental and Social Assessment Documentation."

[12] CRC Committee, GC 16, paras. 62–63.

[13] FAO, *Voluntary Guidelines on the Responsible Governance of Tenure of Land, Fisheries and Forests in the Context of National Food Security* (FAO 2012), Art. 3B.6.

[14] Ibid., Art. 9.9.

[15] FAO, *Respecting Free, Prior and Informed Consent: Practical Guidance for Governments, Companies, NGOs, Indigenous Peoples and Local Communities in Relation to Land Acquisition* (FAO, 2014), p. 5.

environmental and social safeguards, it does not cover non-indigenous communities.

The UNGPs note that the identification and assessment of human rights risks that business operations and decisions may give rise to should "involve meaningful consultation with potentially affected groups and other relevant stakeholders, as appropriate to the size of the business enterprise and the nature and context of the operation."[16] The Commentary to Principle 18 underscores that special attention should be paid to human rights impacts on those from groups or populations more prone to marginalization, which would include children.[17] Furthermore, human rights and environmental and social impact assessments should include all internationally recognized human rights, including by inference children's rights. In fact, such assessments should be conducted regularly and on an ongoing basis as well as in response to any changes foreseen to the activity or the project.

The OECD Guidelines also put an emphasis on meaningful engagement with stakeholders in the decision-making processes and planning of projects or business activities that may have significant impacts on local communities.[18] It is noted that stakeholder engagement may be especially beneficial for projects "involving, for example, the intensive use of land or water."[19] The OECD Guidelines do not clarify whether this requirement for stakeholder engagement should also include an explicit dimension of engagement with children in the local community or whether the processes should be made child-friendly.

Land Acquisition, Involuntary Resettlement and Compensation for Livelihood Loss

Many major multilateral funders, including the WB Group, the ADB, the AfDB and even newcomers such as the New Development Bank (NDB) of the BRICS countries (Brazil, Russia, India, China and South Africa) and the Asian Infrastructure Investment Bank (AIIB) whose majority shareholder is the Chinese state have safeguard procedures for land acquisition, resettlement and loss of livelihoods linked to the investment projects they finance. While the protections provided by the safeguard procedures may be and have been criticized on adequacy grounds, their existence is crucial in guaranteeing access to remedies. With respect to

16 UNGPs, Principle 18(b).
17 Ibid., Principle 18 "Commentary."
18 OECD Guidelines for MNEs, "II. General Policies," para. 14.
19 Ibid., "Commentary on General Policies," para. 25.

land acquisition and involuntary resettlement issues, children have not been specifically identified as a major stakeholder group for businesses undertaking the large infrastructure projects or their financiers. Most multilateral funders consider children to be among vulnerable groups in the context of their safeguards.

Children's Rights and Business Principle 7 regarding environment and land acquisition and use notes that the corporate responsibility to respect, which is the minimum requirement incumbent upon businesses, means that they should:

i. Where possible, avoid or minimize displacement of communities affected by land acquisition or land use for business purposes. Engage in meaningful, informed consultation with potentially affected communities to ensure that any adverse impact on children's rights is identified and addressed and that communities participate actively in and contribute to decision-making on matters that affect them directly. Seeking the free, prior and informed consent of indigenous peoples is specifically required for any project that affects their communities, and it is a desirable goal for any community impacted by a company's use or acquisition of land.
ii. Respect children's rights – especially their right to education, protection, health, adequate food and adequate standard of living and participation – when planning and carrying out resettlement and providing for compensation.[20]

In fact, the requirements pronounced under CRBP 7, if integrated in a meaningful way into regulations applicable to businesses through host- or home-state regulation or enforceable requirements at the international level, for instance, through lender frameworks, would resolve many of the issues that children affected by involuntary resettlement would encounter.

The CRC Committee GC 16 notes that "selling or leasing land to investors can deprive local populations of access to natural resources linked to their subsistence and cultural heritage" and hence adversely impact children's right to life, survival and development under Article 6 CRC.[21] Although the GC does not address involuntary resettlement in the context of business operations as such, it highlights that when businesses are conducting consultations with project affected

[20] CRBPs, Principle 7.

[21] CRC Committee, GC 16, para. 19.

populations, specifically seeking children's views with regard to business decisions with a potential to affect them may be crucial. The process of consultation with children must be conducted under child-friendly conditions and "be accessible, inclusive and meaningful to children and take into account the evolving capacities of children and their best interests at all times."[22]

3.2 Case 3: Bujagali Hydropower Project in Uganda

3.2.1 Bujagali Hydropower Project (HPP): From Appraisal to Completion

Bujagali HPP Project was designed as a 250 MW power-generating facility to be built on the Victoria Nile River near Jinja, Uganda to remedy the country's shortage of electricity.[23] In 1994, the government agreed to construct the power plant[24] and two years later signed a 450 million USD agreement with AES Corporation (USA).[25] In 2001, the WBG Board of Directors approved the project and extended IFC loans of up to 100 million USD and a risk management facility of up to 10 million USD in addition to a – 115 million USD partial risk guarantee from the International Development Association (IDA) to commercial banks.[26] When announcing the approval of the project, IFC noted and denied allegations of corruption that had been raised.[27] Starting in November 2000, a number of complaints were lodged with the IFC/MIGA Compliance Advisor/Ombudsman (CAO). By July 2001, the WB Inspection Panel had also received an inspection request about the HPPs in Uganda and the new Bujagali HPP Project.[28] In fact, the inspection was already underway at the time

[22] Ibid., para. 23.

[23] Website of Bujagali HPP, "About us," www.bujagali-energy.com (accessed 15 April 2019).

[24] IFC, "Press Release – WB's Board Responds to Uganda's Energy Needs – Approves Support for Bujagali HPP," 19 December 2001.

[25] Emma Mutaizibwa, "Bujagali: Finally, Light at the End of Tunnel," *The Observer (Uganda)*, 9 October 2012, www.observer.ug/component/content/article?id=21445:bujagali-finally-light-at-the-end-of-tunnel- (accessed 15 April 2019).

[26] IFC, "WB's Board Responds to Uganda's Energy Needs."

[27] Ibid.

[28] WB Inspection Panel Database, "Uganda: Third Power Project, Fourth Power Project, and Proposed Bujugali HPP," http://ewebapps.worldbank.org/apps/ip/Pages/ViewCase.aspx?CaseId=54 (accessed 15 April 2019).

the project funding was still being approved by the WB Board of Directors.[29]

The first project sponsor, US-based AES Corporation, pulled out of the project in 2002, just after the resettlement process had taken place. Behind the decision were allegations that WB's then Alternative Director Richard Kaijuka had received a bribe to support the project in his previous role as Uganda's Energy Minister,[30] the export credit agency's withdrawal of its support and alleged economic difficulties faced by AES Corporation.[31] Bribes were reportedly also offered to Ugandan Members of Parliament by a UK-based consultancy firm, Amisa Consultants Ltd., hired by the main contractor of the project Nordic Consortium Norpak Power to induce them to vote in favor of the Bujagali Project in lieu of an alternative project.[32] An investigation was launched by the US Department of Justice in 2003 into bribery allegations surrounding the project for violations of the Foreign Corrupt Practices Act.[33] Investigations by the UK Serious Fraud Office, Norwegian and Swedish anti-fraud institutions as well as the Ugandan Inspector General followed.[34]

After the initial project was halted, the Ugandan government reopened the tender and contracted Bujagali Energy Limited (BEL) as the new project sponsor.[35] BEL is owned by a consortium of SG Bujagali Holdings Ltd, which is an affiliate of the US company Sithe Global Power, LLC, and Industrial Promotion Services (Kenya) Limited, the industrial development arm of the Aga Khan Fund for Economic Development (AKFED).[36] The consortium has ownership and operation rights of the power plant for thirty years under the Build-Own-Operate-Transfer (BOOT) scheme, after which time it will transfer the plant to the

[29] Carl Bruch et al., "Compendium of Relevant Practices for Improved Decision-Making, Planning and Management of Dams and Their Alternatives: Compliance" (Prepared for UNEP"s Dams and Development Project), April 2007, p. 154.

[30] Roger Tangri and M. Andrew Mwenda, *The Politics of Elite Corruption in Africa: Uganda in Comparative African Perspective* (Routledge, 2013), p. 99.

[31] WB and IFC, "Project Completion Note (Guarantee No. B-003-0-UG) – the Bujagali HPP in the Republic of Uganda Report No. 33722-UG" paras. 5 and 6; and Mutaizibwa, "Bujagali: Finally, light at the end of tunnel."

[32] David Pallister, "Africa Dam's Passage 'Eased by Bribes'," *Guardian*, 3 November 2003, www.theguardian.com/uk/2003/nov/03/davidpallister (accessed 15 April 2019).

[33] Tangri and Mwenda, *The Politics of Elite Corruption in Africa*, p. 100.

[34] Pallister, "Africa Dam's Passage 'Eased by Bribes'."

[35] Website of Bujagali HPP, www.bujagali-energy.com (accessed 15 April 2019).

[36] Website of Bujagali HPP, "About Us," www.bujagali-energy.com/bujagali_aboutUs1.htm (accessed 15 April 2019).

Ugandan government.[37] The new Bujagali HPP was approved in April 2007 by the Ugandan government as well as the WBG and other lenders.[38] Bujagali Energy Limited has argued that the project has numerous benefits for Uganda, including an increased electricity supply, lower electricity costs, improved air quality, jobs and improvements for nearby villages.[39] The project is also registered as a Clean Development Mechanism (CDM) project (in fact, the largest in a "Least Developed Country") under the Kyoto Protocol of the UN Framework Convention on Climate Change (UNFCCC), due to offset 900 thousand tons of carbon emissions.[40]

The Bujagali HPP was completed on the same site as the first cancelled project. The area had been prepared for the project during the first phase, including through the resettlement of the communities inhabiting the land on which the dam was to be built.[41] Although BEL was not involved with the project when the resettlement process took place in 2001, it took over the commitments to the affected persons that extend to providing in-kind or in-service compensation to resettled villagers after the project was resumed: "[a]lthough resettlement activities for the project were largely completed by the previous sponsor in 2001 through 2003, completion of resettlement related activities are the responsibility of BEL."[42] According to the IFC, in addition to commissioning the new Social and Environmental Assessment, BEL also "conducted additional formal and informal consultations in Uganda regarding the new circumstances of the project."[43] Bujagali Energy Limited committed to running a social program and "spending 2.8 million [USD] on projects ranging from environmental conservation to health, from water to sanitation to education, agriculture to income-raising programmes,

[37] AKDN, "Press Release – President Museveni and the Aga Khan Inaugurate Bujagali Hydropower Plant," 8 October 2012.

[38] CAO puts the project value at 750 million USD while the EIB estimates it to be at 900 million USD.

[39] Website of Bujagali HPP, www.bujagali-energy.com.

[40] Alstom-Kaplan, "Advertorial – Bujagali: Powering Uganda from the Nile," *International Water Power & Dam Construction* (www.waterpowermagazine.com), March 2013, 20.

[41] Phiona Nampungu and Diana Kasabiiti, "The Impact of Involuntary Resettlement on Children – A Case Study of the International Development Association Funded Bujagali Hydro-Power Dam – Naminya Resettlement Area," BIC, 2012, p. 5.

[42] IFC, "Bujagali Energy Ltd. – Environmental & Social Review Summary," http://ifcext.ifc.org/ifcext/spiwebsite1.nsf/ProjectDisplay/ESRS24408 (accessed 15 April 2019).

[43] IFC Projects Database, "Bujagali Energy Ltd. – Environmental & Social Review Summary (accessed 15 April 2019)."

reforestation to rural electrification."[44] The most notable of these projects included a piped water provision project, construction and upgrading of health clinics, and the construction of schools.

The Project Appraisal Process

The Bujagali project appraisal process consisted of two cycles of appraisal for the two projects. Bujagali was designed as a public-private partnership (PPP), entailing an equity contribution from the national government as well as from project sponsors and loans from donors. As such, each of the cycles of appraisal was due to be subjected to two levels of scrutiny: scrutiny at the national level to secure state backing for the project and scrutiny at the international level, in order to be able to secure financing from international investors and institutions. When projects based on PPP and financed through international loans are appraised, this second stage of scrutiny at international level is also needed as a fail-safe for the first level.

The first Bujagali project's appraisal at the domestic level was tainted with allegations of corruption and bribery, barring the existence of any credible and objective scrutiny at the national level.[45] The second level of scrutiny at the international level depended notably on the appraisal of the WBG, which had been considering supporting the project through IDA and IFC loans and a MIGA equity guarantee. As later evidenced, the appraisal by the WBG had not adequately addressed transparency concerns and possible social impacts. Nevertheless, scrutiny at the international level is all the more pivotal in ensuring that proposed projects deliver promised development benefits and do not cause adverse impacts on communities and the environment when scrutiny at national level is ineffective, not sufficiently objective or absent due to resource constraints or corruption. The potential results of a proposed project on the social and environmental plane, that provide a background to appraisal by potential financiers at the international level, are covered by environmental and social impact assessments (ESIA) as required by these institutions. When adverse impacts on communities are projected or suspected, impact assessments are usually accompanied or followed by consultations with local populations on how best to address these adverse impacts and accompanying grievances.

[44] BEL, "Clean, Sustainable Hydropower for Uganda," 2012, www.akdn.org/assets/1/1510.pdf (accessed 15 April 2019).

[45] Tangri and Mwenda, *The Politics of Elite Corruption in Africa*, pp. 98–100.

The Bujagali HPP ESIA was conducted jointly for the numerous lenders, although the different lenders have different safeguard policies or internal rules regarding acceptable impact. In fact, because the project was launched twice, two rounds of impact assessments were undertaken, first in 2001 and later in 2005 and 2006.

First Project The Environmental Impact Assessment (EIA) for the first project noted that initial assessments undertaken in the late 1990s had listed "main impacts on the natural environment" as the inundation of Bujagali falls and land, and a positive impact on fisheries.[46] Major concerns of the local population regarding social impacts were concentrated on resettlement and compensation for lost property and crops. Project-affected persons were defined as those losing assets, including land rights, structures, crops or any combination of the three.[47] The 2001 WB Project Appraisal Document (PAD) noted that the construction of the hydropower facility would result in the physical displacement of 101 households with 714 individuals and that the total number of households affected would be 1,288 with 8,700 people.[48] The integrated transmission project would affect 522 households with 1,867 individuals and physically displace 326 households with 1,522 individuals.[49] It was considered that relocation to new houses nearby would be immediate and economic displacement would be minimal.[50]

The Resettlement Action Plan (RAP) of the first project concluded that the rights of children and women within the displaced households would be guaranteed in line with the protections accorded by the Ugandan Constitution and the 1998 Land Act Section 40, which require prior written consent of spouses before land transactions can take place.[51] It was further noted that cash compensation for lost assets would put women "at risk of being deprived of the productive assets they use for their and their children's subsistence."[52] "Women and children at risk of being dispossessed of their productive assets – land" and orphans were

46 ESG International Inc. and WS Atkins International for AES Nile Power, "Environmental Impact Assessment," E464 Vol. 2, March 2001, p. 145.

47 ESG International and WS Atkins International, "EIA," p. 307.

48 WB, "Bujagali HPP – PAD," p. 37.

49 Ibid.

50 Ibid., p. 38.

51 ESG International Inc. and WS Atkins International for AES Nile Power, "Bujagali Project Hydropower Facility Resettlement and Community Action Plan," March 2001, p. 18, para. 3.43 at 15 and para. 3.57.

52 ESG and WS Atkins, "Bujagali Project Hydropower Facility RAP," p. 57, para. 7.6.

considered among vulnerable people for the purposes of the project.[53] These so-called vulnerable people would have to first of all be identified because they did not routinely participate in the community's meetings.[54]

The PAD included "the adoption of appropriate environmental and social safeguard policies and an environmental management plan" as one of the values-added of the involvement of WBG in the project.[55] The WB Project Information Document (PID) noted that the staff of project sponsor AESNP would be in charge of monitoring the resettlement and community action plans, "reinforced by external, independent evaluations" as well as supervision through third-party review.[56] The "technical, economic, financial, environmental and social due diligence" aspects of the project appraisal process were led by the IFC in cooperation with the IDA, while the IDA worked directly with the government on the "power sector reform program."[57] The PAD asserted that the IFC and IDA's due diligence had been extensive and discounted any criticism of the insufficiency of environmental and social baseline data.[58] Children were not an operative focus of the WB PAD beyond the two references to the protection of the rights of child landowners.[59]

Second Project The second project's impact assessment documents included an analysis of the compliance of the project with "relevant international environmental treaties and agreements"[60] as required per WB's Operational Directive 4.01 on Environmental Assessment applicable at the time.[61] As WB regulations required compliance only with international environmental treaties, no similar assessment of the social

[53] Ibid., p. vii.

[54] Ibid., para. 10.3 at 86.

[55] WB, "Uganda: Bujagali HPP – Project Appraisal Document" (PAD), 2001, p. 19, http://documents.worldbank.org/curated/en/2001/11/1631763/uganda-bujagali-hydropower-project (accessed 24 April 2019).

[56] WB, "Bujagali HPP – Project Information Document" (Report No. PID8803), 2001, p. 10, www-wds.worldbank.org/external/default/WDSContentServer/WDSP/IB/2000/04/13/000094946_00032106082737/Rendered/PDF/multi0page.pdf (accessed 24 April 2019).

[57] WB, "Bujagali – PAD," p. 20.

[58] Ibid., p. 39.

[59] Ibid., pp. 111 and 117.

[60] R.J. Burnside International Ltd, "Bujagali Energy Ltd (BEL) Bujagali HPP Social and Environmental Assessment Main Report" (SEA Main Report), File No: I-A 10045, December 2006, pp. 323–324.

[61] WB, Operational Directive 4.01 – Environmental Assessments, January 1999 (Revised April 2013), para. 3.

impacts in line with Uganda's other international obligations, including on human rights, was undertaken. This goes to demonstrate the importance of designing standards and safeguard policies that require comprehensive assessments of obligations covered by national law and international treaties. Unless the assessment procedures explicitly require it, relevant international treaties or conventions are often sidestepped.

The impact assessment of the second project noted that the IFC had introduced new requirements through its Sustainability Policy since the completion of the impact assessments for the first project, which included the need for an overall "Broad Community Support" (BCS) for projects that pose risks of significant adverse impact.[62] While the project sponsor company is required to prepare the impact assessments and resettlement plans, the IFC itself is tasked with ascertaining BCS for a project, through its own investigation.[63] The IFC concluded that BCS for the project was present.[64] The impact assessment of the second project included information on the resettlement activities undertaken by the previous project sponsor in 2001 by surveying a sample of affected people. The definition of Project-Affected Persons was based on the complete or partial, temporary or permanent loss of the "right to own, use, or otherwise benefit from a built structure, land (residential, agricultural, or pasture), annual or perennial crops and trees, or any other fixed or moveable asset."[65] Consultations with resettled people reflected a number of common complaints related to unfulfilled promises of a refurbished school at the resettlement site as well as a health clinic providing adequate service. Not all resettled persons expressed satisfaction with livelihood restoration; while some considered themselves better off as a result, others had complaints relating to the small size or lack of quality of the resettlement land offered.

Bujagali Energy Limited (BEL) offered to strengthen health facilities on both sides of the riverbank to improve the access to healthcare of "the wider project-affected-population" and providing assistance to existing health centers on either bank by "construction and/or procurement of accommodation facilities for health workers" to ensure that they reside in the communities and not commute from outside.[66] BEL also made promises of a commercial area/market to

[62] Burnside, "Bujagali SEA Main Report," p. 274.
[63] IFC, "IFC Sustainability Framework Policy and Performance Standards."
[64] Burnside, "Bujagali SEA Main Report," p. 274.
[65] Ibid., p. 346.
[66] Ibid., p. 335.

create economic opportunities for women. The impact assessment concluded that the development of modern water schemes was needed because boreholes developed by the previous sponsor and most hand pumps had ceased to function by 2006. The same assessment recognized that the community's electrification by connection to the grid in the short term was unrealistic. BEL's other commitments included improvements to existing school structures, the construction of new ones and the provision of educational equipment.[67]

The second project's impact assessments listed children and in particular orphans as a vulnerable group alongside women, the elderly and persons with disabilities. Because the resettlement had already taken place, the second project was not considered to cause significant impacts on vulnerable groups. While women in the community were responsible for many of the daily tasks related to food supply as well as childcare, fetching water and collecting firewood, they did not own family land and were at a disadvantage. Although the specific situation of children in the community was not addressed in the impact assessment, safety concerns around children included risks related to the fluctuation of water levels during the day and more indirectly, concerns over pedestrian safety. In addition, prohibition of forced and child labor through the verification of employer age was among the requirements imposed on BEL and its contractors.[68]

Consultations

Consultations with project-affected communities as well as a broader group of stakeholders were carried out for both projects. The Public Consultation and Disclosure Plan (PCDP) developed for the second project considered that applicable law and frameworks in the consultation process included the WB Safeguard Policy Framework, IFC Sustainability Policy and Performance Standards, MIGA Policy on Social and Environmental Sustainability, AfDB's Integrated Environmental and Social Assessment Guidelines and other relevant policies on private sector projects and involuntary displacement, EIB policy requirements, DEG's social and environmental requirements

[67] Ibid., pp. 335–338.
[68] Ibid., pp. 137, 145 and 419.

and the Equator Principles.[69] The Assessment of Past Resettlement Activities and Action Plan (APRAP) within the context of the PCDP identified various shortcomings in the preparation and execution of the resettlement activities. The focus-group discussions conducted for the APRAP uncovered various discontents among the affected population, including those who were resettled, those who chose compensation instead of resettlement and those who were originally living in locations where affected communities were resettled.[70] The most common grievances involved the unfulfilled promises of a school, adequate health facilities, a market place and electricity supply to the resettlement villages, in addition to the questions about the fairness of compensation and resettlement packages, the poor quality of the resettled land and constructed houses, and the lack of availability of clean potable water.[71] It was noted by APRAP that the database prepared for the 2001 resettlement plans had not adequately identified vulnerable people, creating a possible point of noncompliance with WBG operational policies. Although "orphans, widows and people with disabilities" were already considered vulnerable, the 2001 plans did not adequately identify such persons within the community, rendering it "virtually impossible to identify, locate and monitor vulnerable people" in the lead-up to the second project.[72] Vulnerable people were defined more broadly for the second project as those that "may be more adversely affected by resettlement than others and who may be limited in their ability to claim or take advantage of resettlement assistance and related development benefits" given their background.[73] Child-headed households, disabled persons, female-headed poor households, widows, orphans, elderly and the seriously ill were explicitly identified as vulnerable by the report. In addition, the community's involvement in the identification of vulnerable people was considered essential in order to avoid grievances.[74]

[69] Burnside International, Canada Dillon Consultants Ltd, Canada et al., "Bujagali HPP, Uganda Public Consultation and Disclosure Plan (PCDP) DRAFT," File No: I-A 10045, November 2006, pp. 3–6.

[70] Frederic Giovannetti, "Assessment of Past Resettlement Activities and Action Plan (APRAP)," in R.J. Burnside International, Canada Dillon Consultants Ltd, Canada et al., "Bujagali HPP, Uganda Public Consultation and Disclosure Plan (PCDP) DRAFT," File No: I-A 10045, November 2006, p. 73.

[71] Ibid., pp. 62–93.

[72] Ibid., p. 24.

[73] The bases for vulnerability were listed as "gender, ethnicity, age, physical or mental disability, economic disadvantage, or social status." (Ibid., p. 32.)

[74] Ibid.

Focus-group discussions, conducted separately with women and with men, also revealed great discrepancies between the level of information given to affected men and to women as well as clear indications that women's free and informed consent had not been formally or explicitly sought. Women in families that sought compensation in lieu of resettlement reported that the compensation had in many instances been directly given to men and spent at their discretion.[75] The women in the Naminya resettlement village had not been consulted before the new villagers were settled, while the men reported being notified.[76]

Children were not directly identified prior to and consulted for either of the resettlement action plan preparations. The APRAP noted that Ugandan law required prior consent of spouses and children of affected persons and the second project would comply with this requirement. But the impacts of the 2001 resettlement on children, including those heading households, were not reported or tracked. The focus-group discussions also revealed that children's diets had deteriorated as a result of resettlement, since the reported poor quality of the new lands given to resettled families only allowed the cultivation of cassava (tapioca) and beans, and the readily accessible fruits at their original residence location were no longer available.[77] Some children were reportedly unable to attend school because they were resettled in a remote location.[78] In addition, the lack of adequate staff and availability of medications at the healthcare center were considered an additional disadvantage for children, especially if children fell ill in the evenings or weekends.[79]

Impacts on Local Communities and Children

The US-based NGO Bank Information Center (BIC) prepared a case study of the negative impacts of resettlement on affected children during the first Bujagali project. The findings related mostly to thirty-five households with approximately 350 members resettled in Naminya in 2001. Accordingly, most benefits promised to resettled communities such as "electricity in their homes, clean water, land titles, schools, a health centre, markets and roads" did not materialize.[80] The project-affected communities were reportedly not consulted prior to the planning and

[75] Ibid., p. 79.
[76] Ibid., p. 73.
[77] Ibid., pp. 51, 67, 73, and 80.
[78] Ibid., p. 104.
[79] Ibid., p. 63.
[80] Nampungu and Kasabiiti, "Impact of Involuntary Resettlement on Children," p. 3.

implementation of the resettlement but "rather informed about the choices available once the plan was already in place."[81] Two types of compensation schemes, a full resettlement package including new land allocations or cash compensation, were made available. Those opting for the first option were resettled to Naminya and given a plot of land with a house as well as cash for crop losses and a moving allowance while others choosing the cash compensation would relocate by themselves. The main allegation centered on the loss of livelihoods especially with respect to access to food and under-compensation. The insufficient diet had reportedly increased children's susceptibility to disease in the absence of means to include protein sources.[82] Prior to resettlement, the affected persons had several sources of income including fishing, coffee trading, farming and shop-keeping or other services, which were not available post-resettlement. The overall sentiment was that living standards had declined. Another complaint centered on the lack of access to safe drinking water, often resulting in girl children having to travel long distances to fetch and carry water back to the village, which allegedly had detrimental effects on school attendance and exposed these children to the risk of sexual violence.[83]

Access to healthcare facilities being a part of the resettlement package had led to a clinic being opened at one of the unoccupied houses but this clinic was reported as lacking essential equipment, a maternity ward and access to adequate medicines as well as experiencing issues with regard to the consistent presence of personnel.[84] The households had no access to electricity, (this was not a part of the resettlement package) and lacked the means to obtain it themselves.[85]

The residents of the resettlement village also reported that access to education for affected children had been severely curtailed as a result of the nearest Universal Primary School being nearly five kilometers from the village. Although BEL ensured this primary school would accommodate resettled children, the distance was considered an insurmountable impediment. The distance issue was even more problematic for secondary school-aged children, as attending school required, in some cases, relocation to other towns. According to the report, BEL had built a nursery school in the village following the persistence of the parents,

[81] Ibid., p. 4.
[82] Ibid., p. 5.
[83] Ibid., p. 10.
[84] Ibid., p. 9.
[85] Ibid., p. 6.

but this school could not be registered in the UPE program of the Ugandan government, despite the villagers' contention that this had in fact been promised. The school was being operated as a private school with a fee per term, which some resettled families reportedly could not afford. The quality of the education was called into question, owing to the lack of resources to accommodate the 200 children attending and the lack of proper certification for some of the teachers, while the opportunities for access to education in the resettlement village for children with disabilities were deemed even more limited.[86] This case study was submitted to the WB Safeguards review team to underscore the need for revised safeguards to consider the needs of children

> particularly by requiring environmental and social impact assessments to specifically assess the unique impacts of projects on children and by explicitly including provisions in the resettlement policy that require that the resettlement action plan to adequately provide for children's unique needs, rather than simply including children in a laundry list of vulnerable groups.[87]

The BIC also carried out a consultation round with children from the Naminya resettlement village, who also confirmed their concerns around the unavailability of adequate food supply, the difficulties resulting from the inexistence of secondary schools, the inadequacy of primary schools, the long distances children need to travel to reach school, as well as school dropouts due to the inability of parents to afford sending children to school.[88] Some children reported that they had to start working to contribute to their families' livelihood. The participating children maintained that WB involuntary resettlement policies should be improved "to guarantee access to education, shelter, health care, water, and adequate nutrition."[89]

A 2008 report by Uganda-based NGO National Association of Professional Environmentalists (NAPE), one of the most vocal opponents of the project, alleged that project-affected individuals "were not

[86] Ibid., pp. 11–12.

[87] BIC, "Press Release – Case Study on Bujagali Dam's Negative Impacts on Children Submitted to the WB," 11 April 2013, www.bankinformationcenter.org/case-study-on-bujagali-dams-negative-impacts-on-children-submitted-to-the-world-bank/ (accessed 15 April 2019).

[88] BIC, "The Need for Child Protection Measures in the WB Safeguards – Naminya Children's Consultation," 2013, www.bankinformationcenter.org/wp-content/uploads/2013/10/Uganda-consultation-report.pdf (accessed 15 April 2019).

[89] BIC, "Children's Voices on WB Safeguards," 2013, p. 12.

adequately educated and informed about their rights, entitlements and the standards of compensation and resettlements associated with such projects as the Bujagali project."[90] The NAPE claimed that houses in the resettlement village were badly built, which was also noted by the children consulted by BIC in 2013, and NAPE has claimed that the consultation process was "carried out more as a formality to secure approval to secure approval of WB funds" with limited participation of women.[91] During a visit of the resettled communities by WB officials in November 2013,[92] concerns were raised around the inadequacy of the resettlement situation for persons with disabilities.[93] The project was also controversial from the beginning because of its location as the area had been a major tourist destination for white-water rafting and the project would effectively mean an end to revenues for those involved in the tourism sector. In response, the sponsor argued that it was working with the Ugandan government and tour operators to develop additional tourism activities in the lake formed behind the dam.[94]

3.2.2 *Legal Analysis*

Domestic Legislation and International Commitments

Article 34 of the Ugandan Constitution of 1995 guarantees specific rights to children that include the right to basic education, right to health and protections for orphaned or vulnerable children.[95] In addition, Uganda enacted "The Children Act" in 1997, which designates the welfare principle as the guiding principle in decisions related to children and bases a child's right to "education and guidance, immunisation, adequate diet, clothing, shelter and medical attention" on the parental duty to maintain

[90] NAPE, "Facts About Violated WB and AfDB Policies in the Controversial Bujagali Project: A Civil Society Perspective," January 2008, p. 20.

[91] Betty Obbo, "Where Are Women's Voices in Uganda's Dam Planning?" *International Rivers Review*, March 2011.

[92] The Bretton Woods Project, "Safeguards Review Neglects People with Disability, Children," 23 January 2014, www.brettonwoodsproject.org/2014/01/safeguards-review-neglects-people-disability-children/ (accessed 15 April 2019).

[93] The Bretton Woods Project, "Safeguards Review Neglects People with Disability, Children."

[94] BEL, "Clean, Sustainable Hydropower for Uganda."

[95] The Republic of Uganda, "Constitution of the Republic of Uganda," 1995, "Chapter IV: Protection and Promotion of Fundamental and Other Human Rights and Freedoms," Art. 34.

a child.[96] The Ugandan Education Act of 2008 designates education as the joint responsibility of a child's parents/legal guardians and the state with basic education deemed a right for all persons.[97] Although universal primary education (UPE) is deemed by this legislation to be free of charge,[98] it is only these UPE public schools that are entitled to government financing. Uganda ratified the CRC in 1990 and became a party to the African Charter on the Rights and Welfare of the Child (ACRWC) in 1994.

Children's Rights Violations Linked to the Bujagali Project

Specific children's rights impacted by the Bujagali projects include the right to information, the right to express one's views, the right to health and the right to education.

Article 12 CRC states that children capable of forming their views have the right to express those views "freely in all matters affecting the child" and that those views are to be "given due weight in accordance with the age and maturity of the child." Article 7 ACRWC also states that children capable of expressing their views have the right to do so freely. No effort had been made – systematic or otherwise – to ensure that children within the project-affected community were given an opportunity to express their concerns, needs or opinions in relation to the project. The CRC Committee has further noted that the right to express their views means, from a practical standpoint, that children have to be given the opportunity "to speak, to participate, to have their views taken into account."[99] The children impacted by the Bujagali project, including the resettled children, were not consulted during the lead-up to the first or the second project. Even in the cases of child-headed households within the affected population, where children did not have parental support and advocacy on their behalf, their views on the project and how it might impact their livelihoods were not sought.

The CRC Committee considers a child's right of access to information covered under Article 13 CRC as quintessentially linked to that child's right to express their views.[100] It was alleged by BIC that project-affected

[96] The Republic of Uganda, "The Children Act," s. 3 (First Schedule) and s. 5, respectively.

[97] UNICEF and FIDA Uganda, "A Simplified Handbook on International and National Laws & Policies on Children – Uganda," 2014, p. 46.

[98] Ibid.

[99] CRC Committee, "Report on the Forty-Third Session, Day of General Discussion, Recommendations," September 2006, Preamble.

[100] CRC Committee, "2006 Day of General Discussion, Recommendations," para. 12.

children's right of access to information had been neglected in the preparation of the resettlement, rendering children's adjustment to their new circumstances more difficult.[101] The first project's RAP and the renewed RAP for the second project did not envisage informing children on the process and the impact of the project on their daily lives and livelihoods, although separate information sessions and consultations were held with men and women in the community. The attention to gender issues, especially in the context of the second project, can be traced back to the fact that the WB has had policy guidance on gender from the late 1980s onwards and adopted a specific policy on gender in the late 1990s. As no similar WB policy on children exists and there are no explicit requirements to include impacts on children in the appraisal process, children have categorically fallen through the cracks in the information and consultation process. The Bujagali experience demonstrates that even when clear disruptions to children's everyday lives such as the resettlement of homes, change of schools attended, disturbances in the provision of healthcare are foreseen within the application of a project, children's rights of access to information and of expressing their views may be wholly ignored in the absence of clear guidelines and policies ensuring compliance with them.

The overarching concerns related to children's health in the context of the Bujagali project were the inadequacy of healthcare facilities in the Naminya resettlement village and the lack of a balanced diet for children due to the loss of habitual fruit staples and fish from their diets. The main community concerns around access to healthcare facilities in the Naminya resettlement village included the unavailability of healthcare staff outside of limited time periods and the lack of access to adequate medicines and supplies. According to CRC Committee's GC 15, primary health services have to be available "in sufficient quantity and quality, functional, within the physical and financial reach of all sections of the child population."[102] One important parameter for the quality and quantity of available health services is the existence of a sufficient and "appropriately trained workforce."[103] The physical existence of a healthcare center, therefore, is not enough to suggest that the right to health of children is being respected.

[101] Nampungu and Kasabiiti, "Impact of Involuntary Resettlement on Children," p. 4.
[102] CRC Committee, GC 15, para. 25.
[103] Ibid., para. 27.

The other health-related concern, expressed especially by mothers in the community, was the loss of access to a balanced diet that previously included a variety of fruits as well as fish. As CESCR's GC 12 notes, the "core content" of the right to food is not limited to the availability of any type of nourishment but means "the availability of food in a quantity and quality sufficient to satisfy the dietary needs of individuals."[104] A state's "failure to regulate activities of individuals or groups so as to prevent them from violating the right to food of others" amounts to a violation of the right to food, while the private business sector has a responsibility to respect the right to adequate food.[105] As a component of children's right to health, the right to adequate food requires not only that children do not suffer from hunger but also that they are able to enjoy a balanced diet from a diversity of sources. The CRC Committee's GC 15 also underscores the obligation of due diligence to respect all human rights on the part of the private sector, allowing businesses to "identify, prevent and mitigate their negative impact on children's right to health including across their business relationships and within any global operations."[106]

The resettled communities from Bujagali had to wait for almost a decade for an operational primary school. They had been resettled in 2001 and the school only became operational in 2010.[107] The school, however, was considered a private school and therefore not covered under Uganda's UPE support system. Although it was later argued by AfDB's IRM Monitoring Mission that the private company BEL had carried out all the commitments undertaken by itself and the previous sponsor under the RAP with regard to education of resettled community children, the community no longer had access to a free of charge primary school within the village covered under UPE. In addition, resettled families had to privately fund the primary schooling facilities not out of choice but out of necessity because young children were unable to walk the required long distances to physically access existing school facilities. Article 28.1(b) CRC and Article 11.3(a) ACRWC underscore that the right to education includes free and compulsory primary education. In addition, Article 28.1(b) CRC states that secondary education (either as general or vocational education) should be "available and accessible to every child," while Article 11.3(b) ACRWC

104 CESCR, GC 12, para. 8.

105 Ibid., paras. 19 and 20, respectively.

106 CRC Committee, GC 15, para. 80.

107 AfDB IRM, "2nd Monitoring Report on the Implementation of Findings of Non-Compliance and Related Actions to Be Undertaken by the ADB Management on the Bujagali Hydropower and Interconnection Projects," 28 July 2010, p. 7.

aims at making secondary education progressively accessible and free of charge. The UN Committee on Economic, Social and Cultural Rights' (CESCR) GC 13 requires both physical and economic accessibility. Accordingly, education must be "within safe physical reach" and "affordable to all," or in the case of primary education, "free."[108] Coomans, for instance, argued early on for the core content of the right to education to be realized immediately as a minimum claim includes compulsory and free primary education being "so fundamental for the development of a person's abilities."[109] Likewise, CESCR has recognized that the "obligation to provide primary education for all is an immediate duty of all States parties."[110]

3.2.3 *Involvement of Businesses*

The second Bujagali HPP's sponsor BEL is jointly owned by Industrial Promotion Services Ltd (Kenya) which is a part of the Aga Khan Fund for Economic Development (AKFED) arm of AKDN and SG Bujagali Holdings Ltd, an affiliate of Sithe Global Power (USA). The two companies have jointly invested 180 million USD of private equity in the project.[111] Sithe Global Power is majority-owned by Blackstone Capital Partners, which is a US publicly traded private equity firm.[112] Blackstone owns two-thirds of the Bujagali HPP, having invested twice the sum invested by AKDN (120 million USD).[113] AKFED is self-described as "an international development agency dedicated to promoting entrepreneurship and building economically sound enterprises in the developing world," focusing on regions lacking "sufficient foreign direct investment" and "makes bold but calculated investments in situations that are fragile and complex."[114] The commercial operations of the Bujagali HPP commenced in August 2012. In addition to the project sponsors, the Italian

108 CESCR, GC 13, para. 6(b).

109 Fons Coomans, "Clarifying the Core Content of the Right to Education," SIM Special n° 18: The Right To Complain About Economic, Social and Cultural Rights: Proceedings of the Expert Meeting on the Adoption of an Optional Protocol to the International Covenant on Economic, Social and Cultural Rights, 25–29 January 1995.

110 CESCR, GC 13, para. 51.

111 IFC, "Uganda: Bujagali Hydropower Project A Case Study on Risk Mitigation Through PPP Structuring," 15 November 2011, p. 1.

112 Ryan Dezember and Nicholas Bariyo, "Private-Equity Firms Build Instead of Buy," *Wall Street Journal*, 14 May 2013, www.wsj.com/articles/SB10001424127887323628004578461223864870026 (accessed 15 April 2019).

113 Dezember and Bariyo, "Private-Equity Firms Build Instead of Buy."

114 AKDN Website, "Aga Khan Fund for Economic Development (AKFED)," www.akdn.org/akfed.asp (accessed 15 April 2019).

construction firm Salini was contracted to build the infrastructure for the HPP. Moreover, the electricity transmission operations are a public-private partnership (PPP) between BEL on the one hand, and the Government of Uganda and the state-owned Uganda Electricity Transmission Company Limited on the other.[115] The other private companies involved in the Bujagali project are private financial institutions ABSA Capital, an affiliate of Barclays, which extended a commercial loan with a sixteen-year maturity[116] and Standard Chartered Bank.

Financing the Bujagali HPP

The financing structure of a large-scale infrastructure project such as the Bujagali HPP tends to be complex. In the case of the Bujagali HPP, the project sponsor BEL extended 172.5 million USD in equity with a credit guarantee from Multilateral Investment Guarantee Agency (MIGA) of 115 million USD.[117] The MIGA equity investment guarantee acted as insurance against the riks of contract breach and covered Sithe Global's equity investment in the project through its subsidiary World Power Holdings Luxembourg S.à.r. l.[118] The project was supported by the WBG, through loans from the IDA of 115 million USD and IFC of 130 million USD. Other lenders included the African Development Bank (AfDB) with 110 million USD in loans, the European Investment Bank (EIB) with 136 million USD in loans and several European development finance institutions: FMO – Netherlands (83 million USD in loans), Proparco and AFD – France (60 and 12.8 million USD in loans, respectively), DEG and KfW – Germany (30 and 15 million USD in loans, respectively).[119] In addition, Barclays/ABSA Capital and Standard Chartered Bank provided commercial loans under an IDA Partial Risk Guarantee (115 million USD).[120]

[115] Sithe Global Website, "Bujagali Project," www.sitheglobal.com/projects/bujagali.cfm (accessed 15 April 2019).

[116] ABSA Capital, "Press Release – Absa Capital, Barclays Plc Team Up on $867m Uganda Hydropower Project," 17 January 2008.

[117] IFC, "Uganda: Bujagali Hydropower Project (Bujagali HPP) A Case Study on Risk Mitigation through PPP Structuring," 15 November 2011. (Estimated on the basis of reports that the total equity level was 192.5 million USD while the public equity contribution was 20 million USD. Other sources have put the BEL equity at 180 million USD.)

[118] MIGA, "Power Brief – MIGA: Fortifying Power Investments," April 2008.

[119] AKDN, "President Museveni and the Aga Khan Inaugurate Bujagali HPP."

[120] The numbers have been modified with latest information from the different finance institutions. The original numbers are taken from: CAO, "Ombudsman Assessment Report, Fifth Complaint (Bujagali Energy-05) Regarding the Bujagali Energy Ltd. Project (IFC #24408 & MIGA #6732)," December 2011, p. 6.

The original financing plan of the Bujagali HPP set the project at 798 million USD,[121] although by the completion of the project in 2012, the estimated financing had reached close to 900 million USD.[122] According to the original financing plan, the project would run on a total debt of 627 million USD and equity of 171 million USD (provided by BEL and the Government of Uganda). During the course of the project, the additional debt came from the commitment of different European development finance institutions, which increased their credit from a cumulative 142 million USD to 200.8 million USD.[123]

The IDA provided the Partial Risk Guarantee of 115 million USD for loans provided through ABSA Bank and Standard Chartered Bank. The aim of the IDA Partial Risk Guarantee was to reduce the risk perception of the project so that commercial debt from private sources would be mobilized and to improve the terms which would accompany such mobilization for the benefit of the project sponsor of access to low-cost, long-term financing. In essence, the IDA guarantee covers the loans provided by ABSA and Standard Chartered Banks to BEL as these loans mature and are due, in cases of political force majeure, legislative changes rendering BEL's activities unlawful or the "agreements unenforceable or void," restrictions on the transfer of funds beyond borders and government failure to discharge its payment obligations.[124] The IDA is bound by WB's safeguard policies. In fact, the Partial Risk Guarantee Agreement in the Bujagali HPP includes a Project Agreement between the IDA and BEL, "under which the company covenants that it complies with WB environmental guidelines and other applicable requirements."[125]

The Bujagali HPP was deemed a category A project with the highest level of social and environmental sensitivity within the IFC's classification scheme[126] designated for projects that are expected to have "significant adverse social and/or environmental impacts that are diverse,

121 WBG Finance, Economics & Urban (FEU) Department, "Financial Solutions: Partial Risk Guarantee – IDA Partial Risk Guarantee (PRG) to Promote Uganda's First Independent Power Producer," December 2007.

122 CAO, "Ombudsman Assessment Report, Fifth Complaint," p. 6.

123 WBG FEU Department, "IDA PRG to Promote Uganda's First Independent Power Producer."

124 Ibid.

125 Ibid.

126 IFC Projects Database, "Bujagali Energy Ltd. – Environmental & Social Review Summary."

irreversible, or unprecedented."[127] The IFC's assessment noted that the rating was linked to the environmental impact of the inundation of eighty hectares of land, including the Jinja Wildlife Sanctuary and Bujagali Falls and the displacement of local populations. In addition to resettlement and inundation, other key issues identified included adverse impacts on small-scale fisheries used by villagers, on commercial white-water rafting and recreational activities and the inundation of cultural/religious sites.[128]

3.2.4 Accountability for Business Involvement in the Bujagali

The Bujagali HPP has involved a number of companies including the first sponsor AES, the second sponsor BEL and the contractor Salini. The project sponsors have undertaken contractual commitments and concluded concessional agreements with the Government of Uganda as well as with the WBG for the loans and investment guarantees offered. These commitments require the sponsors to respect the laws in Uganda as well as WB's policies on social and environmental safeguards. The contractor is also obliged to abide by other financiers' social and environmental policies in addition to Uganda's laws and regulations. Even if the contractor is a foreign company, such as Salini in the Bujagali case, the Ugandan laws on labor, safety and environmental standards apply to this contractor equally. The crucial question is what happens when these domestic rules and regulations are not implemented effectively or adequately by the domestic state.

In addition to the project sponsors, large private businesses in the financial sector Barclays and Standard Chartered Bank are also linked to the project through funding provided by their subsidiary ABSA Capital. There is universal agreement that private companies operating anywhere have an obligation to comply with that state's laws and regulations. It is unclear, however, how a country could hold the financiers incorporated and operating abroad accountable for financing projects that adversely impact their citizens through its domestic legislation.

Uganda's domestic legal system remains the primary site for seeking accountability for corporate practices that result in violations of human

[127] IFC Website, "Definitions of Project Categories," www.ifc.org/wps/wcm/connect/corp_ext_content/tobedeleted/definitionofprojectcategories/projectcategoriesdefinitions (accessed 15 April 2019).

[128] IFC Projects Database, "Bujagali Energy Ltd. – Environmental & Social Review Summary."

rights, in particular of those like children that are more at risk of marginalization. Yet domestic legal systems may be weak or compromised – Uganda being a case in point based on the later substantiated corruption and bribery allegations surrounding the first project that resulted in its cancellation. In the absence of domestic recourse, affected populations seeking accountability have made appeals regarding their grievances first to the IFC/MIGA Compliance Advisor/Ombudsman (CAO) as the only redress mechanism providing direct access to businesses involved in the project.

Cases at the CAO

The first complaint regarding the first project submitted to the CAO in 2000 by NAPE was deemed ineligible on the grounds that the impact assessment report had not yet been released and the IFC's role in the project had not yet been formally determined. The ineligibility decision also noted that the complaint would in fact "fall within the mandate of Ombudsman's role, if still warranted" when the IFC's role was determined.[129] A second complaint was launched on 19 June 2001 and raised a number of issues around consultation and disclosure, environmental impact assessment as well as compensation and resettlement.[130] The complaint made allegations of important defects in the public consultation process and unsubstantiated claims about widespread support for the project using unrealistic sampling. Furthermore, the resettlement and compensation of the project-affected persons had started prior to the final approval of the project by the government and the lenders. In addition, the area affected by the project was spiritually important as the location of important shrines and spirits that were integral to the Busoga faith, affecting those of the faith not only in the project area but also outside it. The complaint highlighted the allegations of bribery and corruption in the press as well as concerns over the effectiveness of the project over alternatives and the tendering process. Previously, one of the complainant organizations NAPE had unsuccessfully applied for an injunction at the Ugandan High Court against AES. The objective had been to prevent the government from signing the Power Purchase Agreement before Uganda's National Environmental Management Authority (NEMA) had completed its evaluation of the EIA.[131]

129 FIVAS and NAPE, *Unsettling Business: Social Consequences of the Bujagali Hydropower Project* (FIVAS, 2014), p. 13 and NAPE, "Complaint About the Bujagali HPP," 19 June 2001, para. 1.

130 CAO, "Case Overview: Uganda/Bujagali Energy-02/Bujagali Falls," www.cao-ombudsman.org/cases/case_detail.aspx?id=114 (accessed 15 April 2019).

131 NAPE, "Complaint About the Bujagali HPP," para. 9(i).

Complainants had also attempted – again unsuccessfully – to trigger an investigation through the Prime Minister's Office and to get Parliamentary Committees in the Ugandan Parliament to examine their allegations.[132]

The assessment report by CAO noted that a WBG-commissioned study of alternative energy projects had indicated that Bujagali would be the least costly option.[133] This was considered by the CAO to amount to adequate due diligence. The CAO recommended that the issues related to the activities of the IDA be raised with the WB Inspection Panel, and noted its satisfaction with the work of the IFC's Environmental Department in "maintain[ing] a close watch" and being "diligent in ensuring that the sponsor complies with the IFC Safeguard Policies," given that the project had still not been approved by the Board.[134] The CAO considered AES' implementation of the resettlement plan without first waiting for the IFC clearance, a decision made at the company's own risk. Yet, the CAO also concluded that a borrower's ability to start the resettlement project without having to formally wait for IFC clearance amounted to a weakness in the IFC's system, especially in light of the IFC's claims to have leverage over its financed project at the said stage.[135] Because the IFC had not yet made a final decision on participating in the project, the CAO did not envisage a further facilitation or mediation role and the complaint was thus closed in January 2005 with no further action deemed "useful or productive" as the project had been halted.[136]

The second Bujagali HPP Project led to a total of six complaints at the CAO,[137] two of which were relevant to the social issues including allegations around the negative impacts of resettlement and failure of sponsors to deliver on promises as well as problems linked to the consultation and compensation processes.[138] The CAO's work is limited to an ombudsman and advisory role and does not include a mandate to decide on the

[132] Ibid., para. 9(ii)

[133] CAO, "Assessment Report: Complaint Filed to the CAO Regarding the Uganda Bujagali Hydropower Project," September 2001, p. 3.

[134] Ibid., p. 6.

[135] Ibid., p. 5.

[136] CAO, "Letter from Meg Taylor (Compliance Advisor/Ombudsman) to NAPE – Closing of Complaint: Bujagali HPP," 19 January 2005.

[137] Three complaints (4, 6 and 8) were filed by former employees Salini on workers' health and safety, compensation issues and one was a personal complaint on the inundation of grave sites belonging to family members (Complaint 3).

[138] Bujagali Affected Community, "Complaint to the IFC," 16 May 2011, www.cao-ombudsman.org/cases/document-links/documents/2011_May16Complaint_redacted.pdf (accessed 15 April 2019).

merits of the complaint but offered its good offices to the parties.[139] It was reported that tourism operators previously working in the Bujagali Falls and BEL reportedly reached agreements on issues related to the loss of livelihoods after the CAO assessment.[140]

A seventh complaint linked to the transmission project was launched with the CAO on 3 February 2015[141] on the issue of the "rate and non-payment of young crops" that were damaged due to project activities.[142] Reviewing the submission, the CAO decided to launch an investigation into the allegations. The claims that requirements for compensation for loss of assets had not been met were found substantial and IFC's implementation of Performance Standard 5 on Land Acquisition and Involuntary Resettlement in the context of the Interconnection Project raised questions about adequacy.[143] The investigation concluded that the IFC had acted without assurance that the compensation framework provided met IFC standards or that meaningful consultation with affected communities had been undertaken. The underlying causes for the shortcomings were found to be "(a) a lack of engagement with public sector institutional capacity in IFC's review of the RAP; and (b) an overreliance on other lenders during supervision of the project."[144]

Overall, the CAO provided a venue for attempting to compel businesses to introduce practical modifications to their behavior, albeit in limited ways. Of course, in the absence of explicit human rights provisions in the IFC's safeguard policies beyond the prohibition of forced and child labor, IFC's CAO does not constitute a venue to demand true and farther-reaching human rights accountability. The IFC's policies applicable to its clients are far narrower in scope than what would be required under Uganda's national law and by international legal standards. Nonetheless, the IFC's CAO has allowed affected peoples to directly

139 CAO, "Ombudsman Assessment Report, Fifth Complaint," 7.

140 CAO, "Case Overview – Uganda/Bujagali Energy-05/Bujagali."

141 CAO, "Case Overview – Uganda/Bujagali Energy-07/Bujagali," www.cao-ombudsman.org/cases/case_detail.aspx?id=230 (accessed 15 April 2019).

142 Malindi Village Affected Community, "7th Complaint Regarding the Bujagali Project," 10 January 2015.

143 CAO, "Compliance Appraisal Report: IFC Investment in Bujagali Energy Project (Project #24408) and MIGA Guarantee of World Power Holdings (MIGA Project #6732), Uganda – Complaint 07," 10 November 2016, p. 2, www.cao-ombudsman.org/cases/document-links/documents/CAO_Compliance_AppraisalReport_Bujagali07.pdf (accessed 15 April 2019).

144 CAO, "CAO Investigation of IFC/MIGA Social and Environmental Performance in Relation to: Bujagali Energy Limited and World Power Holdings, Uganda (Bujagali-07)," 15 December 2017.

address accountability by businesses for their actions when they have been immune from such attempts at the domestic level.

Complaints at the WB Inspection Panel

The complaint at the WB Inspection Panel on the first Bujagali project was launched within a week of the complaint at the IFC CAO upon IDA acceptance to provide project co-financing.[145] The requesters alleged that the rights and interests of local populations had been adversely affected through "inadequate involuntary resettlement (including compensation arrangements); inadequate consultation, participation and disclosure of information; and lack of economic and technical analysis" among others.[146] The Inspection Panel launched and completed an investigation into the allegations of requestors and found a number of compliance deficits on the part of the WB management as well as the project sponsor. The Inspection Panel found the assessment of the project's cumulative effects on the environment descriptive and weak and highlighted the shortcomings of the process, including the lack of balance in gender, across sectors and geography, in the evaluation of stakeholder perspectives.[147]

Within the context of involuntary resettlement, the Inspection Panel found that the compensation plans had been "addressed poorly in implementation, leading to enormous confusion amongst the affected people."[148] Although the socioeconomic survey requirement had been formally fulfilled, the Inspection Panel noted that the defects in the underlying analysis could have been at the heart of the failures of the compensation process, which the project sponsor AES accepted during the investigation, agreeing that the "process of valuing crops was initially botched."[149] Furthermore, the investigation revealed that the affected populations considered the witness NGO as being close to the project sponsor and therefore not impartial. Accordingly, WB management was not in compliance with WB Operational Directive 4.30 on Involuntary Resettlement, through its failure to ensure that "not only people physically displaced by projects, but, also those who suffer other

[145] WB Inspection Panel, "Investigation Report- UGANDA: Third Power Project (Credit No. 2268-UG), Fourth Power Project (Credit No. 3545-UG) and Bujagali Hydropower Project (PRG No. B 003-UG) (Report No. 23998)," 23 May 2002.

[146] Ibid., paras. 14 and 16.

[147] Ibid., para. 134.

[148] Ibid., para. 255

[149] Ibid., para. 259.

kinds of losses" were compensated through payment or rehabilitation.[150]

A second request for inspection was made on 5 March 2007 by NAPE, based on concerns on an array of economic, social and environmental issues.[151] The Inspection Panel investigation of the second Bujagali project included an assessment of the process of involuntary resettlement, action with regard to so-called vulnerable persons, and community development. The Inspection Panel found that the management decision to substitute an assessment of past resettlement activities for a proper action plan using the 2001 documentation had "far reaching consequences" and spillover effects on compliance with relevant policies.[152] As a result, the requirements to census all displaced persons, to conduct a meaningful public consultation and to document the effects of the original displacement and the delays on project-affected persons, were not adequately fulfilled.[153] The Inspection Panel noted that resettlement was an ongoing process and could not be considered to have reached a threshold once land was acquired or people were already moved, thus previous resettlement would not preclude compliance with WB policies on resettlement.[154] The cancellation of the first project and its continuation years later had been detrimental on the affected persons:

> [L]ivelihoods of affected people have been disrupted for some seven years, stemming back to the beginning of relocation and resettlement actions under the prior Bujagali dam project. During this period, many of the people that were originally displaced were essentially left in limbo, and did not receive key elements of the resettlement process to which they were entitled under Bank policy.[155]

The Inspection Panel's final assessment was that the Bujagali project did not "improve or at least ... restore, in real terms, the livelihoods and standards of living of the [displaced] people" and therefore, did not comply with the WB's relevant policy.[156] In fact, there was no monitoring

[150] Ibid., paras. 306–307.

[151] WB Inspection Panel, "Notice of Registration – Re: Request for Inspection Uganda: Private Power Generation Project (Proposed)," IPN Request RQ07/1, 7 March 2007, p. 1.

[152] WB Inspection Panel, "Investigation Report Uganda: Private Power Generation (Bujagali) Project (Guarantee No. BOl30-UG)," 29 August 2008, p. xiv.

[153] Ibid., paras. 450 and 454.

[154] Ibid., para. 453.

[155] Ibid., para. 468.

[156] Ibid., p. xiv and para. 517.

of livelihood restoration after 2001 when the partial resettlement activities took place and although WB social staff had recommended a resettlement audit in 2005, the Management had not responded favorably to this request.[157] The Inspection Panel also found that the project did not comply with the WB policies on vulnerable people. These people were not suitably identified until 2007. Neither specific livelihood risks and assistance to vulnerable people including tenant sharecroppers and children nor sustainability of assistance beyond project support were envisaged.[158] The Inspection Panel noted in a footnote that because children had been displaced along the transmission line during the distribution process after school enrolment, they were effectively prevented from enrolling or transferring between public schools. As a result, educational opportunities for children whose numbers were estimated between several hundred to several thousand would be lost. In addition, an affected household would have to spend approximately 23 percent of its income on private school fees but that "[o]ptions such as paying for full enrollment or transportation costs of private schools or adjusting the time of the move had not been considered" during the project planning.[159]

The 4th Progress Report on the Implementation of Management's Action Plan, drafted in response to the Panel Investigation, revealed that focus-group meetings with project-affected persons four years into the release of the investigation report still highlighted issues of crop failure, infertile soil, lack of agricultural inputs, reduced access to fish, high costs of educational and healthcare facilities, lack of access to employment and credit schemes. The Management report noted a number of services initiated by BEL in response, including a microcredit program, the construction of two market stalls, livelihood assistance and agricultural input support.[160] The report took note of the BIC report on the impacts of the Bujagali involuntary resettlement on children but concluded that it did not agree with the findings that children continued to be adversely affected, based on the WB visit to Naminya resettlement village in April 2013.[161]

[157] Ibid., para. 520.

[158] Ibid., p. xlvii and para. 521.

[159] Ibid., Footnote 536.

[160] WB, "Fourth Progress Report on the Implementation of Management's Action Plan in Response to the Inspection Panel Investigation Report (Report # 44977-Ug) on the Republic of Uganda Private Power Generation (Bujagali) Project (Ida Guarantee No. B0130-Ug)," 13 September 2013, p. 8, para. 25.

[161] Ibid., pp. 11–12, paras. 36–37.

The Bujagali complaint was also the first complaint to be brought to the AfDB-Independent Review Mechanism (IRM),[162] which had been introduced in the previous year (2006) and concerned both the power generation project and the interconnection project that was proposed at the time for AfDB funding. Because the WB Inspection Panel also handled a similar complaint at the time, the two institutions conducted their investigations in cooperation.[163] The cooperation included coordinated field investigations, sharing of consultants and technical information with a view to achieving efficient and cost-effective investigative processes.[164] The social concerns in the complaint included alleged failure of the project's impact assessment to take into account the local community's cultural and spiritual sensitivities, the poor quality of the houses and facilities built for resettlement resulting in their rapid deterioration, and the argument that the compensation and resettlement frameworks were outdated.[165] On the consultation process, the requesters alleged that although consultations had taken place, they did not amount to "true participation in a decision making process" and many of those affected by the spiritual issues were not consulted.[166] The findings of AfDB's Independent Review Panel (IRP) included first that the failure of the AfDB and project sponsors to resolve legacy issues remaining from the first project before the start of the new one was in breach of the AfDB's Policy on Involuntary Resettlement.[167] Second, the project's lack of an adequate gender perspective was in breach of the Policy on Gender and Operations Manual 600 (OM 600). Third, the lack of systematically collected and reliable data on project-affected persons and communities was a further breach of commitments under AfDB's policies on involuntary resettlement, gender and poverty reduction. Furthermore, the absence of background information in the project appraisal report on how issues of "cultural property and consultation" had been adequately addressed was considered an instance of management

[162] Laurence Boisson De Chazournes, "Partnerships, Emulation and Coordination: Toward the Emergence of a *Droit Commun* in the Field of Development Finance," in H. Cissé, D. Bradlow, and B. Kingsbury (eds.), *International Financial Institutions and Global Legal Governance, The World Bank Legal Review*, Vol. 3 (The World Bank, 2012) p. 182.

[163] WB Inspection Panel and AfDB CRMU, "Memorandum of Understanding," 28 November 2007, in WB Inspection Panel, "Annual Report – July 1, 2007, to June 30, 2008," Annex 3, pp. 100–102.

[164] AfDB IRM, "Compliance Review Report on the Bujagali Hydropower and Interconnection Projects," 20 June 2008.

[165] Ibid., pp. 5–6.

[166] Ibid., p. 6.

[167] Ibid., pp. 7–8.

and staff noncompliance.[168] The IRP noted its concern that the management's appraisal reports had not addressed the inadequacies of the consultation process, although it was unclear whether these inadequacies amounted to noncompliance.[169] The IRP also found the failure of the management to explicitly and clearly explain the rationale for the selection of the particular location for the project and to pay particular attention to poverty issues during the appraisal to be instances of noncompliance.[170]

The effects of blasting for the dam construction created new grievances in addition to the concerns voiced in the original AfDB complaint.[171] It was revealed in the third monitoring report that the project sponsor BEL had forwarded complaints linked to blasting to its contractor Salini and that Uganda did not have legal regulations on blasting or safety of the population while construction materials were transported.[172] Interestingly, there is no clear chain of responsibility that allows project-affected peoples to identify which actor (the sponsor, the lender or the contractor) has primary responsibility for adverse impacts created during the project implementation and what the fail-safe procedures are when their grievances are not properly handled by one of these actors to whom they appeal.

The monitoring process of the AfDB IRM drew attention to children's poor nutritional situation, which was considered independent of household income levels. Even when project-affected persons reported improved incomes and the ability to purchase more luxury items, the number and nutritional value of meals available to children under the age of five had not improved.[173] While the monitoring report did not conduct an in-depth analysis into the causes, it linked this situation somewhat arbitrarily to behavioral and cultural motivations and recommended "education and nutrition extension services."[174]

168 Ibid., p. 9.

169 Ibid., p. 10.

170 Ibid., pp. 14–15.

171 The blasting grievances later became the subject of other complaints to the IFC and the EIB.

172 AfDB IRM, "3rd Monitoring Report on the Implementation of Findings of Non-Compliance and Related Actions to Be Undertaken by the ADB Management on the Bujagali Hydropower and Interconnection Projects," 6 June 2011, p. 15.

173 AfDB IRM, "4th Monitoring Report on the Implementation of Findings of Non-Compliance and Related Actions to Be Undertaken by the ADB Management on the Bujagali Hydropower and Interconnection Projects," September 2012, p. 4.

174 Ibid.

A third complaint was addressed to the EIB Complaints Mechanism (EIB-CM) on 20 November 2009.[175] The complaint alleged EIB's failure to meet European development objectives in addition to failures to guarantee fair compensation and to mitigate adverse social impacts resulting from the effects of resettlement.[176] In terms of direct impacts on children, the complaint noted problems related to educational facilities. The nursery was completed only in 2009 but the primary school had not been built at the time of the complaint. The local population had been hosting children in houses from 2006 onwards but could not receive public funding as this arrangement was considered private schooling. It was furthermore alleged that BEL was refusing to "pay for material, books or teachers."[177]

The mediation process launched in March 2012 and facilitated by the EIB-CM involved BEL, the Government of Uganda, NAPE and NEMA.[178] The agreement reached at the end of the mediation process dealing with more than 1,000 complaints concluded that cracks in 240 houses resulting from quarry blasting would be repaired though the blasting procedures had been in line with Ugandan standards.[179] In May 2015, the High Court of Uganda adopted the mediation agreement between the representatives of local complainants and the Uganda Electricity Transmission Company Ltd (UETCL) as a judgment.[180] The CAO noted on 14 August 2015 that the UETCL had not "fulfilled its original commitment … to pay complainants … no later than July 31, 2015" but had promised a new date, although no confirmation of the payment had yet been made.[181] The primary school building promised by BEL was only completed in the first quarter of 2010, almost nine years after resettlement. The EIB-CM did not address whether the complainant's allegations about BEL's refusal to pay for school supplies and teacher fees and its claim that such expenses are the government's responsibility had any legitimate basis.[182] The EIB-CM found all

175 NAPE, Counter Balance, CLAI and Association Sherpa, "EIB Complaint Submission – Bujagali Powerplant Project," 20 November 2009.

176 Ibid., p. 4.

177 Ibid., p. 12.

178 EIB CM, "Outcome of Mediation Process: Complaints on Alleged Effects of Blasting on Buildings During Construction of Bujagali HEP," 31 May 2013.

179 EIB CM, "Outcome of Mediation Process."

180 CAO Case Database, "Uganda/Bujagali Energy-05/Bujagali," www.cao-ombudsman.org/cases/case_detail.aspx?id=172 (accessed 15 April 2019).

181 CAO Case Database, "Uganda/Bujagali Energy-05/Bujagali."

182 EIB CM, "Bujagali Hydroelectric Project (Jinja, Uganda) Conclusions Report (Complaint SG/E/2009/09)," 30 August 2012, p. 30.

components of the RAP to have been completed with the exception of the electrification of project-affected households.[183] Although it took the EIB-CM three years to address the Bujagali complaint instead of the six months envisioned in its procedures, its outcome report was not consistent with the findings of the WB Inspection Panel, the IFC CAO and the AfDB IRM. One NGO consequently criticized the EIB-CM for being a "green washing machine."[184] Follow-up consultations with project-affected communities in the Naminya and Kira Bulindo Resettlement sites indicated that the WB Inspection Panel and AfDB IRM's involvement following the complaints had improved the manner in which the project sponsors (AES Nile Power for the first project and BEL for the second) and the Government of Uganda interacted with the project-affected communities, including better compensation and resettlement packages.[185] Concerns over the inadequacy and lack of quality of services offered ensued while complainants also highlighted continued apprehension over the failure of the project to provide "affordable and adequate electricity."[186]

3.3 Case 4: Uganda Transport Sector Development Project

3.3.1 Uganda Transport Sector Development Project: From Appraisal to Implementation

The Uganda Transport Sector Development Project (TSDP) was designed as a 198 million USD project, financed in major part by loans from the World Bank's International Development Association (IDA) to the Ugandan government and implemented by the Uganda National Road Authority, to improve transportation infrastructure in Uganda through road construction. The Project Information Document (PID) for the project noted that the development of roads to provide or improve access to rural parts of Uganda, including villages, community centers and schools, and to link those to national and district roads were among the key development objectives of the

[183] Ibid., p. 8.

[184] Both Ends, "The EIB Complaints Mechanism Is Only a Green-Washing Machine," 25 January 2011.

[185] Henri Mugisha Bazira, "International Reforms of Environmental and Social Safeguards (ESS) for Development Finance," Water Governance Institute, March 2012, pp. 9 and 26. (The author was involved in bringing the two complaints to the WB Inspection Panel as well as the AfDB IRM.)

[186] Ibid., p. 27.

project.[187] The WB's financing engagement in Uganda's transport sector had been ongoing since the early 1990s.[188] The project was launched in 2008, with appraisal documents mostly dating from that time. At the time of the design of the TSDP, only 30 percent of Uganda's road network connecting cities, districts and neighboring countries, had been paved but were carrying 80 percent of all road traffic in the country.[189] The main beneficiary of international funding was the Republic of Uganda and the main implementing agency was designated as the Uganda National Roads Authority (UNRA), which would work with contractor companies for the construction of the roads. In the context of the project, gravel roads in the Gulu–Atiak and Vurra–Oraba axes would be paved, national roads in poor condition would be reduced, road safety would be improved and "[a]ccess of the rural population to all-season roads in the target area [would] increase from 64 percent to 90 percent."[190] Later, the project was extended to include the upgrade of the Fort Portal–Kamwenge Road, which would become a site for allegations of violations of children's rights.

Impact Assessments

The Project Information Document (PID) Concept Note from 2008 considered the WB's then safeguards only on environmental assessment and involuntary resettlement to be applicable to the project.[191] The Project Appraisal Document (PAD) identified several risks, including a moderate risk that the UNRA had limited implementation capacity, a moderate governance risk due to corruption in the road sector, moderate financial management risks and a substantial procurement risk in contracting businesses.[192]

The Integrated Safeguards Datasheet for the Appraisal Stage from 2009 identified key stakeholders as the "[UNRA], the Ministry of Works, the local governments and communities traversed by these roads" with an

[187] WB, Project Information Document (PID) Concept Stage: Uganda Roads Development Program Phase 4, Report No.: AB3605.

[188] WB, Implementation Completion and Results Report (IDA-46790 IDA-49490 TF-11094) – Report No: ICR00002228, 5 June 2017, para. 7.

[189] Ibid., para. 5.

[190] Ibid., para. 11.

[191] WB, PID Concept Stage: Uganda Roads Development Program Phase 4, Report No.: AB3605.

[192] WB, Implementation Completion and Results Report, Report No: ICR00002228, para. 23.

indication that consultations had taken place with these stakeholders prior to the appraisal.[193]

The Environmental and Social Impact Assessment (ESIA) undertaken in 2009 prior to the commencement of the third part of the project on the Fort Portal–Kamwenge Road Upgrade listed relevant legal instruments as the Ugandan Constitution, national environmental, land and labor legislation as well as the safeguard frameworks of different international financiers. In addition, policy frameworks applicable listed included the National Gender Policy of Uganda of 1997 in addition to environmental guidelines and land and resettlement frameworks.[194] Child-related issues identified in the assessment included resettlement as well as the risk of disruption of educational activities where children could be excited and distracted observing construction work or would be impeded by noise. With regard to resettlement, the need to provide adequate assistance to vulnerable households in affected communities, including child-headed households during the process of resettlement and compensation, was highlighted.[195] The risk of increased spread of HIV/AIDS was identified but not linked to children or women specifically. No other issues around children's rights or gender-based issues were noted in the initial ESIA. In 2011, a review of the ESIA was undertaken for the additional funding.

A later assessment of the PAD and the impact assessments undertaken by the WB management prior to the project noted that the capacity of the Ugandan government and its implementing authority "to ensure environmental and social safeguard compliance was not even discussed" while "[r]esources provided to prepare the project were unreflective of the systemic risks."[196]

Impacts on Local Communities and Children

Local community members from the Bigodi and Nyabubale-Nkingo villages, which sit midway on the Fort Portal–Kamwenge Road, brought up allegations of "sex with minors and teenage pregnancy by road

193 WB, Integrated Safeguards Datasheet for the Appraisal Stage – Report No.: AC3648, 2009, para. II.A.5 (typo in the original).

194 AfDB, Environmental and Social Impact Assessment Summary: Road Sector Support Project 3: Nyakahita-Ibanda-Kamwenge Road Upgrading Project P-UG-DB0-020, www.afdb.org/fileadmin/uploads/afdb/Documents/Environmental-and-Social-Assessments/Uganda%20RSSP3%20%20Nyakahita_Ibanda_Kamwenge%20Road%20Draft%20ESIA%20-%20RAP%20Summary%20_PIC_-1.pdf (accessed 21 April 2019).

195 Ibid.

196 WB, Implementation Completion and Results Report – Report No: ICR00002228, para. 23.

workers, increased sex work, the spread of HIV/AIDS, sexual harassment of female employees, child labor, school dropouts, lack of compensation and inadequate compensation, fear of retaliation, lack of participation, poor labor practices, and lack of adequate road and workplace health and safety measures" related to the project.[197]

The benefits of the project such as improvement of market access and employment opportunities especially for women to engage in small business activities were recognized as having led to increased household incomes and positive outcomes for many residents.[198] On the other hand, civil society reports noted that girl children had become susceptible to sexual harassment and abuse resulting in pregnancies and school dropouts as well as to commercial sexual exploitation. Allegations outlined that perpetrators of sexual abuse and assault reported to the police were able to bribe their way out of charges and child survivors of sexual assault were often left without recourse in the community in the absence of pro bono legal counsel and support mechanisms.[199] There were also indications of possible trafficking of girl children for sexual exploitation or child marriage. In addition, boy children were working as casual workers full or part-time, sometimes dropping out of school or skipping school, while girl children were working in the services industries as laborers resulting in dropouts as well as in increased vulnerability to gender-based violence.[200] These working children did not have health and safety protection or medical cover. Other children's right issues included difficulties in physical access to usual school walking routes due to construction, lack of safety measures and signage around construction sites.

3.3.2 *Legal Analysis*

Domestic Legislation and International Commitments

The protection of children "against any form of abuse, harassment or ill-treatment" is deemed a duty of every citizen of Uganda under Article 17 of the Ugandan Constitution. Likewise, Article 34 of the constitution enumerates the particular rights of Ugandan children including

[197] WB Inspection Panel, "Uganda: Transport Sector Development Project – Additional Financing," www.inspectionpanel.org/panel-cases/transport-sector-development-project-additional-financing (accessed 21 April 2019).

[198] Joy for Children, Uganda and BIC, "The Impact of the World Bank Funded Kamwenge – Kabarole Road Construction Project on Children," April 2015, p. 6.

[199] Ibid., pp. 8–9.

[200] Ibid., pp. 7–10.

protection from social and economic exploitation and hazardous and harmful labor of children under the age of sixteen (paras. 4 and 5) as well as special protections to "orphans and other vulnerable children" (para. 7). Uganda's 2016 Children (Amendment) Act prohibits the sexual exploitation of children, making it "unlawful for any person to use – (a) inducement or coercion in the encouragement of a child to engage in any sexual activity; (b) children in prostitution or other unlawful sexual practices; and (c) children in pornographic performances or materials."[201] Uganda's 2007 Gender Policy notes that specific actions related to gender and rights includes "[d]eveloping strategies to sensitise communities about children's rights and responsibilities so as to protect the girl child from abuse."[202] At the international level, Uganda is a party to the CRC and CRC-OPSC, the ACRWC and ILO Conventions 138 and 182.

Children's Rights Violations Linked to the Uganda TSDP

Children's rights violations linked to the Uganda TSDP were related to the violation of the right to protection from all forms of violence and sexual abuse and exploitation as covered under Articles 19 and 34 CRC as well as Articles 16 and 27 ACRWC. In addition, the right of child victims of sexual abuse and exploitation to rehabilitation and recovery under Article 39 CRC is at stake in light of allegations of cover-ups and lack of support for recovery. The commercial sexual exploitation of children as alleged by the affected communities is also prohibited under ILO Convention 182 as one of the worst forms of child labor. Labor that is hazardous or harmful to health or morals or interferes with schooling is also to be eradicated under ILO Conventions 138 and 182.

3.3.3 Involvement of Businesses

Financing the Uganda TSDP

The Uganda TSDP was financed by numerous loans. Initially, WB's IDA provided a 190 million USD equivalent credit and the United Kingdom Department for International Development (DFID) provided an 8 million USD equivalent grant from recipient executed Trust Fund grant.[203] In 2011, IDA extended a further 75 million USD equivalent

[201] The Republic of Uganda, "The Children (Amendment) Act," 2016, S. 8.A.

[202] The Republic of Uganda, "Gender Policy", 2017, para. 5.2(f).

[203] WB, Implementation Completion and Results Report – Report No: ICR00002228, para. 20.

credit, for a final amount of 265 million USD equivalent credit. The AfDB had financed the preparation of Environmental and Social Assessments, Resettlement Action Plans (RAPs) for the Kamwenge to Fort Portal road while the WB had previously financed road designs for the Guluto Atiak and Vurra to Oraba roads. In addition, the Japan International Cooperation Agency (JICA) financed "a condition survey of district and community access roads," supplemented in 2015 by WB funds as the JICA funds were considered insufficient.[204] The financing provided to the Ugandan government was used through international competitive bidding processes in the designation of civil works contractor companies for the three segments of the road project under the supervision of the UNRA.

Businesses Involved

The civil works to upgrade the different sections of the road under the project were opened up to international competitive bidding and eventually contracted to three Chinese companies. The upgrading of the Vurra–Arua–Koboko–Oraba Road for approximately 57.5 million USD was contracted to Chongqing International Construction Corporation; the upgrading of the Gulu–Atiak Road from gravel to pavement in the amount of approximately 36.5 million USD was contracted to China Henan International Cooperation Group; and the upgrading of the Fort Portal–Kamwenge Road was contracted in 2013 to China Railway Seventh Group (CRSG) for approximately 45.5 million USD.[205] In addition, technical assistance and consultancy services were contracted from companies from various jurisdictions, including from Bulgaria, Canada, Denmark, Ethiopia, Germany, Ghana, Greece, Israel, Italy, Kenya, Mauritius, the Netherlands, Sweden, South Africa, Tanzania, Uganda and the United Kingdom.[206]

In addition to the CRSG, various other businesses were involved in the specific segment of the roadworks subject to allegations. Gauff Ingenieure GmbH & Co (Germany) served as the supervising engineer for the project, tasked with ensuring contractor compliance with UNRA terms. A resettlement consulting firm, SURVECO, was hired by the

204 Ibid., p. 7, para. 20.

205 WB, Contracts Awarded for P092837: Uganda Transport Sector Development Project, web.worldbank.org/external/default/main?menuPK=247629&piPK64002403&theSitePK=256299&pagePK=64002408&Projectid=P092837 (accessed 20 April 2019).

206 Ibid.

UNRA. The consulting firm Air, Water, Earth Ltd (Uganda) was contracted to prepare the environmental and social assessments. WSS Services Ltd (Uganda) was hired by CRSG as an HIV/AIDS service provider and First Insurance Company Limited (Ghana) was hired by CRSG to provide workers' insurance.[207] Even prior to the allegations surrounding affected communities and children, the supervising engineer had suspended earthworks and quarry operations in 2014 due to concerns over illegal operation of quarries without environmental licenses, disregard for health, safety and environmental requirements as well as lack of consultation in the context of land acquisition and compensation.[208] The suspension was later lifted on condition of respect of terms in concert with the UNRA but without consultations with the WB. In September 2014, WSS provided the WB with a baseline report on HIV/AIDS awareness and mitigation, citing occurrence of sexual abuse by road workers on the contractor's payroll.[209]

Shareholding Structures

The three Chinese enterprises that were awarded the contracts are subsidiaries of various other Chinese companies. The Fort Portal–Kamwenge Road segment of the Uganda TSDP that was subject to allegations of misconduct and children's rights violations was contracted to the China Railway Seventh Group (CRSG), a fully owned subsidiary of China Railway Group Limited (acronym CREC), a Fortune 500 company traded on the Shanghai and Hong Kong stock exchanges.[210] The majority shareholder of CREC with 54.39 percent of its shares is the China Railway Engineering Corporation (CRECG), a large Chinese state-owned Enterprise (SOE).[211]

3.3.4 *Accountability for Business-Related Harms on Children*

Large investment projects, especially if they involve construction and roadworks, have the potential to cause extended social impacts, including as a consequence of the influx of workers to investment project sites and

[207] WB Inspection Panel, "Transport Sector Development Project – Additional Financing (P121097): Investigation Report," 4 August 2016, para. 9.

[208] Ibid., para. 25.

[209] Ibid.

[210] China Railway Group Limited (CREC), "Investor Relations: Company Snapshot," www.crecg.com/english/2699/index.html (20 April 2019).

[211] CREC, *2017 Annual Report* (CREC, 2018), p. 8.

the vitalization of informal economy around project sites. The risk of gender-based and sexual violence has been considered a particularly relevant issue in the context of conflict-affected areas and situations in the UNGPs (Principle 7[b]). Likewise, the CRC Committee has called on home states to provide current and accurate information to their businesses on the local situations when they invest in conflict or emergency-affected areas as well as to highlight the risk of sexual abuse and exploitation as well as gender-based violence and child trafficking (para. 51). Beyond this specific attention to conflict and emergency-affected areas, however, the business and human rights normative frameworks do not flag the risks associated with investment projects that may themselves lead to increased risks for children's rights violations linked to gender-based violence and exploitation and an increased susceptibility for children in these contexts.

The direct duties of businesses as contractors have not been clarified in the UNGPs but the host states "should exercise adequate oversight in order to meet their international human rights obligations when they contract with ... business enterprises" in service provision including by clarifying expectations from businesses to respect human rights in service contracts as well as in other commercial transactions, including procurement (Principles 5 and 6). Likewise, the CRC Committee has noted that "states must take steps to ensure that public procurement contracts are awarded to bidders that are committed to respecting children's rights."[212] The CESCR, on the other hand, suggests administrative sanctions to discourage companies from being involved in violations of ESC rights, such as denial to award public contracts to businesses that do not provide information on the environmental or social impacts of their activities and that do not have due diligence measures in place to avoid or mitigate negative impacts.[213]

The CRC Committee's GC 16 notes that international organizations engaged in development, finance and trade "should have standards and procedures to assess the risk of harm to children in conjunction with new projects," take mitigation measures against risks and have "mechanisms to identify, address and remedy violations of children's rights ..., including when they are committed by or result from activities of businesses linked to or funded by them."[214] In addition,

[212] CRC Committee, GC 16, para. 27.
[213] CESCR, GC 24, para. 50.
[214] Ibid., para. 48.

GC 16 calls on home states of SOEs to require them to conduct child-rights due diligence and report on their performance as well as to make public support and services conditional upon child-rights due diligence.[215]

The Request to the WB Inspection Panel

The fact that funds for the project originated from the WB's IDA arm to the Ugandan government allowed affected communities to bring their grievances to the WB Inspection Panel after they reportedly were unable to access remedies directly at the company and national levels. The first request for inspection was received by the WB Inspection Panel on 19 December 2014 but not registered because the Panel found that the WB Management had not been made aware of the concerns prior to application to the Panel. Another request, restating the concerns of the local community, was received and registered in September 2015. This time the requesters, who wished to remain anonymous and had designated the local NGO Joy for Children – Uganda (JFCU) as their representative, noted that attempts to raise community concerns with the WB and UNRA officials had not been fruitful.[216]

Two child protection consultants were hired by the WB and an Implementation Support Mission was dispatched to Uganda in October 2015. The mission identified two cases of underage pregnancy linked to road workers, confirmed sexual harassment of female employees, noted highly unsatisfactory safeguards ratings, the contractor's failure to "meet its contractual social and environmental obligations" and the fact that the contractor-hired HIV/AIDS provider WSS had not been paid for six months by the contractor.[217]

World Bank's Cancellation of the Project In awaiting the management response, the Inspection Panel postponed its eligibility visit to Uganda to December 2015. In one of the rare cases of radical measures, the WB decided to pull funding from the Uganda TSDP in December 2015. The WBG President Jim Yong Kim issued a statement recognizing failures

[215] Ibid., para. 64.

[216] Joy For Children–Uganda (as representative), "Request for an Inspection on the Impact of Kamwenge–Fort Portal Road Works Section on the Community," 21 August 2015. www.inspectionpanel.org/sites/www.inspectionpanel.org/files/ip/PanelCases/98-Request%20for%20Inspection.pdf (accessed 21 April 2019).

[217] WB Inspection Panel, "TSDP: Investigation Report," para. 25.

not only on the part of the Government of Uganda and the contracting companies but also the WB, in having failed to adequately supervise investment projects "to ensure that the poor and vulnerable [we]re protected."[218] The Government of Uganda and the UNRA, however, decided to continue working with the same contracting company to complete the roadworks in the most time- and cost-effective way.[219]

The WB Management response noted that the WB missions had been flagging issues of noncompliance with the Bank's environmental and social safeguards in relation to land acquisition and physical impacts of construction to the UNRA to be remedied.[220] The Management acknowledged that measures taken by the WB and the borrower country "to address the identified risks of sexual misconduct were insufficient, and that actions taken in response were inadequate and too slow, given the gravity of the allegations and emerging evidence" and that its management had been insufficient.[221] The management conceded that

> [g]iven the endemic problem of child marriages and teenage pregnancies in Uganda, the Bank should have been especially vigilant in assessing the extent to which the Project might aggravate the problem and ensured that robust mitigation measures were in place, along with appropriate staffing.[222]

In fact, the contractor's Environmental and Social Management Plan (ESMP), which was not provided to the WB until July 2015 although the works had started in August 2013, had identified "*potential negative impacts on women include exposure to HIV/AIDS and STIs and potential increased sexual exploitation of young girls which will likely also lead to unwanted pregnancies, drop-out from school [. . .].*"[223] Unfortunately, the measures stipulated in the ESMP, including the obligation of the contractor "to implement an HIV prevention and awareness program, prohibit child labor, institute and enforce a policy to prevent sexual

[218] WB, "World Bank Statement on Cancellation of the Uganda Transport Sector Development Project (TSDP)," 21 December 2015, www.worldbank.org/en/news/press-release/2015/12/21/wb-statement-cancellation-uganda-transport-sector-development-project (accessed 22 April 2019).

[219] WB Inspection Panel, "TSDP: Investigation Report," para. 24.

[220] WB, "Management Response to Request for Inspection Panel Review of the Uganda TSDP – Additional Financing (P121097)," 17 December 2015, para. 12.

[221] Ibid., paras. 17–18.

[222] Ibid., para. 26.

[223] Ibid., para. 23. (Original emphasis.)

harassment, establish a community liaison, and provide work camp accommodation" were not carried out.[224]

A number of rather drastic measures were decided by the Management including the immediate cancellation of the TSDP, the review of the contractor China Railway Seventh Group and Supervising Engineer performance in other WB-financed contracts, suspension of any civil works where UNRA was the implementing agency, review of the WB's entire Uganda portfolio with "specific focus on sexual misconduct involving minors and child labor," a global review of the WB approach to risk mitigation with respect to issues of labor influx and a thorough review of the project.[225]

The Inspection Panel's eligibility visit to Uganda included meetings with government ministry and UNRA officials in Kampala, WB Country Director and Project staff as well as affected communities and individuals. Based on these findings, the Inspection Panel recommended an investigation into allegations, approved by the WB Board in January 2016. During this time, the WB suspended funding to two other road projects in Uganda "pending a review and strengthening of the capacity of UNRA to adhere to the required environmental and social standards."[226]

Results of the Investigation The Inspection Panel submitted its comprehensive investigation report in August 2016. The investigation report acknowledged the preexistence of persistent poverty and institutional weaknesses resulting in protection gaps for girl children in the community but noted that the "poorly managed" influx of construction workers had exacerbated risks of exposure to sexual exploitaiton.[227] With respect to the work of the contractor, the Inspection Panel pointed at the "[p]oor design and low construction standards," which ignored the needs of communities living around construction sites.[228] The 2011 ESIA, supposedly updated from the 2008 version, was considered substandard by the Inspection Panel, "lack[ing] the required analysis of the risks to women and children caused by the labor influx, in particular those risks related to

[224] Ibid., para. 9.

[225] Ibid., para. xix.

[226] WB, "World Bank Statement on Suspension of Roads Projects in Uganda," 8 January 2016, www.worldbank.org/en/news/press-release/2016/01/08/world-bank-statement-on-suspension-of-roads-projects-in-uganda (accessed 22 April 2019).

[227] WB Inspection Panel, "TSDP: Investigation Report," para. 31.

[228] Ibid., para. 32.

sex with minors and teenage pregnancies, sexual harassment, child labor, and school dropouts."[229] The WB Management was found to be in noncompliance of various WB policies due to its lack of adequate supervision of the project, and timely and effective response to social issues of gender-based violence and exploitation as well as remediation and recovery support for survivors of child sexual abuse. In fact, the Inspection Panel noted that even after measures were taken by the Management, the numbers of victims of sexual exploitation and abuse had kept rising after the registration of the request for inspection.[230]

Review of Project Performance and Country Risks The cancelled project was reviewed in order to identify inadequacies in WB supervision. In response to the cancellation of funding, the Executive Director of the UNRA announced that "a grievance committee, a community education programme, a social safeguard committee, an environment committee" including community members would be set up for every road project in the future.[231]

The WB review of its own performance with respect to the Uganda TSDP identified several shortcomings on the part of the WB as the supervising financial institution over the project. The contractor's failure to give priority to the safeguards was noted, evidenced by its use of safeguard staff only on a part-time basis.[232] In fact, during the lengthy procurement process, the contractor was chosen because it "appeared to be the best of a weak list . . . and was already present in Uganda on an adjacent AfDB-financed road project."[233] There was a tension between the contractor's view of its business performance as measured by the output of delivered services/goods compared to a more holistic view of good performance that would require avoiding or mitigating social externalities:

> At times, the Contractor seemed to disregard the personal property and individual safety of community members . . . reflect[ing] a basic conflict between the perspectives of the Contractor, which saw its main role as

[229] Ibid., para. 356.
[230] Ibid., para. 357.
[231] Billy Rwothungeyo, "UNRA Vows to Work with Communities After World Bank Woes," *New Vision Website*, 21 January 2016, www.newvision.co.ug/new_vision/news/1415395/unra-vows-communities-bank-woes (accessed 15 April 2019).
[232] WB, "Uganda Transport Sector Development Project – Additional Financing: Lessons Learned and Agenda for Action," 11 November 2016, para. 22.
[233] Ibid., para. 45.

> completing a priority road as quickly as possible, and the Bank, which had an obligation to compel UNRA to ensure that the road was constructed in accordance with the required environmental and social standards in its contract.[234]

Another company involved in the project, the supervising engineer Gauff Ingenieure was noted as suffering from high turnover of key staff and for having become ineffective as its decisions and recommendations were ignored by the contractor and UNRA.[235]

Findings from the WB's review of all its projects in Uganda found the country context as high-risk for children but confirmed that ex ante project documents showed "weak identification of potential risks to children during project preparation, resulting in very weak preventive measures," although no other instances of child abuse were found in the other projects.[236] The risks to children from investment projects were noted as "early marriage, sexual abuse, violence against both women and children, trafficking, and child labor within households, particularly among farm families."[237] In addition, grievance redress committees (GRC) as operational-based grievance mechanisms in projects undertaken in Uganda focused on compensation of assets lost but did not consider child-protection risks, also because they did not "include adequate representation of women or community members likely to raise [these] concerns."[238]

The recommendations from the review of WB performance linked to the TSDP included promoting a better understanding of social risks internally in the WB and with respect to borrower's institutions and agencies, instigating stronger cooperation and coordination with borrower country institutions, collaborating with local civil society actors, ensuring adequate community-engagement and grievance-redress mechanisms that include women as well. Specific to children, the recommendations included addressing child-protection risks throughout the project cycle that also comprises implementation, incorporating requirements for "prevention of sexual harassment, child labor, the promotion of community engagement, and adequate grievance redress" in Standard Bidding Documents for borrowers and contractors, improvement of contractor ESMPs to ensure specific, targeted and measurable mitigation

[234] Ibid., para. 46.
[235] Ibid., para. 48.
[236] Ibid., para. 65.
[237] Ibid.
[238] Ibid.

measures for possible impacts on children and providing adequate resources to supervision.[239]

A WB staff guidance note penned in December 2016 on the influx of laborers into project areas identified a number of issues linked to children's rights including risks of child and forced labor, resulting school dropouts as well as gender-based violence extending to child abuse and exploitation as a result of possible fraternization of workers with female members of the local community.[240] According to the guidance, companies undertaking civil works are not to employ children directly or indirectly to prevent the risk of child labor and school dropout. In addition, suggested mitigation measures for contractor companies with respect to gender-based violence, including child abuse and exploitation, are enumerated as "mandatory and regular training for workers on required lawful conduct in host community and legal consequences for failure to comply with law," a commitment to cooperate with local law enforcement in gender-based violence investigations, entering into partnerships with local NGOs to organize complaints mechanisms, providing workers opportunities to return to families regularly as well as entertainment prospects outside of local communities.[241] The guidance also pointed to the importance of local community participation and consultation prior to the start of any project in order to identify risks and existing social problems, as well as the importance of "specifically target[ing] vulnerable groups, including women and children" during the initial outreach stage.[242]

3.4 Intermediate Conclusions on Investment Projects: The Importance of Backing Regulatory Norms with Accountability Mechanisms

Large-scale investment projects in developing countries like the Bujagali HPP and the Uganda TSDP entail the involvement of businesses alongside the domestic state and different financing institutions in ventures that have the potential to adversely impact human rights. In many of these situations, the domestic state may not have the capability or the willingness to guarantee respect for, protection and fulfillment of human

239 Ibid., para. 66.

240 WB, "Managing the Risks of Adverse Impacts on Communities from Temporary Project Induced Labor Influx," 1 December 2016, p. 6.

241 Ibid., p. 22.

242 Ibid., p. 17.

rights. This may be due to the state's relatively dependent position on financing from external sources, which puts it at a disadvantage vis-à-vis funding institutions and corporations involved in the construction and operation. It may be due to a lack of supervision and enforcement capacity by domestic agencies and institutions as in the case of UNRA in the Uganda TSDP. It may also be due, as in the Bujagali case, to the state's decision-making bodies being afflicted by corruption and susceptible to bribery.

In the two cases explored, the failures in the protection of project-affected populations, including children, from social impacts stem not only from shortcomings on the part of the Ugandan State but also inadequacies at the level of business compliance with domestic and international standards. Supervisory shortcomings at the level of financing institutions, including the WB, has been a contributing factor to these failures. For instance, in the case of Bujagali, because WB safeguards and standards did not require the WB staff to evaluate the project with respect to Uganda's international human rights and labor law commitments – unlike the requirement to do so with respect to environmental treaties – the substantive rights of the project-affected individuals, including children, were easily sidestepped. In the case of Uganda TSDP, the prevalence of gender-based violence in the country context was not adequately assessed prior to the implementation of the project's third segment nor reflected in mitigation measures under the ESIA. In addition, the influx of workers into a rural area and the consequences were not scrutinized and adequately addressed. The WB Inspection Panel noted that the issues encountered in the Uganda TSDP were in fact not unique and could potentially recur in other infrastructure projects, negating the benefits to local communities from road construction and instead "intensify[ing] impoverishment, marginalization, and physical and psychological vulnerability."[243]

Both cases bring up interesting issues from the perspective of responsibility for children's rights violations. In the Bujagali case, the Ugandan State initiated the tender and invited businesses to invest in hydropower projects, including in Bujagali Falls. An affiliate (SG Bujagali Holdings Ltd) of the subsidiary (Sithe) of a US-based company (Blackstone) formed a joint venture (BEL) with a Kenya-based company (Industrial Promotion Services Limited) set up by a nonprofit foundation (Aga Khan Development Network) and won the bid. This particular joint venture

[243] WB Inspection Panel, "TSDP: Investigation Report," paras. 407–408.

presents even more questions as it is set up involving several business enterprises that are affiliates or subsidiaries of larger corporations or even philanthropic foundations, rendering issues such as corporate veil or parental duty of care even blurrier than usual. The joint venture was financed by loans from IDA, IFC, AfDB, EIB as well as a number of European development finance institutions. The equity of the company was given a MIGA guarantee. Bujagali Energy Limited's contractor Salini undertook the construction of the project. Yet, none of the actors involved in the case is directly linked to the conduct that has caused the violations. In fact, the involuntary resettlement was initiated by a previous sponsor (US-based AES), which abandoned the project without delivering the services that were promised to the resettled population. Commitments were then taken over by the new project sponsor, with a supervisory role for the WBG.

In the Uganda TSDP case, the WB's IDA arm provided loans to the Ugandan government, in collaboration with DFID, JICA and AfDB, which contributed to the preparatory stages of the project. The Ugandan government opened up an international competitive bidding process and contracted three Chinese companies to undertake civil works related to the project. One of these companies, China Railway Seventh Group (CRSG), a fully owned subsidiary of another large Chinese company, was involved in business-related harm to children. The majority shareholder of this parent company, in turn, is a Chinese SOE. In this respect, the extraterritorial obligations of China as both the home state of the contractor and the majority owner of its parent company may be triggered. While the contractor was directly involved in concerns related to land acquisition, resettlement, appropriate compensation and the mistreatment of female employees, the child sexual abuse incidents were generally committed by individual workers. In addition, a German engineering company was deemed the supervising engineer of the project, bringing yet another level of business involvement in the case.

The Bujagali case and the Uganda TSDP case, when analyzed in comparison, also reveal a divergence in the institutional responses to different children's rights issues.[244] For instance, in the Bujagali case, management concluded after a visit to Naminya that "the ability of

[244] I would like to thank Ms Elena Berger of the Bank Information Center for her time in answering questions about the World Bank's responses to the allegations surrounding children's rights violations in these two projects.

parents to adequately support and educate their children ha[d] not been hindered by the resettlement program" in response to allegations of violations of the right to education and health.[245] There was no recognition that the elapsed decade between the actual resettlement and the reported restoration of living standards may have given rise to irreversible adverse impacts on the human rights of children and adults. The WB's cancellation of funding for an investment project is a rare event and is demonstrably reserved for only the most serious violations of human and children's rights, amounting to criminal behavior such as sexual abuse and exploitation of children in sex work as in the Uganda TSDP. On the other hand, adverse impacts on economic and social rights such as the right to education and health seem to have attracted less scrutiny in the absence of explicit human rights duties incumbent upon businesses and of provisions extending to the respect and protection of the rights of children in the safeguard policy framework of the WB. In the Uganda TSDP case as well, the absence of clear standards obscured possible issues of gender-based violence and child sexual abuse and exploitation identified as early as 2008 until after formal allegations were filed with the WB Inspection Panel.

The conclusions of the AfDB IRM following the four-year monitoring process of the Bujagali complaint highlight one of the most important deficiencies plaguing large projects with multiple lenders: the lack of clarity in the accountability of individual lenders not only in project implementation but also in supervising compliance. Moreover, the conclusions reflect the importance of transparent, realistic and candid resettlement and compensation programs prior to the project start and throughout the project cycle to avoid ambiguities and unfulfilled expectations. Another important insight concerns the need to conduct satisfactory baseline surveys on the living conditions of populations prior to resettlement in order to allow for a meaningful ex post assessment of whether these conditions are improved or at least reestablished.[246]

The other crucial safeguard with respect to large-scale investment projects is "a robust stakeholder engagement process" characterized by "[s]trong and inclusive consultation, combined with effective grievance redress mechanisms," as noted by the WB Inspection Panel in its TSDP

[245] WB, "4th Progress Report – Bujagali," 12, para. 37.
[246] AfDB IRM, "4th Monitoring Report – Bujagali," p. 11.

investigation report.[247] Such engagement has to be coupled with due diligence mechanisms and tools that allow companies and financing institutions involved to "anticipate, analyze adequately, and mitigate ... negative impacts" from an investment project.[248] Both cases explored demonstrate that unless safeguards and standards explicitly include human rights and children's rights due diligence requirements as legal standards, as was proposed by the WB review to be undertaken in the context of Standard Binding Documents, and require compliance with them, it is likely that companies will not automatically take them into account.

247 WB Inspection Panel, "TSDP: Investigation Report," para. 418.
248 Ibid., para. 419.

PART III

Polycentricity, Children's Rights and Business

4

A Polycentric Governance Model of Children's Rights and Business

4.1 The Promise of Governance and Polycentricism

The business and human rights domain is as much a site of political as it is of legal contention and developments. The process of norm legalization in this domain, as explored in this book, is intricately linked to political regulation of interactions between states, businesses, individuals and communities. The landscape around business and human rights extends beyond international law approaches. Assessing and subsequently formulating solutions to the mismatch between children's rights (and human rights) impacts of business activities on the ground and the response of international law as it stands also presents an international policy problem. Incorporating insights from fields outside of the law, in particular International Relations (IR), which has long problematized the role of globalization and the rise of actors besides states may help resolve the mismatch. The last three decades have seen non-state actors, including horizontal subgovernmental networks, epistemic communities, transnational advocacy networks, intergovernmental institutions and MNEs all come to fall within the purview of policy-oriented IR scholarship.[1]

[1] The most influential formulations are found in the work of James N. Rosenau, *Turbulence in World Politics: A Theory of Change and Continuity* (Princeton University Press, 1990); Peter M. Haas, "Epistemic Communities and International Policy Coordination" (1992) 46(1) *International Organization* 1–35; Margaret E. Keck and Kathryn Sikkink, *Activists Beyond Borders: Advocacy Networks in International Politics* (Cornell University Press, 1998); Margaret E. Keck and Kathryn Sikkink, "Transnational Advocacy Networks International and Regional Politics" (1999) 51(159) *International Social Science Journal* 89–101; Robert O. Keohane, "Governance in a Partially Globalized World" (2001) 95(1)

The "response to an empirical world of growing transboundary complexity, seeking to capture both a novel pluralisation and structural density in world politics" came in the form of governance approaches starting in the 1990s.[2] Governance is not necessarily a legal conceptualization of order; it is first and foremost a political one. Governance on the global scale is not satisfied with the "inter-*nation*-al" and therefore seeks to explain how "governing" occurs beyond the space between states. The late IR scholar James Rosenau considered that the "interactive tensions whereby processes of globalization and localization [that are] simultaneously unfolding on worldwide scale" were behind the dispersion of governance capabilities also to actors besides the state.[3] While states continued to be the "central loci of control in the processes of global governance," they had lost a degree of the authority that allowed them to exert dominance and garner compliance.[4]

Governance was conceived as a broad term to comprise state activities as well as "the many other channels through which 'commands' flow in the form of goals framed, directives issued, and policies pursued."[5] Although (global) governance is sometimes portrayed as a solution for global problems in lieu of international law and human rights law, it is not antithetical to a human rights-based international legal order. For instance, Andrew Hurrell's accurate snapshot of the objectives of governance, namely "the management of power, the promotion of common interest, and the mediation of difference"[6] are among the objectives of international law. Governance approaches may complement international legal efforts, in particular those through international human rights law, in delivering global justice goals and upholding human dignity.

American Political Science Review 1–13; Anne-Marie Slaughter, *A New World Order* (Princeton University Press, 2004); Joseph S. Nye, Jr., *The Future of Power* (Public Affairs, 2011).

2 David Coen and Tom Pegram, "Towards a Third Generation of Global Governance Scholarship" (2018) 9(1) *Global Policy* 107–113 at 111.

3 James N. Rosenau, "Governance in the 21st Century" (1995) 1(1) *Global Governance* 13–43 at 19.

4 Ibid., p. 39.

5 Ibid., p. 14.

6 Andrew Hurrell, "Power, Institutions, and the Production of Inequality," in Michael Barnett and Raymond Duvall (eds.), *Power in Global Governance* (Cambridge University Press, 2005), p. 35.

4.1.1 *Defining Polycentric Governance*

Polycentric governance is a broad term that encompasses various governance possibilities at various levels. In polycentric governance, regulatory authority does not reside exclusively, or sometimes at all, with the state. Both states and non-state entities have the capacity to make decisions, produce norms and implementation strategies.[7] Polycentric governance has emerged as a response to tackling global collective action problems by underscoring the promise of bottom-up approaches and self-regulatory governance regimes.[8] As such, it provides a welcome respite from the traditional state-centric bias and emphasis on hierarchy that constrains much of traditional public international law literature and realist international relations scholarship.

Polycentric governance entails a variety of independent decision-making actors of state and non-state nature that "can make [their] own rules and develop [their] own norms within [their] domain of influence," acting in an interdependent manner, cooperating on the basis of networks to achieve a shared objective.[9] Polycentric governance for solving collective action problems was proposed first and foremost by the late Elinor Ostrom, who later used this research strand to propose polycentricity as a solution to climate change action. As sketched out by Ostrom, collective action "occurs when more than one [actor] is required to contribute to an effort in order to achieve an outcome."[10] Collective action problems occur because those actors looking out solely for their short-term interest do not engage in collective action because they "are better off when others contribute to the collective action and they do not, [as] they benefit without paying the costs."[11] Collective action problems become impediments to effectively achieving desired outcomes in bringing about collective benefits, for instance, human rights benefits, when

[7] Jamie Darin Prenkert and Scott J. Shackelford, "Business, Human Rights, and the Promise of Polycentricity" (2014) 47 *Vanderbilt Journal of Transnational Law* 451–500 at 460.

[8] Elinor Ostrom, "A Polycentric Approach for Coping with Climate Change," World Bank, Policy Research Working Paper No. 5095, 2009, p. 12, http://documents.worldbank.org/curated/en/480171468315567893/pdf/WPS5095.pdf (accessed 12 March 2019).

[9] Prenkert, "Conflict Minerals and Polycentric Governance of Business and Human Rights," in Robert C. Bird, Daniel R. Cahoy and Jamie Darin Prenkert (eds.), *Law, Business and Human Rights: Bridging the Gap* (Edward Elgar, 2014), p. 204.

[10] Ostrom, "Understanding Collective Action," 2020 Vision for Food, Agriculture and the Environment, Collective Action and Property Rights for Sustainable Development, *FOCUS 11*, Brief 2 of 16, February 2004.

[11] Ibid.

all actors only operate with short-term, self-serving agendas. To ensure respect for protection and realization of children's rights in situations where businesses are involved, various actors have to engage in collective action. Of course, collective action entails costs and those driven solely by self-interest are likely to try to avoid incurring such costs. The resulting challenge is to overcome the myopic self-interest of some actors and the participation inertia underlying the collective action problem.

Ostrom focused on the difficulties and the long-drawn-out failure in reaching an "efficient, fair and enforceable" international agreement, the risk that too little would be done too late, and the possibility that global-level solutions may not deliver unless supported at "national, regional, and local levels."[12] Furthermore, in the absence of a central regulatory authority, enforcement of obligations depends on how individual actors behave in the collective. Accordingly, "[t]he advantage of a polycentric approach is that it encourages experimental efforts at multiple levels, as well as the development of methods for assessing the benefits and costs of particular strategies adopted in one type of ecosystem and comparing these with results obtained in other ecosystems."[13]

Ostrom had good reason to propose a polycentric approach to tackle climate change by focusing on environment as a global common good. All actors that are willing to or incentivized to cooperate in the face of climate change have a common and clearly defined goal: to reduce carbon emissions through whatever means most appropriate, given that it is within their capabilities. Thus, the primary norm that will effectively solve the global collective action problem – i.e. the reduction of carbon emissions – is already clearly defined and all actors ranging from individuals to states have been designated obligations commensurate with their contribution to climate change and their capability of inducing change. Of course, all actors may not be forthcoming in acknowledging and carrying out their obligations. Nonetheless, a critical mass of actors at multiple levels cooperating towards the objective will likely induce change.

Polycentricity is based on the horizontal, rather than vertical integration of different actors on the international plane. This may constitute an advantage or a weakness, depending on the specific circumstances of the

[12] Ostrom, "A Polycentric Approach for Coping with Climate Change," p. 4.
[13] Ibid., p. 39.

issue being regulated through polycentric governance. Thanks to horizontal integration, there is ample room for flexibility in collaborative norm-creation and implementation and the polycentric governance system can adapt over time to changing realities.[14] Yet, the promise of flexible and adaptable governance is contingent upon the flawless functioning of the polycentric machinery. On the downside, in the absence of rules applying vertically to circumscribe, order and oversee coherent and effective integration of different norms produced by different actors, polycentric governance systems have the propensity to result in fragmentation and competition among the diverse set of norms.

4.1.2 Polycentricism in Business and Human Rights

Prenkert and Shackelford have argued that "problems that transcend the Westphalian conception of national jurisdictional boundaries [such as those in the business and human rights debate] ... need not necessarily be addressed only by comprehensive global regulation or international law."[15] Despite possible shortcomings, they consider "[p]olycentric regulatory action by multiple actors at multiple levels linked together by diverse information networks" to be "preferable to failed or lumbering international initiatives" and to possibly have benefits over top-down regulation.[16] The most adept solution and "a true polycentric approach" to remedying adverse impacts of business on human rights would accordingly be a combination of bottom-up regulatory frameworks that offer flexibility and more legalized hierarchical multilateral instruments to manage free-riders.[17] In the same line, Backer has concluded that the normative underpinnings of the UN Framework and UNGPs in the way they delineate the division of roles between states and businesses foretells the advent of the polycentric governance of business and human rights:

> The elaboration of a corporate governance framework that is meant to apply concurrently with corporate obligations under the laws of the jurisdiction in which they operate is one of the greatest advancements of [the UN Framework and UNGPs]. Polycentricity in governance results, which considerably advances the development of autonomous

[14] Prenkert and Shackelford, "Business, HR, and the Promise of Polycentricity," p. 466.
[15] Ibid.
[16] Ibid.
[17] Ibid., p. 494.

> transnational regulatory bases for corporate governance. Instead of suggesting further fragmentation of law at the transnational level, the framework is an attempt to build simultaneous public and private governance systems as well as coordinate, without integrating, their operations. [footnotes omitted][18]

Joining Backer, Prenkert hails polycentric governance as a solution to the "[g]overnance gaps [around the activities of transnational corporations] result from inadequate national regulatory reach, a nonexistent international regulatory framework, and insufficiently organized and empowered nonstate market and social actors."[19] While states have an important role to play in addressing these gaps, they themselves are incapable of bridging the gaps fully.

Yet, as Penelope Simons reminds, "to address corporate impunity effectively, one cannot simply deal with the governance gaps alone. One must also identify and address the root causes of those gaps."[20] Using Third World Approaches to International Law (TWAIL), Simons argues that the structure of international law as it exists is structurally biased against rights-holders (and developing states) for the benefit of powerful corporate and financial actors.[21] Consequently, using human rights law to build consensus and push for binding corporate human rights obligations alongside the existing nonbinding and voluntary frameworks presents a more adequate panacea to the structural biases and resulting injustices.

The various attempts to bring accountability to the involvement of businesses in the extraction and trade of DRC's conflict minerals have, for instance, been described as of "a polycentric governance regime . . . focused on supply chain transparency and due diligence and intended to limit the access of rebel groups to the deep pockets of the global market."[22] The numerous state and non-state regulators in this polycentric minerals governance regime act "interdependently to complement each other and to add value with their strengths while counterbalancing each other's weaknesses."[23]

[18] Larry Catá Backer, "On the Evolution of the United Nations' 'Protect-Respect-Remedy' Project: The State, the Corporation and Human Rights in a Global Governance Context" (2011) 9 *Santa Clara Journal of International Law* 37–80 at 43.

[19] Prenkert, "Conflict Minerals and Polycentric Governance of Business and Human Rights," p. 207.

[20] Simons, "International Law's Invisible Hand," 11.

[21] Ibid., pp. 35–40.

[22] Prenkert, "Conflict Minerals and Polycentric Governance," p. 211.

[23] Ibid.

4.1.3 The Necessity of Distinguishing Between Primary and Secondary Norms

Using polycentricity to govern collective action problems surrounding the protection and fulfillment of human rights transnationally is, however, not as clear-cut a case. The proponents of polycentric governance sometimes confound the role of governance in addressing what would be distinguished into primary legal norms about human rights obligations and secondary legal norms about responsibility as regards violations of human rights or as regards failures of the realization of these rights. In this regard, the secondary norms about responsibility and their implementation relate to "behavioral or operative norms," defined as "various principles and ideas that guide the practices of governance" and may be guided by norms such as nondiscrimination, "equality, non-intervention, secrecy and transparency."[24] On the other hand, primary norms about children's rights obligations and human rights obligations more generally are "foundational or meta-norms," which are pivotal in "orienting or guiding the various regimes, behavioural norms and cooperative arrangements that comprise practices of global governance."[25] Polycentricity thus comprises the operational aspect of governing foundational norms, which in this case are human rights norms.

Once a primary norm gains widespread recognition (for instance, the corporate obligation to respect human rights), polycentric governance may assist in its implementation and operationalization. Backer and Prenkert, and even Ruggie himself, are onto something in arguing that polycentric governance will result from the implementation of the Framework and the Guiding Principles at the national, international and private levels.

4.1.4 Polycentric Governance of Secondary Norms on Responsibility

Polycentricity in governance may become a valuable tool in creating secondary rules, meaning norms and practices about how to attribute and allocate responsibility for violations of rights. Moreover, the polycentric governance of the access to remedy may allow rights-holders, especially children, to have recourse to some form of

[24] Colleen Carroll and Emilie Bécault, "Global Governance and the Challenges of Diversity," in Jan Wouters et al. *Global Governance and Democracy: A Multidisciplinary Analysis* (Edward Elgar, 2015), p. 208.

[25] Ibid.

remediation when domestic state legal systems are inaccessible. Polycentric governance of access to remedy would thus include, in addition to the use of (home or host) state-based civil law, criminal law or administrative law procedures, mediation and conciliation bodies such as NCPs for OECD Guidelines, private and company- or industry-based remediation systems, internal compliance mechanisms at international financial institutions such as the IFC/MIGA CAO, AfDB IRM or the WB Inspection Panel, as well as any other bodies that may be developed for the specific purpose of addressing business accountability transnationally. To move beyond the constraints of domestic law when the state on whose territory violations occur is unwilling to or incapable of protecting rights and bringing violators to justice, polycentric governance that supplements existing responsibility avenues with new ones will be pivotal.

4.2 Return to Primary Norms: A Dynamic Approach to Duty-Bearing: From Obligations to Responsibility

The effective governance of children's rights and human rights responsibility of businesses through polycentricism is only possible after primary norms, or the common goals to be reached by collective action, applicable to the business – children's rights (and likewise, business – human rights) relationship are clarified. In a system of law, the attribution of responsibility for a wrongdoing is dependent on the existence of obligations of a given actor. The two exercises of the attribution of obligations and the attribution of responsibility have been treated as two essentially different and unrelated processes. Under public international law, responsibility for an internationally wrongful act[26] is only triggered for those actors that have legal obligations and have breached these obligations. Because international law has not traditionally ascribed human rights obligations to businesses, they have frequently been shielded from responsibility for harms resulting from their actions, omissions and decisions. This disconnect has resulted in gaps in human rights protection, which is especially detrimental to children's

[26] An internationally wrongful act is defined in a very skeletal fashion by the ILC's Articles on the Responsibility of States for Internationally Wrongful Acts (ARSIWA) Arts. 12 to 15. Andrea Gattini argues that the definition could and would benefit from more contextualization with regards the structure of the international obligation in question in Andrea Gattini, "Breach of International Obligations," in Nollkaemper and Plakokefalos (eds.), *Principles of Shared Responsibility in International Law*, pp. 31 and 59.

enjoyment of their human rights. By logical inference, if NSAs were ordinarily considered as duty-bearers with international human rights obligations, that they should incur responsibility if they breach these obligations would be largely uncontested. Hence, the first key task at hand of conceptualizing an effective governance of the business – (children's) human rights nexus is one of revisiting the primary norms, i.e. the attribution of obligations to businesses.

The link between a normative assessment of how obligations ought to be attributed to businesses and state actors and a factual verification of that normative assessment's reasonableness may be established by asking two different sets of questions. The first set of questions is designed to serve as a reality check, assessing whether conditions ranging from directly causality to more indirect forms of involvement can be established between the actor and the violation:

Q 1: Has actor X caused the wrongdoing/violation? Can the event/conduct be attributed to actor X?

The existing guidance on the attribution of responsibility through ARSIWA and ARIO treat this question as the only relevant one: once conduct is attributable to actor X, then actor X's responsibility is triggered. In fact, the attribution of the conduct resulting in an internationally wrongful act is equated with causality for the violation.

Q 2: If actor X were not involved, would the wrongdoing/violation still have taken place?

The question that is implicit in the first question of causality but is quite often ignored is that of whether a given breach would have taken place absent the behavior/conduct/decision of a given actor. This second question allows one to look at the broader spatiotemporal context surrounding the violation.

Q 3: Has actor X contributed to the wrongdoing/violation or its perpetuation or continuation?

This question covers instances where strict causation is not at issue. It is especially relevant in cases of violations of economic, social and cultural rights given that these are considered subject to progressive realization. A continuing violation may be a violation that occurs as a result of an identifiable act but continues over time[27] or it may not

[27] For this reason, the question is not only important in cases of violations of economic, social and cultural rights, but also for civil and political rights. For instance, continuing violations of civil and political rights were handled in the case law on right to life (*Cyprus* v. *Turkey*) and on

constitute a single identifiable act but is a culmination of actions, policies and decisions over time. A given actor may be linked to the violation in a less direct fashion for instance, by failing to undertake an obligation to exercise due diligence.

Q 4: Could actor X have reasonably been expected to take any measures/ action to prevent the wrongdoing/violation from taking place and failed to do so?

The fourth question aims to identify the range of permissible action an actor involved in the situation may have at its disposal in terms of influence or leverage to prevent the wrongdoing. The question aims to provide the test for whether responsibility is incurred with respect to an actor's obligation to protect as a result of its failure to prevent other parties from violating a right.[28]

Under the existing conceptualization of international human rights law, these questions are only posed at the second stage: the point of assigning responsibility for violations. There are, however, very good reasons for responding to these questions as a first step in demarcating whether and in what way a given actor is involved in the commission of a wrongdoing/violation. The determination of whether and to what degree an actor is involved in a process with adverse human rights consequences is an essential step in a normative assessment of whether it is warranted to propose an extension of duties beyond the nation state. In fact, any proposal for attributing direct human rights obligations to actors other than the state in a given situation or case will have to first establish that there is a link between that actor and the violation of a specific human rights provision, without commensurate responsibility creating a vacuum in human rights protection. If any of the above questions are answered in the positive, there is then a corresponding need to "reconceptualize" human rights duty-bearers.[29]

forced or enforced disappearance (*Blake* v. *Guatemala* (Preliminary Objections), Ser. C, No. 27, 2 July 1996 IACtHR; *Radilla Pacheco* v. *Mexico* (Preliminary Objections, Merits, Reparations, and Costs), 23 November 2009, Ser. C, No. 209 IACtHR; *Varnava and Others* v. *Turkey* (Applications No: 16064/90, 16065/90, 16066/90, 16068/90, 16069/90, 16070/90, 16071/90, 16072/90 and 16073/90), Judgment, 18 September 2009 ECtHR. For a detailed mapping of continuing violations in the case law of the ECtHR, see: Andy Van Pachtenbeke and Yves Haeck, "De Becker to Varnava: The State of Continuing Situations in the Strasbourg Case Law" (2010) *European Human Rights Law Review* 47–59.

[28] This was the test undertaken by the IACtHR in the *Velazquez-Rodriguez* case.

[29] Vandenhole, Erdem Türkelli and Hammonds, "Reconceptualizing Human Rights Duty-Bearers," pp. 1035–1037.

Of course, nonlegal responses may have a role to play in meeting children's rights (and human rights) challenges posed by businesses. Yet, as Alston once astutely argued, an explicit espousal of human rights discourse matters because

> [R]ights language provides a context and a framework, invokes states' legal obligations, underscores that certain values are nonnegotiable, brings a degree of normative certainty, and makes use of the agreed interpretations of rights that have emerged from decades of reflection, discussion and adjudication. Most important, rights language recognizes the dignity and agency of all individuals and is intentionally empowering.[30]

To empower rights-holders and to use empowerment as a panacea to unchecked power, a new way of conceptualizing obligations and responsibility is necessary.

The case illustrations explored in this book provide ample guidance as to where children's rights protection gaps lie. Only focusing on the attribution of conduct or a causal relationship between an actor in question and the violation would shield businesses from incurring responsibility in almost all cases. In the case of Uzbek cotton, the domestic state is implicated in the violation through a causal link but the other three cases explored in the book are less clear in terms of delineating causation. For instance, if the WB had not provided financing, thus allowing the sponsors to attract other funding, the Uganda TSDP and the Bujagali HPP projects would likely not have seen the light of day. Yet, if the resettlement in the Bujagali case is defined as "conduct," the conduct itself was carried out by the first project sponsor AES. Nonetheless, the initial need to resettle communities in Bujagali is linked to the decisions of a number of actors, including the WB, the IFC, AES. In addition, the subsequent project sponsor BEL undertook commitments once contracted by the Ugandan government and funded by numerous institutions to build and operate the power plant. The wrongful conduct in relation to child sexual abuse and exploitation in the Uganda TSDP was committed by individuals who were employed by the contractor. In addition, the Ugandan state agency UNRA, the supervising engineering company and the WB all had supervisory contractual roles to ensure

[30] Alston, "The Two Words That Scare the World Bank," *The Washington Post*, 7 November 2014, www.washingtonpost.com/opinions/philip-alston-the-world-bank-treats-human-rights-as-unmentionable/2014/11/07/9091dafa-65da-11e4-9fdc-d43b053ecb4d_story.html?utm_term=.5a400e3eabd8 (accessed 24 April 2019).

contractor compliance with standards. The case of mineral extraction in the DRC represents even more complexity in delineating which actor is responsible for conduct resulting in the children's rights violations linked to artisanal mining, in light of the involvement of armed NSAs in addition to various companies in the supply chain.

At this juncture, a second set of questions may usefully guide the determination of what types of human rights obligations ought to be incumbent on a given actor, drawing on the tripartite typology of human rights obligations[31] of respect, protect and fulfil, as put forth by Asbjørn Eide in 1987.[32] The content of these obligations remains constant irrespective of the nature of the duty-bearers or their numbers. While the methods and tools at the disposal of a particular actor for living up to its obligations may differ depending on its nature, the normative content of the obligations themselves are unchanged. The tripartite typology is used in its more detailed form, distinguishing between the limited respect obligation and the comprehensive respect obligation as well as dissecting the obligation to fulfil into the obligation to facilitate and the obligation to provide.[33]

- Should actor X be under an obligation to refrain from violating the right? (Obligation to respect – limited)
- Should actor X be under an obligation to ascertain it did not violate the right through conduct or omission and did not contribute to a wrongdoing/violation by another actor? (Obligation to respect – comprehensive)
- Should actor X be under an obligation to prevent the wrongdoing/violation by others? (Obligation to protect)
- Should actor X be under an obligation to facilitate or assist the realization of the right? (Obligation to fulfill – facilitate)
- Should actor X be under an obligation to provide for the realization of the right? (Obligation to fulfill – provide)

[31] It was Henry Shue who first wrote about how tripartite duties correlate to the rights of subsistence in the form of duties to avoid depriving, to protect from deprivation and to aid the deprived. (Henry Shue, *Basic Rights: Subsistence, Affluence, and U.S. Foreign Policy* [2nd ed] [Princeton University Press, 1996], p. 53.)

[32] Asbjørn Eide (UN Special Rapporteur for the Right to Food), *The Right to Adequate Food as a Human Right: Final Report Submitted by Asbjørn Eide*, UN Doc E/CN.4/Sub.2/1987/23, 1987, pp. 67–69.

[33] CESCR, GC 12, para. 15.

The questions assist first in identifying the necessity for a new framework on human rights duty bearers to address human rights protection gaps, one that does not unduly constrain its scope to states and principally, with respect to their own territory. This need for reconceptualization is even more urgent when the human rights of children are at stake since it is crucial to resolve ongoing violations before they result in severe or permanent harm. The current debate on business and children's rights has in fact departed from this reality but not ventured beyond the respect obligation. The CRC Committee's GC 16 speaks of "duties and responsibilities to respect the rights of children [that] extend in practice beyond the State and State-controlled services and institutions and apply to private actors and business enterprises."[34] Even the UNGPs, which refrained from pronouncing direct human rights obligations for businesses, recognize that "human rights of individuals specific groups or populations [may] require particular attention" and the consideration of "additional standards" such as those contained in the CRC.[35]

4.3 Normative Building Blocks of a Polycentric Governance Model for Children's Rights Duties: A Forward-Looking Proposal

There is no easy way to ensure the spontaneous transformation of the global order to reflect the considerable economic and political power held by private businesses operating transnationally. Although the exercise of such power is indicative of a given entity's reinforced position on the international plane vis-à-vis other actors, which may include states with less economic and political power than this corporate entity, international law as commonly conceptualized continues to operate under the fiction of unbridled state primacy. Hence, law as it stands fails to embrace an actor-insensitive and rights-holder-centered approach to ensure that the exercise of de facto economic and political power triggers corresponding human rights obligations. Likewise, when obligations are breached by the various actors, state and non-state, collectively either through concerted or individual and independent conduct, the law as it stands may pose more questions than it answers, as demonstrated squarely by the four case illustrations. To echo Nollkaemper:

> On what basis do we determine who, out of a multiplicity of involved actors, is to be held responsible, for instance, for harm caused by peace-

[34] CRC Committee, GC 16, para. 8.

[35] UNGPs, Principle 12 "Commentary."

> keeping missions, the global financial crisis, or global environmental problems? While the law of international responsibility provides some answers, it is not well adjusted to situations of shared rather than individual responsibility. The power-breeds-responsibility proposition suggests that power should be a relevant, perhaps even decisive, consideration in allocating responsibility in situations where multiple actors contribute to harm. [footnotes omitted][36]

As responsibility in the legal sense cannot exist in the absence of obligations, it is perhaps more crucial to take a step back and to recognize that without first linking power to obligations, the task of linking power to responsibility in the legal sense is not consequential.

The following section proposes principles for the attribution of direct children's rights obligations to businesses. This proposal, largely based on how the law ought to be (*de lege ferenda*) in order to provide full respect for and protection of children's rights, is not divorced from reality. It builds on the valuable scholarship challenging both territoriality and state-centrism in international human rights law. In fact, the framework proposed hinges on the applicability of the principles to real-life situations with a view to providing the most comprehensive human rights protection to individuals and groups whose rights might be at stake. The children's rights-specific nature of the proposal is informed by the set of four core principles distinguishing a children's rights-based approach, namely those of best interests, survival and development, due deference and evolving capacities.

4.3.1 Attribution of Obligations to Businesses

The fact that an actor, even though it is not a state actor, enjoys political or economic power on a domestic, regional or global scale is a mark both of capacity and of the intent to participate in the global legal order, directly or indirectly. This participation may take the direct form of participation in law-making and standard-setting or it may take more indirect forms such as influence and impact. As Simons highlights, "transnational corporate actors are the privileged insiders of the international legal system, playing key roles in the promotion, negotiation and drafting of these trade and investment regimes and enjoying remarkable success in resisting and avoiding the 'imposition of new human rights norms on their structure and operations'."[37]

[36] Nollkaemper, "Power and Responsibility," SHARES Research Paper 42, 2014, *ACIL* 2014–22, p. 2.

[37] Simons, "International Law's Invisible Hand," 33 (footnotes omitted).

As such, a powerful corporation participates in the global legal order, motivated by its interests and enabled by the privileges it enjoys due to the current asymmetric structure of the international legal order, with the intent to create outcomes favorable to its operational purpose. These businesses are able to benefit from the structures of international trade and investment that are protected by other subfields of international law but do not assume corresponding duties under international human rights law. The basis for attributing direct human rights and children's rights obligations to businesses would thus be their participation in the international legal order with the intent to benefit from interactions underlying this participation.

In summary, businesses should incur legal obligations, including direct human rights obligations by participating in setting the rules of the game, by engaging in practices favorable or detrimental to the realization of human rights and by exerting influence on other actors (state and non-state) with the intent and the purpose to benefit from such influence. The obligations borne by businesses, however, should be circumscribed to reflect the domains of their participation in the legal order. Participation is an indication of a given actor's consent to be brought within the realm of international law as regards the regulation of its activities and decisions.

4.3.2 Obligation to Respect Children's Rights as the Universal Minimum Obligation

The obligation to respect children's rights should be a universal minimum obligation for all participants in international law: it should be the lowest threshold of obligation that any participant incurs by virtue of participating in the legal process. The violation of children's rights or any other human rights by any state or non-state actor, any international organization or any individual cannot be considered lawful if it is intentional or a result of conduct (acts, omissions or decisions) that discounts foreseeable risks to children. This is comprised by the limited respect obligation, which is a negative obligation, colloquially expressed by the 'do no harm' axiom. Here, violations should be distinguished from lawful restrictions on the enjoyment of certain rights such as the freedom of expression (as allowed for under Article 13.2 CRC) or the freedom of association (as allowed for under Article 15.2 CRC).

The obligation to respect children's rights should extend not only to the acts but also to the omissions with foreseeable effects that present a risk for the violation of children's rights.[38] This comprehensive respect obligation would also entail so-called positive obligations such as the elaboration of policies and frameworks for children's rights by a given actor in guiding its conduct and operations.

The minimum obligation to respect would thus be placed equally on all participants in international law, state and non-state alike. For states, this minimum obligation means that states must respect children's rights within their territory and extraterritorially. As such, there would be no need to delineate primary and secondary duty-bearers in the context of the respect obligation, although there may be differentiation at the level of the attribution and distribution of responsibility for specific violations of respect obligations.

The practical implication of the universal respect obligation is that businesses must respect children's rights (in the limited and the comprehensive senses) with respect to their operations, decisions and interactions. This premise entails businesses respecting children's rights wherever they operate, within all their ventures, decisions and policies as well as in all business interactions. The positive component of the obligation to respect is especially pertinent for businesses. For states, requirements in the context of their children's rights obligations are clearly set out in the CRC as well as any domestic legislation on children's rights and given further meaning by the work of the CRC Committee through its GCs and Concluding Observations.

For businesses, however, before the obligation to respect children's rights can be discharged, the content of the obligations must be set out in relevant policies and frameworks given that businesses are not party to children's rights conventions and as there is usually no explicit domestic regulation on children's rights to which businesses must conform from the onset. The identification of children's rights provisions and their content relevant for a given business and the prior assessment of children's rights impacts that go into the development of a children's rights policy and implementation framework would thus be components of the respect obligation as opposed to the protect obligation.

With respect to the four core principles of best interests, survival and development, due deference and evolving capacities informing children's rights as suggested by Tobin and explored in Part I, the obligation to respect

[38] On this point, the guidance provided by the Maastricht Principle No. 13 on the Obligation to avoid causing harm that "Uncertainty about potential impacts does not constitute justification for such conduct" should serve to strengthen the requirements of the obligation to respect.

in the limited sense means that businesses should not take any decisions, make any policies or engage in any activities that may adversely affect the survival and development of children or in line with due deference, impede in any way the capacity of parents, legal guardians or other caretakers to undertake their care duties towards children. The comprehensive obligation to respect would require businesses to take into account the best interests of the child and children's evolving capacities in the preparation of children's rights policies and an implementation framework. In addition, children's best interests would need to be the leading rationale behind designing children's rights impact assessments. Frameworks for the implementation of children's rights policies would be required to address children as rights-holders and involve children in line with their evolving capacities. The designation of a universal minimum obligation of respect, as one that is also incumbent on businesses, is based on two factors related to internationally codified children's rights: the near universal coverage of the children's rights legal framework owing to nearly global ratification of the CRC, and the diversity of addressees of children's rights obligations in the Convention.

Near Universal Coverage Children's rights codified in the CRC have achieved almost universal ratification, notwithstanding that the Convention is a younger instrument than many other key global human rights treaties. The CRC has been signed by all states in the world and has been ratified by all states with the exception of United States.[39] The United States has signed and ratified two OPs to the CRC: OPAC and OPSC (both ratified on 23 December 2002) although it has not ratified the CRC, which it signed in 1995.

In practice, many businesses will be either domiciled or operating in the territory of a state party to the CRC, or both. The direct attribution of children's rights obligations to businesses does not necessitate their implementation directly at the international level through a binding legal instrument, but could also occur through the implementation of international children's rights norms at the domestic level either in host states or home states.

The children's rights provisions of the CRC have been making their way into court decisions even in the United States. In order to be able to invoke

[39] South Sudan ratified the CRC on 4 May 2015 (CRC Committee, "UN Committee Hails South Sudan's Ratification of Convention on the Rights of the Child," www.ohchr.org/EN/NewsEvents/Pages/DisplayNews.aspx?NewsID=15919&LangID=E, Geneva, 4 May 2015).

its provisions, US judges began as early as 1994 to argue that the CRC had attained customary international law status.[40] In 2005, the SCOTUS cited the worldwide acceptance of the prohibition of juvenile death penalty under Article 37 CRC in *Roper* v. *Simmons* and found the juvenile death penalty unconstitutional.[41] The SCOTUS claimed that the United States had been left alone in the international community in its effort to retain the death penalty for minors and concluded that "the express affirmation of certain fundamental rights by other nations and peoples simply underscore[d] the centrality of those same rights within [the US'] own heritage of freedom."[42] The decision did not restrict the scope of these rights to the prohibition of juvenile death penalty and left the door open for other children's rights provisions and fundamental rights to be considered universal as long as global commitments undertaken by an overwhelming majority of states and their relevant practice reflected as such. As a consequence, children's rights standards that enjoy worldwide acceptance reflected by practice would be applicable even to a US-domiciled company only operating in the United States, not only through the OPs to which the United States is party but also through the Convention itself, as an expression of the children's rights standards espoused by the international community of which United States is a member.

While universal ratification may not immediately mean that children's rights have attained customary international law status, it is important nonetheless to point out that there is no categorical contestation of children's rights from state parties, thus no persistent objection, that would categorically impede some of the most fundamental children's rights provisions from evolving into custom. The evolution of a norm into customary international law has traditionally been based on two conditions: "general and consistent" state practice and *opinio iuris* or the following of this practice "out of a belief of legal obligation."[43] As Skogly notes, the (state)

[40] John L. Kane, Jr. "Dissenting," in Sadeghi v. INS, 40 F.3d 1139, 1147, 10th Cir. 1994; U.S. Court of Appeals, 2nd Cir. *Nicholson* v. *Williams*, 203 F. Supp. 2d 153, 234, E.D.N.Y., 2002; U.S. District Court for the Eastern District of NY. *Beharry* v. *Reno*, 183 F. Supp. 2d 584, 600–01, E.D.N.Y., 2002.

[41] Elizabeth Bartholet, "Ratification by the United States of the Convention on the Rights of the Child: Pros and Cons from a Child's Rights Perspective" (2011) 633 *The ANNALS of American Academy of Political and Social Science* 80, Special Issue, The Child as Citizen 1–22 at 5.

[42] *Roper* v. *Simmons* (03–633) 543 U.S. 551, 2005, pp. 24–25.

[43] Anthea Elizabeth Roberts, "Traditional and Modern Approaches to Customary International Law: A Reconciliation" (2001) 95(4) *American Journal of International Law* 757–791 at 757.

practice condition of customary international law may be problematic in the case of human rights law or other fields of law that seek to regulate behavior: "the need to alter state behaviour makes it hard to determine customary international law based on state practice."[44]

A number of regional human rights systems have been engaging with the CRC, in their jurisprudence as well as their advisory opinions. In response to a request by the IACmHR, the IACtHR pointed in 2002 to "*opinio iuris comunis*" around the CRC:

> The [CRC] has been ratified by almost all the member States of the Organization of American States. The large number of ratifications shows a broad international consensus (*opinio iuris comunis*) in favor of the principles and institutions set forth in that instrument, which reflects current development of this matter. It should be highlighted that the various States of the hemisphere have adopted provisions in their legislation, both constitutional and regular, regarding the matter at hand; the Committee on the Rights of the Child has repeatedly referred to these provisions.[45]

The ECtHR also concluded in *Sahin* v. *Germany* that the children's rights standards contained in the CRC were of a universal nature:

> The human rights of children and the standards to which all States must aspire in realising these rights for all children are set out in the [CRC]. [...] The convention spells out the basic human rights that children everywhere – without discrimination – have: the right to survival; to develop to the fullest; to protection from harmful influences, abuse and exploitation; and to participate fully in family, cultural and social life. It further protects children's rights by setting standards in health care, education and legal, civil and social services.[46]

Acquiring customary international status may yet be elusive for the CRC. The references to its customary status by judges in the United States may be more linked to creative judicial thinking for invoking its provisions in a country that is not party to it than to its widespread recognition as customary international law. Nonetheless, if the designation of human rights norms as customary international law were to be based on modern conceptions of custom, emphasizing *opinio iuris*,[47]

44 Sigrun Skogly, *Beyond National Borders: States' Human Rights Obligations in International Cooperation* (Intersentia, 2006) pp. 109–110, Footnote 433.

45 *Advisory Opinion 17: Advisory Opinion on the Juridical Condition and Human Rights of the Child* (OC-17/2002) requested by the IACmHR, 28 August 2002 IACtHR, para. 29.

46 *Sahin* v. *Germany*, Application No. 30943/96, 8 July 2003 EctHR paras. 39–40.

47 For a discussion of traditional versus modern custom, see: Roberts, "Traditional and Modern Approaches to Customary International Law," pp. 759–760.

there may be grounds to support the inclusion of certain children's rights norms embodied in the CRC into customary international law.

Diversity of Recognized Duty-Bearers The CRC sets out the relationship not only of the state to individual children and their rights but also the relationship of the child and their rights vis-à-vis and alongside the child's parents, extended family and community.[48] Hence, the argument that the provisions of the CRC create obligations exclusively for states parties and do not recognize other types of duty-bearers (be they private individuals, parents, or business enterprises) is baseless. In fact, the CRC Committee's GC 15 affirms the existence of "[a] wide range of different duty bearers" with a special emphasis on parents and caregivers.[49] The Committee insists, for instance, that the full realization of children's right to health is dependent on the involvement of all duty-bearers and that "relevant stakeholders" in this endeavor include "governmental and non-governmental partners, private sector and funding organizations."[50] Addressed to states, GC 15 does not place direct obligations on the enumerated stakeholders but a direct obligation on the state for the facilitation of the full realization of the right in question by ensuring that all duty-bearers "have sufficient awareness, knowledge and capacity to fulfil their obligations and responsibilities."[51] A contemporary reading of the CRC and its interpretation by the Committee suggests that states have the full range of respect, protect and fulfill obligations for children's rights but that the obligations contained in the Convention and given context and content by the Committee may be imposed on other types of actors (duty-bearers) insofar as their practices and/or policies affect or have the potential to affect the enjoyment of children's rights. The CRC Committee's GC 16, on the other hand, also addresses international organizations directly by noting that they "should have standards and procedures to assess the risk of harm to children in conjunction with new projects and to take measures to mitigate risks of such harm."[52]

[48] See CRC Arts. 5 (responsibilities, rights and duties of parents or, where applicable, the members of the extended family or community), 18 (primary responsibility of parents/legal guardians for the upbringing and development of the child) and 27 (primary responsibility of parents and others to secure adequate conditions of living).

[49] CRC Committee, GC 15, para. 6.

[50] Ibid.

[51] Ibid.

[52] CRC Committee, GC 16, para. 48.

Test Case: Application to Case Illustrations The universal respect obligation would require all businesses to have children's rights policies in place applicable to the entire range of their business ventures, decisions, policies and interactions outlining the risks they are likely to encounter, setting out relevant risk-prevention and mitigation measures, having clear implementation guidance, acting so as to prevent harm from occurring and foreseeing remediation for harm when it is not able to be prevented. While the UNGPs and the linked CRBPs prefer to rely on "societal expectations" and shy away from terming the respect duty as a legal obligation, the human rights and children's right due diligence requirements they put forth are becoming increasingly legalized. A universal respect obligation for children's rights would in fact transform the contents of the children's rights due diligence requirement into harder legal form. In line with the comprehensive respect obligation, businesses would have to thus take reasonable steps to identify risks of children's rights violations linked to their business ventures so as to prevent contributing to violations, as underscored by the UK NCP in Global *Witness* v. *Afrimex*. In addition, once covered by a universal respect obligation, businesses could not claim ignorance of circumstances related to their business ventures and relationships until and unless they assessed risks meticulously and effectively and took steps to prevent or mitigate these risks. This is largely in line with the UK NCP's assessment in *RAID* v. *DAS Air*, which amounts to the position that a company with regular operations and business presence in a given context could not claim to be unaware of the political or economic circumstances in that context. The universality of the respect obligation permits the move beyond constraints such as a direct business relationship as required by the OECD Guidelines or the magnitude test for business transactions as applied by the German NCP in *ECCHR* v. *Otto Stadtlander*. In practical terms, business enterprises involved in trading, manufacturing or retail of any products that contain cotton or the 3TG, for instance, would need to assess their supply chains to uncover the risks related to children's rights, including whether they are directly or indirectly sourcing from locations such as Uzbekistan or eastern DRC where children's rights violations linked to labor conditions or conflict have been widely documented. If such risks are found to be consequential, relevant prevention or mitigation measures would need to be taken. In extreme cases where such measures do not yield results, disengagement from business ventures with unpreventable or unmitigable risks of adverse children's rights impacts would need to take place.

Furthermore, the universal obligation to respect children's rights overcomes limitations linked to the inadequate treatment of concerns linked to economic, social and cultural rights that result in the invisibility of violations, as materialized in the Bujagali case with respect, for instance, to the right to primary education. In addition, issues of child protection arising from child sexual abuse and exploitation as in the Uganda TSDP case would be flagged in contractor companies' children's rights due diligence frameworks. In line with the duty to use children's rights specific principles in carrying out the comprehensive respect obligation, in cases like the Bujagali, resettlement policies would have to take children's best interests as well as survival and development into account, thereby preventing or limiting adverse impacts on schooling or healthcare, among others. In addition, in taking children's evolving capacities and due deference principles into account, businesses involved in projects would need to hold consultations with children mature enough to express their views as well as parents in preparing children's rights impact assessments prior to projects, which would assist in the prevention and mitigation of foreseeable harms to children.

4.3.3 Moving Beyond the Minimum: Obligation to Protect

Moving beyond the minimum obligation to respect requires a careful examination of how each participant in the legal process may be construed to have a farther-reaching duty than respecting children's rights in the limited and comprehensive senses.

The obligation to protect children's rights should be based on the capability on the part of a given actor to influence the behavior of another actor to prevent that actor from violating children's rights through persuasion, dissuasion, compulsion or pressure based on its economic leverage within its domains of activity. This is where the idea of differentiated children's rights obligations depending on the type and operational scope of the duty-bearer becomes pertinent. As such, even if a direct replication of state obligations to be incumbent upon businesses is implausible and possibly undesirable, the scope of obligations for businesses need not be limited to negative obligations.[53] In fact, as

[53] See, for instance, David Bilchitz, "A Chasm between 'Is' and 'Ought'? A Critique of the Normative Foundations of the SRSG's Framework and the Guiding Principles," in Deva and Bilchitz (eds.), *Human Rights Obligations of Business: Beyond the Corporate Responsibility to Respect?* and Olivier de Schutter, "Corporations and Positive Duties."

Bilchitz argues, "imposing *some* positive obligations on corporations [does not require] them to take over *all* such obligations" from the state.[54] Furthermore, such positive obligations need not be extensive and need not cover obligations to provide what would be considered public goods.[55]

With respect to states, the ECtHR's case law on the right to life (Article 2 of the Convention) highlights that the obligation to protect has two components: enacting appropriate legislation and elaborating policies, and the implementation of the said legislation and policies.[56] In addition, when states know or "ought to have known at the time of the existence of a real and immediate risk," they are required to take additional operational measures to avoid that risk.[57] For businesses, the formation of relevant children's rights policies and children's rights impact assessments would need to be covered under the respect obligation as explained above. The implementation of these policies, on the other hand, would constitute the central component of the obligation to protect. Specifically, the obligation to protect would require that ex post children's rights impact assessments be conducted as a means to ensure that business activities and decisions have not resulted in children's rights violations. In case they have, the ex post assessments would prevent the continuation and repetition of violations and allow businesses to duly and adequately provide remedies to those harmed.

This proposed obligation to protect would apply to business interactions with subcontractors and suppliers, among others. The rationale for the proposed obligation to protect is based on a business's participation in business ventures with possible children's rights impacts. The protect obligation would be triggered once a business makes the decision to engage in a venture, whereby demonstrating its capacity and intent to participate in and benefit from this venture. The protect obligation would ensure that a business entity's ventures and interactions do not enable another entity (such as a subsidiary, a subcontractor, a financial intermediary or a state) to do harm or to continue doing harm. This obligation need not presuppose a "prior link between the individual [rights-holder] and the duty-bearer."[58] As such, businesses should have an obligation to protect the rights not only of children to whom they are already linked by

[54] Ibid., p. 135.
[55] Ibid., p. 131.
[56] *Osman* v. *the UK* (Judgment), 28 October 1998 ECtHR, para. 115.
[57] Ibid., para. 116.
[58] This is *contra* Vandenbogaerde, *Towards Shared Accountability*, p. 293.

virtue of participation in a business venture or interacting with another entity (independent of the identity of this entity) but also of children who may foreseeably or likely be impacted by the broader scope of their operations.

Given the specific case made for a heightened duty for children's rights, businesses should take a child-rights sensitive approach to obligations. This means, first, that the obligation to protect should be carried out in line with the best interests of children that may be affected in activities and through business relationships, and with due regard for these children's survival and development. Second, the principle of children's survival and development should be understood in the broadest and most holistic way possible (in line with the CRC Committee's GC 5). Especially for businesses that are involved in ventures presenting a high risk of implication in negative children's rights impacts, the principles of best interests of the child and survival and development create a heightened obligation of care and protection. Third, the due deference principle dictates that children's rights should be protected by businesses within their activities and in their business relationships by ensuring for instance that parents and caregivers are enabled to carry out their duties of providing and caring for children. Finally, in line with the principle of evolving capacities, businesses would be required to ensure that children are able to exercise their agency rights and are not impeded from doing so by other actors with which these businesses have a business relationship.

Although the proposal entails businesses having the obligation to respect children's rights on a par with states, it circumscribes the scale of direct protect obligations of business commensurate with the scope of business operations and interactions. For instance, a company may not be reasonably asked to serve as a public agency for child protection unless these functions have been privatized and are already carried out by the said company. Even in such cases, the obligation to protect would only reasonably be covered within the ventures and business interactions of that company. As a practical example, both a private multinational adoption agency and an advertisement agency would have the obligation to protect children's rights within their ventures and in all business interactions. Yet, this obligation would entail very different content for the two companies in practice. The adoption agency would have to undertake wider-ranging actions and even incur more comprehensive duties (for instance, the protection of children in birth environments as well as adoptive environments) by virtue of its more direct involvement with a public service provided for children, whereas the advertisement agency might have more specific areas of focus (for instance, children as consumers) and more limited business interactions (with product manufacturers). This would still mean, in practice, that the advertisement agency has an obligation to consider the best interests of children when it takes on clients (to ensure that the service or product to be advertised has not caused children's rights violations during its production, i.e. due diligence) and when it designs ads and proposes a dissemination strategy to its clients (to ensure that its services do not result in children's rights violations when used by the client especially as regards children or families as consumers).

Ordinarily, businesses lack a legitimate public-interest mandate to protect children's rights outside of their scope of business operations and interactions. Demanding them to remodel their operations and strategies to protect children's rights from encroachment by other actors beyond the relevant business scope would transcend the reasonable obligation that can be expected of them.

Businesses would thus have a duty to use their influence and leverage in discharging their obligation to protect with respect to their ventures and business interactions to prevent third parties (state or non-state) from interfering with children's rights. Even if their legal mandates do not cover the extent of their de facto business activities, businesses should still incur the obligations to protect children's rights within the entire spectrum of these de facto activities. The duty to use influence and leverage is not meant to equal the attribution of children's rights obligations to businesses in their "spheres of activity and influence" as was suggested by the UN Norms.[59] The UN Norms would attribute the full range of state obligations to businesses in any relationship – business or otherwise – that could be a venue for the exercise of influence.[60]

The use of influence and leverage in business relationships pertaining to their activities is a necessary condition to discharge of the duty to protect children's rights, but may not be a sufficient condition depending on the resources of the business in question. Businesses with greater

[59] Sub-Commission on the Promotion and Protection of Human Rights, "Norms on the Responsibilities of Transnational Corporations and Other Business Enterprises with Regard to Human Rights," UN Doc E/CN.4/Sub.2/2003/12/Rev.2/2003, para. 1.

[60] This vision was heavily criticized and eventually discarded during the mandate of John Ruggie in a number of instances. (See: UN Framework, para. 4; SRSG John Ruggie, "Summary of Five Multi-Stakeholder Consultations," UN Doc A/HRC/8/5/Add.1, 2008, para. 137.)

resources and capabilities may need to be held to higher standards as regards the results of their attempted use of leverage and influence.

The obligations to respect and protect children's rights should be applicable to all businesses, irrespective of their size, composition, structure or sector. Issues of ownership and association structure of a company should not play a role in determining whether that company has children's rights obligations in the first place.[61] Furthermore, these obligations should not be linked to a particular attribute of a company, such as its being a multinational or a transnational one. As a principle, the proposal entails that all companies set up as separate entities within the same conglomerate structure or outside are individually and equally children's rights duty-bearers. Ownership and association structure or the links with subcontractors or suppliers are relevant considerations only in the attribution of responsibility if and when a company is allegedly implicated in breaches of their children's rights obligations. It is also at the stage of attribution and distribution of responsibility that a company's relationship with the rights-holders becomes important. Especially when this relationship is not visibly clear or direct, the contribution of a given corporate entity to a violation ought to be substantiated through the inspection of the links it has with other corporate or public entities or individuals that are directly involved in the wrongdoing. The legal complexities surrounding corporate ownership and association structures are matters of attribution of responsibility to businesses.

In practical terms, the obligations to respect and protect children's rights would mean that all businesses should engage in a threefold exercise similar to what has been suggested by the CRC Committee's GC 16 and the CRBPs:

1. Ex ante and ex post children's rights impact assessments,
2. Children's rights due diligence (meaning that impacts should be assessed during projects and programs),
3. Use of leverage and influence.

[61] This differs from the conclusion of the 2005 Report of the OHCHR, which states: "Defining the boundaries of business responsibility for human rights therefore requires the consideration of other factors such as the size of the company, the relationship with its partners, the nature of its operations, and the proximity of people to its operations." (OHCHR, "Report of the United Nations High Commissioner on Human Rights on the Responsibilities of Transnational Corporations and Related Business Enterprises with Regard to Human Rights," E/CN.4/2005/91, 15 February 2005, para. 27.)

Children's rights impact assessments should focus not only on the impacts of a company's own processes on children's rights but also on those of supply chains integral to its business operations. For instance, an apparel company's children's rights impact assessment should map and seek to mitigate adverse children's rights impacts that may occur in the procurement of raw materials or the processing of these raw materials first into fabric and then into clothing. As all companies would have the obligation to respect children's rights on equal footing, each company would need to ensure that it does not violate or contribute to the violation of children's rights in its sourcing decisions. What the content of children's rights due diligence process should entail has been exemplified in detail in the CRBPs and the guidance produced by UNICEF and Save the Children subsequently.[62] Key components of children's rights due diligence include children's rights impact assessments to identify actual and potential impacts with particular attention to children who may be more vulnerable to harm, the integration of impact assessment findings into all functions of the business enterprise, monitoring as well as reporting.[63]

Test Case: Application to Case Illustrations The direct imposition of the protect obligation would mean that businesses have a duty to use their influence and leverage to protect children's rights within the scope of their business operations and interactions. The Italian NCP's assessment of due diligence in textile and garment supply chains is particularly suitable in putting the protect obligation into perspective: a business enterprise assessing risks of human rights violations in the context of its business relationships would have an obligation to use its leverage to induce a change in the behavior of the party violating human rights, even when there is no contribution to the violation itself on the part of that business. Accordingly, both cotton-trading companies and retailers that identify the possibility of cotton produced by forced child labor entering their value or supply chains would have an obligation to use their leverage and influence to prevent the violations. In general terms, the use of leverage and influence may entail the use of positive reinforcement to change the behavior of violators, for instance, by giving them incentives or the use of more coercive or deterrent measures such as boycotts.

[62] See, for instance, UNICEF and the Danish Institute of Human Rights (DIHR), *Children's Rights in Impact Assessments: A Guide for Integrating Children's Rights into Impact Assessments and Taking Action for Children* (UNICEF, 2013).

[63] UNICEF, UN Global Compact and Save the Children, *Children's Rights and Business Principles*, pp. 7–8.

In the Uzbekistan case, the effectiveness of the boycott in getting younger children off cotton fields is evidence of how the collective use of leverage may induce a change of conduct when supported by a critical mass of actors. This being said, the Uzbekistan case is unique in that the violation can be clearly traced to the conduct of one actor, whose actions determine whether the violation continues. In the DRC case, on the other hand, a boycott may not be the best means to protect children's rights. For instance, in *Global Witness* v. *Afrimex*, the UK NCP noted the failure of Afrimex to take measures to influence the supply chain in addition to its failure to act with due diligence in ensuring that minerals sourced from mines using child or forced labor did not enter its supply chain. When the circumstances resulting in the violations cannot be directly traced to or controlled by one actor, as in the DRC minerals case, leverage and influence may be put to more effective use through engagement with local stakeholders and work on grassroots solutions. In the case of Uganda TSDP, having a protect obligation would mean that the contractor company would have to ensure that road workers it employs do not engage in child sexual abuse and exploitation by identifying such risks prior to commencing its civil works and continuously assessing the situation. In the case of the Bujagali, businesses involved would be required to act with due diligence in ascertaining that benefits promised in the context of the project materialize for the affected populations, including by using their leverage vis-à-vis the domestic state and financial institutions involved.

4.3.4 Obligation to Fulfill

The obligation to fulfill children's rights is one that presupposes a different type of participation in the legal process: it requires the duty-bearer to have a legitimate public interest mandate. States clearly have this public interest mandate both with respect to rights-holders within their borders and beyond through their role as both the builders and the implementers of international and regional human rights protection regimes. For businesses, however, a distinction needs to be drawn. It is uncontested that states always have an obligation to provide for the realization of human rights within their territory. This obligation to provide allows progressive realization with respect to economic, social and cultural rights, as per Article 2.1 ICESCR. Likewise, progressive realization is explicitly permitted under the CRC in the context of the rights to health and education (Articles 24.4 and 28.1, respectively). More generally, Article 4 CRC recognizes that states parties have the obligation to realize economic, social and cultural rights of children "to the maximum extent of their available resources" and "within the framework of international co-operation" when needed. This facility extended to states in the progressive realization of economic, social and cultural rights is not unconditional but limited by two requirements. First, even in the context of rights subject to progressive realization, states continue to have immediate obligations, including minimum core obligations.[64] Second, there is an expectation that states parties will work towards the full realization of rights within a reasonable timeframe, retaining their "specific and continuing obligation to move as expeditiously and effectively as possible towards the full realization"[65] by taking "deliberate, concrete and targeted" steps.[66]

The more progressive assessment of the state of the art, as achieved by the Maastricht Principles, would suggest that states have an obligation to facilitate/assist the realization of human rights territorially and extraterritorially.[67] The obligation to facilitate/assist also comprises the duty to respond to requests for assistance within resource limits. Accordingly, a state has a duty to request international assistance in case it is unable to meet the resource requirements of the obligation to fulfill,[68] while other states have a corresponding duty to respond to requests for international assistance.[69] The CESCR, on the other hand, has noted in its GC 3 on the Nature of States Parties Obligations, that the mention of maximum available resources in the ICESCR refers to "both the resources existing within a State and those available from the international community through international cooperation and assistance."[70] Additionally, the UN CRC Committee's GC 5 underlines that

> [s]tates need to be able to demonstrate that they have implemented "to the maximum extent of their available resources" and, where necessary, have sought international cooperation. When States ratify the Convention, they take upon themselves obligations not only to implement it within

[64] The CESCR and the CRC Committee have clarified core obligations in the context of some of the rights contained in the ICESCR and CRC, respectively. (See: CESCR, GC 3 on the Nature of States Parties Obligations, E/1991/23, 1991, para. 10, CESCR, GC 14, para. 30, CESCR, GC 13, para. 57; CRC Committee, GC 15, para. 73.)

[65] CESCR, GC 14, para. 31.

[66] CESCR, GC 3, para. 2.

[67] The Maastricht Principles, Principle 28.

[68] Ibid., Principles 34 and 35.

[69] De Schutter et al., "Commentary to the Maastricht Principles," pp. 1158–1159.

[70] CESCR, GC 3, para. 13.

> their jurisdiction, but also to contribute, through international cooperation, to global implementation (. . .).[71]

Attributing the obligation to fulfill/provide to an entity that is not a state is more problematic, especially when these entities are of a private character. The OHCHR remarked in 2005 that the human rights "responsibilities" of businesses could not simply be a transfer of state obligations and would need to be "defined separately, in proportion to [their] nature and activities."[72] Likewise, the UN Framework held that the responsibilities of businesses as "specialized economic organs, not democratic public interest institutions . . . cannot and should not simply mirror the duties of states."[73] Private business enterprises are indeed geared for "profit maximization, not to assume broad-based welfare functions."[74] Attributes that states possess but corporations lack in the public domain include the exercise of sovereignty over a territory, the exercise of "jurisdiction over persons and assets," the "power to tax and spend, and thus to provide public services."[75]

Based on these reasons, as a general rule, businesses should not be considered to incur the obligation to fulfill children's rights. This being said, specialized obligations may be incurred by businesses running privatized essential services such as healthcare, education, water and energy supply. For some time, the CRC Committee has been noting its concerns over the privatization of the provision and delivery of essential services and the potential fallout for children's rights.[76] Although a business enterprise is not a public interest entity, if it is involved in providing services that are normally considered public services (for instance, adoption, education, healthcare), then its duties can mirror those of states. With respect to substantive rights, private actors must "deliver those goods and services that are essential to a decent life, in order to ensure that they are adequate and available and accessible to all" in situations where private actors take over public functions of "the delivery of education, housing,

[71] CRC Committee, GC 5, para. 7.

[72] OHCHR, "Report of the United Nations High Commissioner on Human Rights on the Responsibilities of Transnational Corporations and Related Business Enterprises with Regard to Human Rights," E/CN.4/2005/91, 15 February 2005, para. 27.

[73] UN Framework, para. 53.

[74] Kinley and Tadaki, "From Talk to Walk," p. 961.

[75] De Schutter, "Corporations and Positive Duties," p. 8.

[76] CRC Committee, Day of General Discussion "The Private Sector as Service Provider and its Role in Implementing Child Rights," 31st Session, CRC/C/121, 20 September 2002; CRC Committee, GC 16, paras. 16, 33, and 34.

healthcare services or food" in full[77] or in part. The content of what is covered under the heading of essential goods and services may be more comprehensive for children given that impacts of deprivation are experienced differently by children, leading to long-term detriment. In line with the principle of survival and development, private actors that are providing services or goods normally considered public goods and services would be held to the same obligations required of states. The principles of evolving capacities and due deference also demand that private actors performing public functions either provide parents (or other caregivers, legal guardians) with the means to carry out their duties or facilitate the parents' access to these means, as a public entity would be required to do so under such circumstances. De Schutter believes that human rights obligations of corporations need to be defined "commensurate with their ability to influence certain actors with whom they interact or certain situations over which they make decisions, that recognizes the important role they can play in the fulfilment of human rights."[78] Although businesses do not have a general obligation to fulfill children's rights, those that may find it in their interest or within their broader social mission to contribute to the fulfillment of (children's) human rights would not be precluded from doing so.

Finally, businesses that have made a legal commitment to rights-holders to facilitate or provide access to certain services in the context of a business venture should be considered as having assumed specific contractual obligations within the scope of their commitment. This is particularly relevant for businesses that undertake legal commitments to provide or facilitate access to certain services such as health, education or water, when they invest in a community, in exchange for the community's consent for the investment. These contractual obligations may be explicitly or tacitly accepted by the business enterprise. Because businesses have enhanced obligations for children's rights, in line with IACtHR's view in *Girls Dilcia Yean and Violeta Bosico* v. *the Dominican Republic*, when such contractual obligations concern services to child rights-holders, they should be understood as fulfill obligations and guided by the relevant principles surrounding children's rights obligations.

[77] De Schutter, "Corporations and Positive Duties," p. 15.

[78] Ibid., p. 11.

Test Case: Application to Case Illustrations None of the case illustrations explored include instances where business enterprises are running privatized essential services, which would give rise to specialized fulfill obligations. Nonetheless, the Bujagali case provides an interesting background to gauge the specific fulfill obligations of business enterprises. The facts of the case about the promises linked to the provision of electricity, clean water, schools and education are disputed. If such promises were actually made to the project-affected populations who believed these to be commitments linked to the project, the businesses in question would incur a contractual obligation with respect to the realization of these services to the extent of their commitment. Moreover, if commitments linked to the provision of a primary school under a UPE scheme that would be both physically and financially accessible were in fact made, these commitments would trigger – under the current proposal – the sponsors' obligation to fulfill the access of children to primary education under the conditions promised.

4.4 Distribution of Obligations

Having proposed that businesses should be direct children's rights duty-bearers alongside states, the next step in the polycentric governance model is the distribution of obligations among the various duty-bearers.

The notion that the domestic state is the primary human rights duty-bearer, so central to many of the normative frameworks on extraterritorial obligations as well as the obligations of business and human rights, has to be duly scrutinized and reevaluated. As Vandenhole notes, the "distributive allocation of human rights obligations among duty-bearers" remains the "least developed" facet of standard-setting on transnational human rights obligations where

> [T]he primary obligation of the domestic State still seems to be the logical point of departure. Other States and [NSAs] have complementary obligations. When complementary obligations apply simultaneously (eg the obligation to respect), they are called parallel. When obligations are only triggered due to the inability or unwillingness of the primary duty-bearer, they are secondary or subsidiary. As to the distributive allocation of obligations to fulfil among other actors than the domestic State, we propose a *differentiated* human rights obligations regime based on an abstract system of allocation.[79]

[79] Vandenhole, "Obligations and Responsibility in a Plural and Diverse Duty-Bearer for Human Rights Regime," in Vandenhole (ed.), *Challenging Territoriality in Human Rights Law*, p. 129.

Vandenbogaerde has suggested, for instance, that the task of attributing and distributing obligations to NSAs and extraterritorial states would be best served by scrapping the term "primary duty-bearer" and designating the domestic state as the "principal" duty-bearer with "complementary obligations for foreign States and NSAs."[80] The "primary versus secondary" distinction is unhelpful at best and damaging at worst, creating the impression that one set of obligations (the obligations of so-called secondary or subsidiary duty-bearers) is subordinate to the other (the obligations of the primary duty-bearer). In fact, primacy in distribution – even as the law stands – is not a feature of the obligations themselves but of the circumstances of their discharge.

The human rights and children's rights obligations of businesses should not be contingent upon the domestic state's inability or unwillingness to live up to its own human rights and children's rights obligations but be independent of that factor as has also been recognized by the UNGPs.[81] Accordingly, obligations of (extraterritorial) states and businesses exist irrespective and independent of but in addition to domestic state obligations. Yet, it must be acknowledged that under many circumstances, the domestic state is best poised to achieve the respect for, protection and fulfillment of rights for individuals and groups, owing to the control it exerts, the legislative and administrative tools at its disposal and its direct relationship with rights-holders through residency and citizenship links. Thus, the domestic state remains the first locus for rights-holders looking to demand and enforce their rights or seek accountability for violations.

There are nonetheless scenarios where the domestic state may not automatically be considered the primary point of reference at least within its formally recognized territorial borders – due to considerations of control and command. This analysis diverges from the interpretation of the ECtHR in *Ilaşcu* and *Catan* cases. The argument put forth is not that the domestic state is absolved of its full range of children's rights obligations under conditions of inability. Here, a distinction between unwillingness and inability is necessary, as unwillingness is linked to a conscious disavowal of obligations, but inability is linked to a manifest lack of capabilities. As such, conditions of unwillingness would dictate that the domestic state remains the first point of reference with respect to rights claims.

[80] Vandenbogaerde, *Towards Shared Accountability*, pp. 236 and 296.
[81] UNGPs, Principle 11 "Commentary."

While continuing to have its full range of children's rights obligations, the domestic state may no longer be the undisputed primary duty-bearer. For instance, Moldova would continue to retain its full range of human rights obligations in the *Ilaşcu* and *Catan* cases but could not be considered the primary duty-bearer, having lost its effective control over Transnistria. The domestic state may be unable to discharge its full range of obligations due, among other things, to resource constraints, to a lack of effective control over its territory or to a lack of decision-making capacity vis-à-vis powerful businesses. In these cases, the burden of primary duty-bearing may shift to extraterritorial states individually or collectively, to the state or NSAs controlling the said-state's territory or to the businesses that are curtailing a state's decision-making or implementation capacity. This reality check effectively dismisses notions of fixed or permanent primary or secondary duty-bearers for rights. Consequently, the domestic state may not be the unequivocal primary duty-bearer for all rights in all cases and under all circumstances and it certainly is not the only one. When incorporating businesses into the circle of duty-bearers, distribution of obligations should not be based on a permanent hierarchy (e.g. primary, secondary, tertiary) but on layers of concurrent obligations. The effective enforcement of these obligations in practice may dictate one habitual point of first reference, e.g. the domestic state, but does not preclude a case-by-case reevaluation of that reference point in line with particularities of a given situation.

4.5 Responsibility of Businesses for Wrongdoings

The attribution and distribution of children's rights obligations to businesses is but the first step in fostering business accountability for children's rights. The second step is that of modelling responsibility for violations.

The four case illustrations demonstrate that in many real-life situations, the actors involved will include domestic/host states, extraterritorial/home states, several business enterprises of varying sizes possibly including SOEs, and one or more financial institutions. Gattini holds that in order to be able to attribute responsibility for a given breach to multiple duty-bearers, "all concerned subjects must be bound by the same obligation, or at least by formally different obligations, but with an overlapping content."[82] Accordingly, responsibility for a violation of

[82] Gattini, "Breach of International Obligations," p. 2.

the obligation to respect or to protect may be attributable – in theory – to multiple states, businesses and financial institutions, whatever the composition of the group of actors involved. The attribution of responsibility to businesses in practical terms may not be as straightforward as theoretically imaginable. As a first step, a number of legal stumbling blocks need to be identified and surmounted.

4.5.1 Responsibility Upstream and Downstream: Supply and Value Chains

Violations of children's rights usually take place upstream, meaning that they usually take place closer to the provision of raw materials that will be processed further down the supply chains. In the Uzbekistan case, the upstream cultivation and harvest of cotton is the site of children's rights violations. In the DRC, children's rights violations are a common feature of the mining of 3TG upstream. Many of the raw materials or services generated move down the value chain, being passed through different territorial jurisdictions by different corporate entities, in their journey towards end users or beneficiaries. When the violation takes place upstream, there is no direct link between rights-holders whose rights are violated and companies downstream that are in the business of providing the markets with end products or services using the upstream materials. Some supply chains such as those for organic or fair-trade goods allow for a high level of traceability and therefore the possibility to establish more direct links between rights-holders and duty-bearers. Nonetheless, to respond to challenges posed by conventional supply chains, the parameters for the attribution of responsibility to multiple duty-bearers should be equally applicable to indirect links as well as direct ones.

Any violation of the proposed universal minimum obligation to respect children's rights should trigger the corresponding responsibility of the actor that has caused the breach through its acts or omissions. Even in cases where the breach is clearly caused by the acts/omissions of one actor (as in the case of Uzbekistan), the attribution of responsibility to that actor should not preclude the attribution of responsibility to other actors involved. In addition, given that the proposed respect obligation is universal, any actor without whose involvement the violation/breach would not have taken place would also incur responsibility even in the absence of direct causal links between its conduct (acts or omissions) and the violations. The responsibility attributed to an actor that directly causes the breach and an actor that has a necessary but not causal participation in the breach may not be of the same magnitude. These considerations would be pertinent in the distribution of responsibility among the various duty-bearers. Likewise, an actor that does not cause a violation in the first place but that contributes to that violation, to its continuation or perpetuation by openly or tacitly incentivizing it, could incur responsibility.

Here, the contribution would not need be substantial to trigger responsibility as was suggested by the French NCP in the implementation of the OECD Guidelines for the textile and apparel sector. The issue of the magnitude of a contribution to a rights violation is in fact a consideration in the distribution of responsibility and not its attribution. Finally, an actor that is under the obligation to protect children's rights would incur responsibility for a violation when it fails to prevent the breach from taking place or from continuing to occur as per its protect obligation.

While it "may be difficult for the enterprise to systematically monitor the activities of all its business partners,"[83] the responsibility of a business enterprise is still engaged when its contribution to a children's rights violation is an act or an omission resulting from the failure to undertake effective and comprehensive due diligence with regard to its direct and indirect business relationships. For businesses with limited means, the UNGPs offer a workable solution:

> Where business enterprises have large numbers of entities in their value chains it may be unreasonably difficult to conduct due diligence for adverse human rights impacts across them all. If so, business enterprises should identify general areas where the risk of adverse human rights impacts is most significant, whether due to certain suppliers' or clients' operating context, the particular operations, products or services involved, or other relevant considerations, and prioritize these for human rights due diligence.[84]

Mares notes that the decision of "*outsourcing to a risky contractor*, a contractor that poses foreseeable risks of human rights abuse," in other words, "outsourc[ing] to irresponsible contractors without vetting and oversight procedures" is particularly problematic.[85] Furthermore, given that access to information has been revolutionized with the advent of

[83] De Schutter, "Corporations and Positive Duties," p. 22.
[84] UNGPs, Principle 17 "Commentary."
[85] Mares, "Responsibility to Respect," p. 177 (original emphasis).

online services and social media, even business enterprises with the most modest means can reasonably be expected to acquire enough knowledge about the operational contexts of their suppliers and clients to guide their business policies and decisions.

Although due diligence requirements are considered to extend to the use of leverage, CRBPs are reluctant to impose a duty to exercise influence or use leverage in business relationships, preferring instead a softer requirement: "Where a business is linked to an adverse impact by a business relationship, it should use its leverage and consider other relevant factors in determining the appropriate action to take."[86]

The CRBPs define leverage as "the ability of a business to effect change in the wrongful practices of the party that is causing or contributing to an adverse impact on human right."[87] According to the CRBPs, businesses "should" use the leverage they have "to prevent or mitigate an adverse impact on human rights that is directly linked to its operations, products or services by a business relationship."[88] CRBPs note that if businesses lack leverage over business relationships, they might be able to "increase it . . . by offering capacity-building or other incentives, or collaborating with other actors."[89] Accordingly, responsibility of the business enterprise would be engaged for failing to undertake its duty to protect children's rights not only if it fails to exercise its leverage but also when it does not seek to increase the leverage it lacks.

4.5.2 *Corporate Structures and Responsibility*

Parent companies should bear direct responsibility for the wrongful conduct of subsidiaries resulting in children's rights violations when they exercise a considerable degree of control or influence over these subsidiaries. This is because the parent company's obligation to respect and protect extends to the business activities undertaken not just within the core corporate structure but also to all other business structures over which the parent company exercises control. The basis for assigning responsibility to parent companies for the wrongful conduct of the subsidiaries they do not closely control/influence is, on the other hand, a thornier issue. Instead of the "duty of care" in tort law of certain domestic legal systems,

86 UNICEF, UN Global Compact and Save the Children, *Children's Rights and Business Principles*, p. 8.
87 Ibid.
88 Ibid.
89 Ibid.

which is already laden with particular conditions and criteria,[90] a duty of oversight may be preferable. As Mares rightly argues, the parent company could be held responsible "under a due diligence standard" for its initial decision to set up a separate subsidiary for instance in poor governance conditions and grant it autonomy without oversight.[91] The parent company's responsibility would thus be engaged on the basis of its conduct by "commission," or more simply put, action: "The parent company acted when it set up the subsidiary and then left it to its own devices in an environment riddled with risks of human rights abuses."[92] In addition, the parent company "retains some responsibility for . . . on-going oversight" having made the decision that creates risks for rights-holders abroad,[93] especially when these risks are foreseeable and likely not to be remedied if they result in rights violations.[94]

Lord Briggs, writing the UK Supreme Court's lead judgment on *Vedanta Resources PLC* v. *Lungowe* goes on to argue further that the "parent may incur the relevant responsibility to third parties if, in published materials, it holds itself out as exercising that degree of supervision and control of its subsidiaries, even if it does not in fact do so. In such circumstances its very omission may constitute the abdication of a responsibility which it has publicly undertaken."[95] The public commitment to oversight giving rise to responsibility is a very interesting contribution to the debate.

A parent company's proposed respect and protect duties would require it to take into account foreseeable risks of harm to children (and others) in setting up subsidiaries as well as in sourcing decisions and to engage in continued and effective supervision of subsidiary activities and decisions, especially as regards areas of heightened risk and as regards individuals or groups such as children at heightened sensitivity to adverse impacts.

A corporation's decision to set up a joint venture in the form of another legal entity, for instance, BEL in the Bujagali case, and to bid for an investment contract is demonstrative of its intent and capacity to be linked to the actions, decisions and activities of the subsidiary even if

[90] De Schutter, "Corporations and Positive Duties," p. 20.
[91] Mares, "Responsibility to Respect," p. 177.
[92] Ibid., p. 178.
[93] Ibid., p. 177.
[94] Ibid., pp. 180–181.
[95] *Vedanta Resources PLC and another (Appellants)* v. *Lungowe and others (Respondents)*, para. 53.

the subsidiary's operations are poised to run independently of the parent company. Given this intent and capacity, it would be entirely reasonable to expect Blackstone to exercise oversight over BEL.

4.5.3 Considerations About State-Owned Enterprises (SOEs)

State-owned enterprises (SOEs) may need to be treated differently than their privately owned counterparts with respect to responsibility in that while they are subject to the same scope of children's rights obligations, recourse can also be made to state responsibility in seeking accountability for violations. In line with ARSIWA Article 8 on "Conduct directed or controlled by a State," the UN Framework notes, for instance, that "the State itself may be held responsible under international law for the internationally wrongful acts of its SOEs if they can be considered State organs or are acting on behalf, or under the orders, of the State."[96] The Commentary to ARSIWA Article 8 makes it clear that a state's decision to set up a corporate entity does not in itself create sufficient basis for the attribution of that entity's conduct to the state. Conversely, if a state had set up a company in order to carry out a practice that is considered a breach of its obligations, the conduct of the company would be attributable to the state.[97]

The exploration of attribution of responsibility to a state for the conduct of its SOE in ARSIWA is rather limited. In the Uzbekistan case, for instance, the state has set up SOEs to trade in cotton produced by forced child and adult labor. Of course, the SOEs are set up to ensure that Uzbekistan receives the best possible prices for its cotton and maximizes its earnings from cotton exports. Although cotton-trading SOEs are not set up with the purpose of carrying out unlawful conduct, they are made accessory to the unlawful action and by their operations, give continued rationale for cotton cultivation using forced labor to persist. The breach of the obligation on the part of the state is linked to the use of forced child labor but SOEs trading in cotton are also in breach of their own obligations to act with due diligence to ascertain that they are not involved in trading goods produced by one of the unconditional worst forms of child labor.

In the case of Uganda TSDP, the links of the SOE as the majority shareholder of the parent company of the contractor obscures the chain

96 UN Framework, para. 32.

97 ARSIWA, Art. 8 "Commentary," para. 6.

of command even further. The Chinese SOE that holds majority shares in the parent company is also represented strongly on that company's board. The parent company, on the other hand, fully owns the contractor. It is clear that the companies have not been set up to undertake unlawful conduct but it is unclear whether the failure of a fully owned Chinese subsidiary of a Chinese parent company (whose majority shareholder is a Chinese SOE) to carry out proper due diligence could be attributable to the Chinese state.

The UN Framework also contends that it should be easier for states to foster respect for human rights from SOEs especially given that the state has the authority to appoint senior management that reports to the state.[98] The CRC Committee's GC 16 also demands an enhanced expectation from states with respect to SOEs, "requiring all State-owned enterprises to undertake child-rights due diligence and to publicly communicate their reports on their impact on children's rights, including regular reporting" in order to "lead [other businesses] by example."[99]

4.5.4 Distribution of Responsibility

For a responsibility framework to be effective in providing true accountability, it should be able to account for the realities presented by today's constellation of diverse entities with the intent and capacity to participate in ventures and interactions that can foreseeably impact human rights, also of children. Given that existing secondary norms about responsibility do not provide an adequate framework for the distribution of responsibility to multiple duty-bearers that include state and non-state entities, other considerations should become pertinent. One such consideration is power.

The famous dictum that "power breeds responsibility"[100] is all too often quoted as a possible basis for apportioning responsibility to multiple duty-bearers. Although linking power to responsibility is attractive as an idea, its application and applicability is fraught with difficulty. As Nollkaemper notes, the "relatively high threshold" to meet in order for power to engage responsibility likely masks the importance of power in various interactions.[101]

[98] UN Framework, para. 32.

[99] CRC Committee, GC 16, p. 64.

[100] Clyde Eagleton, *The Responsibility of States in International Law* (New York University Press, 1928) p. 206.

[101] Nollkaemper, "Power and Responsibility," p. 21.

The four cases illustrate that when multiple duty-bearers are involved in outcomes, each of the actors may be wielding different types or extent of power. Each of them may be involved in a given violation to varying degrees. Situations with multiple duty-bearers may consist of individual actions by multiple entities, where one entity's action is decisive in the coming about of the violation and the others, individual actions by multiple entities causing cumulative effects as well as concerted action involving multiple duty-bearers. Hence, power alone as an underlying distributive principle for allocating responsibility will not succeed in resolving the complexities surrounding real-life scenarios.

Human rights violations may come about as a result of different permutations of behavior by multiple actors. The two most distinguishable cases are cooperative responsibility and cumulative responsibility as sketched out broadly by Nollkaemper and Jacobs.[102]

Concerted behavior leading to human rights breaches: The conduct resulting in the violation cannot be traced to an act or an omission by one actor. The violation comes about as a result of the concerted action by several actors. All actors involved have played necessary but not sufficient roles in concert in the coming about of the violation. All actors collectively bear responsibility for the violation. Both actions and failure to act when required by obligation constitute bases for responsibility. Each actor may have contributed equally to the wrongdoing or in different proportions. This may be defined as cooperative responsibility. The Bujagali project is a clear illustration of concerted behavior leading to violations, where all the actors involved collaborated with one another in the context of the project and contributed in varying degrees to the violations.

Separate behavior cumulating in human rights breaches: There is no one conduct causing a violation that can be clearly isolated. Multiple actors have played necessary but not sufficient roles, but the violation is the cumulative outcome of these roles. This is also termed cumulative responsibility. An example would be when numerous textile retailers hire subcontractors overseas and individually put pressure on subcontractors to work under tight deadlines while pushing them to keep costs low, resulting in violations of labor standards and human rights for textile workers.

[102] Nollkaemper and Jacobs, "Introduction: Mapping the Normative Framework," p. 14.

In addition to cumulative and cooperative responsibility, the distributive rules for allocating human rights responsibility to multiple duty-bearers should take into account the following scenarios at a minimum:

Contribution in the form of complicity: The rights violation is committed by one actor. Other actors enable this actor or facilitate the violation either through action or omission, thus becoming complicit.[103] This is direct contribution to the harm. In this scenario, those complicit may have knowingly enabled or facilitated the commission of the violation or done so through negligence. Whether complicity arises from intentional engagement or negligence may play a role in designating the level of responsibility attributed to that entity. For instance, if traders or companies that are end-users of minerals unknowingly use minerals originating from the DRC's conflict-affected regions, their responsibility might be engaged based on negligence and therefore limited by the extent of their negligence. On the other hand, if these actors intentionally trade in minerals mined in the DRC and marketed by armed groups, they may incur more extensive responsibility for complicity.

In complex relationships such as those populating supply chains, it is normally difficult to causally link actors higher up the chain of custody to human rights harms occurring at the bottom of the chain. Even if causal links were – for the sake of argument – ascertained, the questions of intent, negligence or knowing and voluntary contribution to the harm would remain relevant in how much responsibility can be assigned to a given agent.

One continued human rights breach, several actors contributing to the continuation: The rights violation can be clearly traced to the acts/omissions of one actor. Other actors have contributed directly or indirectly, through action or failure to take action, to the repetition of the violation or to a continuing violation. In this case, the responsibility for the initial violation is assigned to the actor whose conduct can be causally linked to the violation. Other actors, who have contributed to the recurrence or continuation of the violation, are also responsible for this recurrence or continuation, although they are not directly responsible for the initial violation in the first place. This may be deemed "complementary responsibility," separate from the responsibility of the violation-causing actor. This complementary responsibility is triggered on the basis

[103] Lanovoy, "Complicity in an Internationally Wrongful Act," pp. 144–145.

of the harms incurred by injured rights-holders as a consequence of the perpetuation of the wrongdoing. The involvement of various companies at different levels of the supply chain and of the WB, IFC and ADB as financiers in the Uzbek cotton case is an illustration.

Human rights breaches are a function of social or economic conditions, numerous actors are involved: There is no one isolatable action or omission that can be linked to a violation because the violations are a function of the socioeconomic conditions that result from a series of actions/omissions or decisions by multiple actors. One example is violations of the right to an adequate standard of living under conditions of poverty that may be caused by a sovereign debt crisis.

In these situations, the late political theorist Iris Marion Young postulated a forward-looking model of political responsibility instead of the backward-looking liability model.[104] In fact, "[r]ecent CSR discussions like those on human rights violations in supply chains and on societal concerns such as obesity also signal a shift from a retrospective to a prospective approach to responsibility."[105] Young's interpretation of shared responsibility is "a personal responsibility for outcomes or the risks of harmful outcomes, produced by a group of persons" where "[e]ach is personally responsible for the outcome in a partial way, since he or she alone does not produce the outcomes; the specific part that each plays in producing the outcome cannot be isolated and identified."[106] Through assigning political responsibility, existing regulatory institutions may be reformed and new ones created in order to engender structural change and remedy structural injustice.[107]

Young theorized "a social connection model" to supplement a legalistic liability model, employing the concept of shared responsibility as an antidote to structural injustice.[108] This model is dubbed the social connection model because responsibility is derived from social connections or "participation in the diverse institutional processes that produce structural injustice."[109] The model is acutely appropriate for divorcing the responsibility of participants

[104] Iris M. Young, "Responsibility and Global Labor Justice" (2004) 12(4) *The Journal of Political Philosophy* 365–388 at 368.

[105] Schrempf-Stirling, Palazzo and Phillips, "Ever Expanding Responsibilities: Upstream and Downstream Corporate Social Responsibility," p. 360.

[106] Ibid., p. 380.

[107] Ibid., p. 387.

[108] Young, "Responsibility and Global Justice: A Social Connection Model" (2006) 23(1) *Social Philosophy & Policy Foundation* 102–130.

[109] Ibid., 118.

from constraints such as international legal personality or jurisdiction. The need for an alternative model of responsibility lies in the complexity of relations between actors at different levels, which no longer reflect a "direct interaction between the wrongdoer and the wronged party."[110] In the case of the apparel industry, for instance, because the responsibility for poor labor conditions is diffused and "firms higher up the chain . . . often have no legal responsibility for the policies and operations of the firms below with which they contract," the liability model is difficult to apply.[111] Young delineated four variables for assessing each actor's station in relation to structural injustice:

- ***Power:*** the "degree of potential or actual power or influence over the processes that produce the outcomes,"[112] correlated with that actor's position,
- ***Privilege:*** holding or acquiring "relative privilege" by virtue of unjust social structures,
- ***Interest:*** interest in maintaining or transforming social structures resulting in injustice,
- ***Collective ability:*** ease in influencing a process more easily than another process through a coincidental combination of power, interest and organization.[113]

Here, power is an important consideration but only in conjunction with the other parameters.

Applied to the apparel industry, workers making garments are the ones that have the least amount of power, do not enjoy any privilege but have the highest level of interest in transforming the rules although they may not have the collective ability to do so. There are several layers of subcontractors between the workers and the retailers. In fact, those small subcontractors closer to the bottom of the chain "in developing countries frequently operate right at the edge of solvency."[114] These small contractors do not have the power, are not privileged, and are unlikely to have an interest or the collective ability to induce or influence change. It is in fact at the top of the supply chain, at the level of "major logo retailers" who "usually make handsome profits from this system"[115]

[110] Ibid.
[111] Ibid., 110.
[112] Ibid., 127.
[113] Ibid., 127–129.
[114] Ibid., 111.
[115] Ibid.

that power and privilege lie. These actors are also the ones that have perhaps the least amount of interest inherently to rectify the system but also some level of collective ability, by virtue of their power and organization, to do so. In fact, the relative success of the boycott in getting children off the cotton fields in the Uzbek case is illustrative of the fact that retailers at the end of the supply chain hold considerable power and privilege and are able to sway decision-making in favor of their desired goals in a given local situation. Of course, it must be noted that, in this world of prospective approach to responsibility, those actors at the end of the supply chain will increasingly come under pressure as conscious consumers seek to make purchasing choices that seek to avoid causing adverse impacts on human rights, the environment and labor standards.

Young argued, using the textile and apparel industry as an example, that "scope of issues of justice corresponding to political responsibility derives not from the boundaries of a state or political jurisdiction, but from the connections generated by the structural processes."[116] Her policy-oriented conclusion is one that hardly seems revolutionary in political philosophy scholarship but may well be deemed as such in traditional legal scholarship: "Where [the scope of issues of justice] is beyond existing regulatory and political institutions, there may be need to construct some to correspond to that scope."[117] The philosophical roots of Young's approach are to be found in Beitz's response to Rawls on global justice, extending the principles of justice globally on the basis of what he calls "a global scheme of social cooperation" that renders national boundaries as morally insignificant in determining "the limits of social obligations."[118]

In thinking about models to apportion legal responsibility that is both forward-looking and able to address violations that have already happened, elements of the social interaction model need to be combined with the traditional liability model to create a workable hybrid to encompass all situations where not only actions by particular actors but failures to act can also be brought within the scope of responsibility.

116 Young, "Responsibility and Global Labor Justice," p. 388.
117 Ibid.
118 Charles Beitz, *Political Theory and International Relations* (Princeton University Press, 1979), p. 151.

5

Polycentric Governance of Responsibility

The practicalities of working through the distribution of responsibility, when human rights of children and adults are violated by several actors that contribute to the violation in different ways, may not be self-evident. As Nollkaemper notes, international law may not be able to best resolve the question of how responsibility ought to be distributed among different actors because its currently accepted standards are not adequately developed:

> While practice shows many examples where states and other actors together factually caused harm, it is only in rather rare situations that international law recognises that each of these contributing actors shares in the eventual responsibility. . . .
>
> In some cases, while not necessarily precluding the determination or implementation of shared responsibility, international law provides little or no guidance as to exactly how responsibility (or reparation) is to be allocated between multiple actors. (footnote omitted)[1]

Thus, a one-model-fits-all approach may not be workable in real life for attributing and distributing responsibility among wrongdoers. In fact, a feasible hybrid for distributing responsibility for violations of children's rights may not, at this point in time, be attainable through one overarching model. A case-by-case approach to deal with actual instances may be preferable. This is precisely the reason why polycentric governance models for human rights responsibility are useful. In fact, the existing landscape of responsibility is already one of polycentric governance by private and public actors at the subnational, governmental and supranational levels.

The polycentric governance of human rights responsibility already exists in an imperfect fashion as explored in Part I through home state regulation and judicial mechanisms, domestic regulation with

[1] Nollkaemper, "Introduction," in Nollkaemper and Plakokefalos (eds.), *Principles of Shared Responsibility*, p. 13.

extraterritorial effects and multilateral proxy avenues such as the IFC's CAO as well as sectoral certification and operational-level mechanisms.

5.1 Improving State-Level Governance of Responsibility

Part I explored the various venues at the domestic level available to extraterritorial states to govern compliance with human rights obligations of businesses when these actors engage in business dealings abroad, including through the use of subcontractors or through sourcing decisions. Beyond the specific issues around the prevention of child sexual exploitation abroad and conflict minerals due diligence, broader uses of civil liability, tort law and criminal law approaches have been proposed by various frameworks as responsibility mechanisms.

5.1.1 Civil Liability and Tort Law

The use of civil liability and tort law approaches essentially valorizes the use of home state judicial systems primarily with a view to fostering compliance with internationally recognized human rights norms in the extraterritorial business operations and activities. As there is currently no generally recognized duty for home states to allow domestic redress for violations committed outside of its territory, whether individuals or groups can seek justice for violations committed abroad by corporate entities that are domiciled or have their main place of business in a home state's jurisdiction depends entirely on that home state's legal system.

Home state civil liability and tort law approaches are increasingly becoming proposed as effective mechanisms, especially in the European context. The 2016 CoE Recommendation on Human Rights and Business calls on CoE states to take appropriate measures (legislative or otherwise) as necessary to allow for civil liability under their laws against human rights abuses caused by businesses and "ensure that their domestic courts have jurisdiction over civil claims concerning business-related human rights abuses against business enterprises domiciled within their jurisdiction. The doctrine of *forum non conveniens* should not be applied in these cases."[2]

In addition, it recommends states to consider allowing their domestic courts to exercise their jurisdiction over civil claims regarding allegations of "business-related human rights abuses"

[2] CoE, "Recommendation on Human Rights and Business," paras. 32 and 34.

> [A]gainst subsidiaries, wherever they are based, of business enterprises domiciled within their jurisdiction if such claims are closely connected with civil claims against the latter enterprises[;]
>
> [A]gainst . . . a business enterprise [not domiciled within its jurisdiction], if no other effective forum guaranteeing a fair trial is available (*forum necessitatis*) and there is a sufficiently close connection to the member State concerned.[3]

The inclusion of the doctrine *forum necessitatis* as a legal basis for allowing civil claims against businesses not domiciled in a state in the presence of a "sufficiently close connection" is rather interesting from a practical standpoint as it may allow rights holders to pursue their accountability claims in Europe. According to the Explanatory Memorandum of the Recommendation:

> [t]he doctrine may also serve as a safeguard to avoid a denial of justice, for example in cases where victims of alleged human rights abuses involving business enterprises which occurred outside of Europe cannot reasonably be expected to receive a fair trial in the domestic courts of the country where such abuses allegedly occurred . . . [if] . . . the proceedings in the courts of the third country where the alleged violations occurred can be expected to manifestly contravene fair trial guarantees, and that there is a sufficiently close connection to the member State that would exercise such jurisdiction.[4]

The Memorandum also recognises that jurisdictional difficulties may arise with respect to MNEs operating transnationally in attempting to bring their activities within the reach of home state civil law processes. Accordingly, the Brussels Regime and the Lugano Convention, which is open to ratification by non-EU states as well, are detailed as legislation embodying rules on jurisdiction on which to base "legal disputes of a civil or commercial nature between natural and/or legal persons resident or located in" different states.[5] Bernaz has previously noted, however, that "some features of the law of European states make business and human rights civil litigation difficult and less likely," including lower damages and virtual nonexistence of punitive damages as well as the "absence of a conditional fee system, which means that an unsuccessful claimant has to pay the respondent's legal fees."[6]

[3] Ibid., paras. 35–36.

[4] CoE, "Explanatory Memorandum to Recommendation CM/Rec (2016) 3 of the Committee of Ministers to Member States on Human Rights and Business," 2 March 2016, para. 59.

[5] Ibid., para. 56.

[6] Nadia Bernaz, *Business and Human Rights: History, Law and Policy – Bridging the Accountability Gap* (Routledge, 2017), p. 282.

In addition, possibility for bringing civil law liability claims against business enterprises that a state owns, controls or contracts for the provision of public services should be ensured.[7] The Recommendation is also clear that it is the duty of the Member States to guarantee that domestic courts do not apply "law that is incompatible with their international obligations, in particular those stemming from the applicable international human rights standards."[8]

The French law on the duty of vigilance foresees periodic penalty payments for failure to comply with vigilance obligations. Any claimant can, with three months of prior notice, "ask the competent court to order the company to comply."[9] The law also foresees civil law penalties for failure to abide by vigilance obligations as well, these failures would be covered by French tort law and conditional on whether claimants can establish civil liability. It has been noted that this is dependent on three conditions: "a damage, a breach of one of the obligations defined in the law and causation between the two."[10] Nonetheless, it does exist as a possible recourse.

5.1.2 Criminal Law Approaches

Domestic criminal law approaches may have a more limited but much clearer function with respect to accountability for corporate action amounting to crimes under domestic law and quite ostensibly under international law. For businesses, it is rather clear that corporate behavior amounting to crimes (under domestic law or international criminal law) is justiciable and will be dealt with by domestic courts, if the domestic state is willing and capable to bring corporate perpetrators to justice. The use of criminal law in home states for crimes committed extraterritorially by businesses domiciled in their territory remains more contentious but may be done through the establishment of extraterritorial jurisdiction based either on active or passive nationality principles.

The 2016 CoE Recommendation on Human Rights and Business advises states to allow criminal liability of businesses for crimes under

7 CoE, "Recommendation on Human Rights and Business," para. 38.

8 Ibid., para. 40.

9 Stéphane Brabant and Elsa Savourey, "France's Corporate Duty of Vigilance Law: A Closer Look at the Penalties Faced by Companies," *Revue Internationale De La Compliance et De L"Ethique Des Affaires – Supplément A La Semaine Juridique Entreprise Et Affaires N° 50 Du Jeudi 14 Décembre 2017*, p. 4.

10 Ibid., p. 2.

international law and serious human rights violations as well as offenses such as corruption, cybercrime, human trafficking, sexual exploitation and abuse, violence against women and organized crime in addition to offenses covered under CRC-OPSC. Accordingly, criminal liability should cover not only causing a crime or violation but also "participation in the commission of such crimes."[11] The criminal liability for international crimes or serious violations of human rights is to be applicable to representatives of business enterprises "[i]rrespective of whether business enterprises can be held liable under criminal or other equivalent law."[12] Although no explicit mention of extraterritoriality is made, the references to international crimes as well as treaty-based crimes of a transnational nature such as human trafficking, offenses under the OPSC or cybercrime imply that the use of criminal law mechanisms of extraterritorial states would also be covered under the Recommendation.

Under CRC-OPSC Article 3 state parties are required to ensure that offenses relating to the sale of children, child prostitution and pornography are covered by criminal or penal law "whether such offences are committed domestically or transnationally or on an individual or organized basis." In addition, Article 4.2 allows for a state to establish extraterritorial jurisdiction over these offenses, either based on the nationality or habitual residence of the alleged perpetrator in its territory, or based on the nationality of the victim. Moreover, CoE's Convention on the Protection of Children against Sexual Exploitation and Sexual Abuse (the Lanzarote Convention) Article 26 on Corporate Liability obligates states to take all necessary measures to "ensure that a legal person can be held liable" under criminal, civil or administrative law "without prejudice to the criminal liability of the natural persons who have committed the offence" for offenses

> 1. . . . committed for its benefit by any natural person, acting either individually or as part of an organ of the legal person, who has a leading position within the legal person, based on:
>
> a. power of representation of the legal person;
> b. an authority to take decisions on behalf of the legal person;
> c. an authority to exercise control within the legal person.

[11] Ibid., para. 44.
[12] Ibid., para. 45.

2. . . . [as well as] the lack of supervision or control by a natural person referred to in paragraph 1 has made possible the commission of an offence established in accordance with this Convention for the benefit of that legal person by a natural person acting under its authority.[13]

Coupled with Convention's Article 25 on jurisdiction, which requires a state to establish its jurisdiction over the offenses on its territory including on board a ship or aircraft, on the nationality or habitual residence of the "person" having committed the crime, Article 26 would amount to an obligation on the home state of a business (as a legal person) to provide legal liability for the children's rights violations enumerated under the convention. The Lanzarote Convention has been signed by all forty-seven CoE member states and ratified by forty-four of them.[14]

5.2 Improving Supranational Governance of Responsibility

Possibilities for the use of mechanisms at the supranational level for fostering compliance with corporate human rights obligations and ensuring responsibility at this time remain much more limited.

5.2.1 Human Rights Treaty Bodies and International Courts

Existing human rights monitoring mechanisms may provide an entry point for rights claims of children involving businesses either via home or host states, particularly with the newest complaint mechanisms under CRC-OPIC.[15] Complaints to human rights treaty bodies would essentially

[13] CoE Convention on the Protection of Children against Sexual Exploitation and Sexual Abuse, 25 October 2007, Art. 26.

[14] COE, "Chart of Signatures and Ratifications of Treaty 201," www.coe.int/en/web/conventions/full-list/-/conventions/treaty/201/signatures?p_auth=mirLPa4k (based on the ratifications as of 24 April 2019).

[15] How issues related to businesses may arise and be dealt with by the ESCR and CRC Committees has been illustrated by several alternative judgments: Gamze Erdem Türkelli, "Putting an End to Victims Without Borders: Child Pornography (Committee on the Rights of the Child)"; Rachel Hammonds and Gorik Ooms, "Shared Responsibility for the Right to Health (Committee on Economic, Social and Cultural Rights)"; Jernej Letnar Černič, "Economic, Social and Cultural Rights of the Purak Peoples (Committee on Economic, Social and Cultural Rights)"; Arne Vandenbogaerde, "Labour Rights in a Transnational Perspective (Committee on Economic, Social and Cultural Rights)" in Mark Gibney and Wouter Vandenhole (eds.), *Litigating Transnational Human Rights Obligations: Alternative Judgments* (Routledge, 2014).

respond to requirements of state responsibility for violations resulting from business behavior and may render treaty bodies a new venue for polycentric governance of children's rights responsibility. Besides and beyond human rights treaty bodies, proposals for developing new governance mechanisms at the supranational level would provide the benefit of also allowing businesses to be directly brought into the circle of duty-bearers against whom effective enforcement and implementation mechanisms for rights claims exist, beyond what is internally available at such institutions. The proposals for such supranational governance mechanisms are not children's rights specific but could incorporate rules and procedures that provide for child-friendly access to remedy if they were ever to see the light of day.

The use of existing human rights courts at the supranational level for advancing rights-holder claims against businesses remains problematic even in cases that do not span different territorial jurisdictions due to *ratione personae* restrictions. One proposed means for ending corporate impunity and overcoming existing *ratione personae* limitations is by replicating domestic justice systems globally by allowing corporations to be defendants in international courts for human rights violations.

For human rights violations amounting to international crimes, one proposal has been to designate the International Criminal Court (ICC) competent to hear cases on alleged business violations amounting to international crimes. The inclusion of "corporate criminal liability for international crimes" in the Rome Statute was considered during the negotiations but finally not adopted, and now its inclusion in the business and human rights treaty has been called a "unique opportunity not to be missed."[16] It is true that if recognized, corporate criminal liability for international crimes may provide accountability especially if the liability extends to wrongdoing based on complicity in the broader sense, for instance, by facilitating the commission of international crimes by financing armed groups through commercial transactions – as in the case of companies engaged in mineral trade from the DRC's conflict-affected zones. Although refashioning ICC's mandate to include corporate criminal liability may be elusive for the time being, domestic criminal legal systems –with ICC assistance – may serve to bridge the gap in the

[16] Nadia Bernaz, "Including Corporate Criminal Liability for International Crimes in the Business and Human Rights Treaty: Necessary but Insufficient," Business and Human Rights Resource Centre, https://business-humanrights.org/en/including-corporate-criminal-liability-for-international-crimes-in-the-business-and-human-rights-treaty-necessary-but-insufficient (accessed 15 March 2019).

meanwhile. In fact, a 2016 policy paper by ICC's Office of the Prosecutor notes that where it has not selected a case for investigation or prosecution, the Office will continue to cooperate with and assist domestic jurisdictions not only with respect to crimes under the Rome Statute but also – upon request –

> with respect to conduct which constitutes a serious crime under national law, such as the illegal exploitation of natural resources, arms trafficking, human trafficking, terrorism, financial crimes, land grabbing or the destruction of the environment.[17]

For all other violations not amounting to international crimes, the creation of a "World Court on Business and Human Rights" has been suggested as a panacea. The proposal has its roots in the original idea for the establishment of a World Court of Human Rights, which dates back virtually to the establishment of the UN Human Rights Commission.[18] As the World Court of Human Rights as an idea, a concept, and a project has been elaborated in ample detail by others,[19] this study only explores what the proposal envisaged with respect to accountability for business behavior. The "draft Statute" for this proposal for a standing World Court of Human Rights, to be established by an international treaty and able to render binding and final judgments, envisages a number of actors beyond the state called "entities" to be able to accept the Court's jurisdiction by declaration (Article 51). These entities are defined as "any inter-governmental organization or non-State actor, including any

[17] International Criminal Court – The Office of the Prosecutor, "Policy Paper on Case Selection and Prioritisation," 15 September 2016, para. 7.

[18] For a detailed account of how the idea evolved through time, including the most recent proposals: International Commission of Jurists, "Towards a World Court of Human Rights: Questions and Answers," December 2011, http://icj.wpengine.netdna-cdn.com/wp-content/uploads/2013/07/World-court-final-23.12-pdf1.pdf (accessed 24 April 2019).

[19] See particularly: Manfred Nowak, "The Need for a World Court of Human Rights" (2007) 7(1) *Human Rights Law Review* 251–259; Martin Scheinin, "Towards a World Court of Human Rights: Research Report Within the Framework of the Swiss Initiative to Commemorate the 60th Anniversary of the Universal Declaration of Human Rights," June 2009, www.enlazandoalternativas.org/IMG/pdf/hrCourt_scheinin0609.pdf (accessed 24 April 2019); Julia Kozma, Manfred Nowak and Martin Scheinin, *A World Court of Human Rights: Consolidated Statute and Commentary* (Neuer Wissenschaftlicher Verlag, 2010) as well as Manfred Nowak, "It's Time for a World Court of Human Rights," in M. Cherif Bassiouni and W. Schabas (eds.), *New Challenges for the UN Human Rights Machinery: What Future for the UN Treaty Body System and the Human Rights Council Procedures?* (Intersentia, 2011), and Geir Ulfstein, "Do We Need a World Court of Human Rights?," in O. Engdahl and P. Wrange (eds.), *Law at War: The Law as It Was and the Law as It Should Be* (Brill, 2008).

business corporation."[20] Scheinin has clarified that the term "entity" is intended to comprise among others,

a) International organizations constituted through a treaty between States, or between States and international organizations;
b) Transnational corporations, i.e. business corporations that conduct a considerable part of the production or service operations in a country or in countries other than the home State of the corporation as a legal person;
c) International non-governmental organizations, i.e. associations or other types of legal persons that are not operating for economic profit and conduct a considerable part of their activities in a country or in countries other than the home State of the organization as a legal person.[21]

The draft Statute lists the CRC, OPAC and OPSC among applicable law for the Court.[22] According to the Statute, the Court would have the specific mandate to first "determine whether an act or omission is attributable to a State or Entity" in order to attribute responsibility to it for the alleged violation, specifically applying "the principles of the international law of State responsibility ... also in respect to Entities subject to its jurisdiction, as if the act or omission attributed to an entity was attributable to a State."[23] Such a proposition may well imply that the so-called entities having accepted the jurisdiction of the World Court would be covered by the same human rights obligations by which state actors are bound. It must be noted, however, that while many prominent human rights practitioners and scholars have lent support to the idea for a World Court of Human Rights, it by no means enjoys universal backing among human rights and international law scholars.[24]

Practically, as the four case illustrations demonstrate, it is very unlikely for any business to voluntarily accept the jurisdiction of a court and open itself up to possible lawsuits when they would escape such binding legal scrutiny simply by remaining in the status quo. The one solution to

[20] Kozma, Nowak and Scheinin, "Statute of the World Court of Human Rights," in Kozma, Nowak and Scheinin, *A World Court of Human Rights*, Art. 4.

[21] Scheinin, "Towards a World Court of Human Rights," 19.

[22] Kozma, Nowak and Scheinin, "Statute of the World Court of Human Rights," Art. 5.1.

[23] Ibid., Art. 6.1.

[24] For critical and negative assessments, see, for instance, Stefan Trechsel, "A World Court for Human Rights?" (2004) 1(1) *Northwestern Journal of International Human Rights*, scholarlycommons.law.northwestern.edu/njihr/vol1/iss1/3 and Philip Alston, "Against a World Court of Human Rights" (2014) 28(2) *Ethics and International Affairs* 197–212.

corporate unwillingness to submit to a world court might be found by engaging mandatory jurisdiction of the Court, as granted by home states, in cases where transnational corporations domiciled in their territory are involved in human rights violations extraterritorially. Yet, this solution is far more a theoretical solution than a practical one.

The specific proposal on the World Court on Business and Human Rights is a successor to the idea of a World Court of Human Rights, being discussed in reference to the process exploring the possibilities of a binding legal instrument on business and human rights under the auspices of the UN.[25] Accordingly, the World Court on Business and Human Rights would be linked to – and perhaps established by – the international treaty on business and human rights as an access to remedy mechanism for those whose rights have been violated by businesses. The World Court is seen as an umpire in "resolv[ing] conflicts arising from the law in different jurisdictions" and operating under the "international principle of subsidiarity," meaning that its jurisdiction will be engaged only after an exhaustion of remedies at the domestic level or if domestic legal systems are unable or unwilling to deliver justice to rights holders."[26] This idea for a world court as a venue to litigate claims of human rights violations against corporate entities is likely to find traction among civil society and academia to an extent but also to be fiercely debated and opposed first and foremost by many states and business representatives.

5.2.2 *International Arbitration*

One way of connecting the theory and practice of responsibility is through the establishment of a body or bodies mandated with resolving children's rights/human rights conflicts that are related to the acts of businesses and financial institutions. These bodies would then essentially be governance bodies, responding to the challenges linked to the absence of an international court with a similar mandate.

Claes Cronstedt and Robert C. Thompson have come up with a one such proposal, still in nascent stages, for an international arbitration tribunal on business and human rights, in order to resolve the questions of attribution and distribution of responsibility for alleged human rights

[25] Luis Gallegos and Daniel Uribe, "The Next Step Against Corporate Impunity: A World Court on Business and Human Rights?" (2016) 57 *Harvard International Law Journal* Online Symposium 7–10.

[26] Ibid.

violations committed by businesses.[27] According to the proposal, a team of international and human rights law experts representing different stakeholders would evaluate existing arbitration rules and procedures and introduce necessary changes to be used by the "International Arbitration Tribunal on Business and Human Rights." This tribunal's advantages would include reduced transaction costs both value and time-wise, the use of qualified mediators to resolve human rights conflicts at earlier stages, the flexibility to hold proceedings anywhere including online and the possibility to create a sort of jurisprudence on business and human rights "through the publication of a body of reasoned arbitration decisions."[28] The incentives for joining such an arbitration tribunal would range from corporate social responsibility to reputational and business risks for not being a part of such a conflict-resolution system. A further proposal for companies is to place human rights clauses in their contracts with suppliers and other business partners, along with an "escalation clause" which outlines dispute resolution processes.[29] The authors go on to underscore that investors and financiers may consider adding "a requirement that their supply chain and other contracts include human rights and arbitration clauses" to their lending/investing requirements, which could even entail access to third party beneficiaries such as rights-holders who want to start or join proceedings.[30] The proposal has been transformed into a project of The Hague Institute for Global Justice to draft The Hague International Business and Human Rights Arbitration Rules.[31] Once drafted, the rules could be offered to the Permanent Court of Arbitration and other standing arbitration bodies to be implemented in cases of human rights claims against business enterprises.[32]

[27] Claes Cronstedt and Robert C. Thompson, "A Proposal for an International Arbitration Tribunal on Business and Human Rights" (2016) 57 *Harvard International Law Journal* Online Symposium at 66–69.

[28] Ibid., 68.

[29] According to this "escalation clause," the conflict settlement process may start with direct negotiations, continue with mediation and eventually be referred to arbitration.

[30] Ibid., 68–69.

[31] Center for International Legal Coordination, "The Hague Rules on Business and Human Rights Arbitration," www.cilc.nl/project/the-hague-rules-on-business-and-human-rights-arbitration/ (accessed 24 April 2019).

[32] Julianne Hughes-Jennett and Alison Berthet, "Arbitrating Business and Human Rights Disputes: Uncharted Territory," *Thompson Reuters Arbitration* Blog, 30 August 2018, http://arbitrationblog.practicallaw.com/arbitrating-business-and-human-rights-disputes-uncharted-territory/ (accessed 24 April 2019).

The proposed "International Arbitration Tribunal on Business and Human Rights," either using a standing body or a new venue, would in fact have the advantages of allowing for a case-by-case assessment of human rights impacts of companies not just for allegations of adverse human rights impacts ex post facto but also in real time as they happen on the ground. This may facilitate mitigation and prevention of further harm, if the procedural rules of the arbitration allow for administrative measures, such as injunctions. This type of arrangement, allowing rights-holders to access justice expeditiously and without suffering further harm, may be preferable in the context of projects such as Bujagali that entail several stages and span several years.

One of the drawbacks of such an international arbitration process is related to the confidentiality requirements that often characterize arbitration. For this reason, unlike an international court, such an arbitration tribunal would likely not be an arena for advancing norms through strategic litigation. Furthermore, the tribunal envisages an "opt-in" approach, which may shield, due to the absence of compulsory jurisdiction, the worst human rights performers from scrutiny just the same. In addition, from the specific viewpoint of children's rights, it is unlikely for such an arbitration tribunal to be accessible to children or be designed in a way that children concerned by the proceedings are able to have their voice heard.

The proposed arbitration tribunal would be a welcome addition to the polycentric governance of responsibility for violations by providing another platform for rights holders to access remedies. It would, however, play a negligible – if any – role in advancing norm clarification and internalization on the global plane.

5.3 Children's Rights in the Polycentric Governance of Responsibility

The use of polycentric governance in operationalizing responsibility when children's rights are adversely affected necessitates a tailored approach that not only allows children access to these governance mechanisms but also their meaningful participation in the very processes that aim to provide accountability. In the specific domain of criminal law, for instance, the EU Directive No. 2012/29 provides important benchmarks, including the best interests of the child being a primary consideration in the implementation of the benchmarks themselves when child rights-holders are victims of crimes.[33] In addition, in establishing the rights of indirect victims of crimes, due deference to parents – unless this is not in the best interest of the child – is considered a key principle.[34] More importantly, the Directive states: "The right of child victims to be heard in criminal proceedings should not be precluded solely on the basis that the victim is a child or on the basis of that victim's age."[35]

Beyond criminal law approaches, responsibility for children's rights breaches under a polycentric governance system may imply the use of remediation at different levels. A guide authored by UNICEF and the Danish Institute of Human Rights in relation to the operationalization of the CRBPs puts an unequivocal accent on the effectiveness and accessibility of remediation measures in relation to adverse business impacts on children's rights. Accordingly, grievance mechanisms aimed at providing remediation should be guided by the primary question: "Does the company have effective and accessible grievance mechanisms in place to address alleged child rights violations?"[36] The criteria attached to effectiveness and accessibility include making the grievance mechanisms "publicly available and communicated in a way so they can be easily understood by children and their families," putting in place processes "to assist children in reporting allegations of rights violations," taking measures to ensure that obstacles to remediation are addressed, as well as "cooperat[ing] with legitimate processes, including judicial mechanisms" of redress.[37]

While accessibility and effectiveness are prerequisites to building any true remediation mechanism, making such mechanisms child-sensitive or even more ambitiously, child-friendly requires closer engagement with children's rights. The influential CoE Guidelines on child-friendly justice may provide inspiration in this respect. Guidelines define child-friendly justice as "justice systems which guarantee the respect and the effective implementation of all children's rights at the highest attainable level . . . ."[38] The particular attributes of child-friendly justice are that it should be

[33] Directive 2012/29/EU of the European Parliament and the Council of 25 October 2012 Establishing Minimum Standards on the Rights, Support and Protection of Victims of Crime, and Replacing Council Framework Decision 2001/220/JHA, para. 14.

[34] Ibid., para. 19.

[35] Ibid., para. 42.

[36] UNICEF and DIHR, *Children's Rights in Impact Assessments*, p. 19.

[37] Ibid.

[38] CoE, Guidelines of the Committee of Ministers of the Council of Europe on Child-Friendly Justice, 17 November 2010, CoE, Guidelines on Child-Friendly Justice, II. Definitions (c).

> accessible, age appropriate, speedy, diligent, adapted to and focused on the needs and rights of the child, respecting the rights of the child including the rights to due process, to participate in and to understand the proceedings, to respect for private and family life and to integrity and dignity.[39]

In sum, child-friendly justice needs to be driven by the principles of participation, best interests of the child, protection from discrimination, dignity and the rule of law.[40] Participation requires information, access, consultation and due weight to views (recognized in Articles 12 and 13 CRC) as well as full exercise of participation rights based on the child's evolving capacities (in line with Article 5 CRC). Best interests are to be a primary consideration (Article 3 CRC), respecting all of a child's rights at all times while approaching those rights comprehensively. Protection from discrimination requires special protection and assistance to children who may be more vulnerable or marginalized due to their circumstances. Dignity and rule of law are especially important for children in conflict with the law but applicable to all children involved in the justice system. In line with the principle of dignity, children are to be treated with "care, sensitivity, fairness and respect throughout any procedure or case with special attention for their personal situation, well-being and specific needs."[41] The dignity principle entails freedom from torture, inhuman or degrading treatment, while all rule of law principles are to be applied fully to the procedures or cases and due process is to be guaranteed.

It has been noted that in addition to these attributes, child-friendly justice "listens to children, takes their views seriously and makes sure that the interests of those who cannot express themselves (such as babies) are also protected. It adjusts its pace to children: it is neither expeditious nor lengthy, but reasonably speedy."[42] The attributes of child-friendly justice and the principles guiding it constitute the minimum basis for ensuring that frameworks within a polycentric governance of responsibility respond to the needs of children, when their rights are not respected, protected or fulfilled.

[39] Ibid.

[40] Ibid., III. Fundamental Principles.

[41] Ibid.

[42] Maud de Boer Buquicchio, "Foreword," in CoE, Guidelines of the Committee of Ministers of the CoE on Child-Friendly Justice: Adopted by the Committee of Ministers of the CoE on 17 November 2010 and explanatory memorandum, October 2011, p. 8.

6

Children's Rights, Multiple Duty-Bearers and Polycentric Governance: Conclusions

The last quarter of a century has been one of the most prolific in terms of the astonishing rate of new human rights challenges posed by economic globalization, leaps in technologies, including those linked to information and communications, and the rise of actors besides states with considerable economic, political, social and even military power on the international arena. The rise of these actors has not obliterated states as organizing units in international life but has done away with their monopoly. This loss of organizational monopoly is linked closely with the erosion of state monopoly over previously public services through privatization, which have now expanded to include not only privatized education, healthcare, telecommunications or foreign aid, but also the use or threat of use of force, something previously considered a unique state prerogative. Rapidly deployable military capabilities of private contractors, and privately owned and operated detention facilities attest to this trend of the rapid erosion of state monopoly in the field of defense.

Against this backdrop, the normative mission of international law generally and of human rights law more particularly in enhancing human dignity has come under threat. The threat comes from the largely unregulated nature of these 'not a state' actors[1] and their often-unchecked ability to impact the rights that should be enjoyed by individuals and communities. International Relations literature, for instance, has defined these unregulated spaces where these actors exercise power without applicable norms to prevent risks of abuse as gaps in global governance. In human rights law, these unregulated spaces create human rights protection gaps. The impacts of these human rights protection gaps are greatest and gravest on individuals and groups, such as children, that tend to be more prone to vulnerability, marginalization and exclusion.

[1] Recalling, once again, Alston's "not-a-cat" syndrome.

The recognition of threats posed by unchecked spaces or governance gaps to the realization of human rights has led to a corresponding proliferation of efforts aiming to regulate 'not-a-state' actors and to prevent and remedy the adverse impacts resulting from their increasing role and power on the international stage. This recognition has also resulted in calls to expand the definition of duty-bearers under international human rights law beyond the domestic state to include, among others, businesses and international organizations (including financial institutions) as well as extraterritorial states.

Ideally, human rights governance gaps should not exist. This is to say, ideally, domestic states as the recognized primary duty-bearers under the existing international human rights legal framework, should be able to guarantee respect for, protection and fulfillment of human rights within their territory, including vis-à-vis businesses, international organizations and third states. Yet, reality paints a very different picture: many states are incapable of abiding by their human rights duties in practice, while others are simply unwilling.

Within the broader heading of rising actors that are not states, the position of businesses is particularly important to the realization of economic, social and cultural rights. The particular focus on businesses is warranted not only because of the superior economic power they wield vis-à-vis a great number of developing states but also because their operations usually defy territorial jurisdictions and do so purposefully in order to reap the benefits of reduced costs, taxes or regulatory requirements, or of maximized influence.[2] This purposeful instrumentalization of state boundaries needs to be counterbalanced by a normative demarcation of the acceptable limits of the exercise of corporate power and the advancement of corporate interests.

A two-pronged normative process is currently underway in the context of this counterbalancing exercise: the albeit 'non-conventional' scholarly push to expand the duty-bearer side of human rights law and the various regulatory frameworks that have been adopted or proposed in recent years, especially in the business and human rights domain. These frameworks, ranging from the UNGPs to the work on a legally binding instrument, reflect various degrees of legalization. Within this context, children's rights have only more recently been attracting attention as

[2] Robert W. Cox, "Global *Perestroika*," in Ralph Miliband and Leo Panitch (eds.), *New World Order? The Socialist Register 1992* (Merlin, 1992), reprinted in Rorden Wilkinson (ed.), *The Global Governance Reader* (Routledge, 2008), p. 143.

a specialized area of implementation in the business and human rights domain. That more recent attention is evidenced by the adoption of CRBPs as guidelines for business behavior and the CRC Committee's GC 16 on state obligations regarding the impact of the business sector on children's rights.

The ongoing process of legalization seeking to move beyond the legal fiction of (domestic) states as the primary and only human rights duty-bearers and to close the governance gaps by directly addressing business duties is similarly relevant for children's rights as a specialized subfield of human rights. It goes without saying that the activities, decisions, policies and omissions of businesses also impact children's lives and wellbeing. In fact, because these impacts on children's lives and wellbeing are experienced differently both in terms of magnitude and of longitude, it may well be argued that addressing business duties with respect to their involvement in children's lives is even more vital and urgent.

There are a number of reasons for focusing specifically on children's rights in the normative appraisal of direct human rights obligations for business enterprises. As explored in detail in Part I of this book, childhood is a period of rapid physiological, psychological and social development that dictates different survival and development needs. In fact, early childhood when children's capacity for self-expression and the recognition of their agency are at their lowest is the single most important period for this rapid development. For instance, the brain is most sensitive in the acquisition of linguistic, numerical, visual, audio and social skills in the first five years of childhood.[3] Accordingly, deprivations experienced during childhood – whether material or emotional – may have lifelong or intergenerational consequences, by determining health, reproduction, education or employment outcomes. Children are also impacted differently and disproportionately by the effects of harms, not only through exposure to factors such as chemicals or pollution but also through deprivations linked to poverty or disruptions due to conflict situations. Physiologically speaking, children's exposure to chemicals or pollution is different and more severe because children's bodies absorb chemicals more readily, the effects of exposure may be irreversible, and delayed or altered effects of exposure have ample time to manifest themselves.[4] When children are disadvantaged due to poverty, the

[3] Council for Early Child Development, "The Science of Early Child Development."

[4] IPCS, "Principles for Evaluating Risks from Chemicals During Infancy and Early Childhood" and Bearer, "Environmental Health Hazards," p. 20.

impacts of such material deprivations may be exacerbated by the effects of multiple and intersectional discrimination.[5] In conflict conditions and humanitarian situations, children are exposed to the long-lasting consequences of violence and the lack of access to basic services. Under such conditions, children's lives are more acutely threatened when exposed to malnutrition and diseases such as diarrhea.[6] Moreover, children are at a higher risk of exposure to harm because they often remain invisible, lack a public voice and are not consulted even in decisions that intimately concern them. The misconception that children are incapable of forming informed opinions and expressing them because of their immaturity is clearly refuted by research, which has found that children from very young ages are able to reason, comprehend moral values and express their views on abstract and complex matters.[7] Children's rights, in this context, serve as empowerment rights to balance children's inherent and developing capacities for self-expression against social, political or legal limitations placed on the exercise of these capacities.

The framing of children's rights obligations for businesses, as a complement to their human rights obligations, is also important because children's rights have manifest protection, provision and participation dimensions. Nondiscrimination and participation are important principles and should guide all duty-bearers in their human rights obligations. This being said, children's rights obligations are distinguished by the application of best interests, survival and development, due deference and evolving capacities as guiding principles specific to children's rights, as has been proposed by Tobin.[8]

A transposition of constructivist insights from International Relations on how norms become internalized and how identities are shaped reveals that norms regulating the behavior of businesses as actors are still being transformed. More particularly with respect to the regulation of businesses, a biopic of the last fifty years attests to the disintegration of the consensus on MNEs functioning immune from regulatory pressures, the disintegrated consensus leading to numerous regulatory attempts to constrain these enterprises (at first through host state oversight and later through accountability to individuals) and finally, the culmination of these attempts in the construction of a new consensus in the form of the UNGPs. This new consensus is currently being put to the test through

[5] Tarki and Applica, *Child Poverty and Child Well-Being in the EU: Vol. 4.*
[6] UNICEF and WHO, "Diarrhoea," p. 10.
[7] Helwig and Turiel, "Children's Social and Moral Reasoning," pp. 486–487.
[8] Tobin, "Understanding a Human Rights Based Approach to Matters Involving Children."

the wide-ranging uptake of the UNGPs by other frameworks such as the OECD Guidelines and their NCPs, the ILO MNE Declaration, and the CoE Recommendation. A number of states are implementing the UNGPs through NAPs, and business and civil society actors are doing so through sector-based or company-level policies. The normative transformation, however, seems far from complete. Norm entrepreneurs aiming for binding legal rules and currently supporting a treaty process at the UN Human Rights Council are fiercely competing with those that support nonbinding standards for preeminence. In context of this normative journey, children's rights obligations of actors besides and beyond the domestic state are an additional field of inspection within the broader debate.

Various normative frameworks on the responsible regulation of businesses (UN Framework and UNGPs, the OECD Guidelines, the ILO MNE Declaration, the CoE Recommendation or the IFC Performance Standards applicable to private sector clients) now recognize a corporate responsibility to respect human rights as both complementary to and independent of states' full range of obligations. In essence, these frameworks distinguish between duties of (host) states and those of corporations with respect to the softer or legally binding nature of the duty (thus, responsibility versus obligation) and with respect to the extent of this duty (respect versus respect, protect and fulfill). In fact, such characterization is an expression of the distribution of obligations: host states remain the primary human rights duty-bearers while businesses have subsidiary but independent duties.

The two regulatory norms that have achieved the highest degree of internalization around business duties with regard to human rights are due diligence and remediation. The requirement to adopt human rights policies and to conduct human rights impact assessments for projects and programs prior to their launch has been accepted as a key component of the due diligence norm in all normative frameworks on business and human rights. Ensuring access to remedy and the provision of effective remediation to rights-holders in cases of harm is the second norm that has achieved the highest degree of internalization.

Neither mainstreamed nor targeted in the frameworks on business and human rights, children's rights are often subsumed within the broader heading of groups that are at a higher risk of marginalization or disadvantage. For these groups, the frameworks on business and human rights foresee a heightened general duty as well as a possible need to introduce additional and differentiated measures. Children's rights specific normative frameworks on business duties adopt the UN Framework and UNGPs' normative outlook while fashioning the two key norms as children's rights due diligence (including, by way of children's rights impact assessments) and child-friendly access to remedies.

Currently the most legalized aspect of businesses' relationship with children's rights is the most readily visible labor aspect. Businesses' use of the worst forms of child labor such as forced or bonded labor and commercial sexual abuse of children, as well as hazardous forms of child labor or child soldiers are prohibited as a common feature of standards on corporate behavior, including under internal regulations of development finance institutions providing funds to businesses. Fortunately, the potential impact of businesses on all aspects of children's rights, including those beyond a direct or indirect labor dimension, has been recognized not only by the CRC Committee's GC 16 and the CRBPs but also by broader human rights frameworks such as the OECD Guidelines and the CoE Recommendation. These business and human rights normative frameworks recognize the relevance of children's rights issues beyond child labor, including children as consumers, children as a part of the broader community in which businesses operate, and children as stakeholders and future employees.

The need to bring children's rights issues to the forefront of the debate and the ongoing process on expanding the duty-bearer side of human rights law is corroborated by research and insights from numerous disciplines. This need is also increasingly recognized in the various normative frameworks on business and human rights as well as through the elaboration of specific children's rights dimensions of the business and human rights nexus within the ongoing legalization process. On the other hand, the numerous inadequacies and limitations of existing normative frameworks and regulatory mechanisms in providing human rights and children's rights protection and accountability for breaches are still very much visible when confronted with real-life situations. Real-life cases provide much needed grounding to measure whether, how and to what extent the existing norms expressed in the various frameworks are able to respond to real-life children's rights challenges, especially when multiple actors hitherto not recognized as children's rights duty-bearers are involved in violations to varying degrees. The four real-life cases explored in this book are particularly illustrative of these children's rights challenges presented by the involvement of businesses alongside other actors in adverse children's rights impacts. They clarify the need for the evaluation of business activity impact on individuals and communities prior to, during and after business decisions and actions.

The case on the use of forced child labor in Uzbekistan's cotton sector illustrates that there is no conceptual clarity as to the obligations of businesses in the face of a domestic state unwilling to abide by its children's rights obligations. In fact, even when children's rights violations amount to one of the worst forms of child labor that is clearly regulated within self-regulatory frameworks of the multilateral development finance providers such as the WB, ADB and the IFC and is considered one of the clearest links between children's rights and corporate behavior, it is still difficult for rights-holders to assert their claims and to induce behavioral changes to the policies and operations of businesses. In addition, even in seemingly clear-cut situations where the initial violations can be traced to the conduct of one actor, other actors may play necessary roles with respect to ongoing violations.

The DRC case illustrates a set of conditions under which the domestic state may not be fully capable of regulating the conduct of private actors and NSAs and prevent violations of children's rights due to a lack of territorial or administrative control, conditions of violent armed conflict as well as resource constraints, among others. The case is also interesting from the point of view of regulatory efforts put into place to curb profits from mineral exploitation going to armed groups, including home state legislation with extraterritorial effects such as the Dodd-Frank Bill Section 1502, private certification schemes and the sector-specific due diligence guidelines.

The Bujagali case brings together a wide array of diverse actors, including the domestic state, several private companies, the WBG's arms IDA, IFC and MIGA, AfDB, EIB and national development finance institutions from three different European countries. The Uganda TSDP and the Bujagali case are demonstrative of the challenges brought about by large-scale infrastructure projects that require the involvement of several businesses in sponsorship or contractor roles, invoking issues of parent-subsidiary relationships, the relationship of home states of SOEs to subsidiaries as well as financing by various institutions that range from global to national. While the Bujagali case highlights the importance of specifically addressing children as rights holders within a broader community setting in cases of involuntary resettlement, the Uganda TSDP showcases the heightened risks children, especially girl children, face in infrastructure investment projects. Both cases are illustrative of the importance of assessing the potential impacts of investment projects in a comprehensive fashion before their implementation and of continued supervision and mitigation of risks.

It is uncontested that domestic states have the full range of obligations for realising children's rights through respect, protection and fulfillment. However, as the four cases illustrate, domestic states may be unable or unwilling to comply with their obligations, leaving rights-holders susceptible to adverse impacts of private activity, including the projects, policies and operations of businesses. Gaps related to the realization of children's rights will not be bridged unless other actors such as businesses that have an impact on children's enjoyment of their rights besides domestic states are considered children's rights duty-bearers in their own right. The expansion of the duty-bearer side of human rights law to include businesses is a nontraditional, non-statist, dynamic and normative exercise, all at once. It is also a necessary one.

Obligations have routinely been attributed to entities under international law using two notions: jurisdiction and personality. Jurisdiction as a concept is both fascinating and unsettling: it can be permitting or prohibiting, allowing or requiring depending on the circumstances. In human rights law, jurisdiction has largely been used in relation to territoriality, as the habitual basis for attributing human rights obligations to a given state. As such, all other circumstances where a state ought to be attributed human rights obligations so as to prevent impunity are portrayed as exceptional. This is particularly true of the case law of the ECtHR that put forth conditions such as effective control over territory or control over a person,[9] also when the control over a person coincides with exercise of elements of public power[10] or when that control is carried out by a state's agents.[11] Of course, jurisdiction as an attributional principle may be divorced from territory as was done by IACmHR by linking it to alternative and broader conceptions such as "authority and control" that are not physically delimited[12] or by the Maastricht Principles, based on the "foreseeable effects" of actions or omissions and the ability to "exercise decisive influence."[13] When multiple duty-

[9] ECtHR used the effective control over territory condition in landmark cases such as *Loizidou* v. *Turkey* and *Cyprus* v. *Turkey*, whereas the control over individuals has been a common ground to establish the mandatory jurisdiction of a state party to attribute obligations (see, for instance, *Öcalan* v. *Turkey*, *Issa and Others* v. *Turkey*, *Al-Saadoon and Mufdhi* v. *the UK*, *Medvedyev and Others* v. *France*).

[10] *Al-Skeini and Others* v. *the UK*.

[11] *Hassan* v. *the UK*.

[12] IACmHR, "What Is Terrorism? Report on Terrorism & Human Rights."

[13] The Maastricht Principles, Art. 9(b) and (c).

bearers and possible overlapping obligations come into play, the implementation of jurisdiction as an attributional principle becomes even more complex as concepts such as concurrent jurisdiction may need to be explored.[14]

Personality and subjecthood under international law are linked to one another in almost a "chicken or the egg" manner ever since the ICJ rendered its circular reasoning in the *Reparations Advisory Opinion*. Subjecthood means possessing rights and duties under international law, which is contingent upon the attribution of international personality, which in turn is evidenced by rights and duties on the international plane. ICJ's reasoning in the *Reparations Advisory Opinion* allows those not-a-state entities established by states through international contractual means, including regional and global financial institutions, to be designated international legal persons with rights and obligations. On the other hand, using international legal personality, as a principle to attribute human rights obligations to businesses, is much more complicated and still very much disputed. Ultimately, the usefulness of the concept of personality is unclear when actors that are not routinely considered international legal persons, such as corporations, can in fact acquire rights and take part in the creation of legal mechanisms either directly or through the proxy of states.[15]

The constraints linked to the use of jurisdiction and personality as attributional principles for human rights obligations are manifold. First, both notions come with statist baggage that links them to a certain type of actor. More specifically, jurisdiction is linked to state actors, while separate personality is linked to institutions created by state actors. Second, their use has created a metaphorical straightjacket restricting the normative development of the law to include duty-bearers besides the domestic state by impinging on the law's dynamism. Third, the notions of jurisdiction and personality do not as such provide an understanding of how different actors interact within and across different regimes under international law, such as human rights law, economic law and environmental law. Finally, jurisdiction and personality are not comprehensive measures of the influence or power a given entity wields on the global plane and the way this influence or power may affect rights-holders.

[14] Again, the ECtHR hinted at the possible need to develop the concept of concurrent jurisdiction further in *Jaloud* v. *the Netherlands* but shied away from doing so itself.

[15] Shaffer, "How Business Shapes Law."

The alternative to jurisdiction and personality as a metric for measuring entitlements on the international plane and assigning corresponding obligations, including human rights obligations, is the use of the notion of participation. The use of participation as a basis for a given actor's acquisition of rights and duties on the international plane is able to overcome the subject versus object dichotomy. Participation has the benefit of being an inclusive as opposed to exclusive notion, and is also more reflective of political, economic, social and legal realities. Furthermore, participation in international legal processes is indicative of two metrics: the intent to participate and the capacity to participate. Thus, the notion of participation presents a more adequate basis for attributing human rights obligations.

Once participation becomes the basis for any entity's ability to assume obligations under international law, including international human rights law, the second step in closing the rights protection gaps is to conduct a reality check to identify to what extent responsibility for violations, thus accountability, is guaranteed within the existing normative structures on obligations. Of course, responsibility comes at a second stage once it is established that obligations have been breached. Routinely, rights-holders are left in limbo where violators are allowed to enjoy impunity because when there is no obligation, there is no corresponding responsibility. Yet, this premise is both untenable and antithetical to the very rationale of human rights law.

The reality check proposed in this book is intended to reveal whether an actor's possible involvement in rights violations, which may take different forms or magnitudes, is covered by its existing obligations. This may be done by asking several questions that seek to clarify the relationship between the rights violation and any given actor with potential involvement:

> Has this actor caused the violation? Can the conduct be attributed to it?
>
> If this actor were not involved, would the violation still have taken place?
>
> Has this actor contributed to the violation or its continuation/perpetuation?
>
> Could this actor have reasonably been expected to take measures to prevent third parties from causing the violation and has failed to do so?

If any of these questions receive an affirmative response but are not backed by obligations to ensure responsibility when violations occur, the resulting impunity can be defined as a human rights protection gap. Yet, the vocation of the human rights law should be to enhance human dignity. One way of doing so is to close gaps between the letter of law and the realities on the ground. This instrumental but ultimately normative proposition is likely highly contentious.

Providing the best possible rights protection to children when they are affected by the decisions, policies or projects of businesses necessitates the extension of direct children's rights obligations to these actors and the recognition of extraterritorial children's rights obligations for states besides the domestic state. The fundamental premise upon which this extension is proposed is linked to the intent and the capacity of businesses to participate in legal processes to advance their interests in line with their operational rationale. This participation in turn elicits a burden to bear duties towards individuals or groups for whom this participation results in or is likely to result in impacts.

Different configurations of obligations may and should be ascribed to different businesses, depending on their particular relationship to children as well as on whether they undertake the provision of public services. Rights of children do require a heightened duty on the part of businesses, as recognized by the numerous frameworks, linked not only to children belonging to a group that is at a higher risk of being disadvantaged and marginalized but also to their uniquely rapid development dictating different survival and development needs and resulting in disproportionate and different effects when harms occur. Children also enjoy a singularly important status as future drivers of socioeconomic development. Businesses' heightened duty should be reflected in a child-rights sensitive approach to obligations, by fully integrating the principles of best interests, survival and development, due deference and evolving capacities into action and commitments taken to comply with their obligations.

The near universal ratification of the CRC and the diversity of recognized duty-bearers under the Convention (recognized explicitly both in the Convention and in the CRC Committee's interpretation) are bases for proposing a universal minimum obligation of the respect for children's rights. Being a universal minimum obligation, the respect obligation should be incumbent upon all participants in the legal process by virtue of that participation. This is to say, it should apply to states both territorially and extraterritorially and to businesses wherever they operate, in all activities, decisions and policies as well as business relationships. The obligation to respect should cover all acts and omissions with foreseeable adverse consequences for children and their rights. Practically, the universal minimum obligation to respect children's rights would mean that businesses must first set out their children's rights obligations in relevant internal and external policies and frameworks, guided by the principles of best interests, survival and development, due deference and evolving capacities. The respect obligation would also mean that businesses should conduct children's rights impact assessments to uncover areas of potential adverse impacts prior to starting projects and programs.

In line with other scholarship challenging territoriality and state-centricity in human rights law, this extension should take place with the recognition that entities serving public interest should be distinguished from those that do not. Accordingly, those entities not acting as public-interest institutions or providing public-interest services as a part of their mandate would not be warranted to have children's rights obligations on a par with states. Within this expression of differentiated obligations, businesses should have an obligation to protect children's rights in all ventures and business interactions, which requires that they observe a duty to use their influence and leverage to prevent third parties from adversely affecting the enjoyment of children's rights. This obligation would mean that businesses protect children's rights for instance vis-à-vis subcontractors and suppliers. In practice, the obligation to protect should entail putting children's rights policies and frameworks into action during projects and programs and to conduct ex post children's rights impact assessments to ensure compliance with these policies and frameworks, and remedy any violations.

Businesses cannot reasonably be argued to have a general obligation to fulfill children's rights, either in terms of the obligation to provide or the obligation to facilitate/assist. This being said, some businesses may be attributed specialized fulfill obligations depending on their operations, for instance, if they provide privatized essential public services. In addition, businesses that undertake legal commitments to provide or facilitate access to essential public services for children as a part of their investment transactions could also be attributed fulfill obligations, limited to the extent of their commitments.

The differentiated attribution of children's rights obligations dictates that states continue to have the most extensive obligations in terms of content, given their raison d'être to achieve and promote public interest. In addition, in terms of the distribution of children's rights obligations, the domestic state is usually in the best position to achieve respect for, protection and fulfillment of children's rights not only due to the proximity to individual rights-holders but to the control it exerts and the legislative and administrative tools it possesses. As such, the domestic state is the first locus for rights-holders in addressing their claims. Nonetheless, when the domestic state is experiencing limitations with respect to control and command not only over territory but also over its economy, for instance, it may no longer be the primary duty-bearer. More simply put, when the domestic state is unable to discharge of its full range of children's rights obligations, it can no longer serve as an effective first locus for rights-holders' claims. In these situations, the issue of on whom the burden of duty-bearing falls needs to be evaluated on a case-by-case basis and should not be based on a permanent hierarchy.

The expansion of recognized human rights duty-bearers to include actors besides the domestic state brings with it issues linked to the attribution and distribution of human rights responsibility for the breaches of human rights obligations by a multiplicity of actors. The issue of shared responsibility or the multiple attribution of responsibility for internationally wrongful acts is an area of continuing inquiry in public international law scholarship. The two normative frameworks that are established as bases for responsibility for internationally wrongful acts, ARSIWA and ARIO, focus on the responsibility of states and of international organizations as recognized international legal persons. As such, the two frameworks do not have much to offer in terms of the legalization of non-state responsibility for breaches of international law. Furthermore, the attribution of responsibility in both ARSIWA and ARIO is based on the attribution of conduct either to state organs or to the international organization and that conduct constituting an internationally wrongful act. However, the attribution of conduct and linking of responsibility to strict causation based on the conduct being traced to the representatives of a state or international organization is a limited and limiting conceptualization of responsibility, especially when responsibility for breaches of human rights is at stake. Clapham, for instance, argues: "international law provides that a single event can generate multiple violations by a range of actors."[16]

Alternative conceptualizations of human rights responsibility may be found both in scholarship and jurisprudence. In *Munaf* v. *Romania*, the UN Human Rights Committee attached responsibility to the known risk of (extraterritorial) violations when the "necessary and foreseeable consequence" of a given state's conduct constitutes a "link" in the causal chain that brings about the violations.[17] The Maastricht Principles attach

[16] Clapham, "The Subject of Subjects and the Attribution of Attribution."
[17] *Munaf* v. *Romania*.

state responsibility not only to the conduct of state organs but also to the conduct of NSAs when these are controlled by the state or empowered to "exercise elements of governmental authority."[18] The IACtHR has also accepted state responsibility for the acts of private actors if and when the state in question fails to act with due diligence to protect human rights from being violated by private actors, and when it fails to seriously and thoroughly investigate violations by private actors.[19] Of course, human rights violations may not always comprise singular and distinct violations; they might also be systemic or structural. When human rights violations are of a systemic or structural nature, Salomon's proposal to ground state responsibility on the parameters of contribution, control, capability and interest in a common but differentiated responsibilities scheme is an important contribution.[20]

Shared responsibility under ARSIWA and ARIO comes about when more than one state is involved in the wrongdoing or in cases where the wrongdoing can be traced to the conduct of an international organization and one or more of its state members, through composite acts.[21] Aid and assistance, or "complicity," is another scenario under the two frameworks where shared responsibility might be generated. According to Nollkaemper, shared responsibility under international law may also be triggered on the basis of causal contributions to a wrongful act.[22] Yet, because their inquiry is limited to the exploration of shared responsibility within the scope of law as it is, Nollkaemper and Jacobs concede that many instances of wrongful conduct involving multiple actors may be resolved for the time being under some form of "shared accountability."[23] The attribution of responsibility to multiple wrongdoers is fraught with even more complexity in cases where some or all of these wrongdoers are businesses.

The attribution of responsibility to corporations under international law usually encounters two interlinked stumbling blocks: the doctrine of limited liability, which caps shareholders' liability commensurate with their investment and the so-called corporate veil, which legally separates the corporation as a person from its shareholders. These stumbling

[18] The Maastricht Principles, Principles 11–12.
[19] *Velásquez-Rodríguez* v. *Honduras*, paras. 172 and 177, respectively.
[20] Salomon, *Global Responsibility for Human Rights*, p. 193.
[21] ILC, ARSIWA, Art. 15 and ILC, ARIO, Art. 12.
[22] Nollkaemper, "Introduction," in Nollkaemper and Plakokefalos, *Principles of Shared Responsibility*, p. 9.
[23] Nollkaemper and Jacobs, "Shared Responsibility in International Law."

blocks may very well become obstacles when corporations navigate legal jurisdictions by setting up separate legal entities over which the degree of control they exercise is often unclear. In these parent-subsidiary relationships, piercing or lifting the corporate veil in order to engage the responsibility of the parent company for the wrongdoing of the subsidiary is considered an exceptional exercise.[24] The resulting situation, however, is clearly undesirable when human rights are violated by subsidiaries that are sometimes purposefully set up to de-link the parent company from possible adverse social and environmental impacts of the business activities. While the corporate veil and the doctrine of limited liability continue to be the norm, there are legal developments to suggest that these norms are no longer considered absolute. In fact, legal claims may correspond to situations covered under the tort of negligence, where the parent company has a duty of care with respect to the operations and decisions of its subsidiary based on the foreseeability of damages that may result from these operations or decisions.[25] Recent cases in Dutch courts against Royal Dutch Shell for oil spills in the Niger Delta demonstrate that over time, courts may be more willing to adjudicate on claims against the parent company for human rights violations with respect to the operations or decisions of its subsidiaries when the claims brought against both the parent and the subsidiary are connected and at least partially overlapping.[26] Furthermore, beyond the duty of care, a parent company's substantial degree of control over the subsidiary may lead to its direct responsibility for the violations linked to its subsidiary.

There are other issues linked to corporate responsibility, such as the issue of corporate complicity, which has been brought to the forefront by the UNGPs as a component of the corporate duty to respect human rights. Unfortunately, the law on responsibility has thus far had little to say about corporate complicity. Although criminal complicity of corporations has been explored in scholarship,[27] how complicity for wrongdoings that do not amount to international crimes may be conceptualized is still unclear.

[24] For instance, in *Barcelona Traction*.

[25] The original articulation of the conditions of the tort of negligence are found in *Caparo Industries PLC* v. *Dickman* [1990] UKHL 2, cited by District Court of the Hague, Judgment dated 30 January 2013 – C/09/330891 / HA ZA 09–057, para. 4.20.

[26] Jägers, Jesse and Verschuuren, "The Future of Corporate Liability for Extraterritorial Human Rights Abuses."

[27] See: Clapham, "On Complicity," and Clapham, "Corporations and Criminal Complicity."

The recognition that multiple entities may be attributed legal responsibility within the context of a violation brings with it questions of how responsibility will be distributed among these entities. The distributive aspect of the law on responsibility is also its least developed one.[28] Distribution of shared responsibility may take place in situations of cumulative or cooperative responsibility: cumulative responsibility applying to situations where each actor's individual action or omission results in the harm and this harm is cumulated as a result of multiple such actors' actions or omissions; and cooperative responsibility applying to situations where actors engage actions or omissions that are linked to one another in some respect.[29] There are no universal principles for apportioning responsibility in situations where it is shared by a multiplicity of actors. As such, different parameters may come into play, including the nature of the primary obligations, the causational links to the harm, whether the contributions to harm are one-off or structural, the relative power wielded by the actors or considerations of fairness and equity.[30] Other grounds on which to distribute responsibility in cases of structural injustice may not be linked to legal concepts at all but to the degree of potential or actual power exercised or influence wielded over processes resulting in structural injustice, the relative privilege enjoyed or gained, the interest in maintaining or transforming social structures culminating in injustice and the collective ability to induce change.[31] Of course, proposed theoretical parameters aside, the practice of apportioning responsibility, especially of responsibility for human rights violations, is not easy to conceptualize when it is to be shared by multiple actors that include states and businesses.

There is no normative clarity, as the law stands, on how accountability for rights violations ought to be attributed to and distributed among numerous actors involved in a given situation. The Uzbek cotton case demonstrates that even when violations in the form of one of the worst forms of child labor such as forced child labor take place, complexities arising from supply chains or the lack of transparency around safeguards for financing of certain sectors with possible adverse children's rights fallouts result in accountability gaps. The Bujagali case illustration highlights the accountability challenges that arise when numerous actors, some of which are businesses, are involved in the development,

[28] Vandenhole, "Obligations and Responsibility in a Plural and Diverse Duty-Bearer for Human Rights Regime."

[29] Nollkaemper and Jacobs, "Introduction: Mapping the Normative Framework," p. 14.

[30] Ibid., pp. 22–23.

[31] Young, "Responsibility and Global Justice," 127–129.

construction and financing of large infrastructure projects. These actors may be providing services or financing at different levels to a project and undertake different commitments. The influence they exert over decisions related to the project may be a function not only of their overall financial contributions and commitments but also other variables, such as the global or regional influence they exert, their reputation or financial credibility. The Uganda TSDP case links contractors to the violations of children's rights that result from the behavior of workers employed by this company. The case of the exploitation of so-called conflict minerals in the DRC is also notable for the wide-ranging adverse children's rights impacts of the conflict as well as of mining activities and the involvement of various non-state armed groups and businesses alongside the domestic state. The case illustration also provides a fertile ground to engage with how accountability in a polycentric governance perspective may work through domestic state legislation, host state regulation and industry and sector-specific due diligence guidelines.

The local context in which businesses operate may also create additional risks for rights violations. For instance, complexities arising from supply chains, subcontracting or financing of certain sectors may be further exacerbated when businesses operate within the territory of a state that is unwilling to live up to its children's rights obligations. Likewise, corruption and bribery issues in the domestic setting may present stumbling blocks when rights-holders demand accountability. Finally, when impacts of conflict and corporate activities are coupled, it is often unclear whether violations can be traced to impacts of the conflict or to business activities.

Returning to questions about accountability, in addition to causation, the attribution of responsibility for children's rights violations may be based on a business's contribution to a violation or to the continuation of the violation as well as to the socioeconomic or political conditions that enable the wrongdoer. The proposal is that the responsibility of businesses should be engaged when businesses breach their children's rights obligations by failing to conduct ex ante and ex post children's rights impact assessments, to act with due diligence during their interactions or use their leverage and influence to protect children's rights vis-à-vis third parties in their ventures and business interactions. Furthermore, in specific cases of parent and subsidiary relationships, in addition to direct responsibility incurred by parent companies for the acts/omissions of subsidiaries they closely control, the parent companies should have a duty of oversight. The failure to discharge this duty should trigger direct responsibility of the company for the violations linked to its subsidiary. This duty of oversight would require a parent company to take foreseeable risks of harm to children into account when setting up a subsidiary and the continued and effective supervision of the subsidiary especially with respect to areas of heightened risk that have been identified.

A generalized theory on the distribution of responsibility may not be attainable at present because of the diverse set of circumstances that each individual claim might entail, from cumulative or cooperative responsibility to complicity, contribution and collective causation. Instead, the practicalities of handling individual accountability claims necessitate working through a hybrid of legal and nonlegal approaches at this point in time in order to be able to offer a measure of accountability to rights-holders. Responsibility may be operationalized within a matrix of governance, for instance, as suggested by Keohane and Nye, encompassing private, governmental and third-sector governance at subnational, national and supranational levels.[32] Broadly termed polycentric governance, the horizontal integration of actors on the international plane to solve collective action problems such as human rights challenges transcending national jurisdictions provides the basic groundwork for tackling the issue of human rights responsibility of multiple duty-bearers in practice. Polycentric governance mechanisms include already existing mechanisms such as the use of civil liability and tort law or criminal law approaches in national jurisdictions or domestic regulatory measures with extraterritorial effects. At the international level, polycentric governance may be strengthened through schemes such as the proposed expansion of the mandate of the International Criminal Court to allow it to adjudicate on cases where business enterprises are defendants, through the establishment of new judicial mechanisms such as a World Court on Business and Human Rights, an international arbitration tribunal for business and human rights or through global administrative bodies designed especially for this purpose.

Mechanisms and approaches under polycentric governance should be tailored to meet responsibility challenges arising from the violation of children's rights by ensuring children's meaningful participation in accountability processes in addition to allowing children access to governance mechanisms. Governance mechanisms aiming to provide responsibility for children's rights violations when multiple actors are involved should be child-friendly. This means, extrapolating from the CoE Guidelines on child-friendly justice, that these mechanisms are

[32] Robert O. Keohane and Joseph S. Nye Jr., "Introduction", in Joseph S. Nye, Jr. and John D. Donahue (eds), *Governance in a Globalizing World*, 2000, 13.

guided by the principles of participation, the best interests of the child, dignity, protection from discrimination and the rule of law.[33] In addition, child-friendliness of mechanisms should be ensured, among others, by accessibility, age appropriateness, respect for and protection of the rights and needs of children.[34]

The easiest and most practical way to integrate future conceptualizations of direct human rights obligations of businesses and to enforce them at this point in time is through legislation with extraterritorial reach at the home state level. Likewise, home states may open up their justice systems to cases involving businesses operating from or domiciled in their territory. A second welcome step would be the further advancement of extraterritorial obligations, which require home states to protect human rights when businesses to which they are linked impact rights extraterritorially. The proliferation of domestic legislation seeking to regulate business behavior such as the US Dodd-Frank or the UK Modern Slavery Acts is indicative of a trend whereby some home states are assuming a duty to regulate business activity linked to the most serious human and labor rights violations as well as very serious children's rights violations that include sexual abuse of children abroad. In the future, the home state duty to regulate may extend to instances beyond serious violations and crimes. For instance, children's rights or human rights clauses may be integrated into public procurement contracts, impact assessment requirements and reporting guidelines for all companies with operations in a given territorial jurisdiction.

The case for the extension of direct children's rights obligations to businesses is not mutually exclusive with the premise that these actors may also engage with children's rights constructively. As squarely outlined in the CRC Committee's GC 16, "[b]usiness can be an essential driver for societies and economies to advance in ways that strengthen the realization of children's rights through, for example, technological advances, investment and the generation of decent work."[35]

A constructive engagement with children's rights would need to be mindful of the specific principles guiding children's rights and might foster a forward-looking political model of responsibility in the longer term, if such a model becomes the basis for advancing standards for any ventures or business interactions that are linked to, have a foreseeability or the

[33] CoE, Guidelines on Child-Friendly Justice.

[34] Ibid., II. Definitions (c).

[35] CRC Committee, GC 16, para. 1.

likelihood to affect children's rights. It will not, however, nullify the need to frame legal obligations for businesses that can serve as the basis for legal responsibility. In fact, given the rise of other types of private or hybrid actors on the international plane such as multi-stakeholder partnerships or corporate-linked foundations, the framing of legal obligations for businesses may well be the first step in a growing research and policy agenda.

Identifying deficiencies linked to current standards about business duties in relation to children's rights, exploring workable alternatives for accountability and proposing a normative framework for the future attribution and distribution of direct children's rights obligations and for responsibility of businesses is admittedly an exercise in norm entrepreneurship.[36] Notwithstanding recent developments in the legal process on the extension of human rights obligations to business enterprises, this exercise is still likely to engender resistance from those who believe that black letter law circumscribes the boundaries of legalization. Yet, even the letter of law is a social construct and thus, not static, unchallengeable or unchangeable. When law does not adequately serve justice, quietly endorsing it or refraining from challenging it is in essence acquiescing to law being in service of power and privilege. One vocation of human rights law, on the other hand, is to empower individuals and groups as rights-holders in order to ensure that every human being lives with dignity. Children, who make up an important share of the world's population but often remain disenfranchised, have much to benefit from such empowerment. For this reason, even if the proposal to extend direct children's rights (and human rights) obligations to businesses under international law is controversial, it is also timely and necessary to ensure that enhancing human dignity does not come secondary to material goals. The road ahead may be long and rough but if the progression of the field over the last three decades is any indication, optimism is warranted. In 1987, when he submitted his report on "The Right to Food as a Human Right," Asbjørn Eide wrote that his assessment of the tripartite nature of state obligations of respect, protect and fulfill for ESC rights was "in the nature of de lege ferenda."[37] They have since become widely accepted and legalized. There is no reason to discount that the extension of direct children's rights and human rights obligations to businesses under international law could follow a similar trajectory.

[36] Norm entrepreneurship in the sense of the vocation of norm entrepreneurs as explored in Finnemore and Sikkink, "International Norm Dynamics."

[37] Eide, *The Right to Adequate Food as a Human Right: Final Report*, p. 21, para. 94.

BIBLIOGRAPHY

Literature

Books

Alston, Philip (ed.). *Non-State Actors and Human Rights* (Oxford University Press, 2005).

Aust, Helmut Philipp. *Complicity and the Law of State Responsibility* (Cambridge University Press, 2011).

Beitz, Charles. *Political Theory and International Relations* (Princeton University Press, 1979).

Bernaz, Nadia. *Business and Human Rights: History, Law and Policy – Bridging the Accountability Gap* (Routledge, 2017).

Casesse, Antonio. *International Law in a Divided World* (Clarendon Press, 1987).

Clapham, Andrew. *Human Rights Obligations of Non-State Actors* (Oxford University Press, 2006).

Da Costa, Karen. *The Extraterritorial Application of Selected Human Rights Treaties* (Martinus Nijhoff Publishers, 2013).

Darrow, Mac. *Between Light and Shadow: The World Bank, the International Monetary Fund and International Human Rights Law* (Hart Publishing, 2003).

De Schutter, Olivier (ed.). *Transnational Companies and Human Rights* (Hart Publishing, 2006).

Deva, Surya and Bilchitz, David (eds.). *Human Rights Obligations of Business: Beyond the Corporate Responsibility to Respect?* (Cambridge University Press, 2013).

Eagleton, Clyde. *The Responsibility of States in International Law* (New York University Press, 1928).

Fujita, Sanae. *The World Bank, Asian Development Bank and Human Rights Developing Standards of Transparency, Participation and Accountability* (Edward Elgar, 2013).

Higgins, Rosalyn. *Problems and Process: International Law and How We Use It* (Oxford University Press, 1994).

Jägers, Nicola. *Corporate Human Rights Obligations: In Search of Accountability* (Intersentia, 2002).

Keck, Margaret E. and Sikkink, Kathryn. *Activists Beyond Borders: Advocacy Networks in International Politics* (Cornell University Press, 1998).

Keohane, Robert O. and Nye, Joseph S. (eds.). *Transnational Relations and World Politics* (Harvard University Press, 1971).

Klabbers, Jan. *An Introduction to International Law* (Cambridge University Press, 2002).

Kozma, Julia, Nowak, Manfred and Martin Scheinin. *A World Court of Human Rights: Consolidated Statute and Commentary* (Neuer Wissenschaftlicher Verlag, 2010).

Lanovoy, Vladyslav. *Complicity and Its Limits in the Law of International Responsibility* (Hart Publishing, 2016).

McBeth, Adam. *International Economic Actors and Human Rights* (Routledge, 2011).

Milanovic, Marko. *Extraterritorial Application of Human Rights Treaties: Law, Principles, and Policy* (Oxford University Press, 2011).

Nye, Jr. Joseph S. *The Future of Power* (Public Affairs, 2011).

O'Connell, Daniel Patrick. *International Law, Vol.1* (2nd ed.) (Stevens and Sons, 1970).

Parsons, Talcott and Bales, Robert F. *Family, Socialization and Interaction Process* (Routledge, 2002).

Rosenau, James N. *Turbulence in World Politics: A Theory of Change and Continuity* (Princeton University Press, 1990).

Ruggie, John G. *Just Business: Multinational Corporations and Human Rights* (W. W. Norton, 2013).

Salomon, Margot E. *Global Responsibility for Human Rights: World Poverty and the Development of International Law* (Oxford University Press, 2007).

Shonkoff, Jack. (ed.). *From Neurons to Neighborhoods: The Science of Early Childhood Development* (National Academy Press, 2000).

Shue, Henry. *Basic Rights: Subsistence, Affluence, and U.S. Foreign Policy* (2nd ed.) (Princeton University Press, 1996) (originally published in 1980).

Skogly, Sigrun. *Beyond National Borders: States' Human Rights Obligations in International Cooperation* (Intersentia, 2006).

Slaughter, Anne-Marie. *A New World Order* (Princeton University Press, 2004).

Tangri, Roger and Mwenda, M. Andrew. *The Politics of Elite Corruption in Africa: Uganda in Comparative African Perspective* (Routledge, 2013).

Van Bueren, Geraldine. *The International Law on the Rights of the Child* (2nd ed.) (Martinus Nijhoff Publishers, 1998).

Van Genugten, Willem. *The World Bank Group, the IMF and Human Rights* (Intersentia, 2015).

Vandenbogaerde, Arne. *Towards Shared Accountability in International Human Rights Law: Law, Procedures and Principles* (Intersentia, 2016).

Vandenhole, Wouter (ed.). *Challenging Territoriality in Human Rights Law: Building Blocks for a Plural and Diverse Duty-Bearer Regime* (Routledge, 2015).

Vandenhole, Wouter, Erdem Türkelli, Gamze and Sara Lembrechts. *A Commentary on the Convention on the Rights of the Child and its Protocols* (Edward Elgar, forthcoming).

Wall, John. *Ethics in Light of Childhood* (Georgetown University Press, 2010).

Wyness, Michael G. *Childhood and Society: An Introduction to the Sociology of* Childhood (Palgrave Macmillan, 2006).

Chapters in Edited Volumes

Alston, Philip. "The 'Not-a-Cat' Syndrome: Can the International Human Rights Regime Accommodate Non-State Actors?" in Alston, Philip (ed.). *Non-State Actors and Human Rights* (Oxford University Press, 2005), 3–36.

Amao, Olufemi. "The Practice of Shared Responsibility in Relation to Multinational Corporations," in Nollkaemper, André and Plakokefalos, Ilias (eds.). *The Practice of Shared Responsibility in International Law* (Cambridge University Press, 2016), 799–821.

Arneil, Barbara. "Becoming versus Being: A Critical Analysis of the Child in Liberal Theory," in Archard, David and Macleod, Colin M. (eds.). *The Moral and Political Status of Children* (Oxford University Press, 2002), 70–94.

Bilchitz, David. "A Chasm Between 'Is' and 'Ought'? A Critique of the Normative Foundations of the SRSG's Framework and the Guiding Principles," in Deva, Surya and Bilchitz, David (eds.). *Human Rights Obligations of Business: Beyond the Corporate Responsibility to Respect?* (Cambridge University Press, 2013), 107–137.

Boisson De Chazournes, Laurence. "Partnerships, Emulation and Coordination: Toward the Emergence of a *Droit Commun* in the Field of Development Finance," in Cissé, Hasssane, Bradlow, Daniel and Kingsbury, Benedict (eds.), *International Financial Institutions and Global Legal Governance, The World Bank Legal Review*, Vol. 3 (The World Bank, 2012), 179–182.

Brennan, Samantha. "Children's Choices or Children's Interests: Which Do Their Rights Protect?" in Archard, David and Macleod, Colin M. (eds.). *The Moral and Political Status of Children* (Oxford University Press, 2002), 53–69.

Brighouse, Harry. "What Rights (if Any) do Children Have?" in Archard, David and Macleod, Colin M. (eds.). *The Moral and Political Status of Children* (Oxford University Press, 2002), 31–52.

Cantwell, Nigel. "Are Children's Rights Still Human?," in Invernizzi, Antonella and Williams, Jane (eds.). *The Human Rights of Children* (Ashgate, 2011), 37–59.

Carroll, Colleen and Bécault, Emilie. "Global Governance and the Challenges of Diversity," in Wouters, Jan et al. (eds.). *Global Governance and Democracy: A Multidisciplinary Analysis* (Edward Elgar, 2015), 191–225.

Černič, Jernej Letnar. "Economic, Social and Cultural Rights of the Purak Peoples (Committee on Economic, Social and Cultural Rights)," in Gibney, Mark and Vandenhole, Wouter (eds.). *Litigating Transnational Human Rights Obligations: Alternative Judgments* (Routledge, 2014), 99–115.

Clapham, Andrew. "Corporations and Criminal Complicity," in Nystuen, Gro, Follesdal, Andreas and Mestad, Ola (eds.). *Human Rights, Corporate Complicity and Disinvestment* (Cambridge University Press, 2010), 222–240.

Clapham, Andrew. "On Complicity," in Henzelin, M. and Roth, R. (eds.), *Le Droit Penal A L'Epreuve de L'internationalisation* (LGDJ, 2002),241–275.

Clapham, Andrew. "The Subject of Subjects and the Attribution of Attribution," in Boisson de Chazournes, L. and Kohen, M. (eds.). *International Law and the Quest for Its Implementation: Liber Amicorum Vera Gowlland-Debbas* (Brill, 2010), 44–58.

Cox, Robert W. "Global *Perestroika*," in Miliband, Ralph and Panitch, Leo (eds.). *New World Order? The Socialist Register 1992* (Merlin, 1992), reprinted in Rorden Wilkinson (ed.). *The Global Governance Reader* (Routledge, 2008), 140–155.

d'Aspremont, Jean. "Introduction: Non-State Actors in International Law: Oscillating Between Concepts and Dynamics," in d'Aspremont, Jean (ed.). *Participants in the International Legal System: Multiple Perspectives on Non-State Actors in International Law* (Routledge, 2011), 1–21.

De Brabandere, Eric. "Non-State Actors and Human Rights: Corporate Responsibility and the Attempts to Formalize the Role of Corporations as Participants in the International Legal System," in d'Aspremont, Jean (ed.). *Participants in the International Legal System: Multiple Perspectives on Non-State Actors in International Law* (Routledge, 2011), 268–283.

Deva, Surya and Bilchitz, David. "The Human Rights Obligations of Business: A Critical Framework for the Future" in Deva and Bilchitz (eds.), *Human Rights Obligations of Business: Beyond the Corporate Responsibility to Respect?* (Cambridge University Press, 2013), 1–26.

Erdem Türkelli, Gamze. "Putting an End to Victims Without Borders: Child Pornography (Committee on the Rights of the Child)," in Gibney, Mark and Vandenhole, Wouter (eds.). *Litigating Transnational Human Rights Obligations: Alternative Judgments* (Routledge, 2014), 63–78.

Footer, Mary E. "Human Rights Due Diligence and the Responsible Supply of Minerals from Conflict-Affected Areas: Towards a Normative Framework?" in Černič, Jernej Letnar and Van Ho, Tara (eds.) *Human Rights and Business: Direct Corporate Accountability for Human Rights* (Wolf Legal Publishers, 2015), 179–228.

Freeman, Michael. "The Value and Values of Children's Rights," in Invernizzi, Antonella and Williams, Jane (eds.), *The Human Rights of Children: From Visions to Implementation* (Ashgate, 2011), 21–36.

Gallagher, Anne T. "The Practice of Shared Responsibility in Relation to Human Rights and Human Trafficking," in Nollkaemper, André and Plakokefalos, Ilias (eds.). *The Practice of Shared Responsibility in International Law* (Cambridge University Press, 2016), 556–582.

Gattini, Andrea. "Breach of International Obligations," in Nollkaemper, André and Plakokefalos, Ilias (eds.). *Principles of Shared Responsibility in International Law: An Appraisal of the State of the Art* (Cambridge University Press, 2014), 25–59.

Griffin, James. "Do Children Have Rights?," in Archard, David and Macleod, Colin M. (eds.). *The Moral and Political Status of Children* (Oxford University Press, 2002), 19–30.

Hammonds, Rachel and Ooms, Gorik. "Shared Responsibility for the Right to Health (Committee on Economic, Social and Cultural Rights)" in Gibney, Mark and Vandenhole, Wouter (eds.). *Litigating Transnational Human Rights Obligations: Alternative Judgments* (Routledge, 2014), 79–98.

Helwig, Charles C. and Turiel, Elliot. "Children's Social and Moral Reasoning," in Smith, Peter K. and Hart, Craig H. (eds.). *Wiley-Blackwell Handbook of Childhood Social Development* (2nd ed.) (Wiley-Blackwell, 2010), 567–583.

Hurrell, Andrew. "Power, Institutions, and the Production of Inequality," in Barnett, Michael and Duvall, Raymond (eds.). *Power in Global Governance* (Cambridge University Press, 2005), 33–58.

Johnstone, Ian. "The Power of Interpretive Communities," in Barnett, Michael and Duvall, Raymond (eds.). *Power in Global Governance* (Cambridge University Press, 2005), 185–240.

Keohane, Robert O. and Nye Jr., Joseph S. "Introduction", in Nye, Jr., Joseph S. and Donahue, John D. (eds) *Governance in a Globalizing World* (Brookings Institution Press, 2000), 1–41.

Knox, John H. "The Ruggie Rules: Applying Human Rights Law to Corporations," in Mares, Radu (ed.). *The UN Guiding Principles on Business and Human Rights – Foundations and Implementation* (Martinus Nijhoff Publishers, 2012), 51–84.

Kozma, Julia, Nowak, Manfred and Martin Scheinin, "Statute of the World Court of Human Rights," in Julia Kozma, Nowak, Manfred and Scheinin, Martin, A *World Court of Human Rights: Consolidated Statute and Commentary* (Neuer Wissenschaftlicher Verlag, 2010), 9–28.

Lanovoy, Vladyslav. "Complicity in an Internationally Wrongful Act" in Nollkaemper, André and Plakokefalos, Ilias (eds.). *The Practice of Shared Responsibility in International Law* (Cambridge University Press, 2016), 134–168.

Lesnik-Oberstein, Karin. "Introduction: Voice, Agency and the Child," in Lesnik-Oberstein, Karin (ed.). *Children in Culture, Revisited: Further Approaches to Childhood* (Palgrave Macmillan, 2011), 1–17.

Mares, Radu. "Responsibility to Respect: Why the Core Company Should Act When Its Affiliates Infringe Human Rights," in Mares, Radu (ed.). *The UN*

Guiding Principles on Business and Human Rights – Foundations and Implementation (Martinus Nijhoff Publishers, 2011), 169–192.

Nijman, Janne E. "Non-State Actors (NSAs) and the International Rule of Law: Revisiting the 'Realist Theory' of International Legal Personality," in Noortmann, Math and Ryngaert, Cedric (eds.). *Non-State Actor Dynamics in International Law: From Law-Takers to Law-Makers* (Routledge, 2010), 91–124.

Nollkaemper, André and Jacobs, Dov. "Introduction: Mapping the Normative Framework for the Distribution of Shared Responsibility," in Nollkaemper, André and Jacobs, Dov (eds.). *Distribution of Responsibilities in International Law* (Cambridge University Press, 2015), 1–35.

Nollkaemper, André and Plakokefalos, Ilias. "Conclusions: Beyond the ILC Legacy," in Nollkaemper, André and Plakokefalos, Ilias. *Principles of Shared Responsibility in International Law: An Appraisal of the State of the Art* (Cambridge University Press, 2014), 341–368.

Nowak, Manfred. "It's Time for a World Court of Human Rights," in Bassiouni, M. Cherif and Schabas, William (eds.). *New Challenges for the UN Human Rights Machinery: What Future for the UN Treaty Body System and the Human Rights Council Procedures?* (Intersentia, 2011), 17–34.

Parker, Christine and Howe, John. "Ruggie's Diplomatic Project and Its Missing Regulatory Infrastructure," in Mares, Radu (ed.). *The UN Guiding Principles on Business and Human Rights – Foundations and Implementation* (Martinus Nijhoff Publishers, 2011), 273–301.

Plato. *Laws*, in Hamilton, Edith and Cairns, Huntington (eds.). *The Collected Dialogues of Plato* (Princeton University Press, 1961), 1225–1515.

Prenkert, Jamie Darin. "Conflict Minerals and Polycentric Governance of Business and Human Rights," in Bird, Robert C., Cahoy, Daniel R. and Prenkert, Jamie Darin (eds.). *Law, Business and Human Rights: Bridging the Gap* (Edward Elgar, 2014), 203–229.

Qvortrup, Jens, Corsaro, William A. and Honig, Michael-Sebastian. "Why Social Studies of Childhood: An Introduction to the Handbook," in Qvortrup, Jens, Corsaro, William A. and Honig, Michael-Sebastian (eds.). *The Palgrave Handbook of Childhood Studies* (1st ed.) (Palgrave Macmillan, 2009), 1–18.

Qvortrup, Jens. "Childhood as a Structural Form," in Qvortrup, Jens, Corsaro, William A. and Honig, Michael-Sebastian (eds.). *The Palgrave Handbook of Childhood Studies* (1st ed.) (Palgrave Macmillan, 2009), 21–33.

Risse-Kappen, Thomas. "Introduction," in Risse-Kappen, Thomas (ed.). *Bringing Transnational Relations Back In: Non-State Actors, Domestic Structures and International Institutions* (Cambridge University Press, 1995), 3–34.

Rustemova, Assel. "Rent Seeking and Authoritarian Consolidation in Kazakhstan and Uzbekistan," in Vanderhill, Rachel and Aleprete Jr., Michael E. (eds.), *International Dimensions of Authoritarian Persistence: Lessons from Post-Soviet States* (Lexington Books, 2013), 59–80.

Ryngaert, Cedric. "The Concept of Jurisdiction in International Law," in Orakhelashvili, Alexander (ed.). *Research Handbook on Jurisdiction and Immunities in International Law* (Edward Elgar, 2015), 50–76.

Schrempf-Stirling, Judith, Palazzo, Guido and Phillips, Robert A., "Ever Expanding Responsibilities: Upstream and Downstream Corporate Social Responsibility," in Lindgreen, Adam et al. (eds.), *Sustainable Value Chain Management: Analyzing, Designing, Implementing, and Monitoring for Social and Environmental Responsibility* (Ashgate, 2012), 353–368.

Shaffer, Gregory C. and Pollack, Mark A. "Hard and Soft Law," in Dunoff, Jeffrey L. and Pollack, Mark A. (eds.). *International Law and International Relations: Insights from Interdisciplinary Scholarship* (Cambridge University Press, 2012), 197–222.

Tobin, John. "Understanding a Human Rights Based Approach to Matters Involving Children: Conceptual Foundations and Strategic Considerations," in Invernizzi, Antonella and Williams, Jane (eds.). *The Human Rights of Children* (Ashgate, 2011), 61–98.

Ulfstein, Geir. "Do We Need a World Court of Human Rights?," in Engdahl, O. and Wrange, P. (eds.), *Law at War: The Law as It Was and the Law as It Should Be* (Brill, 2008), 261–272.

Vallentyne, Peter. "Equality and the Duties of Procreators," in Archard, David and Macleod, Colin M. (eds.). *The Moral and Political Status of Children* (Oxford University Press, 2002), 195–211.

Vandenbogaerde, Arne. "Labour Rights in a Transnational Perspective (Committee on Economic, Social and Cultural Rights)," in Gibney, Mark and Vandenhole, Wouter (eds.). *Litigating Transnational Human Rights Obligations: Alternative Judgments* (Routledge, 2014), 135–154.

Vandenhole, Wouter and Erdem Türkelli, Gamze. "Best Interests of the Child," in Todres, Jonathan and King, Shani (eds.). *The Oxford Handbook on Children's Rights* (Oxford University Press, forthcoming)

Vandenhole, Wouter and Van Genugten, Willem. "Introduction: An Emerging Multi-Duty-Bearer Human Rights Regime?," in Vandenhole, Wouter (ed.), *Challenging Territoriality in Human Rights Law* (Routledge, 2015), 1–11.

Vandenhole, Wouter, Erdem Türkelli, Gamze and Hammonds, Rachel. "New Human Rights Duty-Bearers: Towards a Re-conceptualisation of the Human Rights Duty-Bearer Dimension," in Anja Mihr and Gibney, Mark (eds.). *The SAGE Handbook of Human Rights* (Sage, 2014), 1031–1046.

Vandenhole, Wouter. "Obligations and Responsibility in a Plural and Diverse Duty-Bearer Human Rights Regime," in Vandenhole, Wouter (ed.). *Challenging Territoriality in Human Rights Law: Building Blocks for a Plural and Diverse Duty-Bearer Regime* (Routledge, 2015), 115–135.

Williams Crenshaw, Kimberlé. "Mapping the Margins: Intersectionality, Identity Politics, and Violence Against Women of Color," in Albertson

Fineman, Martha and Mykitiuk, Rixanne (eds.). *The Public Nature of Private Violence* (Routledge, 1994), 93–120.

Zermatten, Jean. "Best Interests of the Child," in Mahmoudi, Saïd et al. (eds.). *Child-friendly Justice: A Quarter Century of the UN Convention on the Rights of the Child* (Brill Nijhoff, 2015), 30–42.

Journal Articles

Abbott, Kenneth W. et al., "The Concept of Legalization" (2000) 54(3) *International Organization* 401–419.

Alston, Philip. "Against a World Court of Human Rights" (2014) 28(2) *Ethics and International Affairs* 197–212.

Alvarez, Jose E. "Are Corporations 'Subjects' of International Law?" (2011) 9(1) *Santa Clara Journal of International Law* 1–36.

Backer, Larry Catá. "On the Evolution of the United Nations' 'Protect-Respect-Remedy' Project: The State, the Corporation and Human Rights in a Global Governance Context" (2011) 9 *Santa Clara Journal of International Law* 37–80.

Backer, Larry Catá. "Rights and Accountability in Development ('Raid') v Das Air and Global Witness v Afrimex – Small Steps Towards an Autonomous Transnational Legal System for the Regulation of Multinational Corporations" (2009) 10 *Melbourne Journal of International Law* 258.

Bartholet, Elizabeth. "Ratification by the United States of the Convention on the Rights of the Child: Pros and Cons from a Child's Rights Perspective" (2011) 633 *The ANNALS of American Academy of Political and Social Science* 80, Special Issue, The Child as Citizen 1–22.

Bearer, Cynthia F. "Environmental Health Hazards: How Children Are Different from Adults" (1995) 5 *The Future of Children – Critical Issues for Children and Youths* 11–26.

Bederman, David. "Constructivism, Positivism, and Empiricism in International Law" (2001) 89(2) *Georgetown Law Journal* 469–499.

Brabant, Stéphane and Savourey, Elsa. "France's Corporate Duty of Vigilance Law: A Closer Look at the Penalties Faced by Companies," *Revue Internationale de la Compliance et de L'Ethique des Affaires – Supplément à laSemaine Juridique Entreprise et Affaires N° 50 du Jeudi 14 Décembre 2017.*

Calderon, César and Servén, Luis. "Infrastructure and Economic Development in Sub-Saharan Africa" (2010) 19(1) *Journal of African Economies* 113–187.

Caroll, Archie B. "A Three-Dimensional Conceptual Model of Corporate Social Performance" (1979) 4 *Academy of Management Review* 497–505.

Coen, David and Pegram, Tom. "Towards a Third Generation of Global Governance Scholarship" (2018) 9(1) *Global Policy* 107–113.

Cronstedt, Claes and Thompson, Robert C. "A Proposal for an International Arbitration Tribunal on Business and Human Rights" (2016) 57 *Harvard International Law Journal* Online Symposium at 66–69.

Eekelaar, John. "The Emergence of Children's Rights" (1986) 6 *Oxford Journal of Legal Studies* 161–182.

Engle, Patrice L., Black, Maureen M. et al. "Child Strategies to Avoid the Loss of Developmental Potential in More Than 200 Million Children in the Developing World" (2007) 369 *The Lancet* 229–242 at 236.

Federle, Katherine H. "Review Essay: Rights, Not Wrongs" (2009) 17 *International Journal of Children's Rights* 321–329.

Federle, Katherine H. "Rights Flow Downhill" (1994) 2 *International Journal of Children's Rights* 343–368.

Finnemore, Martha and Sikkink, Kathryn. "International Norm Dynamics and Political Change" (1998) 52(4) *International Organization* 887–917.

Gallegos, Luis and Uribe, Daniel. "The Next Step Against Corporate Impunity: A World Court on Business and Human Rights?" (2016) 57 *Harvard International Law Journal* Online Symposium 7–10.

Goldstein, Judith et al. "Introduction: Legalization and World Politics" (2000) 54 (3) *International Organization* 385–399.

Gratham-McGregor, Sally, Cheung, Yin Bun et al. "Developmental Potential in the First 5 Years for Children in Developing Countries" (2007) 369 *The Lancet* 60–70.

Haas, Peter M. "Epistemic Communities and International Policy Coordination" (1992) 46(1) *International Organization* 1–35.

Hart, H.L.A. "Are There Any Natural Rights?" (1955) 64 *The Philosophical Review* 175–191.

Hathaway, Oona A. et al., "Human Rights Abroad: When Do Human Rights Treaty Obligations Apply Extraterritorially?" (2011) 43 *Arizona State Law Journal* 389–426.

Jägers, Nicola, Jesse, Katinka and Verschuuren, Jonathan. "The Future of Corporate Liability for Extraterritorial Human Rights Abuses: The Dutch Case Against Shell" (2014) *American Journal of International Law Unbound* e-40.

Jochnick, Chris. "Confronting the Impunity of Non-State Actors: New Fields for the Promotion of Human Rights" 21(1) (1999) *Human Rights Quarterly* 56–79.

Kalisya, Luc Malemo et al. "The State of Emergency Care in Democratic Republic of Congo" (2015) 5(4) *African Journal of Emergency Medicine* 153–158.

Karavias, Markos. "Shared Responsibility and Multinational Enterprises" (2015) 62 *Netherlands International Law Review* 91–117.

Keck, Margaret E. and Sikkink, Kathryn. "Transnational Advocacy Networks International and Regional Politics" (1999) 51(159) *International Social Science Journal* 89–101.

Keohane, Robert O. "Governance in a Partially Globalized World" (2001) 95(1) *American Political Science Review* 1–13.

Kinley, David and Tadaki, Junko. "From Talk to Walk: The Emergence of Human Rights Responsibilities for Corporations at International Law" (2004) 44(4) *Virginia Journal of International Law* 931–1023.

Koh, Harold H. "Is There a 'New' New Haven School of International Law?" (2007) 32 *The Yale Journal of International Law* 559–573.

Lalji, Nadira. "The Resource Curse Revised: Conflict and Coltan in the Congo," *Harvard International Review*, Fall 2007, www.globalpolicy.org/the-dark-side-of-natural-resources-st/water-in-conflict/40150.html (accessed 15 April 2019).

Landrigan, Philip J. and Carlson, Joy E. "Environmental Policy and Children's Health" (1995) 5 *The Future of Children – Critical Issues for Children and Youths* 34–52.

Lewit, Eugene M. and Schuurmann Baker, Linda. "Children's Health and the Environment" (1995) 5 *The Future of Children – Critical Issues for Children and Youths* 8–10.

Mantilla, Giovanni. "Emerging International Human Rights Norms for Transnational Corporations" (2009) 15(2) *Global Governance* 279–298.

Mayall, Berry. "The Sociology of Childhood in Relation to Children's Rights" (2000) 8 *The International Journal of Children's Rights* 243–259.

McGillivray, Anne. "Why Children Do Have Equal Rights: In Reply to Laura Purdy" (1994) 2 *International Journal of Children's Rights* 243–258.

Milanovic, Marko. "*Al-Skeini* and *Al-Jedda* in Strasbourg" (2012) 23(1) *The European Journal of International Law* 121–139.

Mills, Alex. "Rethinking Jurisdiction in International Law" (2014) 84(1) *British Yearbook of International Law: 2013* 187–239.

Möldner, Mirka. "Responsibility of International Organizations – Introducing ILC's DARIO" (2012) 16 *Max Planck Yearbook of United Nations Law* 281–328.

Muchlinski, Peter M. "Human Rights and Multinationals: Is There a Problem?" (2001) 77(1) *International Affairs* 31–61.

Murray, Daragh. "How International Humanitarian Law Treaties Bind Non-State Armed Groups" (2015) 20(2) *Journal of Conflict & Security Law* 101–131.

Nollkaemper, André and Jacobs, Dov. "Shared Responsibility in International Law: A Conceptual Framework" (2013) 34 *Michigan Journal of International Law* 359–438.

Nowak, Manfred. "The Need for a World Court of Human Rights" (2007) 7(1) *Human Rights Law Review* 251–259.

O'Neill, Onora. "Children's Rights and Children's Lives" (1988) 98 *Ethics* 445–463.

Ostrom, Elinor. "Understanding Collective Action," 2020 Vision for Food, Agriculture and the Environment, Collective Action and Property Rights for Sustainable Development, *FOCUS 11*, Brief 2 of 16, February 2004.

Panter-Brick, Catherine et al. "Violence, Suffering, and Mental Health in Afghanistan: A School-Based Survey" (2009) 374 *The Lancet* 807–816.

Pomfret, Richard. "State-Directed Diffusion of Technology: The Mechanization of Cotton-Harvesting in Soviet Central Asia (2002) 62(1) *The Journal of Economic History* 170–188.

Prenkert, Jamie Darin and Shackelford, Scott J. "Business, Human Rights, and the Promise of Polycentricity" (2014) 47 *Vanderbilt Journal of Transnational Law* 451–500.

Price, Richard M. "Moral Limit and Possibility in World Politics" (2008) 62(2) *International Organization* 191–220.

Roberts, Anthea Elizabeth. "Traditional and Modern Approaches to Customary International Law: A Reconciliation" (2001) 95(4) *American Journal of International Law* 757–791.

Rosenau, James N. "Governance in the 21st Century" (1995) 1(1) *Global Governance* 13–43.

Schachter, Oscar. "The Invisible College of International Lawyers" (1977–1978) 72 (2) *Northwestern University Law Review* 217–226.

Shaffer, Gregory C. "How Business Shapes Law: A Socio-Legal Framework" (2009) 42(1) *Connecticut Law Review* 147–183.

Shaffer, Gregory C. and Pollack, Mark A. "Hard vs. Soft Law: Alternatives, Complements and Antagonists in International Governance" (2010) 94 *Minnesota Law Review* 706–799.

Simons, Penelope. "International law's Invisible Hand and the Future of Corporate Accountability for Violations of Human Rights" (2012) 3(1) *Journal of Human Rights and the Environment* 5–43.

Slaughter, Anne-Marie. "Filling Power Vacuums in the New Global Legal Order" (2013) 54(3) *Boston College Law Review* 919–936.

Slawotsky, Joel. "Corporate Liability for Violating International Law Under the Alien Tort Statute: The Corporation Through the Lens of Globalization and Privatization" (2013) 6 *International Review of Law*.

Stewart, David P. and Wuerth, Ingrid. "*Kiobel v. Royal Dutch Petroleum Co.*: The Supreme Court and the Alien Tort Statute" (2013) 107(3) *The American Journal of International Law* 601–621.

Trechsel, Stefan. "A World Court for Human Rights?" (2004) 1(1) *Northwestern Journal of International Human Rights*.

Van Pachtenbeke, Andy and Haeck, Yves. "De Becker to Varnava: The State of Continuing Situations in the Strasbourg Case Law" (2010) *European Human Rights Law Review* 47–59.

Verdonck, Lieselot. "How the European Court of Human Rights Evaded the Business and Human Rights Debate in *Özel v. Turkey*" (2016) 2(1) *The Turkish Commercial Law Review* 111–118.

Von Bogdandy, Armin and Steinbruck Platise, Mateja. "ARIO and Human Rights Protection: Leaving the Individual in the Cold" (2012) *International Organizations Law Review* 9–67.

Walker, Susan P., Wachs, Theodore D. et al. "Child Development: Risk Factors for Adverse Outcomes in Developing Countries" (2007) 369 *The Lancet* 145–157.

Wall, John. "Human Rights in Light of Childhood" (2008) 16 *International Journal of Children's Rights* 523–543.

Weisbrodt, David and Kruger, Maria. "Norms on the Responsibilities of Transnational Corporations and Other Business Enterprises with Regard to Human Rights" (2003) 97(4) *The American Journal of International Law* 901–922.

Wendt, Alexander. "Anarchy Is What States Make of It: The Social Construction Of Power Politics" (1992) 46(2) *International Organization* 391–425.

Young, Iris Marion. "Responsibility and Global Justice: A Social Connection Model" (2006) 23(1) *Social Philosophy & Policy Foundation* 102–130.

Young, Iris Marion. "Responsibility and Global Labor Justice" (2004) 12(4) *The Journal of Political Philosophy* 365–388.

Policy, Research and Working Papers

Ahlborn, Christiane. "To Share or Not to Share? The Allocation of Responsibility between International Organizations and their Member States" (2013) 28 *SHARES Research Paper*.

Coomans, Fons. "Clarifying the Core Content of the Right to Education," SIM Special n°18: The right to complain about economic, social and cultural rights: proceedings of the Expert Meeting on the Adoption of an Optional Protocol to the International Covenant on Economic, Social and Cultural Rights, 25–29 January 1995.

De Schutter, Olivier. "Corporations and Positive Duties in the Area of Economic and Social Rights," Université Catholique de Louvain, CRIDHO Working Paper 2013/7, 2013, 15.

De Schutter, Olivier. "Transnational Corporations and Human Rights: An Introduction," Global Law Working Paper 01/05. Symposium – Transnational Corporations and Human Rights, NYU School of Law, 2005.

Guenter, Hans. "The Tripartite Declaration of Principles concerning Multinational Enterprises and Social Policy (History, Contents, Follow-Up and Relationship With Relevant Instruments of Other Organisations)," ILO MNEs Programme Working Paper No. 18, ILO, 1981.

International Criminal Court – The Office of the Prosecutor. "Policy Paper on Case Selection and Prioritisation," 15 September 2016.

Locke, Rick, Amengual, Matthew and Mangla, Akshay. "'Virtue out of Necessity?' Compliance, Commitment and the Improvement of Labor Conditions in Global Supply Chains," MIT Sloan Working Paper No. 4719–08, October 2008 (updated March 2009).

National Scientific Council on the Developing Child (NSCDC). "Persistent Fear and Anxiety Can Affect Young Children's Learning and Development" (2010) Working Paper No. 9.

Nollkaemper, André. "Power and Responsibility," SHARES Research Paper 42, 2014, *ACIL* 2014–22.

Office of the SRSG for Children and Armed Conflict. "The Six Grave Violations Against Children During Armed Conflict: The Legal Foundation," Working Paper No. 1, October 2009 (updated November 2013).

Ostrom, Elinor. "A Polycentric Approach for Coping with Climate Change," World Bank, Policy Research Working Paper No. 5095, 2009, http://documents.worldbank.org/curated/en/480171468315567893/pdf/WPS5095.pdf (accessed 12 March 2019).

Ruggie, John G. "The Social Construction of the UN Guiding Principles on Business and Human Rights," Corporate Responsibility Initiative Working Paper No. 67 (John F. Kennedy School of Government – Harvard University, 2017).

Seay, Laura E. "What's Wrong with Dodd-Frank 1502? Conflict Minerals, Civilian Livelihoods, and the Unintended Consequences of Western Advocacy," CGD Working Paper 284, Center for Global Development, January 2012.

UNICEF. "Discussion Paper: Operational-Level Grievance Mechanisms Fit for Children," 2018.

Treaties

CoE Convention on the Protection of Children Against Sexual Exploitation and Sexual Abuse, 25 October 2007.

International Convention on the Protection of the Rights of All Migrant Workers and Members of Their Families (CPRMW).

UN Convention on the Elimination of All Forms of Discrimination Against Women (CEDAW). UN Convention on the Rights of Persons with Disabilities (CRPD).

UN Convention on the Elimination of All Forms of Racial Discrimination (CERD).

UN Convention on the Rights of the Child (CRC).

Declarations

The Universal Declaration of Human Rights.

UN Declaration on the Rights of Indigenous Peoples.

UNGA. "Declaration on the Establishment of a New International Economic Order," A/RES/S-6/3201, 1 May 1974.

UNGA. "Transforming Our World: The 2030 Agenda for Sustainable Development," A/RES/70/1, 21 October 2015.
ILO. Tripartite Declaration of Principles Concerning MNEs and Social Policy (The ILO MNE Declaration), 2017.
ILO. Declaration on Fundamental Principles and Rights at Work.

UN and ILO DOCUMENTS

CESCR. "Concluding Observations on the Second Periodic Report of Uzbekistan," E/C.12/UZB/CO/2,13 June 2014.
CESCR. GC 12 on the Right to adequate food, E/C.12/1999/5, 12 May 1999.
CESCR. GC 24 on State obligations under the International Covenant on Economic, Social and Cultural Rights in the context of business activities," E/C.12/GC/24, 10 August 2017.
CESCR. GC 3 on the Nature of States Parties Obligations, E/1991/23, 1991.
CRC Committee. "Concluding Observations 2006: Uzbekistan."
CRC Committee. "Concluding Observations 2009: DRC," CRC/C/COD/CO/2, 10 February 2009.
CRC Committee. "Concluding Observations 2009: DRC".
CRC Committee. "Concluding Observations on the Combined Third to Fifth Periodic Reports of the Democratic Republic of the Congo," CRC/C/COD/CO/3–5, 28 February 2017, para. 17(a).
CRC Committee. "Concluding Observations on the Second Periodic Report of the Holy See," 31 January 2014, CRC/C/VAT/CO/2.
CRC Committee. "Report on the Forty-Third Session, Day of General Discussion, Recommendations," September 2006.
CRC Committee. Day of General Discussion "The Private Sector as Service Provider and Its Role in Implementing Child Rights," 31st Session, CRC/C/121, 20 September 2002.
CRC Committee. GC 13 on the Right of the child to freedom from all forms of violence, CRC/C/GC/13, 18 April 2011.
CRC Committee. GC 14 on the Right of the child to have his or her best interests taken as a primary consideration, CRC/C/GC/14, 29 May 2013.
CRC Committee. GC 16 on State obligations regarding the impact of the business sector on children's rights, CRC/C/GC/16, 17 April 2013.
CRC Committee. GC 5 on General measures of implementation of the CRC, CRC/GC/2003/5, 27 November 2003.
CRC Committee. General Day of Discussion 2002 on the Private Sector as Service Provider and Its Role in Implementing Child Rights Recomm. 6, 20 September 2002.
HR Committee. "Concluding Observations 2015: Uzbekistan," CCPR/C/UZB/CO/4, 8–9 July 2015.

ILO CEACR. "Application of International Labour Standards 2014 (I) Report III (Part IA)," International Labour Conference 103rd Session.

ILO CEACR. "Observation – Worst Forms of Child Labor Convention, 1999 (No. 182) – Uzbekistan, adopted 2013, published 103rd Session of the International Labor Conference– Follow-up to the conclusions of the Committee on the Application of Standards, International Labor Conference, 102nd Session, June 2013," 2014.

ILO CEACR. "Observation – Worst Forms of Child Labor Convention, 1999 (No. 182) – Uzbekistan, Adopted 2012, Published 102nd Session of the International Labor Conference," 2013.

International Organization of Employers, International Chamber of Commerce, BusinessatOECD and BusinessEurope. "Business Response to the Zero Draft Legally Binding Instrument to Regulate, in International Human Rights Law, the Activities of Transnational Corporations and Other Business Enterprises ('Zero Draft Treaty') and the Draft Optional Protocol to the Legally Binding Instrument ('Draft Optional Protocol') Annex," October 2018.

OHCHR. "UN Guiding Principles on Business and Human Rights," UN Doc. HR/PUB/11/04, 2011, 1.

Open-Ended Intergovernmental Working Group on Transnational Corporations and Other Business Enterprises with Respect to Human rights (OEIGWG). "Zero Draft," July 2018.

Open-Ended Intergovernmental Working Group on Transnational Corporations and Other Business Enterprises with Respect to Human Rights (OEIGWG). "OEIGWG CHAIRMANSHIP REVISED DRAFT 16.7.2019," July 2019.

Open-Ended Intergovernmental Working Group on Transnational Corporations and Other Business Enterprises with Respect to Human Rights (OEIGWG). Draft Optional Protocol to the Legally Binding Instrument to Regulate, in International Human Rights Law, the Activities of Transnational Corporations and Other Business Enterprises.

SRSG John G. Ruggie. "Summary of Five Multi-Stakeholder Consultations," UN Doc A/HRC/8/5/Add.1, 2008.

Statement on behalf of a Group of Countries at the 24rd Session of the HRC. General Debate – Item 3: "Transnational Corporations and Human Rights," September 2013, https://business-humanrights.org/sites/default/files/media/documents/statement-unhrc-legally-binding.pdf.

UN Department of Economic and Social Affairs Report of the Group of Eminent Persons. "The Impact of MNCs on Development and on International Relations," UN ECOSOC Resolution 1982/68, 27 October 1982.

UN ECOSOC. "Report of the Sub-Commission on the Promotion and Protection of Human Rights – Report of the UN High Commissioner on Human Rights on the

Responsibilities of Transnational Corporations and Related Business Enterprises with Regard to Human Rights," E/CN.4/2005/91, 15 February 2005.

UN HR Council. "Mandate of the SRSG on the Issue of Human Rights and Transnational Corporations and Other Business Enterprises," A/HRC/RES/8/7, 18 June 2008.

UN HR Council. "Resolution 17/4 on Human Rights and Transnational Corporations and Other Business Enterprises," A/HRC/RES/17/4, 2001.

UN HR Council. "Statement on Behalf of a Group of Countries at the 24th Session of the HRC," September 2013, http://business-humanrights.org/sites/default/files/media/documents/statement-unhrc-legally-binding.pdf.

UN HR Council. Draft Resolution, "Elaboration of an International Legally Binding Instrument on Transnational Corporations and Other Business Enterprises with Respect to Human Rights," A/HRC/26/L.22/Rev.1, 24 June 2014.

UN HR Council. Draft Resolution, "Human Rights and Transnational Corporations and Other Business Enterprises," para. 8, www.business-humanrights.org/media/documents/norway_resolution_23_06_14.doc.

UN HR Council. Protect, Respect and Remedy: A Framework for Business and Human Rights Report of the Special Representative of the Secretary-General on the Issue of Human Rights and Transnational Corporations and Other Business Enterprises (UN Framework), John Ruggie, A/HCR/8/5, 7 April 2008.

UN WG on Business and Human Rights. "Guidance on NAPs on Business and Human Rights – Version 1.0," 2014.

UN Working Group on the Working Methods and Activities of Transnational Corporations (UNWG TNCs). "Draft Norms on the Responsibilities of Transnational Corporations and Other Business Enterprises with Regard to Human Rights," E/CN.4/Sub.2/2003/12, 2003.

UNGA/UNSC. "Children and Armed Conflict: Report of the SG," A/72/865–S/2018/465, 16 May 2018.

United Nations Security Council (UNSC). "Report of the Security Council mission to Afghanistan," S/2008/782, 12 December 2008.

UNSC Group of Experts on the DRC. "Midterm report of the Group of Experts on the Democratic Republic of the Congo," 18 December 2018, published on 31 December 2018, S/2018/1133.

UNSC. "Midterm Report of the Group of Experts on the DRC," S/2015/797, 16 October 2015.

Legislation and Legislative Proposals

Australian Government. Crimes (Child Sex Tourism) Amendment Act 1994 No. 105, 1994.

Constitution of the DRC. Kinshasa, February 2006.

Directive 2012/29/EU of the European Parliament and the Council of 25 October 2012 Establishing Minimum Standards on the Rights, Support and Protection of Victims of Crime, and Replacing Council Framework Decision 2001/220/JHA.

Directive 2014/23/EU of the EP and of the Council of 26 February 2014 on the award of concession contracts.

Directive 2014/24/EU of the EP and of the Council of 26 February 2014 on public procurement and repealing Directive 2004/18/EC.

Directive 2014/24/EU of the European Parliament and of the Council of 26 February 2014 on public procurement and repealing Directive 2004/18/EC Text with EEA relevance, 28 March 2014.

Directive 2014/24/EU, Article 18.2; EU, Directive 2014/25/EU of the EP and of the Council of 26 February 2014 on procurement by entities operating in the water, energy, transport and postal services sectors and repealing Directive 2004/17/EC.

Directive 2014/95/EU of the EP and of the Council of 22 October 2014 amending Directive 2013/34/EU as regards disclosure of nonfinancial and diversity information by certain large undertakings and groups.

DRC. "Loi n° 09/001 du 10 janvier 2009 portant protection de l'enfant."

DRC. "Loi No. 09/001 du 10 Janvier 2009 Portant Protection de l'Enfant."

DRC. "Loi-Cadre n° 14/004 du 11 Février 2014 de L'Enseignement National."

DRC. "Strategie Nationale Sectorielle de Lutte Contre Le Travail des Enfants dans les Mines Artisanales et sur les Sites Minières Artisanaux en République Démocratique du Congo 2017–2025," Kinshasa, August 2017.

EU Council. Proposal for a Regulation of the European Parliament and of the Council setting up a Union system for supply chain due diligence self-certification of responsible importers of tin, tantalum and tungsten, their ores, and gold originating in conflict-affected and high-risk areas, 7239/17, 20 March 2017.

Japan. Act on Punishment of Activities Relating to Child Prostitution and Child Pornography, and the Protection of Children (Act No. 52 of May 26, 1999) (Unofficial English translation), www.unodc.org/res/cld/document/jpn/act-on-punishment-of-activities-relating-to-child-prostitution-and-child-pornography-and-the-protection-of-children_html/Act_on_Punishment_of_Activities_Relating_to_Child_Prostitution_and_Child_Pornography.pdf (accessed 12 March 2019).

Republic of France. Loi n° 2017–399 du 27 mars 2017 relative au devoir de vigilance des sociétés mères et des entreprises donneuses d'ordre.

The Government of the Netherlands. "Proposal: Wet Zorgplicht Kinderarbeid/Child Labour Due Diligence Law," https://zoek.officielebekendmakingen.nl/kst-34506-A.html (accessed 24 April 2019).

The Republic of Uganda. "Constitution of the Republic of Uganda," 1995.

The Republic of Uganda. "The Children (Amendment) Act," 2016.

The Republic of Uganda. Gender Policy 2017.
UK Government. The Modern Slavery Act, "Part 6 – Transparency in supply chains etc," Article 54(12), 2015.
US Congress. Dodd-Frank Wall Street Reform and Consumer Protection Act, Section 1502.
US Congress. Foreign Corrupt Practices Act, 1977 (Anti-Bribery Provision
§ 30A of the Securities Exchange Act of 1934 (15 U.S.C. §78dd-1)).
US Government. Federal Acquisition Regulation (FAR), 2005–94,2005–95, 19 January 2017.
US Government. PROTECT Act of 2003 (Prosecutorial Remedies and Other Tools to End the Exploitation of Children Today Act), Public Law 108–21, 30 April 2003.
US SEC. "Final Rule (Rule 13p-1)," 77 Fed. Reg. at 56, 22 August 2012.

Cases

Court and Treaty Body Cases

"2016–36 Termination Order (Redacted)," 17 July 2018 and "2016–37 Termination Order (Redacted)," 17 July 2018 Permanent Court of Arbitration.
Advisory Opinion 17: Advisory Opinion on the Juridical Condition and Human Rights of the Child (OC-17/2002) requested by the IACmHR, 28 August 2002 IACtHR.
Agrotexim and Others v. *Greece, no. 14807/89,* Judgment (Merits), 24 October 1995 ECtHR.
Application of the Convention on the Prevention and Punishment of the Crime of Genocide (Bosnia and Herzegovina v. *Serbia and Montenegro),* Judgment of 26 February 2007 ICJ.
Arrest Warrant of 11 April 2000 (Democratic Republic of the Congo v. *Belgium)* ICJ, Joint Separate Opinion of Judges Higgins, Kooijmans and Buergenthal, Judgment of 14 February 2002.
Banković and others v. *Belgium and others* (Application No. 52207/99), Decision (Grand Chamber), 12 December 2001 ECtHR.
Beharry v. *Reno*, 183 F. Supp. 2d 584, 600–01, E.D.N.Y., 2002.
Behrami and Behrami v. *France and Saramati* v. *France, Germany and Norway* (Applications No. 71412/01 and 78166/01), Admissibility Decision, 2 May 2007 ECtHR.
Blake v. *Guatemala* (Preliminary Objections), Ser. C, No. 27, 2 July 1996 IACtHR.
Caparo Industries PLC v. *Dickman* (1990) UKHL 2, cited by District Court of the Hague, Judgment dated 30 January 2013 – C/09/330891 / HA ZA 09–057.
Case Concerning The Barcelona Traction, Light and Power Company, Limited (Belgium v. *Spain),* Second Phase, Judgment, 5 February 1970 ICJ.

Case of Velásquez-Rodríguez v. *Honduras* (Judgment), Series C No. 4. Case 7.615, 29 July 1988 IACtHR.

Catan and Others v. *Moldova and Russia* (Applications no. 43370/04, 8252/05 and 18454/06) Judgment, 19 October 2012 ECtHR.

Cyprus v. *Turkey* (Application No. 25781/94) Judgment, 10 May 2001 ECtHR.

District Court of The Hague. Commercial team, Judgment dated 30 January 2013 in the matter with case number / docket number: C/09/330891 / HA ZA 09-057.

District Court of the Hague. *Judgment dated 30 January 2013 - C/09/330891 / HA ZA 09-057.*

Eric Barizaa Dooh and Vereniging Milieudefensie v. *Royal Dutch Shell Plc and Shell Petroleum Development of Nigeria Ltd.* (Case c - 200.126.843) and v. *Shell Petroleum N.V. and the "Shell" Transport and Trading Company Ltd.* (Case d - 200.126.848) (translated from Dutch) Court of Appeal at The Hague (Den Haag).

Friday Alfred Akpan and Vereniging Milieudefensie v. *Royal Dutch Shell Plc and Shell Petroleum Development of Nigeria Ltd* (LJN BY 9854), 30 January 2013 District Court of the Hague.

Girls Dilcia Yean and Violeta Bosico v. *the Dominican Republic* (Judgment on the preliminary exceptions, merits and reparations), 23 November 2006 IACtHR.

Hassan v. *The United Kingdom* (Application No. 29750/09) Judgment, 16 September 2014 ECtHR.

Ilaşcu and Others v. *Moldova and Russia* (Application No. 48787/99) Judgment, 8 July 2004 ECtHR.

Jaloud v. *the Netherlands* (Application no. 47708/08) Judgment, 20 November 2014 ECtHR.

Jesner v. *Arab Bank, PLC,* 584 U.S. ___ (2018) Justice Sotomayor, with whom Justice Ginsburg, Justice Breyer and Justice Kagan join. "Dissenting."

Jesner v. *Arab Bank, PLC,* 584 U. S. ___ (2018).

John Doe I v. *Nestle, USA*, No. 10-56739 (9th Cir. 2014).

Kaliña and Lokono Peoples v. *Suriname* (Merits, Reparations and Costs) 25 November 2015 IACtHR.

Kiobel v. *Royal Dutch Petroleum Co.*, 569 U.S. 108 (2013).

Loizidou v. *Turkey* (Application No: 15318/89), Judgment (Merits), 18 December 1996 ECtHR.

Munaf v. *Romania*, CCPR/C/96/D/1539/2006, 21 August 2009 HR Committee.

Nat'l Ass'n of Mfrs. v. *SEC*, 956 F. Supp. 2d 43, 77 (D.D.C. 2013).

Nat'l Ass'n of Mfrs. v. *SEC (NAM 1),* 748 F.3d 359, 370 (D.C. Cir. 2014), overruled by AMI, 760 F.3d 18 (D.C. Cir. 2014).

Nestle U.S.A., Inc., et al., Petitioners v. *John Doe I, et al.*, No. 10-56739 (9th Cir. 2015).

Nicholson v. *Williams*, 203 F. Supp. 2d 153, 234, E.D.N.Y., 2002.

Osman v. *the UK* (Application No. 23452/94), Judgment, 28 October 1998 ECtHR.

Papamichalopoulos and Others v. *Greece*, Application no.14556/89, Judgment, 24 June 1993 ECtHR.

Radilla Pacheco v. *Mexico* (Preliminary Objections, Merits, Reparations, and Costs), 23 November 2009, Ser. C, No. 209 IACtHR.

Reparation for Injuries Suffered in the Service of the United Nations Advisory Opinion, 11 April 1949 ICJ.

Roper v. *Simmons* (03–633) 543 U.S. 551, 2005.

Sadeghi v. *INS*, 40 F.3d 1139, 1147, 10th Cir. 1994 Kane, Jr., John L. "Dissenting."

Sahin v. *Germany*, Application No. 30943/96, 8 July 2003 ECtHR.

Taşkın and Others v. *Turkey* (Application No. 46117/99) Judgment (FINAL), 30 March 2005 ECtHR.

Tatar v. *Romania* (Application No. 67021/01) Judgment, 27 January 2009 ECtHR.

Varnava and Others v. *Turkey* (Applications No: 16064/90, 16065/90, 16066/90, 16068/90, 16069/90, 16070/90, 16071/90, 16072/90 and 16073/90) Judgment, 18 September 2009 ECtHR.

Vedanta Resources PLC and another (Appellants) v. *Lungowe and others (Respondents)* 10 Apr 2019 (2019) UKSC 20.

Yassin Abdullah Kadi v. *Council of the European Union and Commission of the European Communities*, Judgment of the Court of First Instance (Second Chamber, extended composition) 21 September 2005 CJEU.

OECD NCP Instances

ECCHR. "Case Up-Date Agreement with Cargill and ICT in OECD-proceeding," 26 July 2011.

French NCP. "Communiqué du Point de contact national français chargé du suivi des principes directeurs de l'OCDE à l'intention des entreprises multinationals," 21 September 2012, www.tresor.economie.gouv.fr/File/375194 (accessed 24 April 2019).

German NCP. "Joint final statement by the German NCP for the OECD Guidelines for MNEs, ECCHR and Otto Stadtlander GmbH regarding a complaint by the ECCHR against Otto Stadtlander GmbH/Bremen," 17 November 2011.

German NCP. "Statement by the German NCP for the 'OECD Guidelines for MNEs' on the Instance Filed against Bayer CropScience by German Watch, Global March, and Coordination gegen Bayer-Gefahren," 30 August 2007.

Swiss NCP. "Closing Statement – Specific Instance Regarding Cotton Trade by Ecom Agroindustrial Corp. Ltd. in Uzbekistan," 22 December 2011.

Swiss NCP. "Closing Statement: Specific Instance Regarding Cotton Trading by Louis Dreyfus Suisse SA in Uzbekistan," 17 February 2012.

Swiss NCP. "Closing Statement: Specific Instance Regarding Cotton Trading by Paul Reinhart AG in Uzbekistan," 7 March 2012.

UK NCP. "Articles 76, 77, 78 and 79, Final Statement by the UK NCP for the OECD Guidelines for MNEs – Instance from Survival International against Vedanta Resources Plc," 25 September 2009, www.oecd.org/dataoecd/49/16/43884129.pdf (accessed 15 April 2019).

UK NCP. "Final Statement by the UK NCP for the OECD Guidelines for MNEs: Afrimex (UK) Ltd," 28 August 2008.

UK NCP. "Final Statement by the UK NCP for the OECD Guidelines for MNEs – Complaint from the ECCHR against ICT Cotton Ltd (in Uzbekistan)," 11 July 2011.

UK NCP. "Final Statement by the UK NCP for the OECD Guidelines for MNEs – Complaint from the ECCHR against Cargill Cotton Ltd (in Uzbekistan)," 11 July 2011.

UK NCP. "Initial Assessment by the UK NCP for the OECD Guidelines for MNEs – Complaint from the ECCHR against ICT Cotton Ltd (in Uzbekistan)," 8 March 2011.

UK NCP. "Statement by the United Kingdom National Contact Point (NCP) for OECD Guidelines for Multinational Enterprises: DAS Air," 17 July 2008, www.oecd.org/daf/inv/mne/44479531.pdf (accessed 24 April 2019).

Cases at Multilateral Development Banks

AfDB IRM. "2nd Monitoring Report on the Implementation of Findings of Non-Compliance and Related Actions to Be Undertaken by the ADB Management on The Bujagali Hydropower and Interconnection Projects," 28 July 2010.

AfDB IRM. "3rd Monitoring Report on the Implementation of Findings of Non-Compliance and Related Actions to Be Undertaken by the ADB Management on The Bujagali Hydropower and Interconnection Projects," 6 June 2011.

AfDB IRM. "4th Monitoring Report on the Implementation of Findings of Non-Compliance and Related Actions to Be Undertaken by the ADB Management on The Bujagali Hydropower and Interconnection Projects," September 2012.

AfDB IRM. "Compliance Review Report on the Bujagali Hydropower and Interconnection Projects," 20 June 2008.

Bujagali Affected Community. "Complaint to the IFC," 16 May 2011, www.cao-ombudsman.org/cases/document-links/documents/2011_May16Complaint_redacted.pdf (accessed 15 April 2019).

CAO Case Database. "Uganda/Bujagali Energy-05/Bujagali," www.cao-ombudsman.org/cases/case_detail.aspx?id=172 (accessed 15 April 2019).

CAO. "Assessment Report: Complaint Filed to the CAO Regarding the Uganda Bujagali Hydropower Project," September 2001.

CAO. "CAO Assessment Report: Regarding Complaint in Relation to IFC's Indorama Kokand, Hamkor Equity/SL, Hamkorbank RIs, Hamkorbank SL, GTFP Hamkor," March 2018.

CAO. "CAO Investigation of IFC/MIGA Social and Environmental Performance in Relation to: Bujagali Energy Limited and World Power Holdings, Uganda (Bujagali-07)," 15 December 2017.

CAO. "Case Overview – Uganda/Bujagali Energy-07/Bujagali," www.cao-ombudsman.org/cases/case_detail.aspx?id=230 (accessed 15 April 2019).

CAO. "Case Overview: Uganda/Bujagali Energy-02/Bujagali Falls," www.cao-ombudsman.org/cases/case_detail.aspx?id=114 (accessed 15 April 2019).

CAO. "Complaint: Uzbekistan: Indorama Kokand/Hamkor Bank-01/Uzbekistan," 30 June 2016, www.cottoncampaign.org/uploads/3/9/4/7/39474145/160630cao_submission_ifc-indorama_public_version.pdf (accessed 15 April 2019).

CAO. "Compliance Appraisal Report: IFC Investment in Bujagali Energy Project (Project #24408) and MIGA guarantee of World Power Holdings (MIGA Project #6732), Uganda – Complaint 07," 10 November 2016, www.cao-ombudsman.org/cases/document-links/documents/CAO_Compliance_AppraisalReport_Bujagali07.pdf (accessed 15 April 2019).

CAO. "Letter from Meg Taylor (Compliance Advisor/Ombudsman) to NAPE – Closing of Complaint: Bujagali HPP," 19 January 2005.

CAO. "Meeting Communique: Indorama Kokand/Hamkor Bank-01/Uzbekistan," July 2018.

CAO. "Ombudsman Assessment Report, Fifth Complaint (Bujagali Energy-05) Regarding the Bujagali Energy Ltd. Project (IFC #24408 & MIGA #6732)," December 2011.

Joy For Children–Uganda (as representative). "Request for an Inspection on the Impact of Kamwenge–Fort Portal Road Works Section on the Community," 21 August 2015. www.inspectionpanel.org/sites/www.inspectionpanel.org/files/ip/PanelCases/98-Request%20for%20Inspection.pdf (accessed 21 April 2019).

Malindi Village Affected Community. "7th Complaint regarding the Bujagali Project," 10 January 2015.

NAPE, Counter Balance, CLAI and Association Sherpa. "EIB Complaint Submission – Bujagali Powerplant Project," 20 November 2009.

NAPE. "Complaint about the Bujagali HPP," 19 June 2001.

WB Inspection Panel and AfDB CRMU. "Memorandum of Understanding," 28 November 2007, in WB Inspection Panel, "Annual Report – July 1, 2007, to June 30, 2008."

WB Inspection Panel. "Final Eligibility Report and Recommendation on a Request for Inspection – Republic of Uzbekistan: Second Rural Enterprise Support Project (P109126) and Additional Financing for the Second Rural Enterprise Support Project (P126962) – Report No. 93222-UZ."

WB Inspection Panel. "Investigation Report Uganda: Private Power Generation (Bujagali) Project (Guarantee No. BOl30-UG)," 29 August 2008.

WB Inspection Panel. "Investigation Report – UGANDA: Third Power Project (Credit No. 2268-UG), Fourth Power Project (Credit No. 3545-UG) and

Bujagali Hydropower Project (PRG No. B 003-UG) (Report No. 23998)," 23 May 2002.

WB Inspection Panel. "Notice of Registration – Re: Request for Inspection Uganda: Private Power Generation Project (Proposed)," IPN Request RQ07/1, 7 March 2007.

WB Inspection Panel. "Report and Recommendation – Republic of Uzbekistan: Second Rural Enterprise Support Project (P109126) and Additional Financing for Second Rural Enterprise Support Project (P126962), Report No. 83254-UZ," 9 December 2013.

WB Inspection Panel. "Report and Recommendation – Republic of Uzbekistan: Second Rural Enterprise Support Project (P109126) and Additional Financing for Second Rural Enterprise Support Project (P126962), Report No. 83254-UZ, 9 December 2013.

WB. "Fourth Progress Report on the Implementation of Management's Action Plan in Response to the Inspection Panel Investigation Report (Report # 44977-Ug) on the Republic of Uganda Private Power Generation (Bujagali) Project (Ida Guarantee No. B0130-Ug)," 13 September 2013.

Guidelines

Accord on Fire and Building Safety in Bangladesh. "Accord Continuation Beyond May 2018," https://bangladeshaccord.org/updates/2017/10/26/accord-continuation-beyond-may-2018 (accessed 15 April 2019).

AfDB. "Private Sector Development Policy of the AfDB Group," May 2013.

CCCMC. "Chinese Due Diligence Guidelines for Responsible Mineral Supply Chains," 2015.

Council of Europe. Guidelines of the Committee of Ministers of the Council of Europe on Child-Friendly Justice, 17 November 2010.

CoE. Recommendation CM/Rec(2016)3 on Human Rights and Business, 2 March 2016.

OECD. Amendment of the Decision of the Council on the OECD Guidelines for MNEs, I. National Contact Points, 25 May 2011.

CoE. "Explanatory Memorandum
to Recommendation CM/Rec (2016)3 of the Committee of Ministers to Member States on Human Rights and Business," 2 March 2016.

European Group on Tort Law. "Principles of European Tort Law" (PETL), 2 September 2005.

FAO. *Respecting Free, Prior and Informed Consent: Practical Guidance for Governments, Companies, NGOs, Indigenous Peoples and Local Communities in Relation to Land Acquisition* (FAO, 2014).

FAO. *Voluntary Guidelines on the Responsible Governance of Tenure of Land, Fisheries and Forests in the Context of National Food Security* (FAO 2012).

IFC. "IFC Sustainability Framework Policy and Performance Standards."

IFC. Performance Standard 2: Labor and Working Conditions," in IFC, "IFC Sustainability Framework: Policy and Performance Standards on Environmental and Social Sustainability and Access to Information Policy," 1 January 2012.

ILC. "General Commentary to the DARIO," Draft articles on the responsibility of international organizations, with commentaries, 2011, http://legal.un.org/docs/?path=../ilc/texts/instruments/english/commentaries/9_11_2011.pdf&lang=EF (accessed 15 April 2019).

ILC. Articles on the Responsibility of International Organisations (ARIO), 2011.

ILC. Articles on the Responsibility of States for Internationally Wrongful Acts (ARSIWA), (Annex to General Assembly resolution 56/83 of 12 December 2001, and corrected by document A/56/49[Vol. I]/Corr.4), 2001.

OECD. *OECD Due Diligence Guidance for Responsible Supply Chains of Minerals from Conflict-Affected and High-Risk Areas*" (2nd Ed.) (OECD, 2013).

The Maastricht Principles on Extraterritorial Obligations of States in the Area of Economic, Social and Cultural Rights, 2011.

UN Global Compact. The Ten Principles of the UN Global Compact, www.unglobalcompact.org/aboutthegc/thetenprinciples/index.html (accessed 24 April 2019).

UN HR Council. "Protect, Respect, Remedy: A Framework for Business and Human Rights," UN Doc A/HRC/8/16, 2008.

UN HR Council. Guiding Principles on Business and Human Rights: Implementing the United Nations "Protect, Respect and Remedy" Framework (UNGPs), A/HRC/17/31, 2011.

UNICEF, Save the Children and UN Global Compact. *Children's Rights and Business Principles* (UNICEF, Save the Children, UN Global Compact, 2012) www.unglobalcompact.org/docs/issues_doc/human_rights/CRBP/Childrens_Rights_and_Business_Principles.pdf (accessed 25 April 2019).

WB. "Bank Directive Addressing Risks and Impacts on Disadvantaged or Vulnerable Individuals or Groups," 4 August 2016.

WB. "Managing the Risks of Adverse Impacts on Communities from Temporary Project Induced Labor Influx," 1 December 2016.

WB. Environmental and Social Framework, Environmental and Social Standard (ESS) 1: Assessment and Management of Environmental and Social Risks and Impacts.

ADB. "Safeguard Policy Statement," June 2009, in Annex 5: ADB Prohibited Investment Activities List.

The Equator Principles. June 2013.

US Congress. "Consolidated Appropriations Act, 2014," 13 January 2014.

WB. Operational Directive 4.01 – Environmental Assessments, January 1999 (Revised April 2013).

News Articles

Alston, Philip. "The Two Words That Scare the World Bank," *The Washington Post*, 7 November 2014, www.washingtonpost.com/opinions/philip-alston-the-world-bank-treats-human-rights-as-unmentionable/2014/11/07/9091dafa-65da-11e4-9fdc-d43b053ecb4d_story.html (accessed 21 August 2019).

Aulakh, Raveena. "Uzbekistan Shuts Down High Schools, Universities in Forced Cotton Harvest," *The Toronto Star*, 30 September 2014, www.caionline.in/articles/uzbekistan-shuts-down-high-schools-universities-in-forced-cotton-harvest-september-30-2014 (accessed 21 August 2019).

Barbière, Cécile. "EU Institutions Still Divided Over Conflict Minerals," *EurActiv.fr*, 3 February 2016.

BBC Website. "DR Congo: Cursed by Its Natural Wealth," 9 October 2013, www.bbc.com/news/magazine-24396390 (accessed 15 April 2019).

Bird, Chris. "The Hard Road to Healthcare for Eastern Congo's Poor," *Guardian*, 10 April 2012, www.theguardian.com/global-development/poverty-matters/2012/apr/10/hard-road-healthcare-congo-poor (accessed 15 April 2019).

De Coster, Jozef. "Uzbekistan Textiles Appeal to Foreign Investors," www.just-style.com, 24 October 2005, www.just-style.com/analysis/uzbekistan-textiles-appeal-to-foreign-investors_id92504.aspx (accessed 15 April 2019).

Dezember, Ryan and Bariyo, Nicholas. "Private-Equity Firms Build Instead of Buy," *Wall Street Journal*, 14 May 2013, www.wsj.com/articles/SB10001424127887323628004578461223864870026 (accessed 15 April 2019).

Doward, Jamie. "H&M Comes Under Pressure to Act on Child-Labour Cotton," *Guardian*, 15 December 2012, www.theguardian.com/business/2012/dec/15/cotton-child-labour-uzbekistan-fashion (accessed 15 April 2019).

Evans, Jessica. "Asian Development Bank's Money vs. Its Mouth," *The Huffington Post*, 13 May 2016, www.huffingtonpost.com/jessica-evans/asian-development-banks-m_b_9961464.html (accessed 15 April 2019).

Fibre 2 Fashion. "Uzbekistan to Machine-Harvest 90% of Cotton by 2016," 17 October 2013, www.fibre2fashion.com/news/textile-news/newsdetails.aspx?news_id=154101 (accessed 15 April 2019).

Goldhaber, Michael D. "The Global Lawyer: The "Zombie" Alien Tort, Three Years After Kiobel," *The American Lawyer*, 12 May 2016.

Mbendi Information Services. "Copper Mining in Democratic Republic of the Congo," www.mbendi.com/indy/ming/cppr/af/zr/p0005.htm (accessed 15 April 2019).

Mutaizibwa, Emma. "Bujagali: Finally, Light at the End of Tunnel," *Observer (Uganda)*, 9 October 2012, www.observer.ug/component/content/article?id=21445:bujagali-finally-light-at-the-end-of-tunnel- (accessed 15 April 2019).

Nieburg, Olivier. "Nestlé Bid to Throw out Cocoa Child Labor Lawsuit in SCOTUS Rejected," *Confectionerynews.com*, 12 January 2016, www.confectionerynews

.com/Commodities/Supreme-court-rejects-Nestle-child-labor-lawsuit-dismissal-attempts (accessed 15 April 2019).

O'Keefe, Joseph C. and Saperstein, Daniel L. "Third Circuit 'Clarifies' Continuing Violation Doctrine," *Proskauer Client Alert*, 22 February 2013, www.proskauer.com/publications/client-alert/third-circuit-clarifies-continuing-violation-doctrine/ (accessed 15 April 2019).

Obbo, Betty. "Where Are Women's Voices in Uganda's Dam Planning?," *International Rivers Review*, March 2011.

Pallister, David. "Africa Dam's Passage 'Eased by Bribes'," *Guardian*, 3 November 2003, www.theguardian.com/uk/2003/nov/03/davidpallister (accessed 15 April 2019).

Pettersson, Edvard. "Child Slavery Claims Against Nestle, Cargill Get One More Chance," Bloomberg.com, 9 January 2017, www.bloomberg.com/news/articles/2017-01-09/child-slavery-claims-against-nestle-cargill-get-one-more-chance (accessed 15 April 2019).

Rushe, Dominic. "Unions Reach $2.3 m Settlement on Bangladesh Textile Factory Safety," *Guardian*, 22 January 2018.

Rwothungeyo, Billy. "UNRA Vows to Work with Communities After World Bank Woes," *New Vision Website*, 21 January 2016, www.newvision.co.ug/new_vision/news/1415395/unra-vows-communities-bank-woes (accessed 15 April 2019).

Saidazimova, Gulnoza. "Uzbekistan: Cotton Industry Targeted by Child-Labor Activists," Radio Free Europe – Radio Liberty, 19 January 2008, www.rferl.org/content/article/1079375.html (accessed 15 April 2019).

Wachenfeld, Margaret. "The Hidden Impacts of Large Infrastructure Projects on Children," *Guardian*, 3 May 2012, www.theguardian.com/sustainable-business/children-large-infrastructure-honeypot-effect (accessed 15 April 2019).

Wolfe, Lauren. "How Dodd-Frank Is Failing Congo," *Foreign Policy*, 2 February 2015.

Press Releases, Statements and Letters

ABSA Capital. "Press Release – Absa Capital, Barclays Plc Team Up On $867 m Uganda Hydropower Project," 17 January 2008.

ADB. "Press Release – ADB $220 Loan to Help Uzbekistan," 25 September 2013.

AKDN. "President Museveni and the Aga Khan Inaugurate Bujagali HPP."

AKDN. "Press Release – President Museveni and the Aga Khan Inaugurate Bujagali Hydropower Plant," 8 October 2012.

BIC. "Press Release – Case Study on Bujagali Dam's Negative Impacts on Children Submitted to the WB," 11 April 2013, www.bankinformationcenter.org/case-study-on-bujagali-dams-negative-impacts-on-children-submitted-to-the-world-bank/ (accessed 15 April 2019).

Council of the EU (EU Council). "Press Release – Conflict Minerals: Council Adopts New Rules to Reduce Financing of Armed Groups," 181/17, 3 April 2017.

DMCC. "DMCC Response to 'City of Gold' 24.03.2014," 24 March 2014.

European Parliament (EP). "Press Release: Conflict Minerals: MEPs Secure Mandatory Due Diligence for Importers," 16 June 2016.

FIAN International et al. "Statement to the HRC in Support of the Initiative of a Group of States for a Legally Binding Instrument on Transnational Corporations," 13 September 2013, www.stopcorporateimpunity.org/?p=3830.

Human Rights Watch (HRW). "Letter to the ADB President Mr. Takehiko Nakao: Concerns Regarding Forced Labor in the Modernization and Improved Performance of the Amu Bukhara Irrigation System (ABIS) Project in Uzbekistan," 3 September 2013.

Human Rights Watch (HRW). "Press Release – Uzbekistan: Forced Labor Widespread in Cotton Harvest."

Human Rights Watch (HRW). "Press Release – Uzbekistan: Forced Labor Widespread in Cotton Harvest – More Adults, Older Children Required to Work, Abuses Persist," 25 January 2013.

IFC. "Press Release – WB's Board Responds to Uganda's Energy Needs – Approves Support for Bujagali HPP," 19 December 2001.

MIGA. "Power Brief – MIGA: Fortifying Power Investments," April 2008.

OHCHR and Center for Economic and Social Rights. "Who Will Be Accountable? Human Rights and the Post-2015 Development Agenda," 2013.

Ruggie, John G. "Prepared Remarks: Public Hearings on Business and Human Rights Sub-Committee on Human Rights," European Parliament, 16 April 2009.

Sherpa. "SAMSUNG: Sherpa and ActionAid France File a Second Lawsuit Following the Closing of the Case by the Public Prosecutor," 25 June 2018, www.asso-sherpa.org/samsung-sherpa-and-actionaid-france-file-a-second-lawsuit-following-the-closing-of-the-case-by-the-public-prosecutor (accessed 15 April 2019).

The Cotton Campaign. "Letter to the ADB President Mr. Takehiko Nakao," 11 September 2013.

UN Secretariat General. "Press Release: Secretary-General Proposes Global Compact on Human Rights, Labor, Environment, in Address to World Economic Forum in Davos," 1 February 1999.

UNSG. "Press release: Secretary-General Appoints John Ruggie of United States Special Representative on Issue of Human Rights, Transnational Corporations, Other Business Enterprises," SG/A/934, 28/07/2005.

US Treasury. "US Position: WB Inspection Panel's Report and Recommendation Uzbekistan – Rural Enterprise Support Project Phase II and Additional Financing for the Second Rural Enterprise Support Project," 23 January 2015.

WB. "Press Release – WB Continues Supporting Agricultural Diversification in Uzbekistan," 7 February 2014.

WB. "Press Release – WB Continues Supporting Productivity and Sustainability of Agriculture in Uzbekistan," 11 September 2012.

WB. "World Bank Statement on Cancellation of the Uganda Transport Sector Development Project (TSDP)," 21 December 2015, www.worldbank.org/en/news/press-release/2015/12/21/wb-statement-cancellation-uganda-transport-sector-development-project (accessed 22 April 2019).

WB. "World Bank Statement on Suspension of Roads Projects in Uganda," 8 January 2016, www.worldbank.org/en/news/press-release/2016/01/08/world-bank-statement-on-suspension-of-roads-projects-in-uganda (accessed 22 April 2019).

National Action Plans

Belgium – Commission Interdépartementale pour le Développement Durable. "Plan D'Action National Entreprises et Droits de l'Homme'" (Belgian NAP), 2017.

Colombia. "Plan Nacional de Acción sobre Derechos Humanos y Empresas," 2015.

Finland. "NAP on the Implementation of the UN Guiding Principles on Business and Human Rights," 2014.

Germany. "German National Action Plan – Implementation of the UN Guiding Principles on Business and Human Rights 2016–2020," 2016.

Gobierno de España. "Plan de Empresa y Derechos Humanos," 2014.

Government of Italy. "The Foundations of the Italian Action Plan on The United Nations 'Guiding Principles on Business and Human Rights'" 2014.

Government Offices of Sweden. "Action Plan for Business and Human Rights," 2015.

Poland. "Polish National Action Plan for the Implementation of the United Nations Guiding Principles on Business and Human Rights 2017–2020," 2017.

Republic of Ireland. "National Plan on Business and Human Rights," 2017.

República de Chile – Ministerio De Relaciones Exteriores. "National Action Plan on Business and Human Rights Chile," 2017.

República de Colombia. "Plan Nacional de Acción sobre Derechos Humanos y Empresas," 2015.

République Française. "Plan National D'action Pour La Mise En Œuvre Des Principes Directeurs Des Nations Unies Relatifs Aux Droits De L'homme Et Aux Entreprises," 2017.

Switzerland. "Report on the Swiss Strategy for the Implementation of the UN Guiding Principles on Business and Human Rights," 2016.

The Danish Government. "Danish NAP – Implementation of the UN Guiding Principles on Business and Human Rights," 2014.

The Netherlands. "NAP on Business and Human Rights," 2013.

UK HM Government. "Good Business: Implementing the UN Guiding Principles on Business and Human Rights," 2013.

United States of America. National Action Plan on Responsible Business Conduct, 2016.

Reports

ADB. "Proposed Loans – Republic of Uzbekistan: Amu Bukhara Irrigation System Rehabilitation Project, Project Number: 44458-013," August 2013.

ADB. Concept Note – Uzbekistan: Amu Bukhara Irrigation System Rehabilitation, 4 November 2011.

AfDB. Environmental and Social Impact Assessment Summary: Road Sector Support Project 3: Nyakahita–Ibanda–Kamwenge Road Upgrading Project P-UG-DB0-020, www.afdb.org/fileadmin/uploads/afdb/Documents/Environmental-and-Social-Assessments/Uganda%20RSSP3%20%20Nyakahita_Ibanda_Kamwenge%20Road%20Draft%20ESIA%20-%20RAP%20Summary%20_PIC_-1.pdf (accessed 21 April 2019).

African Resources Watch (Afrewatch) and Amnesty International (AI). "'This Is What We Die For': Human Rights Abuses in the Democratic Republic of the Congo Power the Global Trade in Cobalt," 2016.

AI and Global Witness. "Digging for Transparency: How U.S. Companies Are Only Scratching the Surface of Conflict Minerals Reporting," April 2015.

Alston, Philip and Tobin, John (with the assistance of Darrow, Mac). *Laying the Foundations for Children's Rights: An Independent Study of Some Key Legal and Institutional Aspects of the Impact of the Convention on the Rights of the Child* (UNICEF, 2005).

Baby Milk Action. "Nestle, the UN Global Compact and OECD Guidelines – What Happened When Nestlé Was Reported for Violating the UN Global Compact and OECD Guidelines for Multinational Enterprises?" 21 May 2010.

Bank Information Center (BIC) and the Human Rights Society of Uzbekistan (Ezgulik). "The Need for Child Impact Assessments: A Case Study of the International Development Association Funded Uzbekistan Rural Enterprise Support Project–Phase II," April 2013.

Barrett, Paul M., Baumann-Pauly, Dorothée and Gu, April. "Five Years After Rana Plaza: The Way Forward," NYU Stern Center for Business and Human Rights, April 2018.

Bazira, Henri Mugisha. "International Reforms of Environmental and Social Safeguards (ESS) for Development Finance," Water Governance Institute, March 2012.

Bruch, Carl et al. "Compendium of Relevant Practices for Improved Decision-Making, Planning and Management of Dams and Their Alternatives: Compliance" (Prepared for UNEP's Dams and Development Project), April 2007.

Buck Louis, Germaine et al. *Principles for Evaluating Risks from Chemicals During Infancy and Early Childhood: The Need for a Special Approach* (WHO, 1986).

Burnside International, Canada Dillon Consultants Ltd, Canada et al. "Bujagali HPP, Uganda Public Consultation and Disclosure Plan (PCDP) DRAFT," File No: I-A 10045, November 2006.

Cedillo, Christina. *Better Access to Remedy in Company-Community Conflicts in the Field of CSR: A Model for Company-Based Grievance Mechanisms* (Institute for Environment Security, 2011).

Changing Markets Foundation. *The False Promise of Certification: How Certification is Hindering Sustainability in the Textiles, Palm Oil and Fisheries Industries* (Changing Markets Foundation, 2018).

China Railway Group Limited (CREC). *2017 Annual Report* (CREC, 2018).

Council for Early Child Development. *The Science of Early Child Development* (Council for Early Child Development, 2010), cited in Naudeau, Sophie et al. *Investing in Young Children: An Early Childhood Development Guide for Policy Dialogue and Project Preparation* (World Bank, 2011).

Cuvelier, Jeroen. "Introduction," in Cuvelier, Jeroen (ed.), *The Complexity of Resource Governance in a Context of State Fragility: The Case of Eastern DRC* (IPIS and International Alert, 2010).

De Boer Buquicchio, Maud. "Foreword," in CoE, Guidelines of the Committee of Ministers of the CoE on Child-Friendly Justice: Adopted by the Committee of Ministers of the CoE on 17 November 2010 and Explanatory Memorandum, October 2011.

Djanibekov, Nodir et al. *Pros and Cons of Cotton Production in Uzbekistan – Case Study # 7–9 of the Program: Food Policy for Developing Countries: The Role of Government in the Global Food System* (Cornell University, 2010).

Doherty, Gillian. *Zero to Six: The Basis for School Readiness* (Applied Research Branch R-97-3E) (Human Resources Development Canada, 1997).

ECCHR. *Forced Labor of Children and Adults in Uzbekistan: How Effective Is the OECD Complaint Mechanism?* May 2013.

EIB CM. "Bujagali Hydroelectric Project (Jinja, Uganda) Conclusions Report (Complaint SG/E/2009/09)," 30 August 2012.

EIB CM. "Outcome of Mediation Process: Complaints on Alleged Effects of Blasting on Buildings During Construction of Bujagali HEP," 31 May 2013.

Eide, Asbjørn (UN Special Rapporteur for the Right to Food). *The Right to Adequate Food as a Human Right: Final Report Submitted by Asbjørn Eide*, UN Doc E/CN.4/Sub.2/1987/23, 1987.

EJF. "Alternative Report Child Labour in Cotton Production in Uzbekistan for the 42nd Session of the Committee on the Rights of the Child," 2006.

EJF. *Somebody Knows Where Your Cotton Comes From: Unravelling the Supply Chain* (EJF, 2009).

Environmental Justice Foundation (EJF). *White Gold: The True Cost of Cotton* (EJF, 2005).

ESG International Inc. and WS Atkins International for AES Nile Power. "Environmental Impact Assessment," E464 Vol. 2, March 2001.

ESG International Inc. and WS Atkins International for AES Nile Power. "Bujagali Project Hydropower Facility Resettlement and Community Action Plan," March 2001.

FIVAS and NAPE. *Unsettling Business: Social Consequences of the Bujagali Hydropower Project* (FIVAS, 2014).

Free the Slaves. "The Congo Report: Slavery in Conflict Minerals," June 2011.

French NCP. "NCP Report on Implementation of the OECD Guidelines in the Textile and Clothing Sector" (Following a Referral from Nicole Bricq, Minister of Foreign Trade), 2 December 2013.

Giovannetti, Frederic. "Assessment of Past Resettlement Activities and Action Plan (APRAP)," in R.J. Burnside International, Canada Dillon Consultants Ltd, Canada et al. "Bujagali HPP, Uganda Public Consultation and Disclosure Plan (PCDP) DRAFT," File No: I-A 10045, November 2006.

Global Witness. *City of Gold: Why Dubai's First Conflict Gold Audit Never Saw the Light of Day* (Global Witness, 2014).

Global Witness. Global Witness, *"Faced with a Gun, What Can You Do?," War and the Militarisation of Mining in Eastern Congo* (Global Witness, 2009).

Government of Canada et al. "Child Rights and Security Checklist," 2017.

Harvard Humanitarian Initiative and WBG. "Ressources et ingéniosité: genre, droits de l'homme, et resilience dans certaines centres miniers artisanales a l'est de la République Démocratique du Congo," July 2015.

Hughes, Kai. "The Cotton Report: Cotton Production & Trade Trends," International Cotton Advisory Committee, November 2017.

IEH – Ethical Trading Initiative Norway (with funding from the Norwegian Ministry of Foreign Affairs). *A Guide to Human Rights Due Diligence in Global Supply Chains* (IEH, 2013).

IFC. "Uganda: Bujagali Hydropower Project (Bujagali HPP) A Case Study on Risk Mitigation through PPP Structuring," 15 November 2011.

ILO CEACR. "Report of the Committee of Experts on the Application of Conventions and Recommendations," 100th Session, 2011.

ILO. "Third-Party Monitoring of Measures Against Child Labour and Forced Labour During the 2018 Cotton Harvest in Uzbekistan," 2019.

ILO. "Time-Bound Programme Manual for Action Planning – TBP MAP Guidebook II: Time-Bound Programmes for Eliminating the Worst Forms of Child Labour – An Introduction," 2003.

ILO. *Global Estimates of Child Labour: Results and Trends, 2012–2016* (ILO, 2017).

Inter-American Commission on Human Rights (IACmHR). "What is Terrorism? Report on Terrorism & Human Rights," OEA/Ser.L/V/II.116 Doc. 5 rev. 1 corr. 22 October 2002.

Italian NCP. "Report on Responsible Business Conduct in the Textile and Garment Supply Chain: Recommendations of the Italian NCP on Implementation of the OECD Guidelines for MNEs," 2014.

ITUC. "Violence Against Women in Eastern DRC: Whose Responsibility? Whose Complicity?" November 2011.

Jackson, Stephen. "Fortunes of War: The Coltan Trade in the Kivus," Background research for HPG Report 13, Overseas Development Institute, February 2003.

Joy for Children, Uganda and BIC. "The Impact of the World Bank Funded Kamwenge – Kabarole Road Construction Project on Children," April 2015.

Lansdown, Gerrison. *Evolving Capacities of the Child* (Save the Children/UNICEF, 2005).

Marx, Axel and Bright, Claire (in collaboration with Nina Pineau). *Access to Legal Remedies for Victims of Corporate Human Rights Abuses in Third Countries* (European Parliament Sub-Committee on Human Rights – European Union, 2019).

Matthysen, Ken and Zaragoza Montejano, Andres. "Conflict Minerals Initiatives in DR Congo: Perceptions of Local Mining Communities," IPIS, November 2013.

Muradov, Bakhodyr and Ilkhamov, Alisher. *Uzbekistan's Cotton Sector: Financial Flows and Distribution of Resources* (Open Society Foundations, 2014).

Nampungu, Phiona and Kasabiiti, Diana. *The Impact of Involuntary Resettlement on Children – A Case Study of the International Development Association Funded Bujagali Hydro-Power Dam – Naminya Resettlement Area* (BIC, 2012).

National Scientific Council on the Developing Child (NSCDC) and the National Forum on Early Childhood Policy and Programs (NFECPP). *The Foundations of Lifelong Health Are Built in Early Childhood* (Center on the Developing Child – Harvard University, 2010).

National Scientific Council on the Developing Child (NSCDC). "Children's Emotional Development Is Built into the Architecture of Their Brains" (2004) Working Paper No. 2.

NGO Baby Milk Action. *Nestlé's UN Global Compact Cover Up: How Nestlé's Shared Value Reports Cover Up Malpractice and Bring the UN Voluntary Initiative for Corporate Responsibility into Disrepute* (Baby Milk Action, 2009).

Norrie McCain, Margaret and Mustard, J. Fraser. *Early Years Study* (Publications Ontario, 1999).

OECD. *Environmental Labelling and Information Schemes: Policy Perspectives* (OECD, 2016).

OECD. *Implementing the OECD Guidelines for Multinational Enterprises: The National Contact Points from 2000 to 2015* (OECD, 2016).

OECD. *Mineral Supply Chains and Conflict Links in Eastern DRC: Five Years of Implementing Supply Chain Due Diligence* (OECD, 2015).

Office of the SRSG for Children and Armed Conflict in collaboration with UNICEF. *Machel Study 10-Year Strategic Review: Children and Conflict in a Changing World* (Office of the SRSG for Children and Armed Conflict and UNICEF, 2009).

OHCHR. "Report of the United Nations High Commissioner on Human Rights on the Responsibilities of Transnational Corporations and Related Business Enterprises with Regard to Human Rights," E/CN.4/2005/91, 15 February 2005.

OHCHR. *The Corporate Responsibility to Respect Human Rights: An Interpretive Guide* (OHCHR, 2012).

PACT. "PROMINES Study: Artisanal Mining in the DRC," June 2010.

Partnership Africa Canada. *All that Glitters is Not Gold: Dubai, Congo and the Illicit Trade of Conflict Minerals* (Partnership Africa Canada, 2014).

Perks, Rachel and Vlassenroot, Koen. "From Discourse to Practice: A Sharper Perspective on the Relationship between Minerals and Violence in DR Congo," Cuvelier, Jeroen (ed.). *The Complexity of Resource Governance in a Context of State Fragility: The Case of Eastern DRC* (IPIS and International Alert, 2010).

R.J. Burnside International Ltd. "Bujagali Energy Ltd (BEL) Bujagali HPP Social and Environmental Assessment Main Report" (SEA Main Report), File No: I-A 10045, December 2006.

Rees, Caroline. *Piloting Principles for Effective Company-Stakeholder Grievance Mechanisms: A Report of Lessons Learned* (Harvard Kennedy School Corporate Social Responsibility Initiative, 2011).

RSN. "From the Field: Travels of Uzbek Cotton Through the Value Chain," 2012.

RSN. "Mining the Disclosures 2015: An Investor's Guide to Conflict Minerals Reporting in Year Two," 2015.

Shift. *From Audit to Innovation: Advancing Human Rights in Global Supply Chains* (Shift, 2013).

SOAS. "What Has Changed? Progress in Eliminating the Use of Forced Child Labour in the Cotton Harvests of Uzbekistan and Tajikistan," November 2010, www.soas.ac.uk/cccac/centres-publications/file64329.pdf (accessed 15 April 2019).

SOAS. *Invisible to the World? The Dynamics of Forced Child Labour in the Cotton Sector of Uzbekistan* (SOAS, 2009).

Sub-Commission on the Promotion and Protection of Human Rights. "Norms on the Responsibilities of Transnational Corporations and Other Business Enterprises with Regard to Human Rights," UN Doc E/CN.4/Sub.2/2003/12/Rev.2/2003.

Swinkels, Rob, Romanova, Ekaterina and Kochkin, Evgeny. "Assessing the Social Impact of Cotton Harvest Mechanization in Uzbekistan," The World Bank, June 2016.

Tahlil and Save the Children. "Child Labor in Uzbekistan," 2002, cited in EJF, *White Gold* (EJF, 2005).

Tarki Social Research Institute and Applica. *Child Poverty and Child Well-Being in the European Union: Volume 1 – Main Report* (European Commission Directorate General (DG) Employment, Social Affairs and Equal Opportunities, 2010).

The Enough Project. "A Comprehensive Approach to Congo's Conflict Minerals," April 2009.

Tostensen, Arne et al. *Supporting Child Rights: Synthesis of Lessons Learned in Four Countries* (Edita, 2011).

Tsurukawa, Nicolas, Prakash, Siddharth and Manhart, Andreas. "Social Impacts of Artisanal Cobalt Mining in Katanga, DRC," November 2011, 31–32, www.oeko.de/oekodoc/1294/2011-419-en.pdf (accessed 15 April 2019).

UGFHR. Human Rights Due Diligence and World Bank Funding in Uzbekistan's Agricultural Sector, June 2014.

UN Department of Economic and Social Affairs Report of the Group of Eminent Persons. "The Impact of Multinational Corporations on Development and on International Relations," E/5500/Rev.1 ST/ESA/6, United Nations, 1974.

UN Global Compact and BSR. *A Guide to Traceability: A Practical Approach to Advance Sustainability in Global Supply Chains* (UN Global Compact, 2014), www.bsr.org/reports/BSR_UNGC_Guide_to_Traceability.pdf (accessed 24 April 2019).

UN Global Compact. "Note on the UN Global Compact and Business and Human Rights," 13 January 2009.

UN Global Compact. *A Guide for Business: How to Develop a Human Rights Policy Second Edition* (UN Global Compact, 2015), www.unglobalcompact.org/docs/issues_doc/human_rights/Resources/HR_Policy_Guide_2nd_Edition.pdf).

UN Panel of Experts on the Illegal Exploitation of Natural Resources and Other Forms of Wealth of the DRC. "2002 Report," S/2002/1146, 8 October 2002.

UNICEF and FIDA Uganda. "A Simplified Handbook on International and National Laws & Policies on Children – Uganda," 2014.

UNICEF and the Danish Institute of Human Rights (DIHR). *Children's Rights in Impact Assessments: A Guide for Integrating Children's Rights into Impact Assessments and Taking Action for Children* (UNICEF, 2013).

UNICEF and WHO. *Diarrhoea: Why Children Are Still Dying and What Can Be Done Globally?* (UNICEF and WHO 2009).

UNICEF Innocenti Research Centre. *Measuring Child Poverty: New League Tables of Child Poverty in the World's Rich Countries* (UNICEF Innocenti Research Centre, 2012).

UNICEF, The Global Compact and Save the Children. "Executive Summary of Mapping of Links Between Business and Children's Rights," 21 April 2011.

UNICEF, The Global Compact and Save the Children. "The Children's Rights and Business Principles Initiative – Draft Principles Consultation Feedback Analysis & Report," August 2011.

UNICEF. "Children's Rights and the Mining Sector: UNICEF Extractive Pilot," March 2015.

UNICEF. *A Future Stolen: Young and Out-of-School* (UNICEF, 2018).

UNICEF. *Children are Everyone's Business: A Practical Workbook to Help Companies Understand and Address Their Impact on Children's Rights* (UNICEF, 2012).

UNICEF. *Children are Everyone's Business: Workbook 2.0 – A Guide for Integrating Children's Rights Into Policies, Impact Assessments and Sustainability Reporting* (UNICEF, 2013), www.unicef.org/eapro/Workbook_2.0_231213_Web.pdf (accessed 24 April 2019).

UNICEF. *Children at Risk in Central and Eastern Europe: Perils and Promises – A Summary* (UNICEF, 1997).

UNICEF. *Tracking Progress on Child and Maternal Nutrition: A Survival and Development Priority* (UNICEF, 2009).

United Nations High Commissioner for Refugees (UNHCR). *Missing Out: Refugee Education in Crisis* (UNHCR, 2016).

US SEC. "Report of the Securities and Exchange Commission on Questionable and Illegal Corporate Payments and Practices," May 1976.

Uzbek-German Forum for Human Rights (UGFHR). *Cotton – "It's Not a Plant, It's Politics" – The System of Forced Labour in Uzbekistan's Cotton Sector: Evidence from the 2011 Cotton Harvest* (UGFHR, 2012).

WB and IFC. "Project Completion Note (Guarantee No. B-003-0-UG) – The Bujagali HPP in the Republic of Uganda Report No. 33722-UG."

WB Inspection Panel. "Transport Sector Development Project – Additional Financing (P121097): Investigation Report," 4 August 2016.

WB. "Bujagali HPP – Project Information Document" (Report No. PID8803), 2001, www-wds.worldbank.org/external/default/WDSContentServer/WDSP/IB/2000/04/13/000094946_00032106082737/Rendered/PDF/multi0page.pdf (accessed 24 April 2019).

WB. "DRC Growth with Governance in the Mining Sector," Report No. 43402-ZR, May 2008.

WB. "Management Response to Request for Inspection Panel Review of the Uganda TSDP – Additional Financing (P121097)," 17 December 2015.

WB. "Uganda Transport Sector Development Project – Additional Financing: Lessons Learned and Agenda for Action," 11 November 2016.

WB. "Uganda: Bujagali HPP – Project Appraisal Document" (PAD), 2001, http://documents.worldbank.org/curated/en/2001/11/1631763/uganda-bujagali-hydropower-project (accessed 24 April 2019).

WB. Implementation Completion and Results Report (IDA-46790 IDA-49490 TF-11094)- Report No: ICR00002228, 5 June 2017.

WB. Implementation Completion and Results Report, Report No: ICR00002228, para. 23.

WB. Integrated Safeguards Datasheet for the Appraisal Stage – Report No.: AC3648, 2009.

WB. Project Information Document (PID) Concept Stage: Uganda Roads Development Program Phase 4, Report No.: AB3605.

WBG Finance, Economics & Urban (FEU) Department. "Financial Solutions: Partial Risk Guarantee – IDA Partial Risk Guarantee (PRG) to Promote Uganda's first Independent Power Producer," December 2007.

Women's Commission for Refugee Women and Children. *Global Survey of Education in Emergencies* (Women's Commission for Refugee Women and Children, 2004).

Women's Refugee Commission. "Education for Refugee Children Fact Sheet," 2010.

World Commission on Dams. "Dams and Development: A New Framework for Decision-Making," November 2000.

World Health Organization. *Summary of Principles for Evaluating Health Risks in Children Associated with Exposure to Chemicals* (WHO, 2011) www.who.int/ceh/health_risk_children.pdf (accessed 15 April 2019).

Online Sources

AKDN Website. "Aga Khan Fund for Economic Development (AKFED)," www.akdn.org/akfed.asp (accessed 15 April 2019).

Alstom-Kaplan. "Advertorial – Bujagali: Powering Uganda from the Nile," *International Water Power & Dam Construction* (www.waterpowermagazine.com), March 2013 (accessed 15 April 2019).

BEL. "Clean, Sustainable Hydropower for Uganda," 2012, www.akdn.org/assets/1/1510.pdf (accessed 15 April 2019).

Bernaz, Nadia. "Including Corporate Criminal Liability for International Crimes in the Business and Human Rights Treaty: Necessary but Insufficient," Business and Human Rights Resource Centre, https://business-humanrights.org/en/including-corporate-criminal-liability-for-international-crimes-in-the-business-and-human-rights-treaty-necessary-but-insufficient (accessed 15 March 2019).

BIC. "The Need for Child Protection Measures in the WB Safeguards – Naminya Children's Consultation," 2013, www.bankinformationcenter.org/wp-content/uploads/2013/10/Uganda-consultation-report.pdf (accessed 15 April 2019).

Business and Human Rights Resource Centre. "UN Human Rights Council 26th Session (Geneva, 10–27 June 2014)," http://business-humanrights.org/en/binding-treaty/un-human-rights-council-sessions#twenty_six_session (accessed 15 April 2019).

Center for International Legal Coordination. "The Hague Rules on Business and Human Rights Arbitration," www.cilc.nl/project/the-hague-rules-on-business-and-human-rights-arbitration/ (accessed 24 April 2019).

China Railway Group Limited (CREC). "Investor Relations: Company Snapshot," www.crecg.com/english/2699/index.html (accessed 20 April 2019).

Civil Society Activists of Uzbekistan. "Purge the Uzbek Cotton of the Stains of Forced Child Labor!," 15 November 2007, www.reports-and-materials.org/sites/default/files/reports-and-materials/Call-for-Uzbekistan-cotton-boycott-15-Nov-2007.pdf (accessed 15 April 2019).

CoE. "Chart of Signatures and Ratifications of Treaty 201," www.coe.int/en/web/conventions/full-list/-/conventions/treaty/201/signatures?p_auth=mirLPa4 k (based on the ratifications as of 24 April 2019) (accessed 15 April 2019).

CRC Committee. "UN Committee Hails South Sudan's Ratification of Convention on the Rights of the Child," 4 May 2015, www.ohchr.org/EN/NewsEvents/Pages/DisplayNews.aspx?NewsID=15919&LangID=E (accessed 25 April 2019).

Danish Institute of Human Rights. "National Action Plans on Business and Human Rights," https://globalnaps.org/. (accessed 24 April 2019).

DMCC Website. "Gold," www.dmcc.ae/gateway-to-trade/commodities/gold (accessed 19 February 2019).

DMCC. "Responsible Sourcing of Gold and Precious Metals," www.dmcc.ae/gold-responsible-sourcing-precious-metals (accessed 15 April 2019).

Eurostat. "People at Risk of Poverty or Social Exclusion," May 2018, https://ec.europa.eu/eurostat/statistics-explained/index.php/People_at_risk_of_poverty_or_social_exclusion#Number_of_people_at_risk_of_poverty_or_social_exclusion (accessed 24 April 2019).

German Federal Institute for Geosciences and Natural Resources (BGR). "Certified Trading Chains (CTC)," www.bgr.bund.de/EN/Themen/Min_rohstoffe/CTC/Concept_MC/CTC-Standards-Principles/ctc_standards-principles_node_en.html (accessed 15 April 2019).

GeSI. "The Value of Membership" (gesi.org, 2018). https://gesi.org/uploads/pdf/GeSI_membership_value_document_2018.pdf (accessed 15 April 2019).

Global Affairs Canada. "Responsible Business Conduct Abroad – Questions and Answers," www.international.gc.ca/trade-agreements-accords-commerciaux/topics-domaines/other-autre/faq.aspx?lang=eng (accessed 15 April 2019).

Government of Canada. "The Government of Canada Brings Leadership to Responsible Business Conduct Abroad," www.canada.ca/en/global-affairs/news/2018/01/the_government_ofcanadabringsleadershiptoresponsiblebusinesscond.html (accessed 15 April 2019).

Hughes-Jennett, Julianne and Berthet, Alison. "Arbitrating Business and Human Rights Disputes: Uncharted Territory," *Thompson Reuters Arbitration* Blog, 30 August 2018, http://arbitrationblog.practicallaw.com/arbitrating-business-and-human-rights-disputes-uncharted-territory/ (accessed 24 April 2019).

IFC CAO. "CAO Cases," www.cao-ombudsman.org/cases/ (accessed 24 April 2019).

IFC Website. "Definitions of Project Categories," www.ifc.org/wps/wcm/connect/corp_ext_content/tobedeleted/definitionofprojectcategories/projectcategories definitions (accessed 15 April 2019).

IFC. "Bujagali Energy Ltd. – Environmental & Social Review Summary," http://ifcext.ifc.org/ifcext/spiwebsite1.nsf/ProjectDisplay/ESRS24408 (accessed 15 April 2019).

IFC. "IFC Project Information Portal: Indorama Kokand," https://disclosures.ifc.org/#/projectDetailSII/5133 (accessed 15 April 2019).

ILO Website. "ILO: Origins and History," www.ilo.org/global/about-the-ilo/history/lang–en/index.htm (accessed 24 April 2019).

International Commission of Jurists. "Towards a World Court of Human Rights: Questions and Answers," December 2011, http://icj.wpengine.netdna-cdn.com/wp-content/uploads/2013/07/World-court-final-23.12-pdf1.pdf (accessed 24 April 2019).

IPIS. "Infographic – Mapping Mining Areas in Eastern DRC," www.ipisresearch.be/mapping/webmapping/drcongo/v5/#-3/28/5/2/1/ (accessed 15 April 2019).

Kennedy, David. "Reassessing International Humanitarianism: The Dark Sides," 2005, www.law.harvard.edu/faculty/dkennedy/speeches/TheDarkSides.pdf (accessed 24 April 2019).

McCorquodale, Robert. "Human Rights and Business: Is International Law Relevant?" *OUPblog* (blog.oup.com), 19 December 2016, https://blog.oup.com/2016/12/human-rights-business-law/.

Medecins Sans Frontières. "DRC: Condition Still Critical," 18 November 2011, www.msf.org/en/article/democratic-republic-congo-condition-still-critical (accessed 15 April 2019).

NAPE. "Facts about violated WB and AfDB Policies in the Controversial Bujagali Project: A Civil Society Perspective," January 2008.

OECD Watch Website. "NCPs," http://oecdwatch.org/oecd-guidelines/ncps (accessed 15 April 2019).

OECD. "2011 Update of the OECD Guidelines for Multinational Enterprises – Comparative Table of Changes Made to the 2000 Text," 2012, www.oecd.org/corporate/mne/49744860.pdf (accessed 15 April 2019).

OECD. "CO2.2: Child Poverty – OECD Family Database," 13 July 2018, www.oecd.org/els/CO_2_2_Child_Poverty.pdf (accessed 15 April 2019).

Office of the SRSG for Children and Armed Conflict, "DRC Factsheet 2016," September 2016, https://childrenandarmedconflict.un.org/wp-content/uploads/2016/02/DRC-Fact-Sheet-September-2016.pdf (accessed 25 April 2019).

OHCHR. "Principled Pragmatism – The Way Forward for Business and Human Rights," 7 June 2010, www.ohchr.org/EN/NewsEvents/Pages/PrincipledpragmatismBusinessHR.aspx (accessed 24 April 2019).

Responsible Mining Initiative. "What is the Responsible Mining Initiative (RMI)?" www.responsiblemineralsinitiative.org/about/faq/general-questions/what-is-the-conflict-free-sourcing-initiative-(cfsi)/ (accessed 15 April 2019).

Responsible Sourcing Network (RSN). "The Cotton Pledge," www.sourcingnetwork.org/storage/cotton-pledge-intro-package-2013/RSN%20Pledge%20Agreement2013.pdf (accessed 15 April 2019).

Rights and Accountability in Development (RAID). "Letter to the Rt Hon Patricia Hewitt MP, Minister of Trade and Industry," 28 June 2004, www.oecdwatch.org/cases/Case_41/124/at_download/file (accessed 15 April 2019).

RSN. The Cotton Pledge Package 2013, www.sourcingnetwork.org/storage/cotton-pledge-intro-package-2013/Pledge_Packet_2013.pdf (accessed 15 April 2019).

Scheinin, Martin. "Towards a World Court of Human Rights: Research Report Within the Framework of the Swiss Initiative to Commemorate the 60th Anniversary of the Universal Declaration of Human Rights," June 2009, www.enlazandoalternativas.org/IMG/pdf/hrCourt_scheinin0609.pdf (accessed 24 April 2019).

Sithe Global Website. "Bujagali Project," www.sitheglobal.com/projects/bujagali.cfm (accessed 15 April 2019).

Strohmer, Michael. "Conflict Minerals: Yet Another Supply Chain Challenge," A.T. Kearney, June 2012, www.atkearney.com/metals-mining/featured-article/-/asset_publisher/S5UkO0zy0vnu/content/conflict-minerals-yet-another-supply-chain-challenge/10192 (accessed 15 April 2019).

The Bretton Woods Project. "Safeguards Review Neglects People with Disability, Children," 23 January 2014, www.brettonwoodsproject.org/2014/01/safeguards-review-neglects-people-disability-children/ (accessed 15 April 2019).

The Code of Conduct for the Protection of Children from Sexual Exploitation in Travel and Tourism (The Code). "About," www.thecode.org/about/ (accessed 24 April 2019).

The Code of Conduct for the Protection of Children from Sexual Exploitation in Travel and Tourism (The Code). "Members of the Code," www.thecode.org/who-have-signed/intro/ (accessed 15 April 2019).

The Cotton Campaign. www.cottoncampaign.org (accessed 15 April 2019).

The Holy See. "Comments of the Holy See on the Concluding Observations of the Committee on the Rights of the Child," 2014, www.vatican.va/roman_curia/

secretariat_state/2014/documents/rc-seg-st-20140205_concluding-observations-rights-child_en.html (accessed 21 December 2018).

The International Chamber of Commerce and the International Employers Organization. IOE – ICC Views on UN Norms, 2004, www.reports-and-materials.org/IOE-ICC-views-UN-norms-March-2004.doc) (accessed 24 April 2019).

Townsend, Terry P. on behalf of International Cotton Advisory Committee (ICAC). Letter: 30 November 2007, www.reports-and-materials.org/sites/default/files/reports-and-materials/Intl-Cotton-Advisory-Committee-letter-30-Nov-2007.pdf (accessed 15 April 2019).

UN Global Compact. "Development of the Children's Rights and Business Principles," www.unglobalcompact.org/Issues/human_rights/childrens_principles/development.htm

UN Global Compact. Human Rights and Business Learning Tool, http://human-rights-and-business-learning-tool.unglobalcompact.org) (accessed 24 April 2019).

UN SRSG on Business and Human Rights. "Launch of the Project by the UN SRSG on Business and Human Rights to Pilot Principles for Company-Level Grievance Mechanisms," 19 August 2009, www.reports-and-materials.org/SRSG-grievance-mechanisms-pilot-19-Aug-2009.doc (accessed 24 April 2019).

US Department of Agriculture, Foreign Agriculture Service. "Cotton: World Markets and Trade, December 2018," http://apps.fas.usda.gov/psdonline/circulars/cotton.pdf (accessed 15 April 2019).

US Department of Labor (DoL), Bureau of International Labor Affairs. "2013 Findings on the Worst Forms of Child Labor – Uzbekistan," www.dol.gov/ilab/reports/child-labor/findings/2013TDA/uzbekistan.pdf (accessed 15 April 2019).

US DoL. 2015 Findings on the Worst Forms of Child Labor: Democratic Republic of the Congo, www.dol.gov/sites/default/files/images/ilab/child-labor/CongoDemocraticRepublic.pdf (accessed 15 April 2019).

Vedanta Resources. "Copper," www.vedantaresources.com/Pages/Copper.aspx (accessed 27 April 2019).

WB Inspection Panel Database. "Uganda: Third Power Project, Fourth Power Project, and Proposed Bujugali HPP," http://ewebapps.worldbank.org/apps/ip/Pages/ViewCase.aspx?CaseId=54 (accessed 15 April 2019).

WB Inspection Panel. "Uganda: Transport Sector Development Project – Additional Financing," www.inspectionpanel.org/panel-cases/transport-sector-development-project-additional-financing (accessed 21 April 2019).

WB. "Projects & Operations: Project P126962, Abstract," www.worldbank.org/projects/P126962/additional-financing-second-rural-enterprise-support-project?lang=en (accessed 15 April 2019).

WB. "Projects & Operations: Rural Enterprise Support Project," www.worldbank.org/projects/P046043/rural-enterprise-support-project?lang=en) (accessed 15 April 2019).

WB. Contracts Awarded for P092837: Uganda Transport Sector Development Project, http://web.worldbank.org/external/default/main?menuPK=247629&piPK=64002403&theSitePK=256299&pagePK=64002408&Projectid=P092837 (accessed 20 April 2019).

WBG. "Rebuilding Lives and Infrastructure in Eastern DRC," 11 February 2014, www.worldbank.org/en/news/feature/2014/02/11/rebuilding-lives-and-infrastructure-in-eastern-drc (accessed 15 April 2019).

Website of Bujagali HPP. "About Us," www.bujagali-energy.com/bujagali_aboutUs1.htm.

Website of Bujagali HPP. "About Us," www.bujagali-energy.com (accessed 15 April 2019).

Website of Bujagali HPP. www.bujagali-energy.com (accessed 15 April 2019).

Website of the OECD Guidelines for MNEs. Specific Instances, http://mneguidelines.oecd.org/specificinstances.htm (accessed 20 April 2019).

Website of the UN Global Compact. www.unglobalcompact.org/ParticipantsAndStakeholders/index.html (as of 10 January 2019).

West, Francis. "Leadership and Being First Aren't the Same Things: An Assessment of the UK National Action Plan on Business and Human Rights," LSE Blogs, 3 June 2016, http://blogs.lse.ac.uk/businesshumanrights/2016/06/03/francis-west-leadership-and-being-first-arent-the-same-things/ (accessed 24 April 2019).

INDEX